Southern Journeys

Southern Journeys

Tourism, History, and Culture
in the Modern South

Edited by Richard D. Starnes

UNIVERSITY OF ALABAMA PRESS
Tuscaloosa

Typeface is Goudy and Goudy Sans

∞

The paper on which this book is printed meets the minimum requirements of American
National Standard for Information Science–Permanence of Paper for Printed Library Materials,
ANSI Z39.48–1984.

Library of Congress Cataloging-in-Publication Data

Southern journeys : tourism, history, and culture in the modern south / edited by
Richard D. Starnes.
    p. cm.
Includes bibliographical references (p. 297).
    ISBN 0-8173-1297-8 (cloth : alk. paper) — ISBN 0-8173-5009-8 (pbk. : alk. paper)
    1. Tourism—Southern States—History. 2. Southern States—Social life and customs. I. Starnes,
Richard D., 1970–

G155.U6 S64 2003
338.4′7917504′09—dc21

                                                                            2002156532

British Library Cataloguing-in-Publication Data available

Portions of chapter 2 by Brooks Blevins were previously published in an earlier form in *Hill
Folks: A History of Arkansas Ozarkers and Their Image* by Brooks Blevins. Copyright © 2002 by
the University of North Carolina Press. Used by permission.

Chapter 3 by Harvey H. Jackson III is a revision and expansion of an earlier article entitled
"Seaside, Florida: Robert Davis and the Quest for Community," published in *Atlanta History:
Journal of Georgia and the South* (fall 1998), 41–51. Copyright © the Atlanta Historical
Society. Used by permission.

Portions of chapter 9 by Daniel S. Pierce were previously published in an earlier form in *The
Great Smokies: From Natural Habitat to National Park*. Copyright © 2000 by the University of
Tennessee Press. Used by permission.

Contents

Acknowledgments

As editor, my first thanks must go to the authors. They have faced the long road toward publication with professionalism and good cheer. Their hard work and dedication to this effort have been phenomenal. Through this process, they have become my friends, and I am better for the journey we have taken together. Members of the staff of The University of Alabama Press have been steadfast in their support of this project. Thanks to my colleagues Tyler Blethen, David Dorondo, Clete Fortwendel, Gael Graham, Jim Lewis, Elizabeth McRae, Scott Philyaw, Vicki Szabo, and Curtis Wood, for their interest and advice. Beyond Cullowhee, Gordon E. Harvey, Eric Tscheschlok, Steve Murray, John Inscoe, George Tindall, and David Goldfield have added to this project in numerous ways. Thanks as well to Nicole Mitchell and Mindy Wilson for their early support. Wayne Flynt and Max R. Williams have shaped my ideas in innumerable ways and continue to be powerful influences in all aspects of my life. Their support and encouragement are most dear to me. Most importantly, thanks to Barbara, Emily, and Nathan for the strength and love they give me every day. Ours is the journey I enjoy the most.

Richard D. Starnes

Southern Journeys

Introduction

Richard D. Starnes

Anyone who has seen Rock City, driven down Ocean Boulevard in Myrtle Beach, wandered the grounds at Graceland, camped in the Great Smoky Mountains National Park, or watched the mermaids swim at Weeki Wachee realizes that the South offers visitors a rich variety of scenic, cultural, and leisure attractions. Yet, few would pause to consider tourism's importance to the region itself. Tourism is one of the most powerful economic forces in the modern South. The South is an international tourist destination, drawing millions of visitors each year who come to enjoy the region's natural and man-made attractions. It is a multibillion-dollar-a-year industry, creating jobs, spawning new businesses, and generating much needed revenue. In some states, tourism is a greater economic force than agriculture or manufacturing and is one of the top three economic activities in every state of the former Confederacy. But tourism's reach extends far beyond economics. It is a force that has wrought pronounced changes in the contours of southern society. Local images and culture have been manipulated and marketed to draw more visitors, regardless of the effects of this process on native residents. Developers transformed or even created whole communities designed to serve the needs of visitors. The South is one of the leading retirement and resort home locations in the country, a fact that has contributed to changing demographics within the region. Despite its economic power, tourism bypassed many with its benefits, forever changed the composition and culture of communities large and small, and created tensions between residents and visitors that manifested itself in many ways. A recent bumper sticker illustrated the animosity many residents feel about the intrusive nature of tourism when it asked, "If It's Tourist Season, Why Can't We Shoot 'Em?"

Southern tourism falls into three broad categories, with some attractions fitting neatly in one category or another while others incorporate elements of all three. The first and oldest is environmental tourism. The land and climate, defining characteristics in so much of southern history, define this form of tourism. Simply taking in the scenic beauty of the southern landscape has drawn visitors to the region for nearly two centuries. Such tourism ranges from enjoying the natural grandeur of mountains or beaches while on a walk or a drive to participating in activities defined by the environment itself, such as camping, hiking, fishing, or white-water rafting. But some visitors require more than scenery to entertain them. In destination tourism, developers, outside corporations, or even communities themselves establish attractions designed to draw visitors for entertainment, shopping, gambling, or any of a host of other diversions. Destination tourism can rely on the land and climate as well but most often is based on attractions created by man. Walt Disney World in Orlando, the nation's single largest tourist attraction, is a shining example of destination tourism. The casinos on Mississippi's gulf coast use the landscape, well-known entertainers, and other attractions to create a travel destination appealing to more than just gamblers. Likewise, Pigeon Forge, Tennessee, uses its location in the Great Smoky Mountains to build a tourist destination that offers amusement parks, outlet shopping, music, and a long list of other diversions. In a region obsessed, sometimes haunted, by its past, it is little wonder that the region's distinctive culture and history form an important component of regional tourism. Cultural and heritage tourism, concepts recently tossed about by preservationists and economic developers alike, actually have a long history in the South. Attractions such as Colonial Williamsburg, Old Salem, historic districts in cities such as Charleston and Savannah, and countless state and federal historic sites across the region draw visitors interested in everything from colonial architecture to Civil War battlefields. Regardless of what brings visitors south, they come, forming a catalyst that has shaped the region's history for over two centuries.[1]

Despite the fact that scholars throughout the world have explored the role of tourism in shaping history and culture, until recently American tourism received little attention among historians.[2] Instead, sociologists, anthropologists, and economists examined tourism's role in economic development, the multifaceted relationship between hosts and guests, and the social and environmental impact of a tourist economy.[3] By the mid-1980s, historians recognized the study of tourism as a way to better understand the interplay of social and economic forces in the American experience. These scholars focused on tourism as a causal force in history, as a lens through which to examine history and culture, and as a way to ask questions about national and regional identity. Southern historians had been urged to ask these same questions about twenty years earlier.[4]

In his presidential address to the Southern Historical Association in 1962, Rembert W. Patrick called for historians to pay more attention to what he termed "the mobile frontier." He noted that tourism had been a long-standing, powerful social and economic force in the South. Tourism served as a catalyst for economic development, introduced new demographic and cultural forces to the region, shaped the ever-changing image of the South for visitors and natives, and served as an important force of conflict and change in countless communities across the region. In short, he argued that tourism "has been important long enough for the past-conscious historian to give respectability to the study of its cause, course, and result." But, even as tourism emerged as one of the most important industries in the South, few scholars heeded Patrick's call to examine its historical development on a local, state, or regional level.[5]

As Patrick suggested, southern tourism has a long history that encompasses the major themes of the larger regional experience. Perhaps this is not surprising given the traditional importance of hospitality and leisure in southern culture. As early as the late eighteenth century, the first tourists appeared in the South. Southern planters, the only people within the region with the means for leisure travel, began to take extended sojourns to upland resorts and mineral springs. Some even relocated their entire households to elaborate summer homes to escape "the fever season." At these early resorts, the wealthy mingled, took in the natural attractions, engaged in faddish treatments for various diseases, and generally were entertained in a manner accorded to their station. Even in its earliest phase, southern tourism had important cultural and economic implications. In places such as White Sulphur Springs, Virginia, Asheville, North Carolina, and elsewhere, these elites injected cash into the local economy, contributed to a powerful cosmopolitan atmosphere that existed in stark contrast to the areas surrounding the resorts, and influenced changing ideas about slavery, regional identity, and, ultimately, secession.[6]

After Reconstruction, tourism emerged as an important but overlooked industry of the New South. Resorts took their place alongside the spindle, the sawmill, and the forge as the economic tools that reshaped the region after the Civil War. Tourism offered, according to historian Edward L. Ayers, "a way for places that had languished for years with unpromising agriculture finally to come into their own." The railroad opened new areas of the South to visitors, and by the 1880s, health and pleasure-seekers from both North and South enjoyed a growing number of resorts in the mountains and along the coast. Their leisure was made possible by black and white southerners from the lowest rungs of the social ladder who labored in low-paying and demanding service jobs. The region's resorts emerged as important forums for social and economic exchange. Northern capitalists sometimes blended business and pleasure, using their holiday to explore places to invest their wealth. Likewise, southern elites took advantage of the access tourism afforded them to affluent outsiders, using leisure time as an opportunity to build business relationships. The South became, in the words of historian Nina L. Silber, "something other than a social problem," but rather "an accepted sojourn on the tourist's itinerary," and one with important implications for the region's economy, image, and culture.[7]

By the early twentieth century, southern tourism began to change. The region's landscape and climate remained the primary attractions, but like many antebellum planters, some visitors wanted to make their southern tourist experience permanent. Wealthy visitors from both North and South built or acquired homes in resort towns such as Charleston, Pinehurst, Coral Gables, Panama City, Jekyll Island, and elsewhere. In 1895, George Vanderbilt began construction on Biltmore, his palatial mountain chateau near Asheville, North Carolina, perhaps the most ostentatious example of this trend. This permanent presence of nonresidents began to alter the character of resort communities. At the same time, the landscape and climate also attracted visitors with different purposes. Around the turn of the century, churches and organizations with religious affiliations began building retreats, summer meeting grounds, and other recreational facilities in mountain and coastal communities across the South. On the surface, these religious resorts seem to contradict the traditional southern religious ethos and its emphasis on salvation, self-denial, and an aversion to worldly pleasures in favor of those in the world to come. Some of these were merely recreational, but others took on larger roles that brought important changes to southern religious life. Montreat, a Presbyterian retreat in the North Carolina mountains, became a test bed for civil rights, a center for missionary training, and a place where major theological issues were debated. Nearby Lake Junaluska served similar purposes for southern Methodists. Still, the Protestant evangelical culture discouraged frivolous travel among the faithful and contributed to attempts to regulate tourism-related amusements for all others through the use of blue laws and other means. The contrast between resort communities of wealthy capitalists immersing themselves in worldly pleasures and resorts where church people refined their practice of faith indicates the conflicts and contradictions that often accompanied tourism within the region.[8]

The burgeoning middle class and the advent of the automobile began the process of democratizing southern travel. Middle-class visitors wanted to enjoy many of the same leisure pursuits as elites but were limited by time and finances. Slowly, the tourist court began to replace the resort hotel, as communities across the region made conscious decisions about which class of visitor to serve. Before the First World War, local and state leaders envisaged the important role this class of visitor would play by including tourism as a major justification for the good roads movement. Tourism was a natural avenue of economic development for these "business progressives" to pursue. Imagemaking, a cornerstone of both tourism and the spirit of the New South, took on new life as business and political leaders crafted elaborate advertising campaigns to draw larger and larger shares of the tourist market. During the Great Depression, local boosters and state leaders worked successfully with federal officials to secure federal funding for tourism-related projects. "Come south is the solid refrain," as one historian noted that "promoters use[d] warm weather, beautiful gardens, ladies in bathing suits, and food-aplenty to lure people southward." It was hoped a vibrant tourism industry would spawn new businesses, enhance reputations, and spur the migration of people and money to southern states.[9]

The larger issues that shaped the region affected tourism as well. As with other aspects of southern society, race defined tourism in several important ways. Black southerners were far less likely than whites to travel for leisure for most of the twentieth century. Poverty prevented most from recreating away from home, and the rigid restrictions of Jim Crow made travel difficult for those who could afford it. Segregated train cars and a shortage of hotels, restaurants, and other facilities made the black traveler's experience somewhat less than ideal. In *Darkwater: Voices from Within the Veil*, W. E. B. Du Bois lay bare the humiliating, dehumanizing conditions black travelers were faced in the region. From Du Bois's descriptions of unscrupulous ticket agents, pointedly inhospitable conductors, and the wretched conditions in segregated railcars, it was little wonder that a black woman remarked to a white visitor, "No, we don't travel much." That does not mean that black southerners were completely excluded from tourism. As with other aspects of southern society, segregation gave rise to resorts and accommodations that catered exclusively to black visitors. American Beach, Florida, and Atlantic Beach, North Carolina, catered to black vacationers as early as the 1930s, and the Gulfside Assembly resort in Mississippi linked religion and leisure for black southerners. Such resorts gave African American entrepreneurs opportunities to tap into a growing tourist trade but also reinforced the power of the color line as a force in southern society.[10]

For blacks and whites, economics determined who could travel and who engaged in more homegrown leisure pursuits. Tourism required money and status that, for many southerners of both races, remained out of reach. Those southerners who lived close to the land did not tour, as poverty and the rhythm of the agricultural year put leisure travel out of their reach. Lower- and lower-middle-class southerners did not venture into the tourist ranks until after World War II. Those who lived in cities or near resorts were not completely excluded from the region's tourism industry. Employment in tourism-related jobs offered some opportunities they might not find in agriculture or industry, but there was a wide gulf between visitors and those who served them. For the maids, bellmen, waitresses, and other workers tourism offered employment and sometimes even meals and a place to live. Such work was demanding, and often workers labored for low wages or tips alone. Tourism employment might also be demeaning, as a woman from a resort town in North Carolina noted. She remarked that tourists "want local people to provide things for them to spend money on, and that's the beginning of dependency. The spiral begins, and you begin to wait for the tourist, although you don't like them. . . . Catering to people is something you don't like to do, a certain amount of self-respect is lost." Moreover, tourism work was seasonal, forcing some workers to find other employment in the off-season, seek work at other resorts, or simply endure unemployment until the change of seasons brought visitors back.[11]

Following the Second World War, regional tourism grew in scope and variation. Postwar affluence opened leisure travel to more people, and the South was conveniently located within one or two days' drive from the majority of the nation's population. Cities large and small took greater notice of the economic opportunities tourism offered, developing visitors' bureaus to coordinate tourism development efforts. Tourism business owners began to target middle- and lower-middle-class visitors through more affordable accommodations, popular attractions, and advertising campaigns. Amusement parks such as Opryland and later Dollywood drew visitors by appealing to the traveling public's fascination with southern culture, or at least, southern stereotypes, while others like Six Flags over Georgia provided visitors with the same thrills found in parks across the nation. Attractions of all types proliferated. Historic home tours such as the Pilgrimage in Natchez entertained visitors with a sanitized view of southern history, and Stone Mountain beckoned visitors to celebrate Confederate heroes while roadside shops filled with cheap souvenirs asked travelers to empty their pockets. In southern resorts, music, crafts, history, food, or combinations of all these were put forth as attractions to draw larger numbers of visitors. Golf courses soon dotted the southern landscape, and southern cities pursued professional sports teams at least in part to boost tourist appeal. Such ploys bore fruit, as the number of tourists grew steadily. Vacation and retirement communities sprang up across the region; an old trend tailored anew which tempted more affluent visitors. Thomas D. Clark noted that by the late 1950s, tourism's economic impact had eclipsed agriculture in several southern states and predicted that it might be "a more profitable and dependable source of income than cotton ever was." Perhaps the biggest change was that black tourists emerged as an important component of the post–Civil Rights South's tourist economy, a fact brought to national attention during debates over the future of the Confederate flag in Georgia and South Carolina in 2000. Though increases in the tourism industry benefited some, others felt threatened by it. Controversies over the use of culture as an attraction, land use and land prices, and decisions to put image and visitor needs ahead of those of local residents divided resort communities across the region.[12]

The essays that follow do not attempt to survey the complicated history of tourism in the region. Instead, they draw together the latest research on the subject, introduce tourism as a causal force in southern history, and assess its influence in a variety of different localities and contexts. They range from broad state-level studies of tourism development to examinations of how local communities experienced tourism's social and economic power. Taken together, they represent the first attempt to trace and interpret the history of southern tourism.

The first essay explores one of the oldest and most notorious southern tourist destinations. Alecia P. Long argues that New South boosterism, tourism, and the particularities of local urban culture came together in New Orleans during the late nineteenth century. Long argues that sex, particularly "sex across the color line," was a fundamental component of tourism devel-

opment in New Orleans between 1897 and 1917. Through the establishment of Storyville, the city's attempt to restrict sex-related businesses, city
leaders actually created a "sexual amusement park" of regional and national
reputation. The development of sex tourism in New Orleans exposed tensions over race, sexual mores, public images, and competing economic visions of the city. Reformers, saloon owners, madams, and other parties often
clashed over the activities taking place in Storyville and its future within the
city. But as long as city leaders promoted tourism as a key element of New
Orleans's economic development strategy, Storyville was safe. When they
courted other forms, such as military bases in 1917, the city's reputation as
a sexual tourist attraction threatened the city's economic future and had to
go. But during its twenty-year existence, Storyville influenced urban development and stamped New Orleans with an exotic and erotic image that still
lingers in the public imagination.

Tourism shaped the contours of rural life as well. Brooks Blevins argues
that in the Arkansas Ozarks, tourism emerged as a modernizing influence,
as a mode of economic development, and as the focal point of a conflict in
the politics of culture. He argues that beginning in the nineteenth century,
tourism developers and local colorists marketed the region to outsiders as a
majestic, rugged place populated by quaintly primitive people. As tourism
emerged, these images took on economic importance in the form of "traditional" handicrafts, regional music, and amusement parks that portrayed locals as stereotypical hillbillies. Even though these images stood in stark contrast to social realities, tourism promoters recognized that the idea of the
backward, impoverished, ignorant Ozark mountaineer resonated with visitors. In the end, Blevins argues, tourism did more damage to the region than
good. The cultural exploitation, changes in land ownership, political infighting, and indignities of the tourism economy far outweighed the economic benefits. Still, tourism remains one of the most powerful forces in the
Ozarks, one that is poised to assume even greater importance.

Tourism has demonstrated the power to transform communities, but the
nature of tourism itself has also changed over time. In a study of Jekyll Island,
C. Brenden Martin and June Hall McCash examine the history of a resort
that experienced tremendous change in purpose and clientele, a case that
reflects larger themes in the history of southern tourism. Tourists first came
to the island during the late nineteenth century, as wealthy northern capitalists sought respite from their daily pressures. Men such as J. P. Morgan,

William Rockefeller, and Marshall Field joined the exclusive Jekyll Island Club, built elaborate beach retreats, and spent winters enjoying the scenery and the company of their peers. Although the club thrived during the early twentieth century, the economic crisis of the 1930s spelled the end to elite tourism on the island. Taken over by the state after World War II in order to create a seaside state park, the island saw changes in its purpose and its visitors. State leaders established the Jekyll Island Authority to manage the resort for Georgia residents and to attract the growing numbers of white, middle-class tourists who flocked south after the war. Jekyll Island soon became a divisive political issue that brought matters of race, class, the role of the state in economic development, and the environment to the forefront. Although unique in many ways, Martin and McCash demonstrate that Jekyll Island's experience illuminates many common themes in the complex, often emotionally charged history of resorts across the South.

Despite extensive cooperation between private tourism developers and government officials across the region, these two groups did not always share a common vision. In a study of the Blue Ridge Parkway, Anne Mitchell Whisnant examines the case of one business owner who successfully challenged state and federal limits on tourism development. As construction began on the Blue Ridge Parkway in the 1930s, Heriot Clarkson, owner of the Little Switzerland resort in the mountains of North Carolina, saw the new scenic byway as a way to connect his isolated development to the rest of the state and region. Federal and state officials hoped that the Parkway would provide visitors a road from which to view and appreciate the natural wonders of southern Appalachia, vistas unmarred by industrial or commercial development. Clarkson seemed willing to accept the annexation of some resort land in exchange for the economic opportunities offered by the Parkway. However, when Clarkson realized that Parkway restrictions on advertising, development regulations such as scenic easements, and limited access to the Parkway by other roads meant the new road might serve to further isolate Little Switzerland from potential visitors, he protested the Parkway as a limit on, not a boon to, regional tourism. Whisnant argues that Clarkson mobilized every legal and political power at his disposal to circumvent the true purpose of the Parkway. He fought for larger payments for the Parkway right-of-way, for direct access from his resort to the new road, and for the right to advertise along the Parkway route. Clarkson even became something of a populist, claiming he was fighting for his right, and the rights of all people, to benefit from public tourism projects. Clarkson refused to accept state and federal visions of acceptable tourism, a fact Whisnant argues points to larger issues surrounding tourism as a route of local economic development.

Elsewhere, other southerners also protested when one vision of tourism seemed to leave them behind. Although developers like Clarkson wielded the political and economic power to push their agendas, those at the other end of the economic spectrum also stood up to fight for a voice when their communities became havens for people from elsewhere. Hilton Head Island is one such case. Margaret Shannon and Stephen Taylor argue that the politics of tourism development created a great gulf between the island's black residents on one side and tourism leaders, second-home owners, and state economic officials on the other. As tourism developed on Hilton Head in the years after World War II, African Americans were increasingly left out of the political process and left behind economically. Shannon and Taylor demonstrate that Hilton Head's African American population was deprived of a meaningful political voice, ancestral land, and the economic benefits of local tourism by white developers who wished to create for their white customers an exclusive, secure, and largely segregated resort. Opposition to tourism development served as a unifying force for Hilton Head's black community as they attempted to gain more from their community's economy than low-paying service jobs fraught with discrimination. This essay raises important issues about the exploitative nature of tourism, as well as the relationship between race and economic development in the modern South.

Part of Hilton Head's appeal rests in the image of exclusivity exuded in its resort communities. Portraying southern resorts as idyllic havens isolated from the problems of modern life is common, but reality sometimes does not measure up to advertising. Harvey H. Jackson III examines tourism on Florida's gulf coast through a study of resort developers and their quest to create and sell the ideal vacation retreat. While resorts such as Miami Beach, St. Petersburg, and Key West catered to northern snowbirds, resorts on Florida's panhandle tended to draw southerners who sought rest and relaxation close to home. Jackson argues that three of these gulf coast resorts, Seagrove Beach, Seaside, and Watercolor, reflect changing sophistication among developers and increasingly exclusive tastes among southern visitors. Each resort emerged during a period of great national and regional prosperity, and all had distinctive visions of the ideal visitor experience. Seagrove Beach began as an unassuming place for southerners seeking an enjoyable but affordable haven from the pressures of modern life. Seaside, on the other hand, was developer Robert Davis's experiment in creating the perfectly planned community—a tourist experience he hoped many part-time residents would make permanent. Watercolor, a development that attempted to merge the most appealing aspects of both earlier resorts, raised the ire of earlier residents, who saw it as a threat to the image for which they had already paid good money. Whether marketed as isolated getaways in tropical climes or as models of regional urban living, Jackson argues that the experience of these three Florida resorts help to understand the process of resort development, the importance of image, the class-based nature of southern tourism, and the conflicts tourism can cause, even among tourists themselves.

Although resort communities have been important, the South's natural attractions remain some of the region's most popular. Since before the Civil War, flora and fauna have drawn visitors to resorts throughout the South. But many tourism promoters see greater profits in amusement parks, outlet malls, and other man-made attractions. These types of attractions depend on visitor access, something that communities reliant on scenic tourism often do not enjoy. The case of Swain County, North Carolina, illustrates this paradox. During the 1930s and 1940s, Swain County saw the creation of the Great Smoky Mountains National Park and Fontana Lake, two large, federally funded attractions that could bring this small mountain community much needed economic development. According to Daniel S. Pierce, such hopes rested on the federal government fulfilling a promise of rebuilding a highway destroyed by the lake. Such a road would give residents access to family homesteads and cemeteries cut off by the reservoir, but also would link the county seat, Bryson City, with the emerging tourist mecca of Gatlinburg, Tennessee. After building a few miles of the promised road, Pierce argues that federal officials abandoned their promise in the face of rising construction costs and environmentalist protests that such a road would damage the fragile ecosystem in the Great Smokies. Poverty and unemployment rates remained high in Swain County, a fact leaders blamed on the lack of access and the fact that the federal government owned over three-quarters of the county's land. Pierce argues that conflict over "The Road to Nowhere" illustrates the paradox faced by southern communities dependent on scenic tourism: how to attract more tourists and the prosperity they often bring, while preserving the environment that brought them in the first place.

Of course, tourism's social and economic effects spread beyond local communities. After World War II, tourism emerged as a key component in state economic strategies across the South. In a survey of the origins, course, and effects of North Carolina's tourism development, I argue that a coalition of politicians and tourism leaders, faced with the deepening economic crisis of the Great Depression, promoted tourism as a partial solution to the state's economic woes. Publicity campaigns, state and federal parks, and an increasingly vocal tourism industry emerged before World War II. By the 1950s, state leaders and tourism developers had created "A Variety Vacationland," albeit one that was ever evolving to serve the changing desires of visitors. Natural attractions gave way to amusement parks, tourist courts replaced exclusive resorts, and seasonal visitors often became second-home owners. Local culture in places like the Cherokee Indian Reservation was depicted not as it was, but in ways calculated to rake in more tourist dollars. Although viewed as an economic panacea, tourism altered land ownership patterns across the state, created intense conflicts between those who benefited from tourism and those who did not, and created tension over race, class, and culture. Using the Old North State as a case study, I call for even more extensive study of tourism in order to better understand the social and economic history of states across the South.

Returning to New Orleans, J. Mark Souther takes the story of Crescent City tourism a bit further, examining the reemergence of tourism in the city after the Second World War. Although the city continued to be a haven for those visitors seeking sins of the flesh, leaders sought a different image to broaden New Orleans's appeal. After 1945, boosters seized on the city's music, architecture, and history to fully establish tourism as a key element of the urban economy. From jazz clubs to the eccentricities of the French Quarter to Creole cuisine, leaders promoted the most distinctive elements of the city's culture to form an interesting and lucrative new twist on heritage tourism. By the 1960s, New Orleans tourism was highly profitable and appeared to many to be the best hope for a city facing severe internal divisions and economic uncertainty. Seeking a larger share of the white, middle-class tourist market, businessmen and politicians attempted to soften the city's image and standardize the tourist experience, in the belief that visitors preferred more sanitized, packaged attractions to more authentic local culture. Ironically, Souther argues, this caused New Orleanians to rebel against new tourism projects and visitors to seek other destinations. As Souther makes clear, New Orleans offers lessons for cities examining heritage tourism as a development policy.

But in no city has tourism wielded as much power as in Atlanta. Harvey K. Newman argues that historically Atlanta was a city built on boosterism, tourism, and hospitality. According to Newman, the 1996 Olympics represent both a high-water mark in the city's long tourist tradition and the mechanism used by Atlanta elites to catapult the city to international standing. Although there were many elements of southern culture showcased during the games, Newman argues that neither the Olympics, nor the city of Atlanta, are uniquely southern. Regional culture was something Olympic promoters applauded or abandoned, depending on whether or not it fit their larger purposes. Embraced as a way to build on the city's image and as a catalyst for economic development, the Olympics had many effects men like Olympic organizer Billy Payne did not envision: destruction of minority neighborhoods, a larger reliance on service-industry jobs, and profound changes to the urban landscape. The Olympics were an important step for a city whose history has been defined by image-making and economic development, and the experience reveals the immense power of tourism as an agent of change.

Historian Ted Ownby ends the collection by placing the preceding essays in context, while speculating on the complex intersection of history, culture, and tourism in the South. By examining the themes suggested in earlier essays, as well as the recent history of southern tourism, this piece provides an articulate coda suggesting that tourism remains a controversial and complex force that both obscures and illuminates the region's history and culture. He concludes by speculating that tourism developers and historians might work together to achieve common purposes. Tourism developers seek variety and uniqueness in their quest for visitors. Historians seek a truthful past. In a call for cooperation, Ownby suggests that by developing attractions that tell a broader, deeper story about the South, southern tourism might be a route for the region both to develop economically and to come to terms with its own past.

As the first foray into the study of southern tourism, these essays cannot hope to provide a comprehensive history of this complicated and powerful social and economic force. Instead, they introduce tourism as a new window through which to view the course of southern history and culture. As such, these essays suggest interpretations, approaches, and ideas that should move the study of southern history in fresh new directions. The study of tourism workers offers new possibilities for labor historians, while the study of cultural and heritage tourism holds significant promise for students of historical memory and the politics of culture. Scholars of environmental history, business history, and social history can all benefit from a consideration of the place of tourism in southern life. On a larger level, the study of southern tourism addresses some of the long-standing questions asked by scholars of the region. Tourism has emerged as an important forum for identifying, creating, and perpetuating a distinctive southern culture, a fact that presents a number of challenging issues. Who benefits from southern distinctiveness? Who is harmed? How do the fundamental tensions between southern hospitality and southerners' traditional aversion to outsiders shape the course of tourism development? To what degree are southerners willing to change in order to court tourist dollars? Will the economic promise of tourism cause southerners to alter attitudes about race, economic development policies, and even outsiders themselves? By suggesting such questions, these essays help to integrate the study of tourism into the broader history of the South and better integrate the history of tourism into the larger national and international historical experience. By better understanding the process and effects of southern tourism, scholars can ask new questions about the South's social and economic history and the links between them.[13]

I
"A Notorious Attraction"
Sex and Tourism in New Orleans, 1897–1917

Alecia P. Long

In 1886, well-known Gilded Age author and travel writer Charles Dudley Warner came to New Orleans to gather information for an article that appeared in the *Harper's* January 1887 issue. Warner's review of the city and its charms was so pastoral and complimentary that it led one local newspaper to comment that his "glowing description of the city . . . is enough to crowd our shores with tourists anxious to see this bower of roses, this perfumed elysium of luxury and perpetual sunshine." Warner, aware of the city's potential as a tourist destination, predicted that "the region around the city would become immediately a great winter resort if money and enterprise were enlisted to make it so."[1]

Although Warner emphasized the city's more sedate, natural attractions, he also dedicated a large portion of his article to a discussion of past and present race relations in the city. Conceding that "no other city of the United States so abounds in stories pathetic and tragic . . . growing out of the mingling of races," he assured his readers that the city's long history of racial amalgamation was at an end. From Warner's perspective, it was "quite evident that the peculiar prestige of the quadroon and the octoroon is a thing of the past." He also remarked, though only in passing, that there were "plenty of *café chantants*, gilded saloons, and gambling houses, and more than enough of the resorts upon, which the police are supposed to keep one blind eye."[2]

Apparently Warner's coverage of such haunts did not satisfy the editors of the city's muckraking organ, *The Mascot*, which dedicated its January 22, 1887, issue to "Sights of New Orleans, The Harpers [*sic*] Did Not See." *The Mascot*'s coverage began with "the slums and dives of Franklin [S]treet,"

The cover of a city guidebook depicts a wide variety of amusements awaiting visitors in the Big Easy. (Courtesy of the Louisiana State Museum, New Orleans, Louisiana.)

home to what it called "the most loathsome, filthy, hotbeds of vice and de-
bauchery ever permitted to befoul the moral or physical atmosphere of any
city." The promiscuous racial mixing that took place in the Franklin Street
"gambling hells" and dance halls was prominent among *The Mascot*'s complaints. According to the paper, these were places where "male and female,
black and yellow, and even white, meet on terms of equality and abandon
themselves to the extreme limit of obscenity and lasciviousness."[3]

The contrast between the respectable, genteel, and increasingly segregated New Orleans described by Warner and the "abominable hovels and
palaces of sin" frequented by racially mixed clientele described in *The Mascot*
lay at the center of a tension that would both bedevil and benefit those
who sought to develop the tourist trade in New Orleans over the next four
decades. The debates over what kind of tourist industry the city ought to
develop and promote had both economic and moral dimensions. Perhaps
not surprisingly, the city's bawdy reputation had its own group of boosters.
These were men and women who understood the economic advantages to be
gained from appealing to those who wished to visit the city's many "palaces
of sin."

There were other parties who also wished to enhance the city's reputation
as a tourist destination, but from their perspective tourism had to be respectable as well as remunerative. In 1910, for example, local businessman, reformer, and Progressive Union president Phillip Werlein complained bitterly
that New Orleans's vice district, located in the same area *The Mascot* had
complained about twenty-three years earlier, had become "a notorious attraction." Werlein admitted that many visitors were drawn to the district's
dance halls and prostitutes, but he argued, "those who come here for more
commendable purposes should not be compelled to look at them." Echoing
The Mascot's comments, Werlein contended that "the open association of
white men and [N]egro women on Basin [S]treet, which is now permitted by
our authorities, should fill us with shame as it fills the visitor from the North
with amazement."[4]

Although the observations made by Warner and *The Mascot* were separated from Werlein's by more than two decades, all contain references to two
themes that preoccupied reform-minded businessmen and boosters as they
sought to shape the city's growing tourist trade at the turn of the century.
First, all three observers focused on the question of race and what role it
played in the city's history and future. Strikingly, all of the parties made a
direct connection between race relations in general and sex across the color

line in particular as the most troubling yet telling manifestation of racial interaction in the city's past and present. Second, all of these observers made suggestions about what kinds of "proper" attractions ought to lie at the heart of the city's appeal to tourists and what role city leaders should play in promoting tourism.

Although the Franklin Street dives were not on Warner's list of must-sees, nor prominent in his coverage, a decade after his article appeared the city chose to segregate its brothels, dance halls, and other sexually oriented businesses into the exact geographic area *The Mascot* had complained about in 1887. What had been, at least from that paper's perspective, a little-discussed but shameful part of the city became home to its quasi-legal vice district in 1897. Over the next two decades that vice district, commonly called Storyville, became a regional and national attraction, and some would say a disgrace. Disgraceful or not, the district had its own contingent of supporters, some of whom were powerful state and local politicians. For many of them promotion or toleration of Storyville made good economic sense. For others, like long-time mayor Martin Behrman, segregation of the city's prostitutes and vice establishments was the best way to control activities that he believed were inevitable.[5]

While the city's vice district was by no means a singular phenomenon, during the twentieth century Storyville gained a reputation as unique. Of course, the city's last and most notorious vice district was not sui generis, but New Orleans's southern identity, complex history of race relations, and repeated attempts to organize urban space through sexualized segregation schemes did make Storyville distinctive. The district's notoriety was also due to the inextricable links between constructions of race and sexuality in the Jim Crow South.[6]

An exploration of the connections between tourism and sexuality in New Orleans suggests that the region's largest contiguous vice district acted as a safety valve, in deference to the widely held belief that male sexuality was necessarily rapacious and required an outlet in order to protect the virtue of respectable white women. The existence of a ribald, racially mixed place like Storyville also allowed visitors to take a vacation from the requirements of Jim Crow, yet maintain the pretension that white supremacy and racial segregation were absolute necessities in their own communities. Storyville was, after all, one of the few places in the turn-of-the-century South where blacks and whites from all classes mingled intimately, casually, and continuously in the pursuit of sex and leisure activities.[7]

Competing economic visions also underlay disagreements about the district's prominence. As a tourist attraction dedicated to the pursuit of illicit sexual behavior, Storyville became an important but contested center of economic activity for the city. Ironically, Storyville was the creation of a reform administration whose members believed that strict segregation of brothels and sexually oriented entertainment venues would limit their visibility and impact on the city's economy while making it easier to control undesirables by forcing them to inhabit a tightly defined geographic space. Those men, whose economic hopes for the future lay in further development of the port, real estate, railroads, and manufacturing concerns, did not anticipate that segregation of vice would have exactly the opposite effect from the one that they had intended. Over time the district became an economic powerhouse that generated graft, enhanced the city's erotic reputation, and helped it to become one of the South's most popular tourist destinations. The quest to develop the city's nascent tourism industry exposed tensions over sexuality, race, class, and collective identity and solidified New Orleans's reputation as "Sin City" in the regional and national imagination in ways that are still apparent today.

How, exactly, did the reformers' plans go so terribly awry? After all, local officials spent several months in 1896 and 1897 trying to determine which area of the city was the most appropriate for designating a vice district. Their ultimate choice was located in a section known as the "back o'town." This area began at the edge of the higher, natural levee grounds that were home to the French Quarter and the uptown business district and was largely populated by people without the resources to afford homes in more desirable geographical areas. The *Daily Picayune* referred to this area as "obscure," and a section "where decent people will not be constantly offended by [the] open and shameless flauntings" of prostitutes and their compatriots.[8]

Why did the neighborhood that was home to Storyville not remain obscure as reformers had planned? First, the reform administration that created Storyville in 1897, with the intention of making prostitution and sexually oriented businesses a less visible part of the city's landscape, economy, and appeal to tourists, was soundly defeated by the Democratic machine in the 1899 election. For the next two decades, the Ring, as its opponents called it, dominated city government. Perpetually successful mayoral candidate Martin Behrman, who was later credited with making the statement, "you can make prostitution illegal in Louisiana but you can't make it unpopular," held that office continuously from 1904 to 1920. His single-term predecessor, Paul

Capdeville, also heartily supported the Storyville solution. Moreover, both men made allies and decisions that helped the district become a cornerstone of the city's economy through its appeal to tourists and its concomitant notoriety. All of these events chagrined the reformers who had created the district, and many of them fought to control the district's growth and visibility in the years to come.[9]

A 1903 ordinance that provided significant grants of land and rights-of-way to the New Orleans and San Francisco Railroad Company helped forge a lasting link between tourism and Storyville. In exchange for the right to bring extensive rail lines and support facilities into the heart of New Orleans, the company agreed to construct "a passenger depot on the neutral ground of Basin Street," where it intersected with Canal. Although the extraordinarily detailed ordinance was adopted February 10, 1903, more than a year elapsed before a design for the terminal building was accepted, and it was four more years before the building itself was completed. In the meantime, there was a great deal of real estate speculation, jockeying among the railroad companies themselves, and uncertainty over how many rail lines the Frisco Ordinance, as it was popularly known, would ultimately bring into the city.[10]

The editors of New Orleans's own architectural digest commented in 1905 that if negotiations were successful, "the New Orleans Terminal Company's enterprises will practically change the face of the city in some respects." They could not have been more correct. Not only did the city's modern railway terminal bring it up-to-date with other New South cities, but multiline railway access into the heart of the city made it easier for people from all across the country to visit the city with speed and convenience. Completion of the terminal also meant that, in geographic terms at least, the back o'town became more integrated into the heart of the city than it had been when the Mississippi River was the main point of arrival and departure for visitors. In significant ways, the back o'town was transformed by the decision to place one of the city's central rail stations along its edge. And, as the back o'town became a vital part of the city's center, so did Storyville.[11]

Once the New Orleans Terminal station opened in 1908, several railroad lines brought their passengers into the city on a route that directly abutted the main street of Storyville. On the station's opening day, the *Times-Democrat* reported that the trains would now arrive "in the heart of the city" and celebrated the fact that "the depot is so near to all the leading hotels that it will not be necessary for passengers to take either cars or cabs to reach

Basin Street Brothels. Prostitutes in the Basin Street brothels helped give New Orleans a reputation among visitors as a sexual playground. (Courtesy of the Louisiana State Museum, New Orleans, Louisiana.)

them." Nor would it be necessary for anyone to look very hard to find the district reformers had worked so hard to hide away.[12]

Another reason the district became such a notorious attraction lies in the simple but seemingly unanticipated effects of concentration. With so many brothels, cribs, prostitutes, dance halls, cabarets, and saloons crammed into a single, contiguous area, the resulting landscape was remarkable simply for its size and the number of its dens of iniquity. At the time it was established in 1897, the blocks that made up Storyville contained 360 structures. Over the next decade that number actually increased as prosperous brothel and bar owners built flashy and sizable new establishments, especially on Basin Street. On the other end of the economic spectrum, greedy but astute property owners subdivided existing buildings into multiple narrow rooms called cribs, which could be rented for sexual encounters by prostitutes who did not actually live in the district full time. Certainly a great many other cities had municipally legislated or unofficially tolerated vice districts in this era, but very few of them were as substantial in size or as concentrated in population as Storyville. In 1900, city officials reported that there were 230 brothels and sixty assignation houses in the district. These figures do not take into account the dozens of other cribs, saloons, dance halls, cafes, and restaurants where prostitutes solicited and sometimes did business. With sixteen city squares largely dedicated to vice and male leisure establishments, Storyville constituted a veritable sexual amusement park.[13]

As with most other amusement parks, Storyville experienced seasonal fluctuations, both in its customer base and its population of prostitutes. According to the mayor and chief of police, as of 1900 there were "about 1500 prostitutes" working in the district. However, they also noted that the number of prostitutes was "largely increased in the winter, say by 500 more." Obviously the population of prostitutes would not have risen so significantly had there not been a customer base in place to support them. But why were so many tourists coming to New Orleans during the winter months and what, if anything, did Storyville have to do with their visits?[14]

Writing in Harper's in 1899, Julian Ralph opined that the city was well on its way to becoming "the chief winter resort of those who journey southward to escape the winters in the North." The author was no doubt correct that the city's temperate winters helped to account for its seasonal appeal, but, like Warner before him, Ralph gave short shrift to the city's more sensual attractions. In addition to balmy days, the winter tourist season featured horse racing and gambling, Carnival festivities, and access to Storyville. While many tourists, especially those from the northern states, were certainly escaping the cold, they were also basking in the many opportunities and outlets available to visitors who wished to indulge in pleasures of the flesh. The city offered its winter sojourners a constellation of sensual delights, and for many of them Storyville was the star attraction. While it was not the focus of articles in genteel magazines or of booster publications, over the course of the next two decades the city's vice district would become one of the city's and one of the South's most prominent and infamous tourist destinations.[15]

Even for locals the Storyville solution worked satisfactorily for a time. Soon after all court appeals were exhausted Mayor Paul Capdeville ordered the ordinance to be uniformly enforced, and the editors of the Daily Picayune claimed that "Nobody, except interested parties, questions the wisdom and propriety of the act." By interested parties, the editors referred to those seeking to enlarge the limits beyond those outlined in the original ordinances. But most of the city's population seems to have acquiesced in the decision, and several even wrote letters to the mayor asking him to make sure the order was enforced in their neighborhoods.[16]

Perhaps Capdeville, like the citizens who lobbied him to enforce the new district's boundaries, felt the enforcement of the Story ordinances would do the two things their advocates promised. One, they would provide an effective way to separate respectable people in the community, especially white women, from their fallen sisters and the rowdy, sexually oriented business establishments such as concert saloons and dance halls that featured casual prostitution on the bill of fare. Second, by moving prostitutes out of other residential neighborhoods, families and property values in those neighborhoods would be protected.[17]

Less than a decade into its existence, however, it was becoming clear that there were serious chinks in the conceptual and physical boundaries of the segregated vice district. The city's increasingly vocal female reformers were among the first to complain about the segregated district and the specious claim that it had been established first and foremost to protect the city's population of respectable women. For example, in 1908, one member of the city's newly formed Travelers' Aid Society "called attention to the danger of having the Frisco depot so near the Redlight District. She said that the boundaries of this district should be removed from this location and should be so clearly outlined." She concluded her remarks by adding that the new boundaries selected "should be far removed from the shopping district." She knew, as did most other locals, that a decade into the vice district's existence, Storyville was a segregated district in the heart of the city that only marginally served its stated purposes. By 1908, Storyville's prostitutes and their customers did business within eyeshot of the city's virtuous white women who shopped in the city's major department stores on Canal Street, while the city's increasingly diverse and numerous tourists were treated to a panoramic view of the district on their way into the new depot.[18]

The women who formed the Travelers' Aid Society in 1908 were keenly aware of the problems presented by the intersection of the city's growing tourist economy and the increasing prominence of its thriving vice district. One history of the organization explains that the association was "instituted for the purpose of fighting the White Slave traffic, an exceptionally flagrant case of which had come to the attention of the women of New Orleans." In response, the women called a mass meeting, after which a consortium of church groups and women's social clubs joined together to "consider ways and means of legally fighting the conditions which, though always existent, had become more heinous than usual." Like Phillip Werlein, the ladies of the Travelers' Aid Society welcomed the economic benefits of tourism but decried those aspects of the tourist trade that interfered with their moral vision for the city.[19]

Not surprisingly, the formation of the Travelers' Aid Society occurred only days after the city's 1908 Mardi Gras celebrations had come to an end. Like so many other reform drives that focused on conditions in Storyville, the events that led to the formation of the Travelers' Aid Society occurred during the city's increasingly popular winter tourist season—a season that reached its disorderly denouement with the celebration of Mardi Gras in February or March. Even reform-minded businessmen like Phillip Werlein, who "promoted their city with New South vigor, us[ed] Mardi Gras as a powerful magnet to attract buyers and investors to their city every winter." But the unruly and sometimes sexually licentious activities that lay at the core of this bacchanalian holiday once again revealed the tensions inherent in attracting visitors to the city considered by many to be the South's greatest sensual playground.[20]

If some tourists came seeking relief from the cold northern winter, for visitors from the immediate region, especially those from the more conservative, largely Protestant states that bordered Louisiana, New Orleans was a place where they could let their hair down with little fear of being censured for activities that would have been out of the question at home. Historian Ted Ownby suggests that even rural southern cities and towns generally set aside an area, either geographically or temporally, for "exclusively male professions, services, and recreations." But, in the context of the evangelical culture that dominated life in so much of the South, these spaces existed in sharp tension with the prevailing Protestant Evangelical religious beliefs held by most people in the community. Questionable "masculine recreations could take place largely unchallenged as long as those who disapproved rarely had reason to see them." While rural towns provided their male residents with occasional and limited outlets for rowdy behavior, New Orleans, and Storyville in particular, acted as a regional safety valve.[21]

Nineteenth-century sexual ideology posited that prostitutes provided men with the kind of physical safety valve that virulent male sexuality required. In many ways, Storyville was a geographic expression of this ideological belief. The district was also a year-round erotic space, inside the boundaries of which men of all descriptions and convictions could indulge in a variety of sensual, even sinful pleasures for days and nights on end free from the moral restraints that their home communities and respectable womanhood required of them. There is even evidence that men who were in the business of subduing Satan in their own communities came to New Orleans to revel with his mignons, even if only for a few days during Carnival each year. Historian Reid Mitchell makes note of the Reverend Charles L. Collins's visit to New Orleans for the 1908 Carnival season. Apparently his work for the Kentucky Anti-Saloon League required him to make at least two visits to the restricted district. In another case, a man from Hazelhurst, Mississippi, reported that he had seen the pastor of his church at "a sporting people's ball" and that the reverend was in the company of a woman wearing "a dress that was simply awful in its short skirts and worse in low neck."[22]

These "sporting people's balls" were also known as French Balls and had been conducted in the city at least since the 1850s. During the period of Storyville's existence these underworld balls reached a level of regularity and notoriety that certainly qualified them as a central tourist attraction. Although they were sponsored by a variety of organizations over the years, most of the balls had significant things in common. First, they were intended for the enjoyment and entertainment of men and offered them the opportunity to mingle with the city's population of prostitutes and fast women, far from the restraints of Victorian sexual mores. Both locals and visitors could revel "in explicit displays of female sexuality for male enjoyment." Second, while some respectable women were certainly able to sneak into these balls over the years, their main female attendees were prostitutes and other women of questionable reputations who received invitations to them at the bars, restaurants, and concert saloons that they frequented in the environs of Storyville. In fact, Tom Anderson, known by many as the mayor of Storyville, was one of the sponsors of the Ball of the Two-Well Known Gentlemen, "the most notorious" of all the French Balls. According to Mardi Gras historian Karen Leathem, "The French ball was a more festive version of a visit to a brothel."[23]

The French Balls were advertised in a variety of ways, including in mainstream newspapers and through production of intricate invitations that aped the high-style versions created by elite, old-line Mardi Gras krewes. But, for the tourist, information about the French Balls could be gleaned from the Blue Books. These small-format, softcover books, which included advertisements for items such as liquor, champagne, cigars, and on occasion even venereal disease cures, listed the names and addresses of some of the district's brothels and some of its individual prostitutes. Blue Books could be found in Storyville's restaurants and bars, and were also distributed to men just leaving the Basin Street train depot. The introduction to several versions of the Blue Book make clear that they were produced for tourists who were unfamiliar with the city's vice district. In one version, the book claims it will put "the stranger on a proper grade or path as to where to go and be secure from hold-ups, brace games, and other illegal practices usually worked on the unwise in Red Light Districts."[24]

According to Pamela Arceneaux, these directories were produced "on a more regular basis" in New Orleans than in "any other city with a sizable red-light district." Multiple versions of the Blue Book, like the business cards and individual advertisements generated by madams and other district entrepreneurs, provide ample evidence of how the district's denizens promoted themselves and their businesses to tourists. Extant advertising materials also demonstrate how the district's promotional schemes mimicked those employed by "respectable" businesses in the city at large. In fact, Joseph Roach argues that through "the normalizing courtesies of business cards and consumer guides," Storyville was "subsumed into the 'legitimate' economy of the city."[25]

The French Balls provide an explicit example of how sexuality played a role in generating tourism in New Orleans, particularly during Mardi Gras, but there is other evidence as well. The names of particular brothels, for example, were meant to entice tourists. Names like The Cairo or Emma Johnson's House of All Nations were intended to project an exotic appeal while names like Mahogany Hall or The Star Mansion evoked the mystique of the Old South and the antebellum mansion and promoted the quality of construction, sumptuous furnishings, and decorative detail one would find in these establishments. Inside upscale brothels, a client could be entertained in themed parlors such as the Turkish or Colonial Rooms in The Star Mansion, the Dutch Room at Hilma Burt's, or the multiple Japanese dens and Chinese parlors located in brothels throughout the district.[26]

The names of other establishments were meant to evoke a sense of familiarity for tourists traveling from other places. Cafés like the Monte Carlo and the Waldorf and bars like the Milwaukee Saloon sought to give their customers a sense of familiarity and convey refined or, in the case of the Milwaukee, casual hospitality. This kind of name recognition was the case with the New World Hotel as well. This sprawling hotel located on Robertson Street in an area of the district considered to be part of its "Negro section," occupied the same building that had housed a school for children of color in the neighborhood prior to adoption of the Story ordinance. Although the exact number of guests the hotel could accommodate is not recorded, 830 children attended the school in 1897. Fire insurance maps indicate that the developers of the New World Hotel made only minor changes to the building's footprint, expanding it slightly when they renovated the school into a hotel. Thus, we can deduce that the building's capacity for guests ran into the hundreds.[27]

While the significance of the hotel's name is not readily apparent, it almost certainly took that name from Clarksdale, Mississippi's, most famous turn-of-the-century brothel. For tourists coming into New Orleans from the Delta, handbills or other advertisements for the New World Hotel would have struck a familiar chord with those who had frequented the Clarksdale brothel of the same name. W. C. Handy described the Clarksdale brothel as a place where "lush octoroons and quadroons from Louisiana, [and] soft cream-colored fancy gals from Mississippi towns," plied their trade. According to Edward Ayers, "the Baptist and Methodist black families living nearby clearly disapproved of the events inside, especially the overt interracial sex," but white officials turned a blind eye to the brothel, probably induced to do so by graft and other favors they received from the New World's owners and resident prostitutes. Handy recalled that the "rouge-tinted girls, wearing silk stockings and short skirts, bobbing their soft hair and smoking cigarets . . . were wonderful clients, especially when important white men were their guests."[28]

The migration of a brothel name from Clarksdale to New Orleans mirrors the way that individual prostitutes used regional identification to draw customers to their doors as well. For instance, the Carnival edition of the *Sunday Sun*, dated February 25, 1906, included this advertisement: "Two sweet girls from Hattiesburg Miss. have come here and have embarked in business at No. 1418 Conti Street . . . visit these girls and they will entertain you in true Mississippi style." Although Mississippi certainly had its own brothels and, according to the prostitutes from Hattiesburg at least, its own erotic "style," the two sweet girls were shrewd enough to know that the most lucrative place to market their erotic wares was Storyville, at least during Carnival season.[29]

In the same issue, Lulu White, the mixed-race madam who was described as "the Queen of Diamonds and the proprietress of Mahogany Hall," assured prospective customers that she was "always surrounded by the finest and prettiest lot of Octoroons to be found in the country." In one version of the Blue Book, she claimed her house was "the most noted pleasure resort in the South." Whether or not she was stretching the truth in claiming that her brothel had "a national reputation," it is clear that the city's erotic notoriety did. Even as far north as Louisville and as early as 1885, southern madams like Sallie Scott bragged about the "famous Creole beauties" she could offer her clients. Twenty years later, W. C. Handy also connected illicit interracial sex to New Orleans when he commented on the quadroon and octoroon women from Louisiana whom he had encountered in Clarksdale.[30]

As the first decade of the new century moved toward its conclusion several things had become clear with regard to Storyville. First, it was obvious to everyone that the goal of limiting the district's visibility had been dashed with the development of the new railroad depot. Second, extant publicity materials and newspaper stories suggest that the district played an increasingly important role in enhancing the city's appeal as a winter tourist destination, particularly during Carnival season. Third, while tourists were the intended recipients of sexually oriented publicity materials generated during Carnival season, it was increasingly apparent that "even respectable people" were willing, even eager, to mingle with the district's denizens and profiteers during Carnival season, even if only "under the cover of masks." Tourists joined town folks to see the spectacles of skimpy dress and sexual license that characterized Storyville every day and, increasingly, at least in the minds of many people, the entire city for at least a single season of the year.[31]

Of course, creating a successful tourist economy required more than an annual, no-holds-barred bacchanal if the city was to become an "attraction the year round." Progressive Union president Phillip Werlein argued as much during his 1909 annual address when he opined that "cooking and the French Quarter" were not sufficient attractions on their own. Nor, he believed was "a one-week Mardi Gras frolic" enough to make the city into a winter resort with national appeal. Under Werlein's leadership the Progressive Union took many practical steps to create the infrastructure for a sustainable tourist economy. "The first accomplishment of any magnitude" came when "the railroads and steamship lines centering [in the city] granted a ten day stop over on all classes of tickets." This concession, for which the organization took credit, went a long way toward "placing New Orleans where it belongs, in the list of great tourist points of America."[32]

Under Werlein's leadership, the Progressive Union played a key role in promoting the city as a tourist destination. The organization routinely sent photographs and press releases to national magazines and newspapers in an effort to generate positive and recurring stories about New Orleans, and in 1909, "Advertise the City" was the organization's slogan. Their commitment to promoting the city as a tourist destination also led to the production of numerous pamphlets that they distributed to visitors during special events. In 1909, for example, Progressive Union representatives distributed twenty thousand copies of their pamphlets, "Fifty Facts about New Orleans" and "Recipes for Creole Cooking," during Mardi Gras celebrations.[33]

Like their underworld counterparts, the Blue Books, the pamphlets produced by the Progressive Union promoted their own agenda for the city's tourists. Although their titles often lacked flash, they reveal the extent to which the organization positioned itself as the authoritative source for information about the city. The revealingly titled pamphlet "I Talk for New Orleans" was followed four years later by "New Orleans: What to See and How to See It." Progressive Union publications promoted the city as "The Winter Capital of America" and "The Convention City of the South," but contextual information makes it clear that the Progressive Union sought to attract a particular kind of visitor to the city. Their target tourist was middle or upper class, certainly white, and, on the surface at least, inclined toward the kind of respectable, healthy pursuits Warner had promoted in *Harper's* nearly three decades before. Their vision for tourism was directed toward those whom they could welcome into their own prosperous and respectable circle. Otherwise, it is difficult to explain how they could promise that "some friend may always be had to obtain privileges [at] the private clubs." The Progressive Union sought to attract tourists who shared their ideas about respectable leisure pursuits and civilized morality, but they were equally interested in the economic benefits to be derived from the members of this demographic sector.[34]

Because Progressive Union members were as interested in attracting capital and industry to the city as they were tourist dollars, promoting tourism among the wealthy was an appropriate strategy. Yet the contradictions of trying simultaneously to emphasize business and pleasure led to some strange suggestions, even from Werlein, who was a tireless and usually prescient planner and activist. For instance, while he wisely suggested that the city find ways to extend its tourist season into the fall, his suggestion that "it should prove very interesting to the visitor . . . [to] be taken through the [city's] different manufacturing plants" was clearly a stretch. Yet it pointed to the dilemma that Werlein and his colleagues faced. How, they wondered, "could they lure outside capital to a city where 'sin,' not the work ethic, prevailed?"[35]

For as much as they tried, coverage about the city in national publications was not always positive. Progressive Union records make mention of several less than flattering articles that appeared in regional and national publications between 1908 and 1910. While some, like the *Chicago Herald Tribune*'s article "New Orleans: A Port Going Backward," related strictly to economic issues, others focused squarely on conditions in the city's vice district. For example, in the February 29, 1908, issue of *Collier's*, New Orleans received a stern reprimand in an article titled "The American Saloon." While many other cities came in for criticism as well, the tight connections the author, Will Irwin, identified among politicians, liquor interests, and the vice district were extremely troubling to men like Werlein who focused on enhancing the city's appeal as a respectable tourist destination.[36]

Irwin complained particularly about Tom Anderson, a man whom he called the restricted district's "law-giver and its king," and he described Storyville's "unblushing" evils in detail, including its "saloons with wide-open poker and crap games" and its "dives where [N]egroes buy for fifty cents five cents' worth of cocaine." Referring to the district as "Anderson County," Irwin charged that "no other city of the country runs vice of every kind so wide open." Irwin also pointed out what he considered the astounding fact that, in addition to serving as unofficial boss of the restricted district, Anderson was perpetually elected to the state legislature where he received important committee appointments and enjoyed enormous influence. He complained that Anderson "does not believe in sumptuary laws; he thinks that it degrades the citizen to take away from him the privilege of choosing for himself between right and wrong."[37]

Irwin clearly suggested that Anderson's position on sumptuary laws was objectionable, but most New Orleanians seemed to agree with Anderson that the privilege to choose between "right and wrong" belonged to them as individuals, especially when it came to indulgence in their favorite vices. But the laissez-faire morality for which New Orleans was so well known had also come under fire from the northern, heavily Protestant areas of the state, where arguments about temperance and vice reform like Irwin's had begun to find a receptive audience by 1908.

During the late nineteenth century, "vice connoted a range of frowned-upon activities, but it especially meant prostitution and alcohol." The conceptual relationship between alcohol and prostitution created substantive problems for Storyville's many alcohol-oriented businesses once prohibition forces began to gain ground in the state. Anderson was the most notorious figure who was openly associated with Storyville, but he was not the only one. Many other less visible and flamboyant businessmen were also heavily invested in the city's reputation for having a permissive attitude toward "vice of every kind." Unfortunately, for the parties who made their money from the potent combination of wine, women, and song, many people in the state, particularly those outside New Orleans, agreed that the time had come for more restrictive liquor laws.[38]

In commenting on that fact, Mayor Behrman remarked that "people from the country were for prohibition at home but when they came to New Orleans they were wet and wanted New Orleans to be saturated." In his own colorful way, Behrman's comment confirms the assertion that the city acted as a safety valve when it came to providing opportunities for tourists to indulge in activities that would be considered vices at home. The state legislature adopted a solution that seemed to reflect this attitude when they passed the Gay-Shattuck Law. According to Leathem, this statute was "designed to forestall prohibition through liquor regulation and to remove women from all places where liquor was sold and consumed." It also stipulated, among other things, that blacks and whites could no longer be served in the same establishments, and it banned musical instruments and musical performances from saloons. The only exceptions to these rules were for restaurants and hotels that served meals.[39]

Of course, the extensive and complicated stipulations of the Gay-Shattuck Law were an indication of how central the saloon had become to entertainment and leisure pursuits for all colors and classes of people in New Orleans and throughout the state. But the law stood to have a particularly dramatic effect inside Storyville, where the potent mixtures of men and women, black and white, and song and dance fueled the majority of the district's activities. Initial enforcement of Gay-Shattuck was swift and surprisingly thorough in New Orleans. At the end of the first week in January 1909, the *Daily-Picayune* reported that the "police put the lid down in the Tenderloin district last night, and saloon men and divekeepers raised a howl which vibrated from one end of the district to the other." The paper also noted that musical instruments were no longer "among the attractions to lure the slummer into the saloons and dance halls." In addition to checking saloons for females and musical instruments, the police also took the opportunity to enforce racial segregation in the district's saloons, suggesting that the racial mixing *The Mascot* had complained about two decades earlier continued to characterize the neighborhood. One saloon proprietor in the district, who was known for serving "refreshments indiscriminately to whites and blacks," was forced to choose one clientele or the other during the early Gay-Shattuck raids. He chose to post a sign that read "For Colored Patrons Only," once again suggesting how integral African Americans were to the district's economy.[40]

Of course, many proprietors sought ways around the law, ostensibly by turning their establishments into restaurants. "The notorious Ada Hayes," for example, installed "a weinerwurst and tamale stand" in the courtyard of her establishment, the New Waldorf Café, which had "a saloon in the front and a dance dive in the rear." Similar so-called restaurants popped up all around the district so that boarded-up dance halls and ladies' entrances to saloon-restaurant combinations were soon back in business. "Minor adjustments, combined with minimal enforcement, left dance hall life relatively untouched" in the long run.[41]

As for activities in the district overall, Storyville's denizens and establishments found many respectable allies in the membership of the newly formed Businessmen's League. The League was established in 1909 "to oppose the organized efforts to put Louisiana in the prohibition column." Within a year, the organization had a membership of nine hundred and was second in size only to the Progressive Union. While defeating prohibition was their goal, the members of the Businessmen's League were vitally interested in tourism, and they understood the tight nexus between the city's reputation for promiscuous good times and the health of its tourist trade. At a meeting held January 5, 1909, members expressed their concerns about recent reform victories like Gay-Shattuck and passage of a state ban on betting associated with horseracing. The members believed that reform legislation had already begun to affect the current winter tourist season. They concluded that "injurious effects have been produced by an erroneous report that has gone abroad that the people of New Orleans are becoming ultra-puratanical [sic] and that they have passed and would still further pass drastic blue laws that would curtail the just liberties of its citizens and make penal what has hitherto been considered legitimate occupations and innocent amusements." Although the members of the Businessmen's League did not overtly support prostitution, they did support the city's reputation for pursuit of good times. Storyville lay at the core of that reputation, both conceptually and physically.[42]

The members of the Businessmen's League sought to protect their economic interest in tourism. In their case, those economic interests were tied to the kinds of businesses, like brewing and hospitality, that profited from tourists no matter what their class background. Their economic interests in combination with their personal convictions led them to defend the laissez-faire morality that characterized the city and made the long-term existence of a vice district like Storyville possible. In a very real sense, the members of the Businessmen's League were progressive reformers, but they believed that the city's tourist economy would only succeed if it remained tied to the city's enduring reputation as the "Great Southern Babylon." Those, like Werlein, who disagreed with the members of the Businessmen's League were similarly concerned about their individual business interests and the city's long-term economic health, but they believed that Storyville was a blight on the city's reputation and that tourism was only desirable insofar as it met their definition of respectability.[43]

While enforcement of the liquor regulations stipulated in Gay-Shattuck ebbed and flowed with the public mood and the intermittent demands of conservative reformers, Werlein launched a direct assault against Storyville in early 1910. Always publicity minded, Werlein was stung by what he believed was the commonly held view that "no other city in the civilized world has permitted such conditions as prevail in New Orleans." His statement was "based upon the observations of travelers and the frequently published comments" in national magazines that criticized the city's vice district. He considered conditions surrounding the Basin Street terminal intolerable, arguing that "the glaring immorality and lack of common decency" is "apparent to everyone who uses the Terminal Station." His first suggestion was to limit the district's visibility by having the city or the railroad companies construct screens to hide the district from view, and he rallied a varied group of supporters to his cause. Members of the Era Club, a women's suffrage organization, agreed to support Werlein as did the largely female membership of the Travelers' Aid Society. Yet one local newspaper reminded readers that the efforts of these ladies would likely be limited "since the horror of the thing will prevent the club[s] from any participation in the warfare other than to give [their] moral support."[44]

Werlein also vowed to "enlist the aid of every minister in" the city. While it is unclear if he meant to include Catholic priests in his vow, it is clear that the bulk of Werlein's support came from members of local Protestant congregations. Some lay members, including women, also showed a willingness to support his crusade. In February, two hundred delegates attended the annual convention of the Laymen's Missionary Movement in New Orleans. They considered adopting a resolution that called on the city and state "to pass laws to drive all immoral establishments from the vicinity of Basin Street, and to wipe out the 'restricted district' if possible." They also declared that the district was "a menace to the city, state, and nation."[45]

Both Werlein and the Laymen's Missionary Association were troubled by the district's increasing visibility on the city's landscape and in nationally circulated newspaper and magazine stories, but they focused their complaints about the district on the availability and apparent popularity of sex across the color line, conflating prostitution in general with sex across the color line in particular. According to both parties, "relations between the races in the district" ought to be "punished by the same penalty as violation of the concubinage law—a term in the penitentiary." If the city did not act, they argued, conditions in the district were "calculated to prejudice the casual visitor against the sacred tenet of the Southern people—racial purity."[46]

The city's district attorney responded to these criticisms in a letter to Werlein. He argued that the recently adopted state concubinage law, which defined the act as the "unlawful co-habitation of persons of the Caucasian and of the [N]egro races whether open or secret," did not "prohibit the conditions on Basin [S]treet." Responding with great vituperation, Werlein declared it was "a shame and a disgrace and it is wrong, law or no law, that [N]egro dives like those of Emma Johnson, Willie Piazza, and Lulu White, whose infamy is linked abroad with the fair name of New Orleans, should be allowed to exist and to boldly stare respectable people in the face." The women of color whom Werlein named were three of the district's most elite and successful purveyors of sex across the color line, but they were not alone. Until 1917 in fact, city authorities took very few meaningful steps to segregate the district racially or to limit white men's access to women of color within its boundaries. African American men and women played vital roles in the district's popularity, as prostitutes, madams, musicians, service personnel, and patrons.[47]

Apparently Werlein and his allies were bothered less by the existence of the district per se than they were by the very profitable and well-known establishments like White's and Piazza's where one could cross the color line sexually with ease. On several occasions during his campaign Werlein reiterated this argument, in one case stating that "the real cancer of the district is the congregation of the whites and [N]egroes under practically the same conditions." He even suggested that if women of color were removed from the district, it would be much easier "after getting rid of the [N]egroes to concentrate the [white prostitutes] in the district."[48]

When the city rejected Werlein's request to screen the district from view, he responded by expanding his campaign and was clearly willing to play the race card in order to generate support for his "War on Basin Street." Led by Werlein, the district's opponents argued that the district in general was a disgrace, but they focused on the visibility of cross-racial sexual liaisons, charging that this aspect of Storyville was primarily responsible for smearing the city's reputation. Yet even this explosive charge barely caused a ripple in the larger body politic, nor was it enough to make city officials waver in their support for the district's continued existence. Although it certainly was not respectable, the district was apparently so profitable that city leaders and those who owned the district's real estate and entertainment venues, and sold alcoholic beverages to its patrons, were able to turn a deaf ear to Werlein's charges of interracial sex and a blind eye to the fact that the city was synonymous with sin and sex across the color line in the minds of many outsiders.[49]

Whether or not there was a collective case of denial or simply a laissez-faire attitude on the part of the populace is not clear, but events in October 1910 created at least a temporary backlash against reformers who railed against the city's vice district. Late in the month the American Purity Congress held a series of lectures in the city, the stated purpose of which was "to arouse among New Orleans purity workers a sentiment for the eradication of the terrible white slave traffic." The lectures failed to draw large audiences but they did attract the attention of many ministers and newspapers. The *Item* ran several stories that suggested, as did one headline, that "This City Is Not So Bad," while the Reverend H. Elmer Gilchrist, pastor of the First Unitarian Church, included "scathing criticism of the speeches of the members of the Purity Congress" in his sermon the following Sunday. Gilchrist strenuously objected to the contention that New Orleans presented reformers with a particularly troubling case of wide-open vice, and he argued that the "manner in which certain subjects were presented before a mixed audience were to say the least embarrassing." He concluded by lambasting the reformers themselves, particularly those "of the Boston type," for their arrogance in believing that they held "a commission from God Almighty to rule the universe."[50]

The *Item*'s editors also denied that the city had an extraordinary vice problem. In fact, they defended the district and suggested that "over-advertisement of the city as a wide-open town" was responsible for the "great deal of evil notoriety" the city had gained in recent months and years. Yet, try as they might to convince themselves and their readers that New Orleans was a big city like any other, no better and no worse, they failed to acknowledge just how deeply indebted the city's tourist industry was to the city's reputation for "evil notoriety."[51]

The always colorful Mayor Behrman recalled in his memoirs that members of the American Purity Congress had dealt the city's reputation a "few wallops." And he, at least, was candid in recalling that "a great deal of [what they charged] was true." Yet Behrman forthrightly defended the city's choice to maintain its vice district. After the Purity Congress adjourned and Werlein's reform drive had fizzled, Behrman issued a statement about the whole affair in which he "declared that this was the best policy and then I waited to hear something from the critics." According to him, there was no reply and "the subject was dropped."[52]

Over the course of the next several years reformers continued to organize locally, occasionally sparred with city officials, and demanded intermittent raids and stricter enforcement of temperance and prostitution statutes. They also sought to pass laws in the state legislature that were designed to trump the surprisingly durable Story ordinance. In late 1913, for example, The Committee of Fifteen for the Suppression of Commercial Vice in Louisiana published "An appeal to the people of Louisiana." The pamphlet's creators reminded readers that "New Orleans—the Metropolis of our State—is one of the very few cities in the United States and in Europe which still maintains a restricted district." They also pointed out that Storyville was "the first thing visitors to the city see when coming into the Terminal Station," and they asked, rhetorically, "are the citizens of the city and State proud of the unique attraction so presented?"[53]

In 1914 this organization managed to have a bill introduced into the legislature that was modeled on the Injunction and Abatement laws that several states had adopted since Iowa passed the first one in 1909. These laws provided local citizens with "an effective legal weapon against the owner, agent, and operator of property used for lewdness, assignation, or prostitution, since such use [was] declared by law, to constitute a public nuisance." In one broadside, supporters of the bill declared that "A vote *Against* the Abatement and Injunction Act . . . is a vote *for the Cribs, its owner and the Pimp.*" Although reformers concluded the broadside with the biblical dictum, "By Their Deeds Shall Ye Know Them," the veiled threat did not produce a legislative victory.

In fact, reformers' victories against Storyville, like their numbers and influence, remained inconsequential, at least until a new kind of tourist came to town in early 1917.[54]

The advent of World War I was a boon to the city's tourist economy. The Association of Commerce, which had grown out of the merger of the Progressive Union and similar organizations in 1913, reported in 1917 that "in normal times New Orleans is a most attractive city in which to hold convention. In war times, with overseas travel impossible, New Orleans has become the mecca of an ever increasing number of tourists." While the outlook was sunny for tourism, the association also worked aggressively to enlarge the presence of military encampments, soldiers, and sailors as the country prepared to enter the war. "With the cooperation of Mayor Behrman the Bureau succeeded in having a naval training station established" in the city. It also lobbied military authorities to make the city an official quartermaster supply depot.[55]

War was good for business on many fronts, and soldiers and sailors, who were both tourists and transients, were a welcome addition to the city's economy, but their presence also created problems and revealed once again how competing economic and moral visions shaped the city's tourism industry. For the women of the Travelers' Aid Society, "problems and difficulties [increased] . . . a thousand fold" as the society went about its mission of "protecting women and girls arriving in the city, who, through ignorance or inexperience, are in danger of being exposed to the influence of the representatives of organized vice." According to their records the "soldiers encamped in . . . City Park and the students enrolled at Camp Martin, on the campus of Tulane University," made their task all the more difficult.[56]

Local reformers were not the only ones who were concerned. Men and women from rural Louisiana also raised concerns during 1917 about the dangers that New Orleans and its vice district posed to soldiers and sailors. For example, M. E. Dodd, pastor of the First Baptist Church in Shreveport, wrote to the national Commission on Training Camp Activities in June. He expressed interest in the "moral and spiritual welfare" of the fifteen boys from his church who had "volunteered for service in the defense of our national honor." He was particularly concerned about the young men who had been stationed near New Orleans and concluded his letter, "it is well known that New Orleans is the sodom of the South and if our boys cannot be protected there, I earnestly request your consideration in moving them."[57]

Mrs. A. C. McKinney of Ruston, Louisiana, wrote a long and impassioned letter to the national office of the Women's Christian Temperance Union that was forwarded to the Commission on Training Camp Activities. She reported in July that officials from New Orleans and Alexandria were in Baton Rouge "doing all in their power to defeat the bill . . . for the protection of the boys that are to be encamped in Louisiana." Why, she asked, "is it that the government makes an exception of New Orleans? They have made other places clean up, or failing in that, have moved the boys. Must the Louisiana boys be sacrificed?" She concluded that "conditions in New Orleans are indescribable and if the Government does not do something to close those saloons and brothels, many of the boys will be rendered unfit for service."[58]

Members of New Orleans's Travelers' Aid Society may have been concerned about protecting young women from seduction, but the military establishment and some in northern Louisiana were more interested in protecting soldiers from venereal disease. In fact, the War Department's efforts focused on penalizing and controlling women, especially prostitutes, as a means to limit the incidence of venereal infection. Under the auspices of the Commission on Training Camp Activities (CTCA), the military services implemented a "rigorous policy of vice suppression" and offered the thousands of soldiers stationed in training camps "wholesome recreational and social opportunities" in their stead.[59]

"The CTCA's authority to suppress prostitution in the communities surrounding military training camps was based on Section 13 of the Selective Service Act, which outlawed any form of prostitution within five- to ten-mile zones around each camp." In order to entice military authorities to locate camps in their locales, many cities closed their districts as quickly as possible. In others, the efforts of reformers had resulted in the eradication of red light districts a few years earlier. But in cities that were reluctant to do so "the threat of moving the training camp to another location was often sufficient to make local officials comply." According to historian Mark Thomas Connelly, "this was often the tactic used in the South, most notably in Louisiana."[60]

Mayor Behrman was convinced that a well-policed segregated district, closely monitored by both civilian and military personnel, was the best means available to protect soldiers stationed in New Orleans from venereal disease, and he went to Washington and made his case before Secretary of War Newton Baker in August 1917. Apparently he was convincing enough that Baker conceded to allow Storyville to remain open until the effectiveness of the proposed patrols could be ascertained. Approximately two months later, however, Behrman received another set of direct orders to close the district, this time from Secretary of the Navy Josephus Daniels. He introduced an ordinance to do so a few days later and Storyville was officially closed on November 12, 1917.[61]

In order to maintain military camps in New Orleans, local officials were ultimately forced to concede to the demands of state and federal authorities. They did so grudgingly, and some local citizens agreed that reform of the vice district would interfere with the city's reputation for good times and thus its appeal to tourists. For example, a writer identified only as R. W. C. expressed the following reservations in a telling letter to the editor. "Are we not in danger of violating the particular 'atmosphere' of our unique city, of dulling the local color, and impairing the individuality of our town, by the institution of 'radical reforms'?"[62]

With the benefit of hindsight we know R. W. C. need not have worried. The downturn in good times, if it ever existed at all, was remarkably brief, indicating that Storyville's demise was much more apparent than real. In fact, in classic New Orleans style, many of Storyville's brothels continued to operate, turning away only sailors and soldiers in uniform. This requirement reportedly gave rise to a new cottage industry in which civilian clothes were rented by the hour to soldiers and sailors on leave. The changed priorities of the nation leading up to entry in the First World War meant that the city's formal collusion in the promotion of sexual tourism had to be traded away, at least temporarily, in order to gain as much patriotic pork as possible in the months leading up to the United States's entry into the war. But, just as Charles Dudley Warner had noted thirty years before, there were still "more than enough of the resorts upon which the police are supposed to keep one blind eye."[63]

The city adopted a policy with regard to prostitution in the years following 1917 that one historian has dubbed "unobtrusive non-observance." The United States Interdepartmental Social Hygiene Board issued a scathing report on vice conditions in New Orleans in 1921 that suggested keeping "one blind eye" on back-room brothels and street-walking or call-girl prostitutes was about all city leaders and police were willing to do. The federal government's report concluded that "immoral houses are operating openly . . . and that the city harbors numbers of women, especially [N]egroes, who openly ply their trade."[64]

Brothels and other less visible forms of prostitution using nightclubs, restaurants, hotels, taxi drivers, and boarding houses as fronts, were thriving in

the city in the 1920s. By the end of that decade one author assured his readers that visitors to New Orleans, a group he referred to as "hell-bound people,"
would find "plenty of liquor . . . gambling dens, cabarets, roadhouses, nightclubs, and a total lack of reformers." If the writer failed to mention prostitutes
specifically, perhaps that was because the business had taken on new and
more surreptitious forms. Yet the city's reputation for openly operating cribs
and brothels reemerged during the 1930s. In 1934, *Vanity Fair*, for instance,
proclaimed New Orleans "a Wicked City" and detailed its history of "quadroon prostitution" in particular. The same year *Real Detective* referred to
the city as a "Vice Cesspool" and described the "nightly saturnalia within
the New Orleans red light district" in graphic detail. According to author
Edward Anderson, the 1930s vice district occupied the same boundaries
Storyville had. Although Anderson claimed that women of all sizes, ages,
races, and skin tones worked in the district, he noted that one of the "most
notorious" places was called "Uncle Tom's Cabin," a venue where sex circuses
were "arranged for those interested." Clearly prostitution continued and, as
the preoccupations of those who wrote about New Orleans's sex trade indicate, so did the conflation between prostitution in general and sex across the
color line as its most troubling and most criticized manifestation.[65]

More than a century after Storyville was established, the city's reputation
for promiscuity and sexually oriented tourist attractions remains intact, as
does the willingness of local entrepreneurs to capitalize on it. Over the decades numerous drinking and entertainment venues have appropriated the
vice district's name. One brass band and two bars currently use the name
Storyville, while the airport has a lingerie shop named after the infamous
octoroon madam, Lulu White. Although this sexualized reputation used to
be controversial, at least among members of booster groups like the Progressive Union, today the city's Chamber of Commerce unabashedly exploits it.
For example, one recent publication described the city as a "corpulent host-
ess, patted and daubed with rouge," reclining "along the banks of the wide
river, straining her corsets of convention and drawing her admirers to her
with a languid gesture." In this iteration, the city itself is portrayed as an
aging prostitute. Such depictions give credence to Joseph Roach's claim that
the city has "somehow constructed itself as the nation's libido (i.e. 'The Big
Easy')."[66]

Although Storyville was established as a place where the city could hide
away its undesirable populations, over time the defunct and now virtually destroyed district has become a beacon that continues to draw tourists to the

city. Today the city's reputation for promiscuous good times manifests itself in the outrageous and often sexually explicit acts tourists engage in during Mardi Gras and Southern Decadence. The city's continuing toleration of street-level lewd and abandoned behavior provides incontrovertible evidence that the city's risqué reputation continues to generate enormous economic dividends. As New Orleans approaches its third century of existence, it remains an island of indulgence where people feel free to explore libidinal longings and illicit sexual desires in a setting that continues to be more permissive than most other places in the South and the nation. While the laissez-faire attitude for which the city is so well known has many sources, its enduring centrality to the development and sustenance of the critically important tourist economy cannot be underestimated. Storyville was and has remained an icon of the city's sybaritic appeal—a sexually alluring beacon to tourists from the Bible Belt and beyond.[67]

2
Hillbillies and the Holy Land
The Development of Tourism
in the Arkansas Ozarks

Brooks Blevins

Harold Sherman, a Wisconsin-born reporter and novelist who had spent most of his adult life in New York City, first traversed the Arkansas Ozarks on a trip from Hollywood to Chicago during World War II. Sherman's first encounter with an Ozarker, a friendly man who made several trips to a creek to fill his hat with water for the city slicker's overheated car, left him with a sudden feeling of "revulsion against the sham of civilization." To ease the stress of his modernized, urbanized conscience, Harold Sherman almost immediately bought an abandoned farm with a little house in Stone County. Like many newcomers to the Ozarks, Sherman found himself torn between an urge to perpetuate and profit from the rustic image of the region and a desire to bring the modern world to the hills in the form of electricity and paved highways. He spent the rest of his life promoting tourist enterprises, including the development of Blanchard Springs Caverns, the Ozark Folk Center, and a failed theme park and hunting refuge called the "Land of the Cross-Bow."[1]

Perhaps no individual exercised more influence on the modernization of the Ozarks and the growth of tourism in the region than Harold Sherman. Sherman's Ozark interests and activities embodied the ambiguity, irony, and often dishonest posturing of the Ozarks' most important post–World War II industry, tourism, and the related business of image development. In spite of sudden and dramatic cultural, economic, and social transformation in the years following World War II, the Ozarks maintained the ambiguous image that had been crafted by travel writers and folklorists during the depression. In spite of the exodus from farms and backcountry communities, in spite of the homogenization of agriculture, the growth of small-scale manufacturing, and the blossoming of retirement villages and wealthy indigenous corporations, the Ozarks and its inhabitants remained in the minds of cold war Americans isolated, independent, contemporary ancestors. But it was only at a point when this image had become even less applicable to the region than ever before that the image spawned a vibrant and diverse tourism industry.

By the time Sherman moved to northern Arkansas, the Ozark region could trace its tourism roots back almost seven decades—to the healing water craze of the 1880s—and a handful of towns had come to depend on tourist-generated revenue as a chief source of income. The region's ambiguous image as both an unspoiled arcadia and an arrested, wild frontier had attracted sightseers and a few urban homesteaders for a generation or more. During the Great Depression growing numbers of articles in national magazines and books about culture and life in the Arkansas and Missouri hills had provided the foundation for a tourist industry based on manipulation and perpetuation of any number of stereotypes of the Ozark region and its inhabitants.

Unfortunately, for the purveyors of the arcadian image of the Ozarks and for the observers of contemporary ancestors, World War II and its aftermath were not kind to their unspoiled region. By the time the smoke cleared in the cold war era, the Ozark hawkers and observers returned to a region quickly being absorbed into regional and national patterns of life and rapidly becoming unrecognizable. But images die slowly, even in the face of damning evidence. Tourism came not as an economic savior to these areas—or at least the ones with such potential—but as a last resort. And this new industry in northern Arkansas was built in large measure on the Ozark image formulated during the depression and perfected in the 1950s, the very image that had attracted Harold Sherman to the region in the first place.

Tourism in the post–World War II Ozarks consisted of an often-complex jumble of activities, practices, and purposes. Nevertheless, major tourism endeavors in the region can be classified into three categories: those capitalizing on the Ozarks' physical and aesthetic attributes (rivers, caves, and man-made lakes), those playing up the presumed cultural uniqueness of this southern highland backwater, and those whose primary thrusts carry no reliance on the region in any physical or cultural sense—in other words—those tourist activities that could very well have taken place anywhere else. The Ozark-themed and general tourist attractions, for the most part located within a twenty-five-mile radius of Mountain View, Eureka Springs, or Hardy, all share to some extent a common faith in the static, innocent image of the region perpetuated by travel writers and folklorists in the quarter-century following World War II. It is with these tourism developments that this essay is primarily concerned.

The recognized center of heritage-based tourism in the Arkansas Ozarks is Mountain View, the once-isolated Stone County seat perched atop the heights where the Boston Mountains collide with the White River Hills. Mountain View and its environs have long attracted a variety of visitors: hunters, fishermen, and campers. Before World War II the Sylamore District of the Ozark National Forest north of the village had served as the state's last best refuge for whitetail deer; consequently, the area around Big Flat became a prime deer hunting destination.[2] The work completed by Civilian Conservation Corps (CCC) crews in the district laid the physical foundation—roads, parks, buildings—for a small camping and resort business in the postwar years. But it was only in the early 1960s that Mountain View and surrounding areas began to be transformed into popular tourist destinations.

A close look at the evolution of the tourist industry around Mountain View, the industry's reliance on both physical- and heritage-based attractions, and the inner workings of various key individuals and groups provides the best window into the complex and political world of modern Ozark tourism. The odyssey that eventually produced northern Arkansas's second most popular tourist destination involved government agencies and private groups, outsiders and native Ozarkers, Washington politicians, and mountain musicians. As has most often been the case, it was an outsider who set in motion the forces of change and the wheels of tourism in Stone County. Harold Sherman arrived in Stone County in the 1940s to find a region quite unlike Hollywood or Chicago. Most of the county's residents lacked electricity and running water, and Stone County was one of the few in the state with no paved highway running through it. Sherman led local efforts to obtain electricity in the early 1950s and later headed up a group of locals who succeeded in getting key highways paved. Like many newcomers, Harold Sherman never truly understood his Ozark neighbors, and most likely he never really sought to.

From the time of his arrival Sherman looked on his new home region as a project. He would lead the silent and thankful natives out of the wilderness in a play scarcely believable outside Hollywood. And he would do so by making Stone County the playground of the rich from Michigan to Texas. Sherman was an ardent supporter of local issues and projects when they were also his issues and projects and a harsh and spiteful critic when local groups failed to share his visions. In a 1957 letter to First District Congressman Wilbur D. Mills, Sherman complained about the state highway commission's decision to pave a twelve-mile stretch of highway in western Stone County rather than his proposed stretch, a road in sparsely settled southern Stone County that was frequently traveled by tourists coming up from Little Rock. In complete earnestness he noted: "Such a road, serves only the local needs."[3]

Sherman's urgency in the spring of 1957 was motivated largely by his first big tourist project—an archery range and hunting resort that he called the "Land of the Cross-Bow." The resort, situated in an isolated, barely accessible area of Stone County, would sport "taverns of early England," bowling greens, and "signs constructed in the old English style to create for tourists an atmosphere of medieval times." The press release for the resort repeated the by now popular mantra of travel writers and folklorists alike, assuring readers that "the rugged country in which it lies is one of the last refuges of original Anglo-Saxon stock which first colonized this country." Visitors were promised native fishing guides, and in case the park sounded too upscale, Sherman assured readers that "there is no question at any time but what you have 'gotten away from it all.'"[4]

Although Sherman's project looked promising in 1957, by the end of the following year the "Land of the Cross-Bow" was a failure. The concept had been far-fetched to start with and, like Gerald L. K. Smith's Eureka Springs projects a decade later, wholly divorced from the tradition and history of the region. The failure of the "Land of the Cross-Bow" further exacerbated political divisions in a county already notorious for its infighting. It was clear that such a project offered no economic salvation for the depressed people of north central Arkansas and that such schemes should be avoided in the future. It was also clear, to most locals at least, that Sherman was either a con man or a kook, perhaps both, and certainly a damn Yankee. As the business and political leaders of Mountain View would soon discover, salvation, if any were to be had, could come only through utilization of the region's physical attributes, through heritage hustling, and through playing up the static image of the Ozarks at the very moment Appalachia's image was experiencing a fundamental makeover.

The growth of heritage tourism and the transformation of Mountain View and its environs can be traced back to 1959. In November the Arkansas cooperative extension service established its first Area Rural Development district for the purpose of formulating plans to address the economic needs of four north central counties, Stone, Independence, Izard, and Sharp. Fulton was added in February 1961. Because the Area Rural Development Committee was under the extension service, the original focus was on improving agricultural methods and marketing and on developing small industry. By the time Leo Rainey arrived in September 1961 as rural development director, the extension service had begun to shift its focus to tourism. Rainey noted in his annual report the following June: "It is true that more emphasis has been placed upon tourism this year as well as crafts. Economists state that tourism probably offers the greatest hope for economic development in the rugged areas of this section."[5]

Only twenty-nine when he arrived in Batesville with the daunting task of practically orchestrating the economic revitalization of an area never known for its financial prosperity, Rainey would soon find himself in the center of a burgeoning tourist industry and heritage revival, a movement that would ultimately revitalize sections of his region but pass over others. Rainey helped launch the tourist movement in September 1961, when he accompanied three other extension service employees and thirty-six community leaders from north central and northwestern Arkansas on an information-gathering trip to the fall fair of the Southern Highland Handicraft Guild in Gatlinburg, Tennessee.[6] Although no Ozark town enjoyed Gatlinburg's unique geographic advantage—it is located on the main thoroughfare leading into the Great Smoky Mountains National Park—the agents and community leaders hoped to emulate the eastern Tennessee city's success as a center of mountain handicraft production.

On the group's return Rainey promptly organized an Area Tourist and Recreation Committee and an Area Craft Subcommittee. The craft subcommittee organized craft fairs in Rainey's five counties as well as in Van Buren and Cleburne Counties in the spring and summer of 1962 to find native talent. To their dismay Rainey and his fellow subcommittee members found a severe shortage of native crafters in the Ozarks. Based on the subcommittee's preconceptions of what constituted mountain crafts, preconceptions largely formed during the visit to Gatlinburg, fifty-five craftspeople were chosen from the seven-county region, all of whom were invited to display and sell their wares at a region-wide fair in Batesville in August. The craft subcommittee selected craftspeople, most of whom were native Ozarkers, on the basis of both authenticity and quality. Crafts displayed in Batesville ranged from woodcarvings to handwoven rugs and from corncob dolls to cornshuck hats. In November the fifty-five craftspeople formed the Ozark Foothills Craft Guild and made plans for the establishment of craft shops. By

1965, with the help of a loan from the Small Business Administration, the guild operated small, seasonal shops at Mountain View, Clinton, Heber Springs, and Hardy.[7]

In addition to its work with the craft guild, the Area Tourist and Recreation Committee organized the first Dogwood Drive automobile tour for the spring of 1962 to capitalize on Stone County's scenic beauty and its recently paved highways. It also organized a series of Tourist Service and Information courses that were offered in towns around the region in 1962. Designed for "persons who have contact with tourists" and taught in three two-hour increments by representatives of the state Department of Vocational Education, the courses offered instruction in Ozark history and legend, fishing, and hunting and provided information concerning tourists' needs and expectations.[8]

The year 1963 witnessed the genesis of three separate but interrelated projects that would transform the county into a traveler's destination. Local craft guild members, Jimmy Driftwood, Rainey, and other leaders organized Mountain View's first Arkansas Folk Festival, which would become a popular annual event. Harold Sherman began efforts to transform Half-Mile Cave into a federally operated tourist site. And local and federal officials launched the movement that eventually produced the state-operated Ozark Folk Center.

Harold Sherman's most important project held better promise for promoting tourism in north central Arkansas than did his earlier medieval village concept. In the early 1960s Sherman was unofficially appointed by local leaders to oversee the development of Blanchard Springs Caverns. According to one participant his active direction of the caverns project served to rid the more important folk center movement of his less than welcome assistance and his negative reputation among many local residents. Nonetheless, Sherman used his media savvy and his friendship with Congressman Mills to guide the project to completion. The project involved the use of a cave (eventually discovered to be a maze of caverns) in the Sylamore District of the Ozark National Forest first explored in 1934 but only recently seriously mapped and charted by two local spelunkers. In 1963, at a Stone County press conference conducted by Sherman, the U.S. Forest Service announced plans to set aside Half-Mile Cave for recreation purposes. Although Sherman's original plan called for private development of the cave, he soon acquiesced to Forest Service control. The Forest Service began construction of a visitors' center in 1970 and opened Blanchard Springs Caverns to the public in the summer of 1973, less than a month after the grand opening of the Ozark Folk Center.[9]

Blanchard Springs Caverns was, like the spring dogwood blooms and autumn leaves, a tourist attraction based solely on the region's physical beauty and uniqueness. The real growth of tourism in the Mountain View area would come to depend on the people, or at least on Americans' image of the people. Utilizing this formula, the Arkansas Folk Festival first attracted large numbers of visitors to Mountain View and directly or indirectly spurred the completion of the other two projects. Mountain View's Arkansas Folk Festival was a straightforward attempt to revive the depressed area's fortunes and funnel tourist dollars into local businesses and into the empty pockets of craft guild members. It was conceived in relative haste and rolled along willy-nilly into snowballing success. In October 1962, even before the establishment of the Ozark Foothills Craft Guild, Rainey, three district extension service employees, and Stone County extension agent Lloyd Westbrook met to plan a craft fair scheduled for April 1963. W. H. Freyaldenhoven, district extension agent, suggested incorporating local musical talent as a complement to the craft sale. Westbrook, the lone Stone County resident of the five, was given the task of convincing the county's most famous citizen, Jimmy Driftwood, to organize musicians for the fair. Driftwood agreed to serve and came on board in January 1963.[10]

Born James Corbett Morris in a Stone County community south of Mountain View in 1907, Driftwood grew up in an atmosphere rich in mountain musical heritage. Neal Morris, Jimmy's father, was a locally prominent folksinger who had learned more than one hundred old ballads from his mother, and Driftwood's maternal grandfather was a traveling merchant who regaled customers with his renditions of ballads both recent and ancient. Driftwood and his wife, Cleda, spent their young adult lives as country teachers. Jimmy served for thirty-four years as a teacher and principal at the little three-room school in Timbo. It was as a teacher during the depression that Driftwood, to aid his students' mastery of American history, wrote the words to his famous "Battle of New Orleans" and set them to the melody of an old Irish fiddle tune, "Eighth of January." "Discovered" by folklorist John Quincy Wolf, Jr., two decades earlier, by the 1960s Driftwood was a commercially successful singer and songwriter.[11]

From the moment Driftwood entered the picture, the project took an unexpected and monumental turn that would alter the destiny of Mountain View and Stone County. The festival's planners had envisioned something along the lines of a small country-and-western music program featuring Driftwood and a few of his fellow musicians from the Grand Ole Opry. Driftwood had other visions. Concerned over the almost complete disappearance of traditional mountain folk music in his home county and region and quite oblivious to the objections of his fellow festival planners, Driftwood decided to use the Arkansas Folk Festival as a project for the resuscitation of his beloved musical heritage.

Driftwood returned to Stone County in early 1963 to discover that a local physician had only recently begun hosting informal, traditional musical gatherings in his Mountain View office. Within two months the weekly gatherings had outgrown the tiny office, forcing the newly formed Rackensack Folklore Society (which Driftwood quickly came to dominate) onto the courthouse lawn. Rainey and the festival's organizers decided to schedule the craft fair and musical to coincide with the second annual Dogwood Drive. Mountain View hosted its first Arkansas Folk Festival on the weekend of April 19–21, 1963. In spite of a general pessimism among the town's business leaders regarding the festival's reliance on unknown, local musical talent, approximately ten thousand visitors passed through town that weekend, and 4,500 jammed themselves into the tiny high school gymnasium to watch the performances of Driftwood's "timber cutters, farmers, housewives, and all plain people of the hills." The craft fair, limited to guild members only, generated more than $2,000 for forty-five craftspeople.[12]

Through word of mouth and promotion by Driftwood and the craft guild, the Arkansas Folk Festival expanded into the state's biggest annual tourist event. By the late 1960s every inch of Mountain View was devoted to the April festival, and for a few years beginning in 1975 festival organizers scattered events over a three-weekend period to maintain enthusiasm, draw larger crowds, and prevent single-weekend traffic jams. By the early 1970s crowds regularly exceeded one hundred thousand people. The thousands of automobiles and tour buses clogged Mountain View's tiny town square, the side streets, and all four roads leading into and out of town. Over time the festival grew beyond the control of its original planners, the members of the Arkansas (formerly Ozark Foothills) Craft Guild. Faced with declining sales due to the proliferation of independent craft dealers who set up tables and booths on every street corner in town, the guild ceased its sponsorship of the Arkansas Folk Festival.[13]

The Arkansas Folk Festival, still conducted each April in conjunction with the Ozark Folk Center, was perhaps the purest and most earnest example, at least in its early years, of Ozark heritage tourism. The driving force was economic revitalization for a poor town and county, and most of the original craftspeople and musicians were native Ozarkers if not residents of Stone County.[14] As the native craftspeople and musicians have died, lost interest, or grown too old to participate they have generally been replaced by non-Ozarkers, many of them counterculture holdovers or urban escapists who came to the Ozarks in the 1960s and 1970s to learn traditional crafts. Most often this process of replacement is by necessity. Few modern Ozarkers are interested in the handicraft and musical skills of their forebears, and fewer still are recipients of such traditional folk knowledge handed down through the generations. Of course, such cultural and generational apathy is not unique to the Ozarks but is common in any modern culture. Ozarkers are no longer bound by isolation and poverty to carry on the unconscious traditions born of necessity, place, and want. The Ozarkers of 1963 were not bound to their heritage, either, which explains the paucity of native craftspeople and the musicians' need to dust off their instruments. The later years of the festival also brought an influx of hillbilly stereotypes into the picture. The wood and plastic caricatured moonshiners and Daisys obscured the original goals and products of the Arkansas Craft Guild, which in part explains the Guild's ultimate disassociation from the event. Furthermore, by focusing so intently on one phase of the region's past, a period assumed to adequately represent the whole of the Ozarks' static history, the festival tended indirectly to perpetuate the image of Ozarkers as "a people without factories, who made everything they used with their own hands and who sang 'Barbara Allen' and other British ballads as in the days of Elizabeth and James I."[15]

The spirit of the Arkansas Folk Festival realized its physical manifestation in the Ozark Folk Center. Nevertheless, the Ozark Folk Center grew out of a separate cause, one infused with more political overtones and less folk earnestness. The Ozark Folk Center was a decade in the making and for a dozen years was racked with political turbulence. The folk center idea came from a young bureaucrat named John Opitz. Opitz, an Arkansan though no Ozarker, first mentioned his idea for a cultural center in 1963 in his capacity as regional director of the Area Redevelopment Administration (ARA), a federal agency created by Congress in 1961 for the purpose of funneling loan and grant monies into rural areas for industrial development, public facilities, technical assistance, and trainee pay. Personally interested in the folk movement himself, Opitz had two goals in mind: the construction of a new water and sewer system for Mountain View, a popular cause in town; and the establishment of a folk culture center for the preservation of traditional music. In order for the town to receive the water and sewer system, Opitz proposed to Jimmy Driftwood and local leaders the building of a music auditorium with ARA assistance. The auditorium would have to come equipped with a new system to pump water from the nearby White River, and, he suggested, the town of Mountain View could hook up to the auditorium's system. Thus began the movement to preserve the Ozarks' culture and dying traditions.[16]

Opitz's offer came as a welcome project, one whose direction Driftwood happily assumed and selfishly maintained. In the dozen years after 1963 he would adopt the center as his personal project. Already recognized around the nation as a leading practitioner of traditional mountain music and a self-taught expert on Ozark culture, Driftwood served as a go-between, though certainly not a universally popular or uncontroversial one, in the drawn out negotiations between Washington politicians and bureaucrats and local officials.

In September 1968, after five years of lobbying, the federal Economic Development Administration (successor to the Area Redevelopment Administration) approved the folk center project, and Wilbur D. Mills's House Ways and Means Committee set aside more than three million dollars, 20 percent of which was to be paid back by the city of Mountain View over a fifty-year period.[17] The original folk center concept called for a center for both preservation and training. The center's leaders soon discovered, as had Driftwood five years earlier, that the traditional crafts and music to be preserved had not been bequeathed to the past couple of generations of Stone Countians. Ozarkers would have to be taught the folk skills and activities that visitors to the Arkansas Folk Festival assumed they already possessed. Consequently, in November 1969, the state Department of Vocational Education agreed to establish a training school at the Ozark Folk Center for the purpose of instructing local young people in the forgotten music and crafts of their heritage. The irony explicit within the nature of the center was further compounded in succeeding years. When the firm awarded the original contract to build and operate what was to be a privately controlled folk center went bankrupt in 1972, the state Parks, Recreation and Travel Commission purchased the operating lease at the behest of Ozark Folk Cultural Commission leaders and Governor Dale Bumpers. The Department of Parks and Tourism had no need for another expensive, non-profitable project and agreed to operate the Ozark Folk Center as a state park only when the Ozark Folk Cultural Commission agreed to scrap the original vocational training mission and convert the center into an outdoor museum charging admission.[18]

When the Ozark Folk Center was officially dedicated in May 1973, the 300-acre complex contained a 1,060-seat auditorium, sixteen craft shops, a tourist reception center, a conference center, a restaurant, a fast-food counter, and a 60-room lodge. The first couple of years of the Ozark Folk Center's existence were racked by numerous problems. The two activities of the center—music and craft making—were originally undertaken by local groups. The Department of Parks and Tourism contracted with the Ozark Foothills Craft Guild to supply Ozark crafts and craft demonstrators. The members of the guild received no salaries or wages, relying instead on sales of their crafts. Because the original center had no gift shop, craft sales were conducted at the individual shops scattered around the compound. This system proved unwieldy for the craft guild and unprofitable for its members, prompting the guild to pull out of the project and open its own craft shop near the folk center in 1975. The Department of Parks and Tourism began contracting directly with individual craftsmen, most of whom were guild members.[19]

Likewise, the Department of Parks and Tourism originally relied on Driftwood's Rackensack Folklore Society to provide musicians. By doing so the Department of Parks and Tourism, perhaps unwittingly, placed the Ozark Folk Center in the middle of a fierce local political conflict. Driftwood and a core group of his original Rackensackers had long demanded that the society's song selection and musical presentations be free of any modernizing influence. The Arkansas Folk Festival in 1963 had made only one concession to modernity: a sound system and microphones were utilized because of the unexpectedly large crowd. Driftwood and his supporters relied on musicologists' definition of southern mountain folk music as premodern country music, which prevented the group from performing any song composed later than 1940 and from using electric or electrically amplified instruments. His enemies, however, challenged Driftwood's authenticity and claimed that his definition of traditional music often depended on his personal appraisal of the musician. In the late 1960s Driftwood's hard-line, traditional approach and his sometimes abrasive leadership resulted in a split within the Rackensack ranks. His opponents, most favoring a more liberal presentation of both traditional and modern sounds, formed the Mountain View Folklore Society and began playing on the courthouse lawn on a different night of the week. The two groups proceeded to align themselves with existing political factions within the county.[20]

By the time the Ozark Folk Center opened in 1973, Stone County's musical scene was a fragmented mess with numerous tastes based on socioeconomic and political differences. When the Department of Parks and Tourism contracted with the Rackensack Folklore Society it implicitly adopted the policies of Driftwood and the minority of traditionalists on Ozark music and by so doing further exacerbated a local rift and alienated a large number of Stone County natives. The center's opponents later accused the first director of the Ozark Folk Center of awarding jobs on the basis of political patronage. This multilayered division could be initially reduced to two sides: those who opposed performances of contemporary country and western music alongside traditional folk music versus those who accepted them.[21] According to H. Page Stephens, the Mountain View Folklore Society and others whose musical tastes were not limited to the songs of their ancestors "remained in the mainstream" of the county's musical tastes, "while those musicians who were recreating older styles of music for a broader market were outside the current local traditions." Thus, states Stephens, "the local revival was not indigenous . . . but a reaction to national trends."[22]

Ironically, the Ozark Folk Center, by virtue of its affiliation with the Rackensack Folklore Society and that society's definition of folk music, excluded a large number of native Ozarkers and Stone Countians whose contacts with wider American culture had rendered them less "authentic." Their unselfconscious and extemporaneous melding of the indigenous and inherited with the external made them in some ways more natural and historically accurate representatives of contemporary Ozark life. They more fully reflected an Ozark heritage of experimentation, change, and adaptation than did Driftwood and the Rackensackers. Ozarkers, though certainly behind the curve of American modernization, had never lived in a timeless vacuum. Many of the songs were ancient, and many were not. Many bore the stamp of the Arkansas hills and of the twentieth century. They had been altered both subtly and completely over the generations so that drawing a boundary in the web of the past was an arbitrary exercise, one marked from the standpoint of those outside the folk tradition. The bottom line was that no one cared to listen to a middle-aged man from Stone County play the guitar and sing about his Ozark life in a style too closely resembling that of George Jones or Merle Haggard. People would listen, and pay to listen, to an Ozarker sing his folk songs.

In September 1975, in an attempt to circumvent the constant political sniping in Stone County, Governor David Pryor fired the center's director and Driftwood and completely removed any local influence from the administration of the center. When Pryor removed the director and Driftwood in September, he offered a compromise to the competing factions. Each of the groups could play two nights a week. Only a group of traditionalists who had broken with Driftwood accepted. Driftwood and his Rackensackers moved to the old Uptown Theater before building the Jimmy Driftwood Barn in 1979.[23]

Increasingly in subsequent years, aging and dying native Ozark musicians and craftspeople came to be replaced by performers and demonstrators from outside the region. Some Stone Countians who "felt the idea of helping the local work force should come first" grew disillusioned in the process. A 1975 *Stone County Leader* editorial sarcastically verbalized the sentiments of many local people who felt alienated by Folk Center decisions. "Only a couple of weeks ago it was announced that a lady from the southern part of the state was hired to cook old-fashioned bread; of course everyone knows none of the unemployed or underemployed local hillbillies can bake those old-time biscuits."[24]

The center was also susceptible to charges of artificial preservation. As Diane O. Tebbetts stated in her study of perceptions of the Ozark Folk Center, a major concern was to avoid a situation in which the presentation of Ozark culture was "related to the real culture in the same way a mounted butterfly collection relates to a living swallowtail." Nevertheless, artificial qualities were inherent to the project. The era in which the handicraft skills and music represented at the center were prevalent in the region had long since passed, forcing a re-creation of a past to be preserved. The lack of training funds or local interest, especially in craft making, also bred an early reliance on non-native demonstrators emulating Ozark pioneers.[25]

Despite the inherent contradictions involved in the conscious display of Ozark folk culture by non-Ozarkers, the Ozark Folk Center stands as a monument to the dream of Jimmy Driftwood and the center's administration. For more than a quarter-century the Ozark Folk Center has by and large maintained the original historical and cultural integrity of its visionaries, regardless of the vision's unrepresentativeness in the 1960s and 1970s. This was after all a cultural preservation that first relied on re-creation. The center achieved an even greater degree of academic integrity in 1976 when it hired professional folklorist and musicologist W. K. McNeil as full-time researcher and consultant. The Ozark Folk Center has successfully avoided the "fast-buck artists" who "jam the streets with gimmicks, Hong Kong trinkets, mass-produced glasswares, and the like."[26] The town of Mountain View and its surrounding areas have been less successful in that regard.

Some local residents still harbor ill will against the center, if not for the three-decades-old political squabble then for the center's indirect role in attracting the typical tourist town's share of flea markets, antique malls, and junk peddlers. Perhaps the most common complaint is that the Ozark Folk Center has not been the economic savior promised by its supporters. By the mid-1980s the center was the county's largest employer, but of its three hundred workers only twenty-three were full-time employees. Two-thirds of the center's workforce was composed of seasonal contract craftspeople and musicians. Furthermore, the success of Branson, Missouri, which was blamed in part on a slumping 1990s tourism market in northern Arkansas, has rekindled old animosities toward Driftwood and the folk purists whose shortsighted meddling in local musical circles, so goes the argument, prevented Mountain View from achieving the same broad-based, musical, family-oriented success enjoyed by Branson. Nevertheless, it is probably the lack of blatant commercialism that continues to make Mountain View eminently more visitor-friendly and livable.

Three other entertainment attractions arose in the late 1960s to capitalize on the region's growing popularity and on images of the Ozark folk, both positive and negative. Although not immediate products of the folk cultural movement in the Ozarks, all three owed their existence at least in part to the heightened interest in the region brought about by the movement. One of the three disappeared almost as quickly as it was conceived. Ozarkland, a small theme park complete with a frontier homestead, was hastily erected in the retirement village of Horseshoe Bend in 1969, primarily to serve as a filming location for the short-lived, syndicated *Ozarkland Jamboree*. The company's creator, Albert Gannaway, an Arkansan who undertook the project at the urging of the Ozarks Regional Commission, hoped to re-create the success he had enjoyed with his earlier *Grand Ole Opry* television program in the 1950s and 1960s. Like the retirement community in which it was built, Ozarkland and *Ozarkland Jamboree* had almost no connection to the local area or to the region. The regular musicians hired for the show were recruited from Nashville and from a West Virginia television program, the *Wheeling Jamboree*. Despite a flurry of activity in the summer of 1969— Ozarkland even constructed an exact replica of *Gunsmoke*'s Dodge City set, called Starr City, in hopes of luring that production to Arkansas for an episode or two—by the end of the year *Ozarkland Jamboree* had folded and

Gannaway had left. In the early 1970s a small-time country music promoter tried to attract visitors to the facilities Ozarkland left behind by presenting musicals and refurbishing the homestead and Starr City into an amusement park called Frontierland. Despite these efforts Horseshoe Bend proved to be a poor location for such tourist attractions.[27]

Horseshoe Bend might have been less than ideal for a theme park and television studio, but one other retirement community proved a perfect location for a more Ozark-themed attraction. In 1968 Leo Rainey decided to put his hard-earned tourism expertise to the test by opening up the Arkansaw Traveller Folk Theatre just below Hardy and near the entrance to Cherokee Village. He and James Bobo came up with the idea—a humorous, musical play based on a nineteenth-century legend—after a 1967 trip to Gatlinburg, Rainey's first journey to eastern Tennessee since 1962. Rainey's involvement in the folk culture movement had spurred his own interest in folk music and had introduced him to enough talented eastern Ozarkers to fill out the cast of a dinner theater troupe. For several years the Arkansaw Traveller Folk Theatre flourished with a captive audience. In the summers of the late 1960s and 1970s Cherokee Village entertained hundreds of guests each weekend, most of them Midwesterners attracted by the free lodging provided as a marketing tool. Most often Rainey's theater was the only entertainment Sharp County's nights offered. The Arkansaw Traveller Folk Theatre was indicative of the Ozark tourist industry in general in that it capitalized on Ozark stereotypes but attempted to redeem the hillbilly. Tourists from Illinois and Ohio got to hear real hillbilly music played by real Ozarkers, and the natives in the play delighted in the assurance that the poor, slovenly squatter outsmarted the city fellow every time. Rainey sold the theater in 1990 after several years of declining attendance. The new owner, from northeastern Arkansas, attempted to revive interest by intensifying the hillbilly quotient. She brought to the stage the barefoot, slack-jawed frontiersman found on postcards in every convenience store and tourist trap in the Ozarks. But the buffoonish Ozarkers could not bring back the crowds, forcing the theater to close its doors in the mid-1990s.[28]

The Arkansas Ozarks' most ambitious tourist project relied from its inception on the cultivation of the more negative aspects of the Ozark image. Dogpatch, U.S.A., was the largest theme park ever developed in northern Arkansas and the most exploitative of American stereotypes of mountain people. The idea for the park originated with a group of Harrison businessmen in 1967. A generation earlier "village patriots" would have fainted at the pros-

Li'l Abner and Daisy Mae at Dogpatch, ca. 1968. (Courtesy of Patricia Mathis Mitchell and Teresa Mathis Russell.)

pect of spending hundreds of thousands of dollars to build a small city whose basic purpose was to empty tourists' pockets by reinforcing their stereotypes of Ozarkers. By 1967, amid the rediscovery of the region sparked by the folk culture movement, middle-class Ozark town dwellers had begun to see dollar signs in the region's image, regardless of the interpretation. There were concerns about the image Dogpatch, U.S.A. would project, but the most vocal opponents were state publicity employees who feared the park would revive Arkansas's "Bob Burns image."[29]

Dogpatch, U.S.A., was based on the long-running Al Capp comic strip "in which rustic yokels cavorted in a manner supposed to have originated in backwoods Kentucky, not Arkansas."[30] The New England–born cartoonist granted permission to use his characters. He was even among the eleven original stockholders of Recreation Enterprises, Inc., the Harrison-based parent company of the park headed by realtor O. J. Snow. Recreation Enterprises, Inc., chose a location on Arkansas Highway 7, midway between Harrison and Jasper near the Boone-Newton county line, as the site for Dogpatch, U.S.A. The 825 Boston Mountain acres lay in one of the most rugged and sparsely settled areas of the Ozarks; nevertheless, Highway 7 was a favorite route for motorists absorbing some of Arkansas's most scenic vistas, and the park site lay only a few miles from the Buffalo River. Despite its isolation the site seemed a perfect place for the theme park. The land contained two natural attractions, Marble Falls and Mystic Cave. Furthermore, the post office and deserted mercantile from the old hamlet of Marble Falls (formerly Wilcockson) stood as a reminder of the small but nearly vanished farming community that once scraped life from these hills and hollows.[31]

Recreation Enterprises, Inc., hired local farmers and carpenters to erect the log and plank buildings of Dogpatch, U.S.A. using old lumber and logs snatched from deserted neighborhood buildings. When the craftsmanship of the Newton and Boone countians turned out to be too superior for the hillbilly image depicted in Capp's fictional Dogpatch, management called the workers back to "smash the ridgepoles and make the roofs look slovenly."[32] Capp made his first visit to Newton County in the fall of 1967 for Dogpatch, U.S.A.'s dedication. When asked by a wary reporter if he thought the new park would hurt the state's image, Capp wryly replied that it certainly could do nothing more to hurt the image and, most importantly, it would bring money to the depressed area. In fact, officials of Recreation Enterprises, Inc., believed they knew just how much money it would bring. A Los Angeles–based firm commissioned to conduct an economic impact study promised that within ten years Dogpatch, U.S.A.'s annual attendance would exceed one million, which would translate into the addition of five million dollars to the local economy each summer. Dogpatch, U.S.A. officially opened on May 18, 1968, again with Capp on hand. Capp's whole crew—Li'l Abner, Daisy Mae, and Mammy and Pappy Yokum among others—were on hand as well to witness the beginning of what he called the "greatest urban renewal project I've ever seen." As Capp addressed the audience, Mammy Yokum hollered from the roof of the country store, and an angry hillbilly with a shotgun chased his daughter and her young suitor across the roof of the railroad station. Most of the other roofs were adorned with statues of goats. Clearly, this was no cultural celebration, but blatant exploitation, and most of the local people knew it. The park's demonstration of Ozark fiddling, singing, dancing, and woodcarving did little to assuage local suspicions.[33]

Dogpatch, U.S.A. underwent a transformation in late 1968 and early 1969 from the merely corny to the bizarre. In October 1968, Little Rock insurance magnate Jess P. Odom purchased Recreation Enterprises, Inc., for

$750,000 and immediately announced plans to spend five million dollars in an effort to bring Dogpatch, U.S.A. to the level of other successful amusement parks such as Six Flags and Disneyland. Three months later Odom hired former governor Orval Faubus to run Dogpatch, U.S.A.—the most caricatured Ozarker alive overseeing an entire estate of hillbilly stereotypes. Odom also brought in a creative director to oversee the actors portraying Capp's characters, added several amusement park attractions such as a roller coaster, railroad, and other rides, and antagonized local residents of Marble Falls by constructing a new post office on park grounds and by officially changing the community's name to Dogpatch. Odom and Faubus advertised nationally and held the first Miss Dogpatch pageant in June in front of the "Korn-vention hall," featuring college students from as far away as Florida.[34]

Faubus eventually left Dogpatch, U.S.A. The park, moderately successful but never in danger of threatening Disneyland or most other American amusement parks for that matter, changed hands a few times before it closed in 1993. Dogpatch, U.S.A.'s various managers could never decide if they wanted a "Six Flags over the Ozarks" or a Newton County version of Silver Dollar City.[35] The park was too far from the currents of American mainstream tourism to succeed as the former, and Dogpatch, U.S.A., was from the beginning too hokey and insincere to emulate the latter. In 1997 residents of Dogpatch, Arkansas, many of them newcomers to the area, perhaps officially brought an end to the Dogpatch odyssey when the U.S. Postal Service granted their petition to change the name of the post office to Marble Falls. The amusement park still sprawls in the hollow as a reminder of failed dreams. It is a testament to America's willingness to exploit the images of an entire culture and of many Ozarkers' willingness to poke fun at themselves. By the early twenty-first century Dogpatch, U.S.A., once a giant living stereotype of mountain life, had become a tawdry symbol of man's struggle in the hills of northern Arkansas. This multi-million-dollar caricature of a region and its image had suffered the same fate as scores of the Ozarks' promising settlements over the past 175 years.

Although most tourism projects have been linked in some direct way to the physical characteristics or the popular image of the region, certainly not all have been. The best example of the superimposition of a generic tourist concept onto the region is also the driving force behind the Ozarks' chief tourist center, Eureka Springs. Despite the fact that the Passion Play and its Christian-themed accoutrements in northwestern Arkansas could have been built anywhere, it is quite fitting that this most un-Ozarkian attraction would spring from the hills of this most un-Ozarkian community. And it was the Ozarks' well-crafted image of a region divorced from the march of time that ultimately brought to Eureka Springs the man who would transform the town into a tourist haven.

From its inception Eureka Springs was a novelty in the Arkansas Ozarks. Built on hucksterism and mineral water peddling, the Victorian-Swiss architecture could not have been more foreign to the hills in the late nineteenth century. The town site itself, with its steep, curving streets and granite ledges, no straight-faced son of the upland South would have chosen. After the depression put a halt to resort business, Eureka Springs began to refocus its efforts in the 1940s and 1950s in an attempt to attract modern midwestern tourists.

Slowly Eureka Springs began to make a disturbing discovery: the town was too modern for its own good, too de-hillbillyized. The vacationers who had been promised electric lights and hot showers in their mountain bungalows had also been promised real hillbillies by the travel writers and incidentally by the folk tales and songs in *Rayburn's Ozark Guide*. They received only the former. In 1948 Eureka Springs revived its Ozark Folk Festival to recapture the hillbilly spirit that the town had never possessed. But the staged musicals and dances and the Indian relics and factory-made corncob pipes were less than authentic. Even most visitors could tell that. And the tourists who did manage to spot a stereotypical hillbilly on the outskirts of town likely fell prey to the area's resident fake anachronism, a bearded native of New York City living the life of a stereotypical mountaineer on a hillside outside of town.[36]

A local resident with origins outside the region suggested improving Eureka's Ozark image by staging appearances by hillbilly stereotypes based on an artist's representation. "You know . . . the girl with the daisy on her hat, the boy with the toothless smile, Pa with his battered hat, red necktie and the stickpin. I think those should be played up more in this region . . . the tourist is always looking for a hill-billy." The recipient of all this advice, Rayburn, knew the last statement was unfortunately—for Eureka Springs at least—correct. "I soon discovered what the tourists from the North want to see in the Ozarks. They are interested in log cabins and the old crafts such as spinning, weaving, woodcarving, blacksmithing, and basket making. They want to see real hillbillies who pick the guitar, play the fiddle, and sing the old traditional ballads that grandfather sang. These tourists are usually disappointed in Eureka Springs, for we have only a few hillbillies to show them. We have killed the goose that laid the golden egg."[37]

Indeed, modernization killed the hillbilly, and Eureka Springs suffered the false advertising of travel writers. The Ozark image no longer described the region by the time of Rayburn's lament in 1957. The only solution, as at least a few saw it, was to make the town conform to the image. But, as Rayburn suggested, that would not work for Eureka Springs, and he would not live to see that solution put to work in Mountain View. Instead, Eureka Springs's economic salvation would come from a more unlikely source, though perhaps one more fitting for the eccentric resort town.

The man who singlehandedly revitalized the slumping Swiss village was Gerald L. K. Smith, an ultra right-wing newspaper publisher. Born in Wisconsin in 1898, Smith enjoyed a varied career as a political organizer for Huey Long in the 1930s, an anti-Communist speaker in the 1940s, and founder of the racist, anti-Semitic newspaper *The Cross and the Flag* in California. In 1964, in hopes of establishing a pioneer farm with an authentic log cabin, furnishings, and frontier farming implements—a sort of museum to America's nostalgic past as interpreted by Smith—he dispatched his assistant Charles F. Robertson to find such a farmstead. Robertson, apparently familiar with the popular image of the arrested frontier Ozarks, journeyed to Eureka Springs. He found no log cabin fitting Smith's description, but he did take a fancy to a Victorian mansion there called Penn Castle. Robertson purchased the mansion as a retirement home for the Smiths. At the time of the Smiths' arrival in Eureka Springs in late 1964, Rayburn, the heart and voice of the village, had been dead four years, and the town's population had dropped to below 1,500 inhabitants, mainly retirees with a sprinkling of writers, artists, and craftspeople.[38]

The wealthy Smith had big plans for his new hometown. He bought 167 acres east of town on Magnetic Mountain and announced plans to construct a statue of Christ on that site. For this project Smith commissioned the elderly Emmett Sullivan, a former South Dakota cowboy and attorney who had settled in Eureka Springs to pursue his love of painting and sculpting. Two years later the "Christ of the Ozarks," a 70-foot-tall concrete behemoth, was dedicated by Smith, Sullivan, and local dignitaries. The statue, almost hideously disproportionate and sadly foreign on the rocky, brushy ridge, stood "masquerading as a monument to Christ, . . . intended . . . in reality as a monument to [Smith.]" The "Christ of the Ozarks" was the first part of

The Christ of the Ozarks attempted to use religion as a tourist attraction for Eureka Springs, Arkansas. (Courtesy of Bob Besom/Shiloh Museum of Ozark History, Springdale, Arkansas.)

Smith's dream of a sort of Christian theme park at Eureka Springs. His most ambitious project followed.[39]

The "Passion Play" transformed Eureka Springs into a thriving tourist town. Smith conceived the idea of staging a Passion Play, which chronicled Jesus' last days on earth from Palm Sunday to the Ascension, and tabbed another South Dakotan, Robert Hyde, to oversee its production. Hyde wrote the play, designed the 6,000-seat amphitheater and set, directed the play, and portrayed Jesus. Two hundred additional actors were brought in for the Passion Play's 1968 opening. By the mid-1970s the Passion Play had become the largest outdoor pageant in the United States. By bringing in tens of thousands of tourists each year, Smith's Passion Play revitalized the main street business district of Eureka Springs. Gift shops opened, hotels sprang up along all the roadsides leading into town, and, ironically, Eureka Springs began to gain a reputation as a center of Ozark craft making.[40]

Between 1964 and 1972 the gross municipal product of Eureka Springs increased from less than one million dollars to almost $15 million. Smith's tourist attractions transformed the town into the most popular tourist destination in the Arkansas Ozarks and the leading tourist municipality in the state. Nevertheless, by the 1990s Eureka Springs was in many respects a typical late-twentieth-century American tourist town. Downtown shops and restaurants offered goods and dishes found elsewhere around the country. The crafts were frequently passed off as authentic Ozark products, but their makers were almost never natives of the region. Eureka Springs's success had been at best indirectly related to the region's image; consequently it offered little in the way of Ozark heritage and tradition. The tourist searching for attractions built on this heritage or the inherited image of the Ozarks could find them in abundance by the 1990s in places both distinctly Ozarkian and generically, buffoonishly nonregional.[41]

Aside from the Passion Play and the Ozark Folk Center, the most ambitious tourism projects in the Arkansas Ozarks eventually failed. By the late 1990s even these two enterprises had begun to feel the effects of Branson's rise to national prominence and the growing popularity of casinos in Missouri and Mississippi. Furthermore, tourism is forever a precarious business. The tastes of travelers are finicky and can change on a whim. By the 1990s the nation's interest in southern mountain folk music had clearly subsided. Many Ozark tourist towns, such as Hardy, Mountain View, and Eureka Springs, had come to rely increasingly on a renewed interest in Ozark crafts, both the tacky, factory-made glasswares and corncob pipes and the high quality handicrafts of artisans in the Arkansas Craft Guild. Most are not particularly Ozarkian, and almost none are handcrafted by Ozark natives.

Tourism has not been a panacea for northern Arkansas's economic woes. Northwestern Arkansas, easily the region's most prosperous area, owes little of its success to the tourism industry. Influential residents and government officials in north central Arkansas, however, consciously hitched their financial wagons to tourism when it looked as if no other approach was feasible. The results have been bittersweet. Certain areas—Mountain Home, Mountain View, Hardy, and Eureka Springs among them—have experienced economic revitalization and tremendous business growth. But this has rarely worked for the benefit of the natives whose depressed status in the early 1960s had originally prompted efforts to lure tourists to the Ozarks. The tourism industry has generated seasonal, minimum-wage, usually retail employment for Ozarkers that barely lifts unskilled workers above poverty level. Skilled occupations such as folk musical and handicraft jobs have been assumed by newcomers drawn to the region by nostalgia for the old days or by currents of the counterculture movement. The Parks, Recreation and Travel Commission's decision to drop the Ozark Folk Center's original and costly

mission of training local young people in the arts and music of their ancestors helped assure this development. Furthermore, the government-operated
and private small businesses created by tourism contribute relatively little to
local tax bases that support schools, hospitals, and other services.

Perhaps the most ironic, and the most predictable, result of the post–
World War II tourism boom has been its modernizing influence. The Arkansas Ozarks' popularity in the 1960s and 1970s grew both from its image of
isolated innocence and from the survival of British folk ballads and the rem-
nants of a frontier existence long vanished in most parts of urbanized America.
The very unconscious quaintness and uniqueness that first attracted visitors
and tourists to places like Mountain View and Hardy quickly disappeared in
the wake of waves of tourism in the late 1960s and 1970s.

Anthropologists Charles F. Keyes and Pierre L. van den Berghe have addressed this phenomenon. The presence of the tourist "transforms the native
into a 'touree,' that is, into a performer who modifies his behavior for gain
according to his perception of what is attractive to the tourist. . . . The tourist quest for authenticity is, thus, doomed by the very presence of tourists."[42]
One writer for the St. Louis Post-Dispatch noted this development during a
trip to the 1974 Arkansas Folk Festival: "The Folk Festival was founded ostensibly to preserve the old mountain ways, but it is very much the child of
change. . . . The Arkansas Ozarks are becoming more and more a bustling,
'progressive' place."[43]

By the 1990s visitors were still invited to "step back in time to the Arkansas that used to be" in Mountain View, but they could also expect to find the
same fast-food franchises, convenience stores, and traffic jams that they had
left behind. One result of this modernizing phenomenon is that areas of the
region infrequently visited by tourists, the locales whose lack of scenic vistas,
folk singers, or log cabins rendered them somehow less Ozarkian and therefore less appealing in the 1960s and 1970s, had become by the 1990s the
truest bearers of unconscious Ozark tradition and life. Towns such as Huntsville, Berryville, Marshall, Salem, and Melbourne and their rural hinterlands
were less adulterated representatives of the modern Ozarks and its agricultural past than were Mountain View, Hardy, and Mountain Home and certainly more so than Eureka Springs or Dogpatch.[44]

For good or bad it appears that the tourist industry has become a permanent and integral part of economic, cultural, and social life in the Arkansas
Ozarks. Along with the related developments of the growth of retirement
communities and the growing in-migration of non-Ozarkers to rural areas

and small towns, tourism has had a transformative effect on an increasing number of areas in northern Arkansas. Harold Sherman has been dead for more than a decade, but his memory and the legacy of others prominent in the Ozark tourist industry live on in institutions and establishments both respectable and tawdry. In many ways the static image of the region that so enamored Sherman lives on because of them.

3
Developing the Panhandle
Seagrove Beach, Seaside, Watercolor, and the Florida Tourist Tradition

Harvey H. Jackson III

Florida has always been a nice place to visit. Folks have wandered in, stayed a while, gotten warm, been entertained, relaxed, and gone home. From such excursions has risen an industry built for and sustained by people who were not interested in any permanent attachment to the state. They came, stayed, spent, and went. If they liked it, they returned. These tourists were searching for something not available back home, and many a Floridian has made a good living providing it for them. The job was easy because the land was sufficiently exotic and romantic to become, in advertising at least, whatever the travelers wanted it to be. Sunny beaches, black-water rivers, clear springs, and unfamiliar flora and fauna promised visitors sights and adventures they could talk about for years to come. And when nature was not enough, promoters enhanced it, created Monkey Jungles, Cypress Gardens, snake-o-ramas, and Indian villages where Native Americans wrestled alligators, all to attract and entertain. Ironically, efforts to entice tourists eventually evolved into the theme park phenomenon, where promotional creations cluttered the land and where the location, except for its climate, was incidental.[1]

Florida is also a nice place to live, so it is hardly surprising that land developers who wanted to sell to a more permanent population have worked hand in glove with the tourist industry. Both groups touted the same things —climate, recreation, and ambiance—but in addition to entertainment, real estate entrepreneurs packaged and sold a way of life, one that often included an escape from the modern world. This is why so many of their schemes contained utopian elements, and why so much that they built had a fanciful quality to it. Moorish architecture, Venetian pools, and even a town laid out on the plan of the mythological Grecian city of Heliopolis were only a few of the innovations imposed on the landscape. Florida was a blank canvas on which anything could be painted—and frequently was.[2]

Developers and their schemes rose and fell with the economy. During the early 1920s investors descended on the state and drove land prices to dizzying heights. Subdivision and speculation became so profitable that sand was sometimes dredged from the bottom of bays to build artificial islands that were sold at inflated prices. In the early 1920s over 1.5 million visitors came down each year, and so many stayed that Florida's population grew four times faster than any other state's. Then, in 1926, the bubble burst. Land prices collapsed, banks failed, and thousands went broke. Three years before the rest of the nation, Florida got its depression.[3]

Although set back when the boom burst, the tourist industry limped along until the crash of 1929, when it joined real estate as an economic casualty. With little money to spend on vacations, many visitors stayed home, and soon hotels and attractions began to file for bankruptcy. Yet, despite it all, those who could afford to travel continued to come, and by the end of the 1930s, the tourist industry was recovering. Real estate, however, remained depressed. World War II and an infusion of military money helped some, but not much. After the war there were still bargains to be had, especially up on the Panhandle, the northwest finger of the state, far removed from trendy resorts in the south. Between the villages of Panama City and Destin one could buy land, including half a mile of pristine beach, for less than $500 an acre, which is exactly what C. H. McGee, Sr., did in 1948.[4]

McGee bought Seagrove Beach, a strip of white sand dominated by an oak-covered bluff that some claimed was the highest point on the Gulf. There had been a hotel there in the 1920s and 1930s, where an Alabama artist colony briefly took up summer residence, but depression and war left the area all but deserted. McGee was essentially starting from scratch. So he laid out the streets, subdivided his acres, put up an office, and began advertising Seagrove as the place "where nature did its best." He priced beachfront lots between $1000 and $2000 each and property back in the grove a little less; "a good investment" he told anyone who would listen. But getting people to listen was no easy matter. It was hard to convince travelers to detour off Highway 98 and drive some five miles of rutted, sandy road, through pine and palmetto, to see what he had to offer. And then he had to convince those who came that the community he was selling would one day become

C. H. McGee in front of his Seagrove Beach office, ca. 1950. (Courtesy of Mrs. C. H. McGee, Jr.)

a reality. That these were the same problems developers had always faced was small comfort. Florida's history was filled with schemes such as his. The landscape was littered with those that had failed, and C. H. McGee knew it.[5]

Like so many developers, McGee was also a contractor, and soon he had built five "spec" houses to give potential investors an idea of what Seagrove Beach could become. Slowly the lots began to sell and one by one other houses appeared. They were simple frame or cement block structures for the most part, with lots of windows and screened porches. Their owners were mostly Alabamians, or at least people with Alabama connections, who were part of the upper middle class that rose in southern towns and cities after the war. Most of them had visited the Gulf before, and being familiar with established beach communities nearby, they saw Seagrove as a less expensive, more exclusive alternative to developments around Panama City to the east and Fort Walton to the west. Undeterred (though inconvenienced) by the lack of telephone or mail service, and willing to accept unpredictable water delivery from the windmill-powered town well, these first investors thought of themselves as pioneers, which, indeed, they were.[6]

Although these primitive conditions would continue for some time (phone service did not begin until 1958), investors were never attracted to Seagrove by its conveniences or amenities. Seagrove Beach was a place to relax, a place to enjoy swimming, fishing, and visiting neighbors who may have been friends back home and may even have bought their lot on another owner's advice—word of mouth was some of McGee's most effective advertising. It was a family place and the developer went to great pains to make sure that anyone who visited could tell, just by looking at it, that people of quality invested there. The key to maintaining this appearance was the requirement that all construction had to be "approved and accepted" by McGee under a code that assured owners that "no trailer, tent, shack, outhouse or temporary structure" would be allowed. To underscore his intention to preserve the natural beauty of the site, the developer set aside some four hundred feet of beachfront as a park for the enjoyment of the community, however his code promised that "no noxious activities, offensive noises or odors, nor any nuisance will be permitted" there, or anywhere else in the village. Peace and quiet was the order of the day. The code added that "not any of the property shall be sold, leased or rented to or occupied by any person or persons other than the caucasian race," a restriction not uncommon to the time and region. However, to assure more affluent investors that they could bring their "domestic servants" with them if they wished, the code added that blacks who were "actually employed by those residing on said property, may reside thereon while thus employed." To some that exception made a difference, and a few of the beachfront houses were built with "maid's quarters" in the back.[7]

Through the rest of the 1940s and on through the 1950s, Seagrove Beach existed in semi-isolated splendor. McGee built a small store to supply milk, bread, bait, and beer for the local population, which was usually enough since owners came loaded with groceries and cooked meals at home. They were seasonal visitors for the most part and the season was the summer. They opened their houses around Memorial Day, brought the kids down when school was out, stayed through the summer (with Dad arriving on Friday and going back to work on Monday), then closed up on Labor Day. Some returned for Thanksgiving, for a few days between Christmas and New Year's, or for Spring Break (which was only a couple of days then), but as often as not the houses stayed vacant the winter months. By the mid-1950s a few

permanent residents had moved in, retirees mostly, but as anyone who re-
members those days recalls, not much happened in Seagrove during the winter. Even Seagrove Manor, an eight-kitchenette motel and coffee shop built
there by an Air Force officer and wife, could not support the owners. The
husband remained on active duty and his wife commuted to a job in the next
county. Making a living at Seagrove Beach was no easy matter.[8]

Still, most owners were not interested in developing Seagrove into anything other than what it was. Although they were happy when the road in
from the main highway was paved, when word got out in 1956 that the state
was thinking of building a beach route that would link Seagrove to other
villages along the coast investors rose in protest. Uniting in a letter writing campaign to the head of the state road department they complained
that their property would be "badly hurt in value" by the "added traffic and
noise" that would result if "a through highway were jammed around the present road site." But it was more than a matter of economics. "The seclusion
of the area was the main reason I selected Seagrove," one property owner
wrote, and that seclusion would be shattered if the road were built. The elder
McGee had died a few years earlier, but his son and heir, C. H. McGee, Jr.,
joined the protest. Even though he knew that a beach route would bring in
more customers, young McGee nevertheless "offered to give [the state] a right
of way for the new road behind" the community. For developer and residents
alike, inaccessibility was part of the charm of Seagrove Beach.[9]

The beach route was not built, at least not then, and for the next decade
Seagrove grew slowly along lines defined by its code and its residents. Although a couple of roads in the eastern part of the development were paved,
most owners moved from house to beach on dirt streets and sandy trails,
pausing from time to time to talk to neighbors sitting on front porches to
catch a Gulf breeze—air conditioning was rare there until the late 1960s.
Perched high above the water, safe from rising tides that came with fall and
winter storms and sheltered by the trees, Seagrove was a world to itself. Teen-
agers found it dull and, when they could, took family cars to hangouts in
Panama City and Destin, but their parents seldom left the community. They
did not come to the beach to do things they could do back home. Seagrove
Beach was a place to relax, to unwind, to escape.

Then things began to change. In the early 1970s, the state built Highway
30-A, the once-opposed beach route. Few residents protested this time.
Original investors were older, some had passed away, and the new ones, sons

and daughters in many cases, were more interested in access to the outside than isolation from it. There were also more permanent residents now, most of whom worked in nearby towns. The highway cut their commute dramatically. Convenience, in turn, attracted more new residents, and while Seagrove hardly experienced a "boom," it was obvious to old-timers that the village was growing faster than before. Then, on September 23, 1975, the spot "where nature did its best" felt nature's fury. Hurricane Eloise, with 130-mile-per-hour winds and a massive storm surge, hit the coast. Seagrove's elevation saved the town from the water damage experienced in lower-lying communities, but despite protection from the ancient oaks, the wind battered buildings and ripped off roofs. Panama City, some thirty miles to the east, suffered over $200 million in damages and the beach from Fort Walton to Port St. Joe was declared a disaster area.[10]

Eloise transformed the coast. In Panama City and Destin old houses and motels collapsed beneath the waves and wind, and when the weather cleared, often all that could be done was bulldoze the splinters and build anew. Although the nation was beginning to feel the inflation that would plague the economy in the 1970s, there was still money to invest and those who had it, or could get it, turned their attention to rebuilding the Panhandle. At first development dollars poured into the larger, harder hit communities, but in time even Seagrove was touched. Since McGee's code had prohibited any building over two stories high, a group of investors bought land just outside the eastern town limits and soon two multi-story condominiums were going up. A restaurant/bar/nightclub opened nearby, and Seagrove Beach began to boogie. Or at least some of it did. Most of the community was far enough from these attractions that, except for a bit more traffic and two new silhouettes on the skyline, residents hardly knew the additions existed. Condominium sales were slow, the honky-tonk went out of business soon after the construction crews left, and by the mid-1980s anyone looking east would have concluded that the old Seagrove, the laid-back, easy-going, nothing fancy, peace and quiet Seagrove, had carried the day.[11]

But meanwhile, off to the west, something else was a-building, something that would change the coast as nothing before. On eighty acres of scrub and sand, Robert Davis was creating Seaside.

The land had been bought in 1946 by Davis's grandfather, J. S. Smolian, for around $100 an acre. Owner of a department store in Birmingham, Alabama, Smolian hoped to build a summer camp for employees, but his business partner vetoed the idea. So the land lay vacant until 1978, when Davis inherited the tract and set about to create what *Time* magazine would later call "the most astounding design achievement of its era."[12]

Robert Davis brought an interesting mix of experiences to the Panhandle. As a boy in Birmingham he had often come to the coast with his grand-father, and as his life grew more complex he looked back nostalgically at those simpler days. A liberal undergraduate education at Antioch College ex-posed him to 1960s utopian thinking, while a Harvard M.B.A. refined his business skills. Eventually he got into real estate development, first in Wash-ington, D.C., and then in Coconut Grove, Florida, where his innovative projects were both critical and financial successes. While in Coconut Grove he became friends with a group of young architects and town planners and together they began to dream of the community they would create, if they could. Then Davis inherited the land and dreams began to become reality.[13]

Davis and his colleagues were not out to build a resort, and the developer (a term he avoided whenever possible) at first recoiled from the suggestion that he might. Their inspiration, and many of their ideas, came from the work of Leon Krier, the London-based urban theorist who advocated a re-turn to small, "traditional" village patterns where the landscape was ar-ranged to encourage community cohesion and social interaction. Finding himself with a plot of land the size Krier considered "ideal" for such a design, Davis decided to create an "old-fashioned town," one that would be popu-lated by neighbors who were also shopkeepers, merchants, doctors, lawyers, teachers, writers, artists, and artisans. He wanted a place where people lived together, worked together, went to church together, sent their kids to school together, attended each other's weddings and, in time, each other's funerals. Seaside, he answered those who asked, would be "a way of life."[14]

Davis's initial plans drew heavily on his experiences as a child visiting Seagrove and other beaches along the coast. Enamored with the architecture of local "cracker cottages," and remembering how people lived in and around them, he and his friends designed the town and its houses in an effort to re-create the way of life he once enjoyed. Unpaved streets were laid out nar-row to force people to slow down, then public places were added for them to slow down in. The town center, with shops the developer would own and rent to merchants, was convenient so residents could park and walk. Houses, built from pre–World War II materials and based on vernacular precedents, were close-constructed so casual strollers could lean on picket fences and talk to friends on front porches. Seaside was designed to be a place free from the isolation, insecurity, and dull sameness that Davis felt were the ills of modern urban life. Seaside was designed to be perfect.[15]

Some, hearing these plans, were skeptical. Bill Wright, one of the early homeowners, recalls Davis telling him how people from all walks of life would settle at Seaside and "love each other . . . like back in the old days," and thinking "that sounds great," but figuring that if it did not happen (and it probably would not) a house at the beach was better than a condo in a high-rise. Others, however, bought the dream with their lot and went to work on cottages whose construction was governed by a code so simple, they were told, that anyone "handy with tools" could design and build their own. They were the sort of people Davis wanted in his town, people like those he met on the coast as a child, down-to-earth folks who, as Davis described them, could "truly enjoy the indolence of the tropics . . . [and] find it delightful to sit under a ceiling fan on a hot afternoon and just talk to passing strangers."[16]

So Davis cleared some lots, and in 1981 built two houses, single story, frame, with the porches and fences that would become Seaside's signature. The one painted red served as the sales office. The yellow one was home for the developer and his wife. Both were models of the sort of houses the town's planners believed investors would and should build. At about the same time the Davises opened a weekend market on the beach side of Highway 30-A. Soon "Seaside Saturday" became an occasion for locals to buy and sell fresh produce, baked goods, arts and crafts, and that stuff that had been piling up in the garage. Beer, wine, and crustaceans were dispensed from a "plywood hut" called the "Shrimp Shack," and the whole operation took on a festival atmosphere. Although "its not sleek," Davis admitted, he liked the way the place reflected the "seedy, vigorous quality" of the built environment of the Panhandle. But "shack-vernac" did not appeal to everyone. In the Seaside files is a letter from some "concerned citizens of Walton County" chiding Davis for the "slung up" appearance of things and asking why he did not build something "with a bit of distinction and class" like, perhaps, the "outdoor gazebo . . . near the Destin East Trailer park"—a telling commentary on popular taste back before promoters tried to replace the area's nickname, "Redneck Riviera," with a more attractive alternative, "The Emerald Coast."[17]

While "concerned citizens" fretted, Robert Davis was hard at work showing locals just what a good neighbor Seaside intended to be. By its second year the village was sponsoring an August "Dog Days Festival," with proceeds going to the Bay Elementary School, which educated the few children who lived in Seagrove Beach. Some folks still have pictures of Davis in drag when he took part in the all-male "Miss Seaside Beauty Pageant," which was part of the celebration. Two former "sharecropper shacks" were found inland and brought to the site. One became the Seaside Grill, whose burgers and barbecued shrimp are fondly remembered, and where happy hour hosted homeowners, construction workers, and visitors from up and down the high-way. Seaside was becoming a social center for the 30-A community. Mean-while, lots sold, houses went up, and Tupelo Street, defined by its colorful cottages, beach pavilion, and gazebo, became a neighborhood. Although few homeowners actually lived at Seaside, many hoped they eventually would, so when they held their first town meeting in 1983, some sensed that a special bond had already formed among them.[18]

But it was becoming apparent that it was not the vision, but the packag-ing, that was getting the most attention. Almost from the start architects and urban planners took note of the town and its design, and professional awards soon came its way. More important from a marketing standpoint was an article that appeared in the summer of 1984 in *Southern Living,* the popu-lar primer on how to be an upscale southerner. Photographed and laid out so that the few houses already on the ground would look like part of a real village, Seaside came across as a place where upper-middle-class Americans could indulge their "pastoral urges." More than that, the town and its color-ful, whimsical cottages caught the spirit of maturing baby boomers. As one of the town's architects later noted, in the "eighties Americans like[d] pretty things," and Seaside was certainly pretty.[19]

Although lots at Seaside were priced considerably higher than those in neighboring Seagrove Beach, early sales were better than anticipated. As awards were received and publicity picked up, property sold even faster, and amid this flurry of activity problems began to appear. Preoccupied with his own utopian vision, things were, by Davis's own assessment, "being run in a less than business-like way." Although the money from sales was substantial, the developer did not appear to be paying much attention to what would happen to his cash flow when all the lots were sold—or as an observer close to the scene bluntly put it, Seaside's founder was "pissing away his assets." Finally realizing something needed to be done, in 1985 Davis brought in a new financial manager who proceeded to fire most of the people working on the project and focus more attention on the rental market and the town's retail center. From a business standpoint, the new strategy was a success.

From the community standpoint, at least according to some early home-owners, the decision changed everything, and not necessarily for the better.[20]

Early information about Seaside made no mention of rental possibilities, but as more cottages were bought for vacations instead of year-round residences, homeowners began to ask about renting their houses when they were not being used. Still interested primarily in sales, Davis picked up on rentals as a way to give potential buyers a chance to live in the town and learn to love it. But after the new manager took over, rentals began to play a more prominent role in the financial planning. Handled through a commission-charging agency set up for that purpose, units were soon going for as much as $750 a week, a tidy sum when an efficiency on the beach down at the Seagrove Motel could be had for around half that. In time, a house to rent in Davis's increasingly popular village became a significant source of income for developer and homeowners and, while some purchasers groused that they could not find a week in the summer when they could use their own house, most took the money without complaining.[21]

Today there are many who believe that entering the rental market changed Davis's focus. Soon less and less was done to make Seaside a "real town" where people lived and worked, and more was done to make Seaside the sort of place people would pay handsomely to visit and spend lavishly while there. Shops in Davis's town center bore this out. Modica Market, the village grocery, began to stock more items for the weekend gourmet than for the family shopper, and L. Pizitz, which opened as "a little garden store" with hardware for the handyman and woman, evolved quickly into a upscale gift shop and home decoration center. Although it was proudly noted that there were no airbrush tee-shirt shacks like those lining Panama City Beach, there was plenty of wearing apparel available with the Seaside logo, just the thing for visitors to take home to the neighbor who fed the cat while they were away.[22]

Seaside's new marketing blitz and the media response to it soon caught the attention of an important group of investors—the rising young urban professionals. Yuppies who came of economic age with the Reagan Revolution loved Seaside. It was unique without being daring, it spoke of quality, taste, and environmental sensitivity, and it dripped money. So it followed that the better-off or better-financed among them bought lots, hired architects, and set out to put their stamp on the village—usually by copying existing houses they liked, which to Davis's distress gave Seaside some of the "numbing sameness" he had seen in other planned communities and hoped to avoid in his. These were very different buyers from those who came first, for they had no intention of becoming residents, not soon, not ever. This was a financial investment. In the short run they expected to reap returns from renting, and it is likely that many could not have paid the mortgage without rental income. In the long run, a house in Seaside was better than money in the bank. For these buyers Seaside became, according to Davis, "a horizontal condominium," and soon the market center, which was to be the focus of community life, became a haven for the recreational shopper. Homeowners who used their cottages only a few weeks out of the year became, in effect, tourists themselves, so they fit right in.[23]

Popularity drove up prices and it was not long before the teachers, shopkeepers, artists, and writers who were to have been residents were priced out of the market. Looking back, Davis realized that at this point the community he first envisioned slipped from his grasp. Reflecting on this he concluded that if he had put less "faith in building topology, in the power of architecture" to diversify the population, he might have designed the town differently, but it was too late. People who worked in Seaside could not even afford to rent there, much less buy. Nearby Seagrove and Grayton beaches enjoyed a booming long-term rental business, while in Seaside the mix of people usually associated with a community was missing.[24]

Some of Davis's early collaborators expressed concern over the direction the dream was taking and despaired at the "populist prettifying" of the town: we set out to "build Kansas," one complained, but now we're "building Oz." But what really seemed to stick in the craw of the architects and urban planners whose ideas Davis had incorporated into the town was that the folks now buying and building, and the folks laying out the money to rent a cottage for a week or so, had their own vision of Seaside. They liked dollhouse cottages, bright colors, and the *Southern Living* touch to interior design. For them, fences were to define limits, not lean against and talk; porches were for piling beach toys and hanging towels, not sitting and swinging— especially in the heat of the day. They did not come to Seaside to meet their neighbors; they came to relax and be entertained. Let others wax eloquent on how Seaside would redefine suburban living for the next century; these folks just wanted to know where to eat, what events were scheduled, and if it was going to rain. The rest was just window dressing.[25]

Through it all Davis displayed a remarkable ability to make changes and alterations in his original design appear to be neither. Though less than enthusiastic when dust-choked homeowners insisted on bricking the streets, when it was done the developer declared the decision "an expression of community pride" and explained how the rough ride caused drivers to slow down and watch for children, as if that had been the plan all along. Such adaptability was possible largely because Seaside's original concept was long on ideals and short on specifics, which made it possible for Davis to take just about any route, so long as it appeared that Seaside was going where he and the homeowners wanted it to go.[26]

Among those ill-defined aspects of Davis's original communitarian vision was the developer's desire to make Seaside a cultural oasis in the coastal desert. Early on, poetry readings and art films were part of the calendar, though the "dog days" festivals and "womanless weddings" were more popular with the locals. But in time a new audience arrived clutching clippings from *Smithsonian* and *Atlantic Monthly,* and for them classier events were scheduled. The days of redneck revues were numbered, and soon brochures were touting Seaside as a place where you could "listen to a chamber group while enjoying strawberries and champagne with neighbors." By the end of the decade the town was playing host to the Alabama Symphony, the North Florida Ballet, art exhibits, wine tastings, and croquet tournaments. A new community was forming within the framework of the old, a community that was, according to the *New York Times,* "as relentlessly tasteful as any place on the planet."[27]

While these events were heavily tilted toward affluent, educated baby boomers, the demographics of this market group revealed that many among them were parents. If these folks were going to visit and buy, Seaside would have to offer something for the little ones to do—with and without grownups. Davis had always spoken of making Seaside a "family place . . . where grandparents could get to know their grand-children, where families and friends could re-acquaint themselves with one another." However, the focus on families became more pronounced in late 1987 when the Davis's son was born. It is hardly coincidental that as Micah grew, so did activities oriented toward the younger set. Yet in many ways Seaside was made for children. The narrow, car-free streets, the public green at the town center, and the paths through the neighborhoods seemed designed with youngsters in mind, and often, when describing the pedestrian flavor of the development, Seasiders told how you could walk anywhere in the village in ten minutes—"with a child in tow." And there was the beach. So what if the faces of the children, like those of their parents, changed every week—the community remained.[28]

Of course, Davis and the homeowners did not see eye to eye on every issue. As the town filled up, neighborhood associations formed and investors united to preserve what they considered a very successful status quo. Since their cottages were first and foremost investments, they opposed anything that threatened the idyllic image of Seaside and, naturally, their property values. This is why they supported cultural events and upscale activities but balked when the developer allowed noted architects to construct homes and town-center buildings that pushed the envelope beyond what conservative homeowners believed the code allowed. Investors did not mind all of Davis's talk about social theories and urban design, but they got nervous when he tried to put talk into action, as he did when he returned from Italy in 1991, where he had been a fellow of the American Academy of Rome. They listened with bemused interest as the developer told them that Seaside should give up trying to be the perfect community and become instead a "holiday town" like those he had enjoyed in Europe. But when they found that this new vision included pony rides and a miniature train in the town center, homeowners (fearing "goofy-golf" was next) rose in protest. Davis set up the concessions anyway, but they were not popular, so the plan quietly died. These issues paled, however, when both sides checked the books. In 1992 Seaside had close to thirty thousand visitors who paid almost $4 million for accommodations and spent $6.6 million at the shops. Despite their differences, homeowners and developer were doing quite well and expected to do even better. A strong balance sheet turneth away wrath.[29]

Seaside's success spread to neighboring villages. In Seagrove Beach to the east and Grayton Beach to the west, restaurants opened to cater to the Seaside spillover. New condominiums were built—smaller, less intrusive, and more quickly sold than the pre-Seaside high-rises. Summer cottages went on the rental market, and local stores began to stock more merchandise for the tourist trade. Davis's development had become an attraction for people all along the beach, and in what might be the supreme irony of the situation, traffic got so bad that some homeowners along Highway 30-A closed in the porches that had been Seaside's inspiration.

Meanwhile, Davis was off to create yet another community in and of Seaside, one that would complement the town's expanding activities and add yet another dimension to its appeal. Robert Davis had created a cultural center on the coast; now he wanted an intellectual center as well.

The idea was actually older than Seaside. Davis's grandfather, from whom he inherited the land, had unsuccessfully tried to get the University of Alabama to build a retreat there, and this inspired Davis to include "an educational component" in his original scheme. The developer even went so far as

Odessa Street in the mature "holiday town" of Seaside, ca. 1995. (Photograph © Steve Brooke, courtesy of Seaside, Florida.)

to have architect Walter Chatham design "a replica of Thomas Jefferson's University of Virginia" for the town, complete with classrooms, an expanded library, and an urban design center. It was his hope, Davis told *Palm Beach Life,* that Seaside would become "an academic village . . . [featuring] small-town studies, more sophisticated musical events and a full range of intellectual activity like that of a college town."[30]

Although Chatham's campus was not built, a town hall was, and in 1987 Seaside held its first symposium on urban design. In the years that followed, this annual event became an important conference for architects and town planners. To seal the connection between cultural and intellectual pursuits the Seaside Institute was set up to sponsor concerts, recitals, exhibits, symposia, conferences, and seminars that (hardly by coincidence) reflected the taste, interests, and vision of Robert Davis. Since most homeowners believed the Institute's activities improved the quality of life in the community, enhanced property values, and brought in renters, they supported its efforts. Just how many homeowners actually attended these events is another question.[31]

But it was on that question—the physical presence of homeowners—that so much commentary and criticism seemed to focus. This, in turn, forced those who really cared about the image of the town (Davis and his most ardent supporters) to go public with their thoughts on what Seaside had become and where it was going. When a 1995 article in the *Wall Street Journal* announced that "Despite Acclaim, Town of Seaside Fails to Become a Cozy Community," some homeowners and merchants wrote back to assure readers that despite its transitory population, in Seaside "community spirit reigns." In another instance Davis himself went into print to explain what happened to the dream, candidly admitted that some things did not turn out as planned, but advised critics that it was still too early to pass final judgment. Indeed it was, for though most who were familiar with Seaside had long since concluded that the town would never be a residential community, Robert Davis had not given up the dream. Although Seaside had strayed from its original route, the destination for Davis remained the same.[32]

Focusing on the educational component, Davis and the Institute found a way to bring the creative folks once envisioned as year-round residents to Seaside for at least a few weeks out of the year. Through the "Escape to Create" program, selected artists, writers, and musicians were invited to spend a winter month in Seaside to live and work under the auspices of the Institute. Some homeowners rallied to the idea and even volunteered their cottages for the "Escapees" to stay in, while others looked at the program as yet another example of the developer improving his development with other people's money.[33]

Of course, Davis had no intention of stopping there. After exploring the possibility that Florida might open its tenth university in Seaside's backyard, and discovering that it would not, he began looking for ways to link his town to an existing institution. The University of West Florida in Pensacola was the obvious choice. Beginning with programs and seminars co-sponsored by UWF and Seaside, cooperative ventures grew, and in 1996 it was announced that the University's Institute for Human & Machine Cognition and Davis's Seaside Institute had embarked on "an effort to create an environment for creative interdisciplinary thought and action called the *Lukeion*"—named, in good Robert Davis fashion, after the school where Aristotle taught.[34]

The idea was pure Seaside. The *Lukeion* would be a school "not bound by geography." Although Seaside would be its "physical place," "the *Lukeion* [would] also be located firmly at the center of the exploding global network of *computer-mediated communication*—and thus, in a sense, be anyplace." Under this arrangement, Davis told a 1996 homeowners meeting, the "information Super Highway" metaphor would be replaced by the "Information

Boulevard, Street and Square," and Seaside would become New U.—the "New University."[35]

At this same meeting homeowners also got an update on the Seaside Neighborhood School, which opened its doors that year to thirty-six sixth, seventh, and eighth grade students. One of Florida's first charter schools, Davis boasted that it "may be Seaside's most significant addition in terms of community building," but anyone expecting a traditional community to coalesce around the school may have a long wait ahead of them. Although it occupied a new, architecturally compatible building with computers and support services as technologically advanced as any in the state, during the 1997–98 academic year what critics derisively refer to as "Micah's School" had only one pupil who actually lived in Seaside. However, to the school's advocates that did not really matter, for the other students came from "neighborhoods" nearby, which reinforced the image of Seaside as the center of a greater coastal community. The school was filled to capacity, parents enthusiastically supported its activities, and soon there was a waiting list. So successful was the middle school that in January 2000 the county school board approved plans for a Seaside Elementary School, based on the "school-in-the-workplace" design and open first to children of Seaside's employees and merchants—which made sense, for few residents had school-age kids. But these Seaside Neighborhood Schools were to be more than places where fortunate students will receive a first-rate education. In time, the schools and their facilities, linked to the *Lukeion* and its facilities, will give Seaside Internet connections that will be the envy of the Gulf Coast. This, in turn, will put Seaside right back on the road to the destination Davis charted for it in the beginning.[36]

Early in Seaside's development Robert Davis often spoke of how he hoped that homeowners would "plug their work more and more into telephone lines and computers" and become year-round residents. Few did, but Davis did not abandon the idea. He took another route to get there. Instead of attracting residents and hoping they would build the infrastructure, Robert Davis sought ways to create an infrastructure (or have one created for him) that would attract enough year-round residents to make Seaside more than a "holiday town." The *Lukeion* and the Neighborhood School are components in the effort. Once in place, Davis told his audience, "living in Seaside will be an increasingly feasible option for many of us." With that he announced the Institute was at that moment planning a symposium to explore the idea and that "Coming Home to Seaside" would be a topic on the agenda.[37]

So then, one might ask, just what is this thing, Seaside, that people will come home to? In his quest for community what has Robert Davis actually produced? Truthfully, it is too early to tell, but in the less than two decades that hold its history, some things about the Seaside experience are coming clear.

On one hand, despite its success, or maybe because of it, there are people who do not like Seaside very much. Journalist Peter Applebome, in his 1996 book *Dixie Rising*, described the town as an "instant Dixie Cape Cod of cobblestone streets, white picket fences, widow's walks, languorous front porches, and New England cottages in Bermuda pastel shades of pink, yellow, and blue, where platoons of Atlanta lawyers and squadrons of Birmingham doctors' wives alight each summer to eat designer corn chips, drink pina coladas, and take seaside yoga classes." To him Seaside seemed symbolic of a South that was losing its identity, a South where "it always helps not to be too sure you know where you are."[38]

But where Applebome seemed unable to decide if Seaside reflected a cultural disorientation or was just a bit of frivolous fluff, others saw the town as the sinister personification of a community built on commercialism and illusion—a place so tightly controlled that "personal taste has been exercised from the plan," nothing was real, and everything was for sale. These critics got a chance to stake out their position when director Peter Weir selected Seaside as the location for his 1997 movie *The Truman Show*. The film told of the story of Truman, a man raised in a village that was, in reality, a stage where, unknown to him, everyone else was an actor. Truman's life was a TV show, scripted by a manipulative director, and broadcast to an audience of millions. Detractors saw Seaside's selection as confirmation of their belief that Davis's "old fashioned town" was a sham, a marketing gimmick, a tourist trap catering to the tastes and tics of visitors who were willing to pay dearly to be part of the latest trend.

Never one to let critics go unchallenged, Davis wrote a spirited defense of the village, in which he acknowledged that Seaside was indeed a stage, but one where homeowner and tourist found themselves "in the communal play," a performance in which they were part of "the spectacle of life on holiday, of life celebrated, of life observed, of life more fully lived." The difference, he suggested, was that where Truman did not realize his situation, folks who come to Seaside "and allow themselves to relax," knowingly become part of the production. Like people in an Italian piazza, "everyone knows that he and everyone else is on stage; they are performing for an audience of neighbors and strangers and that they are also the audience." It was a ringing reaffirmation of the belief that Seaside was, or at least had become, one with "holiday towns like Bath and Brighton," towns that "can bring out this sense of spectacle even among phlegmatic people."[39]

Although the article hammered home Davis's conviction that Seaside's antecedents could be found in European town traditions dating back at least to the Renaissance, the article revealed, perhaps without meaning to, how Seaside's antecedents were also rooted in the Florida tourist tradition. Change the stage, move it to Seagrove Beach, or farther east to Panama City, or down the state to Tampa, Miami, and Key West, it does not really matter. The spectacle of life celebrated, observed, and lived, even for a week, is what a tourist attraction is all about. Seaside was such an attraction. Call it a development, a resort, or a "holiday town," the result was the same. Seaside was popular because it entertained. If the entertainment stopped, the crowd would move on.

But that does not mean that Davis was content to let Seaside's legacy be that of a very profitable tourist destination. Despite the commercial success he has enjoyed, Seaside's "founder" (as he has come to be known) remained the visionary he was at the outset, and though he admitted that Seaside's success as a holiday town has slowed the growth of the community he hoped to create, he still did not give up on the idea. *The Truman Show* paid some $368,000 in location fees to use Seaside for the movie and Davis donated his share to the Neighborhood School, a move that surprised critics who claimed that the "founder" was interested only in the money. But the school was, and remains, one of the essential building blocks in his creation, a visible testimony to Davis's determination to make Seaside more than a resort, to make it real.[40]

In the meantime, until the day when Seaside is finally populated by permanent residents, the founder wants his village to serve as a model of what urban America can be. Under Davis's leadership Seaside has encouraged and given substance to a town planning movement that in 1993 organized itself as the "Congress for the New Urbanism" and set out to promote what its proponents called "neo-traditional town planning." Representing a host of urban design professions, the Congress, according to its charter, stands "for the restoration of existing urban centers and towns within coherent metropolitan regions, the reconfiguration of sprawling suburbs into communities of real neighborhoods and diverse districts, the conservation of natural environments, and the preservation of our built legacy." One of the ways to accomplish this was to "reintegrate housing, workplace, shopping and recreation into compact, pedestrian-friendly neighborhoods" that will allow, indeed require, "people to walk more and rely on public transportation to attend to their daily needs, while reducing automobile use and gasoline consumption." This "alternative to suburban sprawl" is New Urbanism's vision of the future and Seaside is their prototype, which should come as no surprise, since many of the Congress's leading lights began their careers with Davis. If this movement is successful, this little town on the Gulf Coast will be heralded as the place where it all began.[41]

All of Davis's efforts notwithstanding, the power that tourists and investors have over tourism and real estate development was and continues to be difficult to overcome. As the century drew to a close, this control of the purchaser over the product was apparent in a new community that was taking shape next door to Seaside. There the St. Joe Company, Florida's largest private landowner, began work on "Watercolor," a 1,140-homesite development that drew selectively from the Davis design, even as it ignored many of the ideas and concepts that made Seaside what its founder wanted it to be. As a result, Watercolor provided an interesting commentary on the impact Seaside has had on development in the area and offered, perhaps, a glimpse at the Florida of the future.[42]

With lots starting at just under $200,000 and house prices beginning in the mid-$300,000 range, Watercolor did not pretend to seek residents from all strata of society, as Seaside did at the outset. The community Watercolor's developers wanted to build was upscale from the start, much as Seaside had become. Realizing that even a modest house in Seaside was selling for over $500,000, Watercolor's prices did not seem out of line, and in the eyes of some might be counted as a bargain. Following Seaside's successful precedent, Watercolor's houses were to be built according to a carefully constructed code, with "an approved list of architects and builders to simplify the design/built process." Not surprisingly, the houses pictured in promotional literature and models bore an uncanny resemblance to those found in the development next door.[43]

But Watercolor was not a Seaside clone. Spread over nearly five hundred acres, half of which was "devoted to open space and preservation areas," St. Joe's community was not laid out for the pedestrian—though the bicycle promises to become the automobile's alternative there. A town center was planned, as well as conference facilities, a hotel, shops and the like, but there was nothing to suggest at this early stage of things that Watercolor would try to re-create for its residents the "holiday town" atmosphere of Seaside. And why should it, when Seaside is a short walk or bike ride away? Although Davis and many Seaside homeowners were less than thrilled at the idea of so many neighbors nearby, Watercolor's developers saw Seaside as one of the new development's attractions. Acknowledging their debt to Davis and his design, Watercolor representatives told potential buyers that Seaside was their "historic district," the place where residents and visitors could go to see the roots from whence Watercolor sprung. It was an ironic role for what was once touted as the "town of the future," and there were folks at Seaside who were none too happy with this turn of events.[44]

Yet if one wished to compound the irony, a walk through Seaside, into Seagrove, would take the visitor back even further. Although new houses at Seagrove Beach, and some newly renovated ones, looked as if they were constructed under the Seaside code, in Seagrove you could still find ample examples of the sort of vernacular architecture that inspired Robert Davis in the first place. There, in that coastal square mile, are three communities that reveal half a century of Florida land development.

Watercolor's creators have taken what appealed to the people who paid big bucks to own or rent in Seaside, refined it a bit to get rid of the cloying cuteness that the Peter Applebomes of this world disliked, unhitched it from the dreams and theories of the New Urbanists, and presented it to a public that test marketing suggested was ready and willing to invest in a diluted version of Davis's dream. Like Seaside, Watercolor's promoters played on personal nostalgia and told potential buyers that the "old familiar feeling," the "overall tingling sensation you first got as a kid when your family stayed at the beach," could be theirs again. An emphasis on families and children pervaded Watercolor's promotional literature, and its advertisements were so similar to those produced by and for Davis's development that it would be easy to believe they were designed and written by the same people. And down the list of what Watercolor had to offer was the rental program, just to assure anxious buyers that a house in St. Joe's development would help them pay its mortgage.[45]

While such economic safeguards were important, they were not the critical factor for most investors. Going all the way back to mid-twentieth century, Seagrove Beach, Seaside, and now Watercolor have all benefited (or in Watercolor's case hope to benefit) from generational good times. Seagrove attracted affluent folks who had profited from the post–World War II boomlet and the prosperity of the 1950s. Davis's town rose from the palmetto with the help of Reagan Era tax reforms and liberal lending policies that put big hunks of discretionary money into the hands of baby boomers who were financially coming of age. Then Watercolor arrived to offer paradise to people who thrived during the Clinton (or as they might prefer, Greenspan) boom and who, a little wary of Wall Street, wanted to put their money into something a bit more tangible. A quick look at the way the value of property in Seagrove and Seaside has grown over the years makes any beach area investment look attractive.[46]

Attractive to whom? Southerners, which is a point that should not be missed.

Although the developers of Seagrove, Seaside, and Watercolor gladly welcomed investors from anyplace, at the core of each enterprise was the recognition that to be successful they had to attract southerners, and a certain class of southerners at that. So it followed that all three developments stressed the fact that they were culturally as well as physically part of the South. When McGee talked of Seagrove being the place where "nature did its best," he was talking of natural Florida, and the seclusion he offered was southern seclusion. This was revealed in Seagrove's restrictive covenant which, when read from the perspective of mid-twentieth century southerners, assured investors that they would not have to worry about white trash or black folks moving in next door and messing things up. The covenant also made it clear that if buyers from elsewhere did invest, they would be expected, indeed required, to accept the cultural values of the development's southern majority.

Robert Davis targeted the same group. Although he would not have written a racially restrictive covenant even if it had been legal to do so, economics dictated who would buy in Seaside, and that was sufficient to keep the community overwhelmingly white and a cut or two above trashy. True, the "cracker cottages" Davis hoped would line his sandy streets grew to mansion proportions, yet all but a few retained elements that are distinctly southern. Tin roofs (which interestingly enough were prohibited in Seagrove Beach's original covenant), screened porches, and high ceilings with fans stirring the air spoke to a Dixie decadence that attracted without threatening. Despite the founder's infatuation with Italian piazzas and English holiday towns, one did not have to wander far into the residential section to realize that there was more of Charleston than Brighton in Seaside. In his efforts to attract what he described as "increasingly cosmopolitan" southerners, Davis filled his town with folks whose tastes were tempered and trained more by

Southern Living than by *Architectural Digest,* though both probably sat on the coffee table back home. At the end of the century, fully 75 percent of Seaside's homeowners were from the old Confederacy, and visitors from those states dominate the rental market, so it is hardly surprising that southern interests shape what Seaside offers its guests.[47]

Watercolor catered to regional tastes in much the same way. Conscious of its southern location and southern clientele, St. Joe's planners made being southern an important part of Watercolor's marketing strategy, and they singled out potential buyers in Birmingham and Atlanta for particular attention. Residences built in the St. Joe development were described as "classic Southern homes with their wide front porches," set down in a landscape that offered visitors and residents everything "from the coastal pine forest to the marshy shallows of Western Lake to the emerald waters of the Gulf." Clearly Watercolor was in and of the South.[48]

And it is the South that provides the most lasting link between Seagrove, Seaside, and Watercolor. All three, in their time and place, appealed to essentially the same clientele, a group of rapidly rising southerners who yearned for a simpler time, a more secluded world, yet one that would fit into an investment strategy in a culture which, until recently, would have recoiled from the very idea of having one. Today, at the beginning of a new century, these three designs offer insights into the hopes and dreams, and foibles and fantasies that have motivated a particular group of southerners to come down to the Gulf Coast and spend their money. They also serve to show anyone who cares to look how investors and tourists, along with developers and founders, dictated an attraction's design. That lesson should not be lost on the next dreamer who wants to make Florida after his own image.

4
Public and Private Tourism Development in 1930s Appalachia
The Blue Ridge Parkway Meets Little Switzerland

Anne Mitchell Whisnant

When most people think of the Blue Ridge Parkway—winding quietly through Virginia and North Carolina—they seem to conceive of it as a welcome antidote to, and respite from, southern Appalachia's numerous chaotically commercial highway strips such as Maggie Valley and Cherokee, North Carolina, or Gatlinburg or Pigeon Forge, Tennessee, where summer visitors flock to motels, chalets, pancake houses, miniature golf courses, water slides, candy and craft shops, creekside RV parks, outlet malls, casinos, wedding chapels, or tacky western-theme amusement parks. On the face of it, the Parkway seems to share little with such private, entrepreneurial tourist areas, and conventional wisdom about the road usually says, "Thank God it's not another. . . . " Most observers further assume that, in comparison to other tourist developments in the region, the Parkway's impact has been benign and its story interesting mainly for the remarkable engineering feats the construction involved, such as the famous Linn Cove viaduct around Grandfather Mountain.

In truth, however, the Parkway's early development was much more closely intertwined with the broader history of tourism in the mountains than has generally been understood. Conventional wisdom is right in some sense, however: the Parkway isn't Maggie Valley, or Cherokee, or Pigeon Forge or Gatlinburg. Examined more closely, this observation suggests that not all "tourism" looks the same. Indeed, when the Blue Ridge Parkway was built in the southern Appalachians beginning in the 1930s—as well as at other times in the region's history—the shape, scope, accessibility, and impact of "tourism development" were contested by people in various sectors, public and private, who often shared little beyond a general interest in promoting it.[1]

The formative years of Parkway development offer an exceptional opportunity for examining these tangled interactions.[2] Growing out of ideas first promoted by local chambers of commerce and private, business-oriented tourism boosters in North Carolina and Virginia, the Parkway was built when the New Deal brought federal funds from the Public Works Administration to pay for their tourist development plans. Thus, the project originated as a public-private joint venture, with public and private leaders in both states heavily involved in the early route planning, state highway departments in charge of land acquisition from private owners through 469 miles of the southern Appalachians, and design and construction overseen by the federal National Park Service and Bureau of Public Roads. Throughout the 1930s, the local Parkway boosters, adjoining landowners, and tourist developers collaborated and clashed with state and federal officials about Parkway routing, width of the right-of-way, land acquisition, concessions policies, access and use restrictions, and other aspects of Parkway development that determined how the road's significant costs and benefits would be distributed—both to the public in general and to private landowners and entrepreneurs.

Primarily due to stringent action by federal Park Service officials and at least one visionary North Carolina bureaucrat, the road was not completely co-opted by local protourism elites who most fervently promoted the project. Controlling nearly all decisions about the Parkway's design was the premise that the road was to be a *scenic* parkway serving a broad public goal: preserving and making accessible to everyone the beautiful farmlands, high peaks, and breathtaking vistas of the southern Appalachians.

But creating this kind of road involved significant costs, especially to many adjoining rural landowners, who hoped to use the Parkway to transport goods back and forth to market, or to develop their own tourist accommodations. To the dismay of many of them, a parkway differed significantly from a highway. Most importantly, it was to be used by passenger cars only; commercial vehicles (buses and trucks) were prohibited. Roadside development and advertising were severely curtailed in hopes of preventing the congested and unsightly buildup that had already by the late 1920s marred the roadsides of many of America's regular highways. To make matters worse, the Parkway required an unusually wide right-of-way "to provide an insulating

strip of park land between the roadway and the abutting private property"
and preserve scenery. Thus, adjoining landowners were generally permitted
no frontage rights or direct access from their property.[3]

As it turned out, the width of the right-of-way varied considerably at different locations, but it was intended to average about one thousand feet. In
some places, protective green space was preserved through a scenic easement,
which left the land in the hands of the original landowner but imposed strict
usage regulations; in most places, the entire strip of land was bought outright
for the Parkway as the National Park Service came to realize the difficulty of
obtaining and policing easements. No matter which way it was done, the
Parkway (technically "an elongated park . . . to contain the roadway") took
much more land than either an average highway or many previous parkways
had taken, and it kept nearby landowners and residents at a much greater
distance.[4]

Other design requirements intended to enhance safety and enjoyability for
travelers also hindered use of the Parkway by local people. Anticipating innovations that would later become standard with freeways and interstates,
most intersections with other highways were handled via under- or over-
passes. To reduce interruptions in Parkway traffic, access was tightly controlled via widely spaced entrances and exits. In some cases, new regular
highways were built parallel to the Parkway to carry local traffic, and the
states were required to provide landowners who were totally isolated by the
Parkway with alternate access to local roads. In keeping with all of these requirements, the rights of adjoining property owners to connect driveways,
crossing roads, or other access roads to the Parkway were limited, especially
on the North Carolina sections of the Parkway. These regulations guaranteed easy driving and uncluttered, magnificent scenery for auto travelers, and
the public responded enthusiastically to the road. Currently it is the most
popular site in the National Park system, with nearly twenty million annual
visitors.[5]

There were moments when the Parkway might have become just another
commercial corridor resembling Gatlinburg or Maggie Valley, however. No
early conflict illustrates this possibility better than an episode at Little Switzerland, North Carolina, an exclusive resort for well-to-do white lowlanders
developed in the 1910s by North Carolina Supreme Court justice Heriot
Clarkson.[6] In this conflict, dramatic tensions emerged between local and
state-level Parkway boosters, who tended to promote the Parkway largely for
the economic benefits it could bring to established tourist centers such as

Little Switzerland Developer Heriot Clarkson, ca. 1920s. Clarkson welcomed the Blue Ridge
Parkway but fought to maintain his own vision of tourism development in the North Carolina mountains. (Courtesy of the North Carolina Office of Archives and History, Division
of Historic Resources, Raleigh, North Carolina.)

Asheville (and Little Switzerland), and Park Service officials, whose vision
focused on a larger good of opening up areas of exceptional scenery to easy
public view. For state officials charged with obtaining Heriot Clarkson's land,
the dilemma over how both to promote tourism in the state and preserve the
integrity of the tourist-drawing attraction they were creating proved difficult to negotiate. Developer Clarkson brilliantly manipulated the tensions in
the Parkway project. At one level, his complaints about the plans of the
North Carolina State Highway Commission to take eighty-eight acres of
land through Little Switzerland for the Parkway echoed those complaints
expressed by many landowners in the Parkway's path. But as a state Supreme
Court judge, wealthy resort owner, and longtime Democratic party power

broker, Clarkson was positioned to take his fight into North Carolina's news-papers and courtrooms in ways that smaller, less prominent owners could not. His story reveals the complicated class politics as well as the state-federal and public-private conflicts surrounding the early development of the Parkway.

When he clashed with the state Highway Commission over Parkway land acquisition through Little Switzerland in the late 1930s, in a three-year battle that involved several court hearings and ended with a $25,000 settle-ment in his favor, Heriot Clarkson was already well known to government officials and citizens throughout North Carolina. Now seventy-five years old, he had emerged as a fixture first in local and then in statewide Democratic politics in the late nineteenth century, when he took a prominent role in the white supremacy campaign that led to the disfranchisement of African Americans. He had moved on to the prohibition crusade, and then into the "good roads" movement of the 1910s and early 1920s, when he had managed the gubernatorial campaign of Cameron Morrison, North Carolina's "good roads governor." Morrison rewarded Clarkson with a post on the North Carolina Supreme Court in 1923, and there Clarkson remained when the Parkway battle commenced. Through all his many political activities, Heriot Clarkson worked squarely within the group of new "business progressive" Democratic leaders who came to dominate North Carolina by the early twentieth century.[7]

During his years as a powerful Democratic party stalwart, Clarkson es-tablished an exclusive resort in the North Carolina mountains where the wealthy and powerful could retreat in the summers. Riding a mule, he first approached the isolated mountaintop that would become Little Switzerland in the summer of 1909. Admiring the sweeping panoramic view and learn-ing that the area was well supplied with fresh spring water, Clarkson knew immediately that he had found the spot for his planned summer colony. He rushed home to Charlotte and rounded up nine other men—drawn from among Clarkson's associates in Charlotte's professional, business, and real es-tate community—to invest in his venture. Within two months, the investors had signed a contract to buy as much of the Grassy Mountain and Chestnut Ridge property as they could from the mountain families who owned it. By early fall, the investors had incorporated the Switzerland Company to run the development, which soon came to comprise over 1,100 acres straddling Mitchell and McDowell counties.[8]

Planning for "Little Switzerland" began in earnest in early 1910. One hundred acres of the land (purchased by Clarkson for about $11 per acre) would initially be offered in one-acre parcels for $150 (soon $300) for home sites. To ready the lots for cottages, the Company installed a water and sewer system (planned to empty into a stream six hundred feet down the mountain) and set to work improving railroad and wagon road access. Clarkson used his influence to have a Carolina, Clinchfield, and Ohio (CC&O) railroad station moved to within two miles of the resort, and by 1910, a Company-financed toll road connected the station to Little Switzerland. That summer, Heriot Clarkson's widowed sister, Ida Clarkson Jones, opened the resort's first hotel, the Switzerland Inn, which quickly became the center of the new community. In the ensuing months Clarkson Jones advertised the new resort by entertaining both prospective homeowners from the Charlotte area and local residents from the surrounding mountains at a series of parties, picnics, and celebrations.[9]

Cottage construction proceeded slowly at first, with only Heriot Clarkson and his Charlotte law partner building homes by 1911. But before long, about twenty people—like the initial investors, mostly Charlotte-area attorneys and businessmen—had bought land at Little Switzerland, and four of them immediately built summer homes. Road development on the Switzerland Company lands continued apace, and Heriot Clarkson himself built a general store and post office in 1911. He had a telephone line run in 1912—practically the only modern convenience available at the resort until electricity arrived in the 1930s. With ten more cottages built between 1913 and 1916, the colony began to take shape.[10]

The establishment of several other institutions and the enlargement of the water system followed, making the colony a relatively self-sufficient community by the early 1930s. The ardently Episcopalian Clarksons helped organize Church of the Resurrection in 1913, and a South Carolina woman opened Camp As-You-Like-It for Girls the following year. A boarding-house, Echo Cottage, opened several years later, and about the same time, the Raleigh Business and Professional Women's Club built the Swiss Chalet for club members' use. Thomas Dixon, author of *The Clansman*, erected a hotel and started his short-lived Wildacres development next door to Little Switzerland in the 1920s. Little Switzerland's community center, Geneva Hall, rounded out the colony's facilities when it was constructed in 1929.[11]

Meanwhile, several original Switzerland Company investors died or sold out to Clarkson or other members of his family, who gradually consolidated their hold over the resort. When he ascended to the state Supreme Court in 1923, Heriot Clarkson handed over day-to-day management of the company to his son, Charlotte attorney Francis O. Clarkson. Until his death in 1942, however, the elder Clarkson remained the central power within the company.[12]

The years in which he launched Little Switzerland were the same years in which Heriot Clarkson found himself in the midst of North Carolina's "good roads" campaign. In fact, it may perhaps have been partly his concern with improving access to Little Switzerland that brought Clarkson into the campaign, since by 1917 it was clear that the roads built to bring wagonloads of tourists to the colony from the train station were inadequate to allow automobiles into the resort. Throughout the late 1910s and 1920s, Clarkson and the Switzerland Company lobbied energetically, creatively, and effectively to bring county- and state-financed roads through the development, even at the expense of local residents in the nearby Spruce Pine area who argued that they would have been better served by more direct routes that bypassed the resort. These successful manipulations of state road-building plans were critical for Little Switzerland's continued prosperity; by the late 1930s, the colony consisted of about sixty homes.[13]

From the beginning, Little Switzerland cottage owners and summer visitors were an exclusive group. To ensure that the development attracted only the right people, deeds carried restrictive covenants, which were at that time becoming increasingly common tools to separate the wealthy from the poor, black from white, and businesses from residences. Little Switzerland's covenants stipulated that the one-acre lots could not be subdivided or contain more than one home, and that they were to be used only for residences or farming. No business development, other than that authorized by the Company (the post office and general store in the early years), was permitted. And, in keeping with Clarkson's long-held segregationist views, Switzerland Company deeds specified that the land "shall never be owned or occupied by persons of the colored race." Thus, the deeds—and, no doubt, the high prices of lots (by the 1930s, up to $600 per acre)—tended to keep the poor and black out of Little Switzerland, and the restrictions ensured that the community would be exclusively a leisure colony and would not attract the kind of business development that would likely provide significant numbers of year-round jobs for local residents.[14]

Not surprisingly then, most of the cottage owners and tourists at Little Switzerland by the 1930s were, as one ad proclaimed, "prominent and noted people."[15] Several North Carolina lawyers, a state senator, the presidents of several Charlotte-area companies, a Supreme Court judge from Louisiana,

and doctors, musicians, and other professionals from North and South Carolina, Georgia, and Florida built homes at the resort, as did ardent good roads
activist Harriet Morehead Berry.[16]

Nevertheless, the restrictive covenants did not result in a totally homoge-
nous community at the Little Switzerland enclave on the eve of the Parkway
battle. A 1936 advertisement for the resort noted, for example, that "the
most modest" home at Little Switzerland cost $300, and the most expensive
$15,000. These less expensive homes likely belonged to one of the fifteen
"more enterprising" members of local families who had by the 1930s built
"substantial and attractive" homes on farmlands there. Indeed, during the
first decades of the resort's existence, Little Switzerland newcomers developed
relationships of friendship and mutual interdependency with several native
Mitchell and McDowell county families, most notably the Buchanans, the
Hollifields, and the McKinneys.[17]

These relationships rested largely upon the employment Little Switzerland homeowners and the Company itself offered local citizens during the
summer season. Local carpenter and contractor Alphonzo "Fons" McKinney, for example, built a home for his family on Switzerland Company lands
shortly after the community opened and, according to one of the Charlotte-
based homeowners, "was of great service to the growing community." In
the years before automobile travel to the resort was possible, members of
the Hollifield and Buchanan families drove hacks loaded with visitors up the
Switzerland Company's toll road from the train station. Switzerland Company records show that numerous McKinneys and Hollifields built the Kilmichael Tower observation platform in 1935, constructed roads, and performed other labor throughout the late 1930s and early 1940s. Another
member of the large McKinney family lived on Company lands as caretaker
for the Cansler family of Charlotte, who built an expensive two-story "cottage" equipped with a Delco electrical system on their large acreage. According to one longtime Little Switzerland homeowner, the Canslers situated
their caretaker's small home close enough to their own that they could easily
shout requests for assistance down the mountain to the McKinneys.[18]

As the development's historian later remembered, summer cottagers came
to depend heavily on local women and men "for help" in managing house-
hold chores and caretaking at private homes, the Switzerland Inn, the camps,
and the Echo Cottage as well as for the carpentry, plumbing, and masonry
work needed in building new structures for the village. Little Switzerland
visitors also bought handmade products from several local craftsmen, includ-

ing chairs from the Woody family of Spruce Pine and gemstones from Roby Buchanan of Hawk.[19]

Notwithstanding elite residents' obvious dependence on the energy and skills of local people, the resort's historian portrayed the "mountain friends and their ways" in condescending stereotypical terms: as "clans" of noble, "proud and independent" mountain people who spoke "picturesque mountain speech," made quilts, displayed a "natural fatalism" in the face of tragic events, and raised their enormous families in log cabins. The patriarch of the McKinney family, she wrote, had four wives and fathered forty-two children.[20]

News reports in the 1930s characterized Heriot Clarkson as a great friend of the seventy-five or so local families who lived at or near his resort colony. "We's just one big family up here," he told a reporter in 1937.[21] Yet it is clear that the relationship between Little Switzerland homeowners and visitors and local residents was always a lopsided one, with local residents dependent on tourists and cottagers, and with homeowners and visitors displaying a combination of paternalistic concern and outright condescension to local residents.

While mountaineers were said to refer to Clarkson as "the judge," for example, Clarkson "call[ed] every mountaineer by name" as he drove to Little Switzerland in his Model T.[22] Another report noted somewhat disingenuously that local people were "never conscious of Justice Clarkson's official position."[23] A journalist with whom Clarkson drove down the mountain in 1937 recalled that "we encountered seven or eight ruddy-cheeked mountain children. 'Hello, Judge Clarkson!' they all bubbled, affectionately. His face flushed with a warmth of pleasure, he gathered around them, plied them with questions, then gave them all the pennies he could produce from his pockets." The reporter concluded that "that incident reflects . . . the bond of affection existing between him and these mountain children."[24] Another article explained that Clarkson had "consistently strengthened [his mountain neighbors'] faith in his leadership; and he has firmly rooted himself in their esteem. His tutelage of Little Switzerland . . . and his championing of the rights and best interests of its people have been inspiring, to say the least."[25] Looking after the mountain residents, prohibiting alcohol at Little Switzerland, eliminating the possibility of blacks owning homes there, and interesting himself fervently in road development in and around the community, Clarkson created for himself at Little Switzerland a small utopia where he could pursue the elitist, racist, probusiness, and paternalistic social vision he worked for through his activism in the disfranchisement, prohibition, and good roads campaigns.

Members of the Clarkson family portrayed themselves as the saviors and protectors of such mountain people, even at moments when they cleverly merged the interests of the Switzerland Company with those of local residents and disguised political maneuvers designed to manipulate public policy in the Company's favor as activism on behalf of local people. Descriptions written on the eve of the Parkway fight recounting a successful effort years earlier to keep an important state highway open from Marion through Little Switzerland to Bakersville provide a glaring example. While it was clear in 1929 that retaining the state-maintained road was critical for the continued progress of Little Switzerland as a tourist colony, newspaper articles as late as 1937, written with the Clarksons' cooperation, described the battle as one waged by the Clarkson family mainly on behalf of local mountain residents.[26] This portrayal flew in the face of evidence that residents in the nearby town of Spruce Pine had actually called for closure of the road in favor of a more direct route. That earlier episode—which highlighted the Clarksons' unabashed use of their own power to mobilize local citizens and to shape both road policy and public understanding of events—proved eerily predictive of aspects of Heriot Clarkson's later battle with the state Highway Commission over the Blue Ridge Parkway.

Thus, by the late 1930s, Heriot Clarkson had fifty years of experience in local and state politics, more than twenty years of practice in getting what he wanted for Little Switzerland, and a lifetime of portraying himself as a fearless crusader for high principle. As it set out to take some of Clarkson's lands for the new federal Parkway in 1937, the state Highway Commission was dealing with a formidable and experienced foe.

It must have come as something of a shock to North Carolina Highway Commission officials, however, to find themselves in a major conflict with Heriot Clarkson over the Parkway, for Clarkson and his son Francis had from the first been involved in the massive lobbying effort waged by North Carolinians to bringing the Parkway through the western North Carolina mountains on a route that (not coincidentally) would take it near Little Switzerland. Even as relations between the Highway Commission and the Clarksons began to sour in 1937, Francis Clarkson wrote that the Parkway "will be in my opinion the greatest single asset of its kind in the State of North Carolina."[27]

Since he had been involved in the Parkway routing discussions from early on, it certainly came as no surprise to Clarkson that the Parkway right-of-way would take some of his ridgetop resort land. And in fact, Clarkson at first seemed to see the Parkway as a potential asset to his somewhat isolated development. In a cordial 1935 note to the state highway engineer in charge of land acquisition, he suggested a possible route through the development that would bring travelers within a short distance of the (pay-per-view) Kilmichael Tower observation deck he had just had built. His congenial tone continued through mid-1937, when he offered cooperation in land acquisition through Little Switzerland. That summer, glowing Clarkson-approved newspaper articles about the resort advertised the fact that three miles of the Parkway would pierce the development and opined that the new road "doubtless . . . will prove a boost for her, and will serve to bring her added patronage."[28]

Although by many reports Little Switzerland—now consisting of 1,200 acres and approximately sixty homes—appeared to be thriving by the mid-1930s, some evidence indicated that the community needed just such a boost. And while a long article-advertisement in the *Asheville Citizen* boasted that "there is no indebtedness on the Little Switzerland property," many similar resorts had failed as the depression descended. Clarkson rightly worried that a depression-induced drop in tourist travel might bring his development a similar fate. And, indeed, Switzerland Company financial records for 1937 indicated that, even if it was not seriously in debt, the company was losing money. Some records suggested that the Clarksons may have been using their personal funds to keep the development afloat. By Clarkson's account, his family had by this time poured at least $150,000 (and perhaps as much as $200,000) into the resort, which, the family later claimed, had never made a profit. Two years after Clarkson's death in 1942, company records indicated that the company still owed the Clarkson estate over $10,000.[29]

Thus Heriot Clarkson—always eager to advertise and promote his development—must have viewed the coming of the Parkway to Little Switzerland as a great opportunity for opening his resort to more travelers and potential homeowners. Even as Clarkson's conflicts with the North Carolina Highway Commission escalated in the summer of 1938, the *Asheville Citizen* quoted him as saying in regard to the routing of the Parkway through Little Switzerland: "It was the natural action to take. My place enjoys wide recognition as the beauty spot of the Blue Ridge. . . . Now the federal government, by routing its driveway through Little Switzerland, shows its determination that motorists from distant states and places shall have the opportunity to drink in the marvelous sweeping views and natural beauty of this wonderland."[30] But as the negotiations over land acquisition progressed, Clarkson also became intrigued by the possibility of making the land condemnation procedure itself work to the Switzerland Company's advantage. What had begun as a partnership between private tourist promoters like Clarkson and the state and federal governments in creating a new tourist attraction in the Blue Ridge Parkway disintegrated into a conflict that illustrated fundamental differences between the two approaches to tourism development.

With many other area landowners, Clarkson was initially and perhaps legitimately alarmed by the roughly thousand-foot right-of-way to be seized for the Parkway, annoyed by the state's sluggishness in letting him know what parts of the Switzerland Company's property would be affected, and frustrated by the state's delay in working out payment for the lands to be taken.[31] By mid-1936, a visibly worried Clarkson was pushing state officials to lobby the National Park Service for a reduced right-of-way through Little Switzerland. With relations still cordial between Highway Commission staff and the Clarksons, the state obliged—in keeping with its desire to foster the local tourist industry as well as to save money on land acquisition. The Highway Commission chairman advised the Park Service director that narrowing the right-of-way at Little Switzerland "would not reduce the beauty of the Parkway but might enhance it through the furnishment of better opportunity for the right kind of local development. Furthermore, . . . [it] would save this State a very considerable cost."[32]

Park Service officials seemed convinced that trying to acquire a wide fee simple right-of-way through a developed area like Little Switzerland would be prohibitively expensive, so the Parkway superintendent replied that the Park Service would accept a reduced right-of-way through the development. By December of 1936, the state—with federal approval—presented new plans to take a fee simple strip averaging slightly more than the Parkway minimum of two hundred feet in width (accompanied by a small amount of scenic easement) through three miles of Clarkson's resort.[33]

Thus, when the official land acquisition process for the Little Switzerland section of the Parkway finally commenced in the spring of 1937, state and federal officials had already gone a long way to reduce the damage the Parkway might cause at Little Switzerland. Heriot Clarkson, for his part, initially attempted to reach an out-of-court settlement with the state for $300 per acre, while he threatened that the Switzerland Company would demand $500 per acre if the case went to court, because, he claimed, "the road has wrecked the Western part of the Switzerland Company property for any further development for summer visitors."[34]

Having paid an average of just over thirty dollars per acre for all the land thus far acquired for the Parkway, and being simultaneously embroiled in delicate negotiations with the Eastern Band of Cherokee Indians and the nearby Linville Improvement Company for much larger tracts, the Highway Commission was not disposed to settle for $300 an acre, especially when its staff felt that damage to the development would be far outweighed by future benefits.[35]

Unpersuaded, Heriot and Francis Clarkson became more adamant during the subsequent months that the new road would irreparably harm the development. The state, meanwhile, proceeded to acquire title to the Switzerland Company property, transferring control of eighty-eight acres to the federal government (as was the practice for all land acquisition in North Carolina for the Parkway) in the spring of 1938. With this transaction completed, and with their offer for a negotiated settlement rejected, the Clarksons hired a team of prominent lawyers and promptly filed suit in the Mitchell County Superior Court in hopes of getting the $50,000—approximately $575 per acre—in "just compensation."[36]

Following the normal procedures for condemnation cases, the Mitchell County courts appointed three local appraisers to assess the damages. The appraisers awarded the Switzerland Company $27,000 plus some interest, more than the Company's original compromise offer of $22,500. Worried that a large settlement in the Switzerland Company case would push up land prices for other lands in the area, the Highway Commission appealed to the Superior Court, where the case went before a judge and jury in March of 1939. That body awarded the Switzerland Company $25,000, with the stipulation that several access roads from company property to the Parkway be provided. This figure was less than the Switzerland Company's request for $50,000, but the Company was disposed to accept the judgment. Still believing this sum to be excessive, however, the Highway Commission appealed to the state Supreme Court, on which Clarkson himself still sat.[37]

As the case wound its way through the North Carolina courts, the Clarksons consistently argued that the Parkway would hinder Little Switzerland's future expansion and development. "The road," the Clarksons frequently maintained, "is like a Chinese wall or canal."[38] This meant, Francis Clarkson complained, that "You could not get on or off it, and it has bottled up and destroyed the western section of our development . . . making useless for col-

ony development hundreds of acres of land."[39] And indeed, when they initially filed suit in the spring of 1938, the Clarksons had few assurances that
Little Switzerland would be provided with adequate accesses and crossings to
a Parkway that would bisect the resort. Without these, the integrity of the
resort was threatened, as travel within the community's boundaries would be
hindered. Furthermore, the Clarksons—by now owners of 80 percent of
Switzerland Company stock—had poured considerable funds into having
building lots surveyed, roads constructed, sewer and water lines laid, the observation tower built, and other improvements made. The loss of either the
lands and lots themselves, or of access to them, did involve costs and con-
siderations that did not pertain in areas where the lands the Parkway required were largely undeveloped. Thus, the Clarksons argued, the costs of
routing the Parkway through Little Switzerland went far beyond the value
of the eighty-eight acres actually confiscated. The Clarksons also asserted
that the long delay in reaching a settlement had itself crippled the resort's
growth.[40]

Such were Clarkson's reasons, therefore, for asking for what was up to that
time the largest settlement yet demanded for Parkway right-of-way in North
Carolina. Indeed, he estimated the $50,000 asked for in the lawsuit was less
than the real damages to the development, which his more generous ac-
counting set closer to $70,000.[41] Whatever the sum, officials at the state
Highway Commission thought it too high. Their assessment of the Parkway's effects on Little Switzerland differed dramatically from Clarkson's, and
they fought the influential judge with their own set of compelling counter-
arguments.

The Commission contended that Clarkson had wildly overstated both
the value of the lands he was losing and the detrimental impact the Parkway
might have on Little Switzerland. To bolster their claim, they cited tax valuations of Switzerland Company lands, which were vastly lower than what
the Clarksons demanded.[42] Commission officials further contended that, far
from being prime development lots, as much as two-thirds of the lands taken
for the Parkway were undevelopable rugged and steep tracts which, Highway
Commission attorneys noted, had "heretofore been inaccessible and not marketable at any price" and that "in nearly 30 years [had] brought no income
and offered no opportunity of development."[43]

Acknowledging, however, that the Parkway did pose difficulties not encountered with a regular highway, Commission officials reiterated the numerous special accommodations already arranged to minimize the negative ef-

fects of the Parkway on the resort. Most important was the 1937 decision to reduce the right-of-way through Little Switzerland to the bare minimum of two hundred feet, a concession made for no other individual or company and one that left the right-of-way at Little Switzerland narrower than at any other point along the North Carolina sections of the Parkway. Furthermore, contradicting the Clarksons' claims that they had no assurances of being able to get on or cross the Parkway, Highway Commission officials countered— truthfully—that they had worked for months to convince a reluctant Park Service to permit several accesses and crossings along the Parkway through Little Switzerland. One of the access roads, they noted, would allow drivers to visit Kilmichael Tower, and would thus "bring hundreds of sight-seers within reach of this tower to every one that came before." Having made these arrangements, the Commission argued—with considerable merit, as it turned out—that the Parkway would help rather than harm the resort and that, as a result, the Clarksons' proposed settlement sum was too high.[44]

Nevertheless, when the state Supreme Court (with Clarkson recusing himself) split three to three on the Switzerland Company case in the fall of 1939, effectively upholding the Mitchell County Superior Court's verdict, Heriot Clarkson felt vindicated. By December of that year, the Switzerland Company finally had its $25,000 check.[45]

Although defeated in court, Highway Commission officials were right in predicting that the Parkway would benefit Little Switzerland. Rather than suffering "wreckage and ruin," Little Switzerland thrived. In late 1939, the company promptly paid its attorneys and most of its outstanding debts with the receipts from the Parkway settlement. Heriot Clarkson gleefully told relatives and Little Switzerland property owners that "now we will have the Switzerland Company free from debt, except what they owe me," so that "the Company will not have to go into bankruptcy and will remain [a] going concern." "I have been able to beat up the State Highway and Public Works Commission, in seven trials," he gloated, and "we now own this beautiful mountain development."[46]

More than simply rescuing the company from financial difficulty, however, the settlement package markedly enhanced the development's accessibility and potential profitability. And shrewd as he was, Heriot Clarkson knew it. "I have never known such a vindication and victory in the history of the State," he bragged, "$25,000 . . . and then to reduce the damages they give special and general benefits by plastering our section with entrances and underpasses. It shows the wisdom of suing them. We now have everything we

should have." Energized by his victory, Clarkson set out immediately to capitalize on the new opportunities. There were new lots to be sold and hundreds
of acres still to be developed, and electric lights were coming soon. Direct
access to the Parkway was plentiful. Switzerland Company advertising in the
wake of the lawsuit touted the fact that Little Switzerland was the "Only
Resort Directly On The Blue Ridge Parkway."[47]

Indeed, the rapid development of Little Switzerland in the decades after
the building of the Parkway bore out the founder's optimism. Little Switzerland's historian wrote in 1982 of the "expansion of Little Switzerland's horizon," which the Parkway had brought by attracting more travelers to the
development and by making interesting destinations near the resort more
accessible to Little Switzerland visitors. The community spilled over onto
neighboring ridges, and new developments sprouted on its fringes. Roads
were paved, and a new lodge (visible from the Parkway) and general store
were constructed.[48]

Dying in 1942, Heriot Clarkson did not see his colony expand in the
aftermath of the Parkway settlement, but he doubtless would have been
pleased. In many ways, his vigorous fight against the Highway Commission
set the resort up for its later vitality. Indeed, Clarkson turned the coming of
the purportedly "non-commercial" new road directly to his private company's commercial advantage. Instead of fighting what he had frequently portrayed as a defensive battle to *save* his development from disaster, Clarkson
in fact waged his anti-Parkway campaign mainly with the hope of maximiz-
ing his company's return in the short run by getting a high payment for his
seized acreage, and in the long run by assuring that Parkway tourists could
not miss Little Switzerland. His complex but brilliant array of strategies and
his ultimate victory underscored the ambiguous and multidimensioned nature of the Parkway project and revealed once again the multiple agendas
that shaped its early development. How did a private developer manage to
manipulate the Parkway project so completely in his favor when so many
other Parkway landowners—often making identical complaints and har-
boring similar hopes of benefiting from developing tourist accommodations
alongside the road—were unable to force significant changes in project plans?

The answer lay in Clarkson's personal power, his wealth, his high position
and longtime influence in state politics and government, and his significant
potential to disrupt the progress of land acquisition by forcing a pricey settlement that would set a precedent that might raise land acquisition prices
along a long section of the road in North Carolina. But Clarkson did not

rely on political and personal influence alone to wage his fight. In addition, he employed an intricate and shrewd political and cultural strategy through which he co-opted small landowners' complaints, manufactured a "grass-roots" movement in support of the Switzerland Company, used the state's newspapers to publicize his version of events, and skillfully mobilized several existing discourses to depict his crusade as a contest of good and evil and to generate the maximum possible public and private sympathy for his cause. Finally, he exploited a fundamental tension at the heart of the Parkway project itself between its goals of aiding the ailing tourism industry in western North Carolina and providing an uncluttered, scenic drive through the mountains for the traveling public.

Not surprisingly for a well-connected and wealthy judge and politician, Clarkson's first move in early 1938 was to hire a top-flight team of eight lawyers—including his son Francis. Leading this "dream team" was former North Carolina governor J. C. B. Ehringhaus, who had been in charge of state government a few years before when the state had fought Tennessee to secure the Parkway route. As it turned out, this legal team cost the Clarksons over $6000 of their $25,000 settlement, but it also afforded them maximum flexibility in arguing the case. Ehringhaus's well-known political face gave the case credibility, while Francis Clarkson's involvement allowed Heriot Clarkson to direct the day-to-day legal maneuvers from behind the scenes. Meanwhile, Mitchell County attorneys acted as front men for court actions in that locale.[49]

Clarkson knew, however, that a team of sophisticated lawyers alone would not win his case, particularly when longtime Highway Commission general counsel Charles Ross—an old Clarkson nemesis—was shrewdly arguing the Highway Commission's case in the pages of the Raleigh *News and Observer*. The verbal contest in the press started almost as soon as Clarkson's suit was filed, when the newspaper ran a blistering initial story—based largely on a "confidential tip" and a lengthy interview with Ross—reporting that the Switzerland Company was seeking a "large sum" for damages in Parkway land acquisition. The article stressed the accommodations that Parkway officials had already made to reduce damage to Little Switzerland and reminded readers that the resort already had easy highway access. Taken by itself, the article doubtless left readers wondering what Clarkson was so angry about.[50]

Incensed by the story, Clarkson retaliated immediately with an article that cited his claims in the case. But simultaneous reports undermined his efforts by disclosing the low tax valuations for Switzerland Company lands.

An editorial compared those tax values (amounting, it noted, to a total of less than $16,000 for the company's several hundred acres in Mitchell and McDowell counties), with the $50,000 the Clarksons were demanding in their suit. The pro–Highway Commission *News and Observer* articles continued into the summer of 1938, one of them repeating almost verbatim the text of the Highway Commission's legal briefs arguing that the Parkway would help Little Switzerland.[51]

By July of that year, a furious Heriot Clarkson decided that the Switzerland Company needed to mount a more coordinated response to the unfavorable publicity. A first step was to get the Switzerland Company's own legal arguments published. The *News and Observer* obliged, but it recapitulated the Switzerland Company brief in a mocking tone that doubtless made it difficult for the public to take the company's claims seriously.[52]

The Clarksons also set to work organizing local citizens in the Little Switzerland area in support of their cause. "I am going to get five or six mountaineers here who are willing," Clarkson wrote Francis, "to issue an article, carefully prepared, . . . to the people of the State, especially officials around Raleigh." Instructing Francis to have maps printed that showed the route of the Parkway through Little Switzerland, he added that "Your Aunt Ida [Clarkson Jones] is game[;] she says that she will head the list of mountaineers."[53]

Within two weeks, the Clarksons organized a "mass meeting" at Little Switzerland's Geneva Hall community center, which, the minutes reported, "was attended by a crowd of mountain people from this section." The group's leaders, however, were pillars of the Little Switzerland Community: real estate agent and Little Switzerland postmaster Reid Queen became the group's chairman and Ray Deal, a consultant for the Southern Mining and Development Company who had built at Little Switzerland in 1933, its secretary. In language that could only have come directly from the Clarksons, the "mass meeting" responded to the pro–Highway Commission articles in the *News and Observer*. Resolutions spelled out the alleged damage wrought at Little Switzerland by the Parkway, denounced Highway Commission attorney Ross for his attempt to "muck-rake the Switzerland Company," and asserted that "the amount of damages claimed by the Switzerland Company, on account of the wreckage of its property, is reasonable and just and should be paid." Where the newspaper had implicitly portrayed Heriot Clarkson as a high-handed and greedy businessman, the meeting asserted that "Justice Clarkson has been with us on the mountains for nearly thirty years and he has done more for this section of Western North Carolina than any man that has ever been on it and has built up a development on a plan unequaled in the Nation." The meeting concluded by appointing a committee to "keep up with . . . this case and see that it is not tried in the newspapers of this State." That committee, like others the Clarksons had organized in the past, consisted of members of local families who often worked for the Switzerland Company: three McKinneys, three Hollifields, one Buchanan, and three other men. The Clarksons, who frequently touted Little Switzerland's contribution to the local economy, demonstrated once again that they knew how to portray what was in fact the loyalty of a small and select group of local residents who were beholden to them personally and to the Switzerland Company as the broad consensus of a representative group of "mountain people."[54]

"It was a fine meeting of sturdy mountain men," a pleased Heriot Clarkson wrote in the days after the gathering, as he forwarded son Francis a copy of the group's resolutions to have printed in the *Charlotte Observer*. Not relying on the newspapers alone to present their case, however, the Clarksons also published and had mailed to hundreds of North Carolinians a pamphlet entitled "What Citizens Think About Attorney Charles Ross' Attack On The Switzerland Co., and Its Stockholders," containing the mass meeting's resolutions, the Company's legal brief, and other pro-Company documents. "People are now getting the true facts," a satisfied Heriot Clarkson wrote his son, and "we have [the Highway Commission] on the run." Containing his optimism, however, he cautioned Francis to "be patient—work & win."[55]

The *News and Observer* ridiculed the pamphlet in a series of articles and attempted to expose the mass meeting as the Clarkson-orchestrated exercise that it was. Enjoining the public somewhat jokingly to "Get the pamphlet folks, it is truly spicy reading," it also called attention to the striking similarities between the Clarksons' writings about the case and the language of the pamphlet: "anyone who has read an opinion written by Associate Justice Clarkson will harbor little doubt as to the authorship of a pamphlet entitled 'What Citizens Think.'" Countering the Clarksons' attempts to distinguish between the Switzerland Company's interests and their own, the paper highlighted Clarkson's personal role in the lawsuit: "Little Switzerland is as much Mr. Associate Justice Heriot Clarkson of the state Supreme Court as Mr. Justice Clarkson is Little Switzerland. One is almost of the other."[56]

The newspaper battle raged throughout the rest of 1938 and 1939, as the *News and Observer* defended its coverage and resisted the Clarksons' intensifying efforts to tell their side of the story. Ever persistent, the Clarksons threatened legal action to pressure the Raleigh paper for more balanced reporting.[57] While the threats did force the newspaper to print a long letter to the editor from Francis Clarkson spelling out the Switzerland Company's version of events in excruciating detail, the Clarksons also planned and paid for a large advertisement entitled "A Plea for Simple Truth and Justice" that put forth their case again in early October in advance of the initial hearing of their case before the appraisers.[58]

Although the Clarksons' efforts to correct further "errors" in the Raleigh paper continued into 1939, Heriot Clarkson seemed to feel that the fall publicity campaign had gone far toward rehabilitating his name and the image of Little Switzerland. Charles Ross, he wrote a colleague, "behind closed doors with the 'News and Disturber' tried the meanest piece of assassination that has ever been attempted in the State." Brightening, he added, however, that the Company's public revisions to the newspaper's reports had made the state's "just thinking people sensitive to the fact that our Company is honest and right."[59]

These statements exaggerated both Ross's and the *News and Observer's* transgressions and the ultimate significance of the Switzerland Company's battle, but the hyperbole was entirely typical of Heriot Clarkson. Indeed, the language and imagery he employed in presenting the Company's case were as important a part of his strategy as were his tactical decisions to employ eight lawyers, orchestrate the "mass meeting," and argue his case in the state's major newspaper. Just as he was a master of political maneuvering, Heriot Clarkson had an uncanny instinct for cultural manipulation, and he skillfully drew on several powerful discourses in shaping a narrative of his effort to wring "just compensation" from the Highway Commission for the Switzerland Company's lands.

Clarkson drew cleverly and consistently on the language of war (particularly of the building world tensions in advance of World War II), of the Bible, and of the American creed of freedom, capitalism, and private property. Using dramatic images, he presented himself at once as just one among many aggrieved property owners and entrepreneurs along the Parkway and as a lone and noble freedom fighter in a grand cosmic cause. Combined with his demonstrated political savvy, it was a winning rhetorical strategy that no other Parkway opponents were able to match.

The darkening world situation was much on Heriot Clarkson's mind as he plotted his strategy in early 1938. "The Japs took China, Mussolini took

Ethiopia, Mexico took the British and American oil wells, and Charlie Ross, Frank L. Dunlap and the Highway Commission have taken our land, turned it over to the Government and refuse to pay us anything," Clarkson wrote his son as the case careened toward the courts. Pushing the metaphor further in a later note to Francis, Clarkson labeled Charles Ross a "pygmy Hitler." "Now is the time to collar him," Clarkson continued, observing that "the trouble in Europe is due to the fact that they did not collar a mad-dog before."[60]

This rhetoric, which initially appeared mainly in Clarkson's private correspondence, became central to the Switzerland Company's public discussion of the case in Switzerland Company legal documents, in the Clarkson-sponsored newspaper articles, and in the "mass meeting" pamphlet: "Mussolini took Ethiopia, Hitler took Austria, Japan took part of China, Mexico took $400,000,000 of American and British oil. They have kept their takings, but the Switzerland Company's land has been taken and given away to the U.S. Government, without 'just compensation.'"[61]

If the Highway Commission was Hitler or Mussolini, Heriot Clarkson was—by his account—the last line of defense in the protection of American private property rights, entrepreneurship, and liberty, and he was not about to rely upon a failed appeasement policy. As the Clarksons prepared for the initial hearing of the case in the fall of 1938, Francis wrote former Governor Ehringhaus that "We are getting things lined up for the hearing so that . . . we can shoot both barrels." "We have got to meet force with force for peace," the elder Clarkson told North Carolina governor Clyde Hoey in the final months of the controversy. Basking in the glow of victory in 1940, Heriot Clarkson bragged that "I did not do like Chamberlain—go around with an umbrella in my hand—I took a big stick when I thought we were in danger and they were trying to destroy me." "I am thankful," he wrote Francis, "that we made them come across and shot holes into them and made them realize that they could not take people's property—that this was a land of law and order and not ruled by Hitlerites."[62]

Clarkson's aggressive crusade to "save" Little Switzerland took on special importance in light of the fact that many other mountain resorts had fallen victim to the Great Depression. Clarkson was determined that Little Switzerland would not fall. "Almost every development in Western North Carolina has broken," he observed in the complaint the Company filed in mid-1938, "and if I can help it, by the grace of God and a Mitchell County jury, this development shall not be 'Gone With the Wind.'"[63]

Clarkson seemed instinctively to understand that in order to mute criticism and increase his chances of prevailing, he must tell his story in resonant language. His instincts were confirmed in the midst of preparing the case, when he and Francis sought advice from a fellow attorney with experience in Parkway land acquisition cases. Their colleague encouraged them to manipulate public understanding of the case, observing that "the psychology of these cases is as important as any civil case that I have ever appeared in. . . . There is something inherent, deep-rooted, in most Tar Heels that every man should have and enjoy the fruit of his own labor and when his property is taken for the public . . . he should be fully compensated."[64]

The Clarksons took this advice to heart. "Our development," Francis Clarkson wrote to a Greensboro newspaper editor, "has been the only one that has not gone into the hands of the Receivers." Emphasizing his father's sacrifices, he continued that "the reason for this is that my father has put everything he has ever made into the place and the proceeds of every piece of land sold has gone back into the investment, we have not taken a cent out." Now, he concluded, Highway Commission officials were trying maliciously to "crush the development." Americans, however, had "no right to take other people's property and give it away." Writing to Raleigh editors, Francis aligned the Switzerland Company with "the people of North Carolina who believe in law and order and justice," who "will never submit to having their property confiscated and destroyed for public use without 'just compensation.'" In a letter to the Highway Commission's land acquisition engineer in early 1939, Heriot Clarkson warned that, "'Truth is great and will prevail.' You just cannot destroy and bankrupt the Company and get away with it. A jury of this country will never permit it." An ominous final note added a religious gloss to the free enterprise, private property arguments as Clarkson threatened: "You know you cannot get away from the great stories in the Bible. One is that of Ahab taking Naboth's vineyard. . . . The tragedy came: turned out of office, then death came and his two sons gone. You watch your step." Closing, he quoted Galatians 6:7: "Whatsoever a man soweth that shall he also reap."[65]

When the jury awarded the Switzerland Company $25,000, Heriot Clarkson worked diligently to be sure the verdict was not viewed as a vindication of one man's—or even one social group's—interests. Instead, he broadly labeled the court's decision "a victory not only for our Company but for the people in general." It was even a win for the Almighty, as "the good Lord has blessed us in the contest for God and humanity" and it proved, Clarkson declared, "that men cannot sit back in offices in Raleigh and Washington, like King John of old, and force a free people to accept the injustice of the valuation of the land and not allow a jury to say what was just compensation. It was a victory for the courts and the jury system." Furthermore, in a post-trial letter to the "People of Mitchell County," he assured citizens that the verdict "maintains the fundamental principle that no man's land can be taken for public purposes without 'just compensation.'" Finally, in a statement that served both to conflate Clarkson's personal and business interests with those of average landowners, and hence perhaps obliquely to dissuade local citizens from protesting a future second-home development in which he might have an interest, Clarkson told them that, because of the case's outcome, "when people . . . wish to locate in Mitchell county and purchase homes there, they may do so with the assurance that no crown of thorns will be pressed on their brows and that their property and personal rights will be safe."[66]

Thus, Heriot Clarkson transformed what was mainly a personal quest to wring from the state a generous payment for his resort property into a broad battle on behalf of American liberty and the proverbial "pursuit of happiness." His statements attempted to preempt any criticism of the Switzerland Company's actions either as an abuse of Clarkson's personal political power, an effort to co-opt smaller landowners' legitimate complaints about the Parkway, or a crass attempt to turn the project (and taxpayer dollars) to the service of the interests of a wealthy developer.

Heriot Clarkson persisted in trying to capitalize on Little Switzerland's closeness to the new Parkway right up until his death in 1942, making even more evident the fact that manipulating the new road to his resort's advantage had been one of his central goals all along. One almost comical episode will illustrate.

In the early 1940s, Clarkson placed signs advertising the resort and its Kilmichael Tower observation platform on lands adjacent to the Parkway that he claimed (incorrectly) were not under Park Service control. The Park Service reminded Clarkson that the signs violated its ban on roadside advertising and instructed its ranger to pull them up. Through Francis, the Judge once again cried that his property rights were being violated and his resort destroyed because, without the signs, tourists did not know how to get to either Little Switzerland or to the tower. Before long, what should have been a minor disagreement over three small signs worth about $35 threatened to balloon into another lawsuit.[67] "It looks like," Francis Clarkson wrote the new Park Service director in 1940, "the Government ought to rejoice in helping to build up the property along the new Parkway. Ours is the only development that has not gone broke and we have put hundreds of thousands [of] dollars in it and hope that you will see to it that these matters are adjusted." He threatened to take the case directly to Interior Secretary Harold Ickes.[68]

By this time, though, the tables had turned: the land was in federal hands and federal officials were determined to stop the erosion of Parkway standards. Early in the sign controversy, the Parkway superintendent wrote to his supervisors that "in view of the many troubles that have developed through the Little Switzerland area we believe it is time for the government to take a firm stand on the question of ownership of this tract." Top Park Service officials agreed, noting that—for reasons of fairness and for better preservation of Parkway scenery—the Service could not afford to set an "undesirable precedent" by making an exception to the no-advertising rules. There would be no further alterations made to accommodate Little Switzerland.[69]

The episode—taken together with the two-year land battle that preceded it—illustrated many of the conflicted class and intra- and intergovernmental dynamics that shaped the early development of the Parkway. The two incidents also revealed some unresolved ambiguities within the project caused by the uneasy fit between conservation, transportation, publicly accessible recreation, and different varieties of tourism development.

During his vicious court battle in 1937–39, an astute Heriot Clarkson exploited some of those dynamics and ambiguities. The Parkway as it originated in the minds of most of its North Carolina supporters was intended primarily to be an engine for tourist-oriented economic growth. Understanding this well, Heriot Clarkson portrayed Little Switzerland as the very type of successful and well-run enterprise the road was meant to help. He therefore fought to make the state Highway Commission and the Park Service alter restrictions so that the original broad intention for the Parkway to benefit the state's tourist industry would be implemented.

If the Parkway had been designed simply as an economic enterprise, Clarkson's demands might have caused little stir. The fact that they did, however, brought into the open an unresolved issue at the project's core: how to reconcile the goal of boosting tourism (and the associated demands of private tourism entrepreneurs) with the simultaneous effort to serve a broader public good by building a spectacular, protected, *scenic* road that would also attract the desired tourists. It was a delicate balancing act, for if it catered so obviously to business that it became merely another highway, the new road would likely not draw those visitors.

Officials in charge of Parkway land acquisition for the North Carolina State Highway Commission understood this balance, and they tried to harmonize the two objectives. They generally worked faithfully to implement Parkway land acquisition and design specifications, often to the detriment of adjoining landowners, who were usually disappointed in their quest to make money from tourism along the road. It was fairly easy—in the name of maintaining Parkway standards—for the state to reject the pleas of small mountain landowners for access or frontage rights. But state officials' divided loyalties—and the Parkway project's inherent internal ambiguity—were more sorely tested when the complaining party was a well-connected and well-financed operator like Heriot Clarkson, who had "the right kind" of tourist business.[70] Moreover, as a close friend and associate of many of the state's original Parkway supporters in both Asheville and Raleigh, Clarkson shared the social status and the outlook of many of the "business progressives" who had driven the state's original Parkway movement. When he complained, state officials had to listen.

But federal officials, as the signs controversy indicated, were neither as torn nor as manipulable, and once the Park Service took firm control of the Parkway lands at Little Switzerland by 1940–41, the potential for exploiting internal inconsistency and conflict inherent in the project lessened. As planning became more centralized and the project's course more firmly set, many of Clarkson's earlier strategies were no longer workable. The Park Service, most concerned with fitting the Parkway into the National Park system, with providing new recreational opportunities for eastern travelers, and with preserving or creating beautiful natural scenes, had less patience than did the state with the demands of a persistent and powerful local landowner and entrepreneur like Heriot Clarkson, who threatened to undermine what they believed were the Parkway's guiding principles. Federal officials did, it is true, acquiesce to the state's original request for help in obtaining the Clarkson lands, but once land acquisition was accomplished, they refused to budge further in permitting Little Switzerland's advertising signs to remain on Parkway lands, and this case faded away when Heriot Clarkson died.[71]

The Switzerland Company episode brings to light the cross purposes and conflicting agendas between a variety of protourism groups, between private citizens and the government, and between different *levels* of government, that impinged upon—and were exacerbated by—early Parkway development. It also offers insights helpful in thinking broadly about the history and practice of tourism development. In particular, it makes it clear that there are many varieties of possible "tourism development," serving a number of possible populations, and that all sectors promoting it need not be equally trusted. It also suggests a number of ways in which private interests may co-opt public projects through creative use of resonant rhetoric and tactics that mask the limited scope of the interests at stake. But finally, the Switzerland Company episode illustrates ways in which publicly planned tourist development, while subject to considerable influence by well-connected private interests, can also provide a space for endeavors like the Blue Ridge Parkway—a project which, though flawed in some ways, stands in stark contrast to elite, members-only developments such as Little Switzerland and serves a much broader public good.

5
Making "America's Most Interesting City"
Tourism and the Construction of Cultural Image in New Orleans, 1940–1984

J. Mark Souther

In 1984 New Orleans played host to the world for six months, attracting millions of tourists to the Louisiana World Exposition, an 80-acre compound on the banks of the Mississippi River that etched in tourists' minds a garish kaleidoscope of sights, sounds, and smells of "America's Most Interesting City." From morning to night, tourists soaked up a ceaseless stream of Creole food, Mardi Gras frivolity, and jazz music. The 1984 world's fair marked a watershed in New Orleans's development. The culmination of four decades of constructing a marketable cultural identity, the exposition marked the outer limits of the effectiveness of the "canned history" experiences that New Orleans and other cities had worked for more than a decade to perfect. When the fair ended its six-month run, the Crescent City found itself with thousands of empty rooms in new high-rise hotels. Within weeks the bottom fell out of the oil industry, upon which New Orleans had staked much of its economic fortunes. In the economic near-depression that ensued, city leaders realized that tourism remained the only viable industry and scrambled to re-claim New Orleans's image of distinctiveness, much of which had eroded in four decades of modernization and efforts to standardize the tourist experi-ence to capture a largely white, middle-class, suburban market.

In order to understand the importance of the 1984 world's fair, it is nec-essary to examine how New Orleanians interpreted their city's cultural heri-tage to outsiders over the previous four decades. Although the Crescent City had always attracted tourists, World War II set in motion developments that shaped the contours of the city's tourism marketing. Like many southern cit-ies, New Orleans exhibited new vigor beginning in the war years. As pros-perity swept the South, New Orleans and other southern coastal cities lost ground as a result of their passive reliance on waterborne commerce to carry their economy. Historian David Goldfield argues that older southern cities like New Orleans began to realize the economic potential of focusing on "what southerners are best at—remembering. . . . These were cities that had either no taste for Yankee-style boosterism, or had the ill-fortune to be on the backwater of American economic development in the century after Appomattox." Although New Orleans would continue depending on its port and, increasingly, the oil and gas industry, city leaders became more and more aware that the Crescent City's most dependable natural resource lay in its heritage. Even as the marketing of New Orleans's cultural heritage shaped the course of tourism, the growing pervasiveness of tourism gradually altered the city's distinctive culture. New Orleans exemplifies a tension in the post–World War II South between persistent cultural distinctiveness and the encroachment of standardizing market forces. Ironically, as modernization eroded the South's uniqueness, the exploitation of distinctive culture fueled New Orleans's modernization.[1]

New Orleans had for many years attracted and charmed visitors with its distinctiveness. Since its founding, the city had nurtured an intermingling of diverse peoples, notably French, Spanish, African, Caribbean, Italian, German, and Irish. Architecture, music, cuisine, and other cultural attributes set New Orleans apart as a Latin or Hellenic appendage to a more Anglo-Saxon South. New Orleans fostered a lifestyle that resonated with nonconformists of every ilk, among them literary giants William Faulkner, Truman Capote, and Tennessee Williams. It was a city in which racial lines blurred and permissiveness softened the crisp edges of Jim Crow laws.

Tourist guides in the 1940s and 1950s emphasized that one could in effect visit a foreign land just by traveling to the Crescent City. It was not difficult for tourism interests to call New Orleans "America's Most Different City" in a special segment on the city's attractions in the 1940 city directory. New Orleans was a place where "on every hand may be seen landmarks connected with bold pioneers, swashbuckling pirates, colorful adventurers, famous generals, noted European personages, [and] high-ranking statesmen." The guide drew attention to New Orleans's distinctiveness, but in ways that suggested an active, lively intermingling of diverse peoples. Referring to the riverfront, the description added, "Here is a waterfront bustling with modern trade, teeming with ships and sailors of the 'Seven Seas' and the products of many lands, with a fusion of the odors of the Orient, the atmosphere of the Tropics and the tang of North America." Likewise, the French Market appealed to the same sense of heritage blending with present-day life. One could mingle with natives as they purchased fresh meat, seafood, produce, and an array of other commodities from open-air vendors. As late as 1954, an article in a prominent national magazine noted that on Bourbon Street "it is possible to rub elbows with debutantes, drunks, bank presidents, gamblers, ladies of the evening, actors, collegians, poets, artists, servicemen, beggars and crooks—each with his inhibitions down." Gradually, however, mass culture standardized national tastes, and Americans expected certain predictable standards in their travels.[2]

During World War II, many Americans discovered the Crescent City for the first time. The war stirred a slumbering city that had for a century viewed economic modernization with a mixture of indifference and aversion. It also provided a platform from which the city's tourist trade could catapult itself to new heights. As an Army Port of Embarkation with a number of Army and Navy bases nearby, New Orleans saw a tremendous influx of servicemen and industrial workers in the five years after 1940, many of whom discovered the city's unique charm. One Army corporal noted that while New Orleans's downtown was mostly "just another one" with "neon signs, drug stores, [and] lunch counters," the French Quarter "has history written all over it" and "even in the other parts of the city the old style of living is still evident." Another serviceman averred that the Crescent City was a "gay, brightly lighted, carefree capital of fun." Still another enlisted man visiting in 1944 found that the French Quarter's Creole restaurants were "crowded with people more interested in being able to say they ate at Antoine's or Arnaud's than in getting something to eat." Even as World War II introduced outsiders to New Orleans's distinctiveness, it planted the seeds of the city's transformation into a more standardized tourist destination. Indeed, although Bourbon Street began the transition to an adult playground in the 1920s, its reputation for risqué entertainment crystallized in the crucible of war. The bacchanalia of strip clubs, peep shows, and sleazy bars both added to the city's freewheeling image and encouraged city leaders to restrain that spectacle as tourism became more crucial to the economy.[3]

In addition to painting New Orleans as a city with a vibrant culture closely tied to a romantic past, tourism promoters and city officials prior to the 1960s exploited African American heritage as tourist entertainment. The influence of African and Afro-Caribbean customs on New Orleans culture provided much of the basis for the city's tourist appeal. The Crescent City's allure also relied on the ability to stage a spectacle that other cities could not match. Creating this spectacle entailed emphasizing the city's "Africanness" while also limiting African Americans' standing in society. In particular, it relied on keeping Jim Crow most intact in areas frequented by tourists, especially in the French Quarter and the city's leading hotels. Nevertheless, perceptive visitors doubtless marveled at the complexity of racial interactions that flourished despite the force of Jim Crow. Never a simple black-white division, the New Orleans racial gumbo of subtle color gradations was further complicated by differentiations between uptown and downtown, Protestant and Catholic. Such divisions smoothed the hard edges of racial discrimination but also made it more difficult to forge a cohesive African American front against racism and cultural exploitation.

The common white tourist view of New Orleans blacks as exotic in the 1940s and 1950s had changed little in the century since visitors marveled at what they perceived as savage, primitive displays of black dancers in Congo Square. The exploitation of African Americans to reinforce racial division in a fluid social order and to encourage tourism revealed itself most starkly in the city's Mardi Gras festivities. While most parade organizations in New Orleans were all white, the King Zulu Carnival Club was composed of blacks, mostly working-class uptown blacks. The King Zulu Carnival Club was the most visible part of the Zulu Social Aid and Pleasure Club, a mutual benefit society incorporated in 1916 in part to provide its members a dignified funeral with a proper brass band accompaniment.

While Zulu reflected black agency by appropriating and inverting the symbolic royalty and pageantry of the elite white Carnival organizations, many African Americans came to see Zulu as more of a plaything of white tourism leaders who were learning to package New Orleans as a distinctive, exotic city. Indeed, Zulu became a prized tourist commodity and source of comfort and amusement for an increasingly defensive local white elite. Although Zulu's parade meandered through black neighborhoods, stopping periodically at saloons whose owners had purchased this privilege with contributions to the organization, it drew its largest and most enthusiastic crowds from the white community and white visitors. Understanding the economic benefits of Zulu, white merchants and tourism leaders helped fund the annual parade. One Zulu official remarked that "the merchants want this parade on the street. The Carnival would go on if there was no Zulu, but the life would be took [sic] out of Carnival." Seymour Weiss, general manager of the Roosevelt Hotel and one of the powers behind Huey Long's political machine, admitted that the New Orleans Hotel Association gave money to Zulu every year. His remarks illustrate the commonly held paternalistic white view of Zulu and its role in the tourist trade: "It's an interesting, funny adjunct to Carnival, and the colored people don't have much money." The local press also encouraged the wild spectacle, which preceded the staid Rex parade, in articles with titles such as "Head-Hunters on the Loose."[4] A Dillard University professor likened Zulu's role in Mardi Gras to that of a clown in a circus. "A man going up on a high wire is more effective if two clowns fall off first, and Rex is more beautiful because Zulu is ridiculous. The clown doesn't have to be a Negro . . . but in this area, where we think in terms of black and white, it's logical that it should be a Negro. . . . There's nothing in the South as important as being white or Negro, and you can't have an all-white Carnival or the whiteness wouldn't show."[5] Indeed, the Zulu parade portrayed African Americans in precisely the negative stereotypes that many whites found entertaining. In the tradition of minstrelsy, Zulu members appeared in blackface with jungle costumes, usually grass skirts and black tights. Float riders tossed painted coconuts as souvenirs to tourists. In addition to King Zulu, the parade's most notable dignitaries included Queen Zulu, the Big Shot from Africa, and the Royal Prognosticator.

Although the 1940s and 1950s saw the continuing exploitation of African Americans to entertain white tourists, the arrival of outsiders in the war years heightened local appreciation of New Orleans's rich black cultural heritage. The transition came after the city almost allowed the wellspring of one of its most recognizable cultural exports to dry up. New Orleans had long been known as the birthplace of jazz. With the designation of Storyville as an official haven for prostitution in 1897, New Orleans created a year-round tourist draw that reinforced the image of a "wild spectacle" commonly associated with the Carnival season. Attracting musicians, gamblers, and prostitutes, Storyville solidified in the tourist mind what New Orleans was supposed to be. Jazz figured prominently in that image.

With the closure of Storyville in 1917 and the concurrent exodus of many African Americans seeking better employment and freedom from the harsher manifestations of racial prejudice, jazz music began a long decline and by World War II appeared moribund. For many of the city's best musicians, leaving New Orleans was the only hope of realizing their potential. Far from recognizing jazz music as a tourist attraction, prominent New Orleanians usually either dismissed it as inconsequential or took it for granted as purely a suitable dance music. One critic remarked that "the people of New Orleans enjoyed and sustained the music without the music itself getting more than a passing nod from the local guardians of culture."[6] Jazz practically disappeared from the areas of New Orleans most frequented by tourists. The growing popularity of radio fostered the standardization of national popular music tastes, and French Quarter bars increasingly installed jukeboxes to save the expense of hiring local musicians. By 1940 New Orleans hotels that had once employed local jazz artists for the most part turned to national acts instead. Noted jazz scholar Orin Blackstone concluded that it "might well be true that on an ordinary week end New Orleans would offer no more music than any other city its size."[7]

The transformation of New Orleans jazz into an integral part of tourism marketing took more than twenty-five years to accomplish. Jazz clubs, along with foundations, museums, archives, and concert halls, provided the most effective vehicles for the jazz revival. The most prominent organization in the jazz revival was the New Orleans Jazz Club (NOJC), started in 1948 by a handful of prominent New Orleanians who had developed an appreciation for jazz. Four years earlier a similar organization, the National Jazz Foundation, had been formed, but it lasted only three years. The NOJC staged concerts and assisted tourists who went to New Orleans in search of jazz music, furthering the resurrection of the art form through publicity and the employment of languishing musicians for concerts, festivals, and recording sessions. Although jazz appreciation stood at low ebb in the 1940s, the coalescence of eager jazz pilgrims from around the world with a small cadre of local white jazz enthusiasts fueled a chain of events that eventually made the art form practically synonymous with New Orleans.[8]

Into the 1960s tourism promoters were torn between emphasizing New Orleans's distinctive charms and pushing its modern, cosmopolitan offerings. For many years, the city's leaders had allowed or even encouraged the modernization of the Vieux Carré, replacing a square of nineteenth-century Creole buildings with a marble neoclassical court building in 1904 and removing another square from the regulatory Vieux Carré Commission in 1946 to facilitate the expansion of the Monteleone Hotel. Tourism guides in the 1950s and 1960s illustrate city leaders' faith in New Orleans's modernization as much as in its cultural legacy. In one 1968 guide, Chamber of Commerce president Murray C. Fincher noted that the French Quarter "has been preserved as a living example of what our city was in bygone days." His choice of words, suggesting preservation or freezing of a part of the city as it was at an earlier time, reflected the ambivalence of many New Orleanians toward the brand of progress exemplified by southern cities such as Houston, Dallas,

Atlanta, and Miami. Significantly, such statements implied that it was perfectly acceptable that the mere appearance of distinctiveness was sufficient to compensate for the loss of the lifestyle that fed that uniqueness. Fincher quickly turned his focus to the city's modernization: "We hope also that you will look at our growing city with its bridges and expressways and increasing number of tall buildings. That you will ride to the top of our magnificent new Trade Mart where Canal Street meets the river and from this vantage point gain an idea of how large our city really is."[9]

The guides of the 1950s and 1960s alerted tourists to the excitement of river tours of the city's miles of wharves and ship terminals and listed skyscrapers in the central business district among the points of interest. Hotels vied with each other in offering the latest amenities, such as the Monteleone's new Sky Terrace, with its modern resort atmosphere, and the Fontainebleau Motor Inn, which resembled a Miami Beach resort planted in the middle of New Orleans. The Fontainebleau shunned Creole themes, offering international flair typified by the hotel's Hawaiian Luau Restaurant and Lounge. Clearly, New Orleans had yet to embrace its Creole heritage.[10]

As tourism and gentrification became entrenched in the French Quarter, the neighborhood became a hotly contested urban space, pitting gentrifying residents and tourism leaders against criminals, drifters, and nonconformists who, in their view, could not appreciate the Quarter's real value. Beginning in the 1950s under Mayor deLesseps S. Morrison and peaking two decades later, city leaders tried to take the unpredictability out of the tourist experience in the French Quarter. Accordingly, the city government sought to make the Vieux Carré clean, safe, and attractive for tourists. Reflecting on his two years as president of the Vieux Carré Property Owners and Associates, a French Quarter citizens' watchdog committee, Mark Lowrey described a scene that Crescent City officialdom found troubling. He mused that the French Quarter's "streets and gutters and sidewalks are littered with refuse and filth that would do honor to the back alleys of Zanzibar." City leaders sought to root out anything deemed undesirable within the emerging tourist zone. This effort involved cracking down on vice and crime, attempting to rid the Quarter of "undesirables," cleaning streets and building exteriors, and otherwise creating a suburban-like atmosphere where tourists would feel comfortable. Mayor Victor H. Schiro, Morrison's successor, quipped that the Vieux Carré should be a Coney Island–like "fun spot" and that its residents should expect such an atmosphere.[11]

To the extent that the municipal government cracked down on illegal activities such as gambling and prostitution in the French Quarter, it usually closed down offending clubs for only a day or two in a cursory show of law and order. The first reform wave came in 1958 when police arrested Lilly Christine, a stripper known as "the Cat Girl," and about thirty other exotic dancers. Only Christine went to trial, and she was acquitted in Criminal District Court. Although the district attorney appealed the case to the state Supreme Court—a rarity in New Orleans—that court ruled for Christine, a decision that emboldened Bourbon Street entertainers for a time. However, in 1963 a newly elected district attorney, Jim Garrison, declared war on vice in the French Quarter and padlocked errant clubs indefinitely. In one raid, plainclothes agents outwitted a club barker by boarding a city bus at the corner of Bourbon and Canal, ordering the driver to stop in front of the club, and then dashing inside to arrest a B-girl, a performer who was drinking with a customer. The Garrison raids demonstrated officials' clear sense that the French Quarter was the city's front porch as far as the outside world was concerned.[12]

While Mayor Schiro repeatedly urged cleaning up the Quarter to make it more appealing to tourists, the municipal government was torn between strict policies and the need to accommodate the devil-may-care attitude of the tourist who went to New Orleans to let off steam. In the wake of Garrison's crackdown, tourism-minded New Orleanians feared that Bourbon Street might become no different from any other commercial street in America. The *New York Times* noted that Bourbon Street was becoming "a street where tourists are less likely to get clipped but more likely to get bored." Striptease artists no longer mingled with customers, and some of the racier burlesque clubs closed and reopened as more sedate establishments. The rollicking Moulin Rouge became the tame Whiskey A Go-Go. The Old Opera House Bar and Lounge, where "in 1950 one of the roughest sets of strippers could be found on the runway," became the Ivanhoe Piano Bar, "a Sunday school frolic compared to its predecessor."[13]

New Orleans officials in the 1950s and 1960s walked a thin line between strict and lax enforcement. Accordingly, amid efforts to tighten control over the French Quarter in the 1960s, the New Orleans City Council quietly buried an ordinance planned to ban street drinking in the historic district. In the course of one week in 1969, the hotly contested issue fell into obscurity. The bill's author, Councilman Henry Curtis, withdrew the ordinance and suggested instead a "trial" ban on selling alcoholic beverages from open windows on Bourbon Street, a common practice. Indeed, city leaders understood the utility of nurturing the delicate balance between the French Quarter's decadent, naughty image and its attractiveness to families. Cultural heritage was not yet sufficiently popular or well promoted to warrant abandoning the city's sinful, frolicsome atmosphere.[14]

City Hall and tourism leaders remained too preoccupied in the 1950s and 1960s with making the French Quarter more attractive to tourists to devote much attention to promoting cultural resources that might have begun to lessen New Orleans's reliance on the wild spectacle of Mardi Gras and Bourbon Street for its tourist image. Just as jazz enthusiasts from around the world awakened well-positioned New Orleanians to the possibilities the music offered their city, the rise of tourism shaped the course of the jazz revival. What had started as a reinvigoration of a black music genre by jazz enthusiasts gradually became a cash cow for tourism promoters. While the formation of local clubs devoted to the furthering of jazz and the enthusiasm of outsiders contributed heavily to the jazz revival by awakening native and tourist appreciation for the music, locally orchestrated dissemination of jazz music across the nation proved the biggest catalyst for harnessing jazz to the city's tourist trade. For many years New Orleans exported jazz passively with the emigration of its most promising young musicians to cities such as New York, Chicago, Kansas City, and Los Angeles. There the music adapted to progressive, ever changing tastes while New Orleans remained more insular. Because New Orleans stood relatively isolated from mainstream American culture into the 1940s, its jazz music remained less changed than that elsewhere.

The retention of a distinctive, traditional New Orleans style served as an ideal springboard for cultural tourism. Yet New Orleanians had failed to assert themselves for decades, allowing outsiders to define and adapt the art form. Before New Orleans could lay claim to being the birthplace of jazz and become a mecca for jazz pilgrims, it had to find a way of taking mecca to the pilgrims. A succession of local initiatives in the two decades after World War II brought New Orleans jazz more squarely into the national mind. A combination of recording and touring proved essential in stimulating the city's cultural tourism.

Local recording efforts contributed much to the recrudescence of New Orleans–style jazz. Joe Mares, a French Quarter fur purveyor whose brother played trumpet in a local band, launched Southland Recording Studio and the Southland Records label in his fur company building in 1953. Mares recorded many musicians who would go on to national fame, including Pete

Fountain, Al Hirt, Johnny Wiggs, and Sharkey Bonano. In addition to re-cording New Orleans musicians, Mares took them to perform on the West Coast beginning in 1954, laying the groundwork for what eventually became a favored marketing tool of the city's tourism officials. Mares's musicians played at the Dixieland Jubilee at Shrine Auditorium in Los Angeles. By 1961, Mares's affiliation with the Dixieland Jubilee had led entertainment magnate Walt Disney to take notice. That year Disney hired a six-piece New Orleans jazz band to play aboard the riverboat *Mark Twain* as it plied the Disneyland River in the Magic Kingdom, replacing the rather lackluster sounds of wild animals and the crackling flames of a log cabin supposedly set afire by Indians. Beginning the following year, Mares's musicians appeared in "Dixieland at Disneyland," which succeeded the annual concerts at Shrine Auditorium.[15]

If Joe Mares supplied the prototype of touring as an essential component of marketing jazz to prospective tourists, the founders of Preservation Hall perfected the model. Just as the influx of servicemen and jazz devotees in the 1940s provided essential ingredients for the first wave of the jazz revival, newcomers showed the determination necessary to provide an exception to the rule of the proliferation of strip shows and other cheap thrills in the French Quarter in the late 1950s and after. E. Lorenz Borenstein, the son of Ukrainian immigrants and grand-nephew of Leon Trotsky, came to New Or-leans from Milwaukee in 1941 on the heels of an early career in circuses and sideshows in the Midwest. Thirteen years later Borenstein started Asso-ciated Artists' Gallery adjacent to the famous Pat O'Brien's courtyard bar, where he encouraged musicians to play informal sessions that evolved into Preservation Hall, which officially opened to the public on June 10, 1961. Preservation Hall was essentially unadorned, served no drinks, and provided only a few chairs for patrons. The music itself was the focal point. Preserva-tion Hall's greatest contribution to the jazz revival lay in providing steady employment to forgotten, downtrodden older New Orleans jazz players, who suddenly found themselves in great demand. Although jazz had flourished through the constant replenishment of musicians with young talent, the tourist trade now devoted inordinate attention to the oldest musicians who had played in the early twentieth century. On Bourbon Street, which con-tinued to be the city's most celebrated tourist attraction, nightclubs and bars sought old musicians because tourists "expect to hear an older black man, white shirt open at the collar, suspenders, simply cut trousers, plain black

Jazz Museum. By the 1960s, New Orleans jazz emerged as both a mode of creative expression and a tourism attraction. (Courtesy of Louisiana Division, New Orleans Public Library.)

shoes, and legs crossed." In addition, jazz tended heavily toward New Orleans style, then known as "Dixieland," because that fit tourists' conception of what the music should be.[16]

Preservation Hall soon soared in popularity as tourists became its main clientele. In 1962 Borenstein turned the Hall over to Allen and Sandra Jaffe, jazz enthusiasts who had come to New Orleans from Philadelphia the previous year. The Jaffes observed that tourists believed erroneously that Preservation Hall had been in operation since the halcyon days of jazz and that the musical style remained unchanged since that time. Understanding that perception often was more important than reality when building a tourist attraction, the Jaffes studiously avoided making any changes to either the building or the performances.[17]

Preservation Hall's reputation relied not only on its perceived antiquity but also on its international tours. Touring began in earnest in 1963 with a summer trip to Chicago by train, followed by a three-month tour of Japan. By the late 1960s, several Preservation Hall bands were making regular tours, enabling the Jaffes to plant in people's minds the idea that Preservation Hall was a must-visit site on any future New Orleans itinerary. The Hall's success quickly led to spin-offs such as Dixieland Hall and Southland Hall. Preservation Hall was so successful, in fact, that in later years young musicians, who had come of age during the height of the civil rights struggle and associated traditional jazz with segregation, hard times, and an Uncle Tom mentality, became inspired to take up the traditional style of playing. Preservation Hall was, perhaps, two decades ahead of its time, for only in the 1980s would New Orleans tourism promoters fully tap the potential of authentic heritage experiences to stimulate discretionary or leisure tourism. Nevertheless, even in the late 1960s the music venue began to influence tourism officials, who started sending brass bands among the emissaries on international marketing missions. Even the name Preservation Hall was significant, for it demonstrated the shifting focus of New Orleanians from marketing their culture as an everyday experience toward a more self-conscious presentation of that heritage as a preserved relic.[18]

As tourism officials in the 1950s and 1960s began conceiving of the French Quarter as a sort of outdoor history museum set apart from yet contributing to the city's economic modernization efforts, they also began revising their old view of Jim Crow as beneficial to New Orleans's tourist image. Increasingly after the mid-1950s, they began to see the limitations racism imposed on the city's reputation. Indeed, the race issue constituted one of the most troublesome impediments to economic progress in many southern cities, which increasingly found that attracting outside investment depended on discarding, or at least appearing to discard, the specter of Jim Crow. In the Crescent City, both Morrison and Schiro labored to contain any large-scale racial turmoil while easing their city toward integration, drawing support from economically self-interested business elites.[19]

New Orleans could hardly cultivate an image of being hospitable and forward thinking when its black citizens and visitors were relegated to second-class status. While northern cities had much earlier begun easing restrictions that barred African Americans from public accommodations, New Orleans clung to segregation. Visitors to New Orleans became acquainted with the insidious Jim Crow at every turn. Staffed primarily by blacks, the Crescent City's hotels strove to contain interracial contact within limits acceptable to prevailing views. At the city's leading hotels, black workers were forced to arrive each day by well-concealed rear or side entrances to avoid the embarrassment of unwanted contact in the lobby. None of the Crescent City's leading hotels offered lodging to black travelers, who instead had to try their luck in black-operated inns and rooming houses, often inconveniently distant from the city's attractions. A perusal of the *Louisiana Weekly*, New Orleans's leading African American newspaper, in the 1950s reveals that black accommodations were almost completely set apart from the French Quarter and other areas associated with the city's tourist trade.[20]

Not only did hotel workers and patrons face discrimination, but so did many of the city's jazz musicians. Following the U.S. Supreme Court's 1954 *Brown v. Board of Education* ruling against segregation, bitter southern politicians defiantly passed many particularly harsh new race codes. In July 1956, the Louisiana state legislature passed a law that forbade black and white musicians from performing together. When enforcing the Jim Crow law against integrated bands, New Orleans policemen concentrated on the French Quarter, the area most visible to white New Orleanians and tourists. In January 1957, they arrested black trumpeter Ernest "Punch" Miller and five other men, both black and white, allegedly for disturbing the peace following a performance at a Quarter bar. When they appeared in court, the judge dismissed the case and warned the black jazzmen, "Don't mix your cream with your coffee." African American trumpeter and New Orleans native Louis Armstrong, whose sextet included blacks, whites, and a Hawaiian of Filipino extraction, scorned the 1956 law and vowed not to visit his hometown until the law was repealed. He lamented that "they treat me better all over the world than they do in my own hometown—that even includes Mississippi."[21]

The byzantine intricacies of segregation law in public accommodations even made it problematic to host foreign dignitaries on official visits to the Crescent City. In 1954 the visit of Ethiopian Emperor Haile Selassie and his official delegation to New Orleans tested the city's ability to extend hospitality in the shadow of Jim Crow. The Roosevelt Hotel agreed to lodge Selassie and his cohorts but adamantly refused to allow the black officials to enter the hotel's bar, restaurant, or Blue Room supper club. City leaders planned a harbor cruise, dinners, and receptions to ensure that Selassie and his group would not have time to experience racial discrimination in the city's nightspots. Morrison's public relations director personally sat in the Roosevelt lobby one night until 3 A.M. to be sure the Selassie party would not attempt to venture into the French Quarter. The Selassie visit passed without real trouble, but when city officials considered inviting the president of Liberia to the city a few months later, Morrison refrained, heeding his public relations director's warning that the dignitary "would be just another Negro to most of the people of this city."[22]

The mounting problems associated with maintaining Jim Crow while trying to build the city's tourist trade became clearer in the 1960s. New Orleans suffered a considerable blow to its easygoing image in 1960, when the nation watched as angry white women cursed and spat upon those who pioneered the token integration of the city's schools. Fearing that the city's image might be tarnished, Mayor Morrison wrote a letter to the media in December 1960, suggesting a three-day moratorium on printed and televised news coverage of the school crisis to safeguard New Orleans's tourist trade. The struggle for racial equality had implications beyond simply affecting the city's image. With the help of the NAACP, civil rights leaders worked to desegregate the city's hotels, an important step because it would enable African Americans to secure lodging closer to leading attractions. When the Roosevelt, New Orleans's leading hotel, refused to integrate, activists decided to work with chain hotels instead, reasoning that they would see the futility of upholding Jim Crow in New Orleans while hotels in many other cities had lifted the racial bar. Despite repeated racial incidents and convention cancellations, only with the passage of the Civil Rights Act of 1964 did Seymour Weiss end overt discrimination in the Roosevelt.[23]

Even in the wake of the Civil Rights Act of 1964, which forbade racial discrimination in all public accommodations, New Orleans continued to face embarrassing compliance problems. In 1965, twenty-one African American football players in town for the AFL All-Star Game suffered racial discrimination when they attempted to partake in French Quarter nightlife. Some of the players reported that they had been refused admittance to Bourbon Street clubs while their white teammates experienced no harassment. Most complained that they were denied taxicab service from the New Orleans International Airport to their hotels and between the hotels and the French Quarter. After the players' poor treatment, the AFL promptly rescheduled the game for Houston, dealing a major blow to New Orleans's hopes of attracting a professional football franchise. Persuading league officials to grant New Orleans a team necessitated projecting the idea that it was a progressive city on the move. Accordingly, the New Orleans Hotel Association, a number of leading hostelries, the New Orleans Restaurant Association, and the city's largest taxicab company all agreed to serve all citizens and visitors in accordance with the Civil Rights Act of 1964. Moon Landrieu, a rare voice of moderation in the city council during the late 1960s, pushed successfully for a biracial Human Relations Committee in 1967 and a public accommodations ordinance in 1969, both of which effected careful, strict oversight of the delicate process of racial integration and inclusion so necessary to the advancement of the tourism industry. Freed from the encumbrances of Jim Crow, New Orleans tourism would flourish in the 1970s.[24]

In the 1970s the trend toward packaging New Orleans culture for mostly white, middle-class, suburban tourists accelerated. Like many southern cities after World War II, New Orleans began experiencing an exodus of its white population to the suburbs. As wealth departed central cities, downtown areas often suffered the closure of retailers, departure of manufacturing plants, and onset of urban decay. City leaders scrambled to offset these disturbing trends by retooling their downtown areas with attractions designed to appeal to suburban tastes. The French Quarter, long a model for other cities seeking to boost heritage tourism, became a more standardized tourist experience as New Orleans followed a path of riverfront redevelopment much like that in other southern cities.

The 1966 opening of New Orleans Square, a three-quarter-scale replica of the French Quarter in Disneyland's Magic Kingdom in Anaheim, California, proved the bellwether for what awaited the real French Quarter in the next decade. Walt Disney's creation, which included pseudo-Creole architecture, a tropical courtyard, a grassy area for caricature artists and acrobats patterned after Jackson Square, a haunted house, and a mock Mississippi River with a schooner and a paddle wheeler, became one of the theme park's most popular venues. Disney even staged nightly Mardi Gras parades and planted plastic ferns in artificial cracks in the buildings to lend a sense of age and decadence. Predictably, the Disney version of the Crescent City's most illustrious attraction helped reinforce key elements of tourists' image of New Orleans, shaping their expectations of what the Vieux Carré should be and providing "the most impressive single piece of free tourist promotion the city could ever get." A *Vieux Carré Courier* writer suggested that "a large number of New Orleans civic and political leaders have visited New Orleans Square and apparently have decided they like it better than the original." A *Chicago Daily News* reporter wrote that it would be ironic if "the chief preservationist of beautiful New Orleans turns out to be the California film genius who created Donald Duck and Mickey Mouse."[25]

Indeed, the French Quarter—or perhaps a hybrid of the French Quarter and Disneyland—captivated the imaginations of urban planners around the country, influencing fabricated heritage attractions such as Atlanta's Underground and St. Louis's Gaslight area. Rather than allowing the Quarter to evolve naturally, city leaders believed the district had not reached its true potential as a generator of tourist revenues. With so many choices of safe, secure, clean, and controlled tourist venues appearing around the nation, New Orleans leaders clamored to bring the French Quarter into accord with quickly standardizing national tastes.[26]

In the 1970s, New Orleans and many other cities took advantage of the growing American nostalgia for historic waterfronts at a time when traditional port facilities were quickly decaying and being replaced by newer terminals and wharves in outlying areas. Accordingly, in the Crescent City, tourism stimulated a shift in the focus of tourism promotion away from Bourbon Street and toward the riverfront. The transition from neglecting the riverfront to embracing it in public discourse came in the late 1960s when preservation-minded activists succeeded in blocking construction of a riverfront expressway favored by the business elite that would have severed the French Quarter from the Mississippi River. Several publicly financed projects along the French Quarter riverfront during the 1970s reflected the growing tourist interest in waterfronts.

Moon Landrieu, who succeeded Schiro as mayor in 1970, had little patience with those who argued that the French Quarter should be preserved as a neighborhood. He viewed the French Quarter as a commodity that could harvest tourist dollars for an increasingly cash-starved city. Landrieu saw the Quarter as a blighted slum that needed immediate attention to realize its potential as a tourist attraction. Although the French Quarter continued to lure visitors from around the world to experience its Spanish colonial architecture and revel in its raucous nightlife, Landrieu sought to make the district more like the shinier, safer, more family-oriented attractions found in other cities.

Prominent in Landrieu's transformation of the Quarter were his plans for the riverside French Market and Jackson Square. Landrieu understood well the tourist mentality in which travelers sought unique experiences but only within the confines of what appealed to their sense of comfort, but his revitalization plans stirred controversy. Ardent protest erupted when the mayor announced plans to close three streets around the perimeter of Jackson Square and replace them with a flagstone-paved pedestrian mall and a marble river-viewing platform across Decatur Street. In 1970 the municipal government had floated a trial balloon, barricading those streets to gauge the impact on traffic flow and public sentiment. They observed no adverse reactions from residents, but the transition from temporary to permanent street closures brought a rapid reversal in opinion.[27]

French Quarter residents struggled to prevent the revamping of the heart of their neighborhood into a venue carefully scripted for tourist consumption. Preservationists managed to block the planting of ornamental shade trees at intervals in front of St. Louis Cathedral, which they argued would detract from the simple formality of what once served as a colonial military parade ground. In addition, they forced the scaling down of Landrieu's viewing platform, which detractors likened to an "Aztec temple with hanging gardens." They were unable, however, to stop the permanent closing of the streets for the mall, which gave Jackson Square a virtual "Egyptian bazaar" atmosphere. The municipal government encouraged the sidewalk artists that had plied their trade in the narrow Pirate's Alley alongside St. Louis Cathedral to relocate around the perimeter of Jackson Square. While the city government restricted street vendors in Jackson Square to one ice cream stand and one Lucky Dog wiener stand, it set no limits on the number of artists, street musicians, fortune-tellers, and entertainment sideshows that could set up on the pedestrian mall. City Hall made no effort to require that entrepreneurs using the public space be licensed or pay taxes. All transactions were cash only, and fortune-tellers skirted a state statute against their trade by simply requesting a "suggested donation." Thus, city leaders gave carte blanche to practically anyone who wished to operate a business in Jackson Square, in effect turning a public space into a semi-private carnival midway.[28]

Similarly controversial was Landrieu's plan to transform the city's historic French Market into a festival marketplace of the sort that the James Rouse Company of Columbia, Maryland, was developing at the time in Boston's historic Quincy Market. Such complexes reflected a growing affinity for a sense of heritage in everyday experiences like shopping. The French Market lay on a narrow strip of land between the Mississippi River wharves and Decatur and North Peters Streets, a seedy stretch of seamen's bars, flophouses, and rundown buildings. Skeptical of the market's importance to French Quarter residents, Landrieu scoffed to its defenders, "When was the last time you bought a goose there?" In his view, the market was merely an eyesore that repelled tourists. The mayor undertook a program to revitalize the French Market. Elsewhere, festival marketplaces arose from public-private partnerships between a developer and a city improvement or redevelopment agency. In New Orleans, the public sector pulled the strings through the pre-

New Orleans tourism industry leaders and municipal leaders clearly understood the potential of marketing the city's unique history and culture in the years after World War II. (Permission granted by The Times-Picayune Publishing Corporation. All rights reserved. Reprinted with permission.)

existing city-run French Market Corporation. Exactly as critics predicted, the completion of the market renovation in 1975 led to the departure of neighborhood services such as the Morning Call coffee stand and Battistella's fresh seafood market. As the French Market metamorphosed into a tourist draw, retailers increasingly sold cheap souvenirs, and marketing campaigns centering on New Orleans cultural themes proliferated in the form of festivals.[29]

In addition to worrying about the French Quarter's seedy appearance, city officials and business leaders sought to tame the "wild spectacle." Their efforts reduced the Quarter's unpredictability and presented carefully selected aspects of New Orleans culture, creating a "canned history" experience. Where earlier efforts in the 1950s and 1960s had involved merely ridding the Vieux Carré of unsavory characters, crime, and filth, initiatives in the 1970s added an emphasis on using entertainment to communicate cultural distinctiveness. In keeping with tourism-driven remolding of attractions such as Jackson Square and the French Market, the city government and private interests seized upon the idea of exposing tourists to heritage through entertainment shows.

In 1975, *New Yorker* correspondent Calvin Trillin remarked that New Orleans was in danger of becoming a caricature of itself in its effort to package its distinctive culture in ways calculated to make the city appear more in keeping with bustling regional rivals such as Houston, Dallas, and Atlanta. When Crescent City leaders were lining up support for a downtown domed stadium in the late 1960s, they suggested naming the facility Mardi Gras Stadium and staging the Mardi Gras parades in it for paying customers. In a hollowly democratic gesture (considering that the festivities would likely exclude the city's large, poor black population), promoters hoped to release beads, doubloons, and other trinkets from the dome ceiling for spectators sitting too high in the stadium to catch those thrown from passing floats. Although the scheme faded into obscurity long before the domed stadium opened, it suggested an ongoing indifference toward the accurate portrayal of local culture for tourists.[30]

This conception of the role of cultural heritage in tourism development may also be seen in Mayor Moon Landrieu's scheme in the early 1970s to offer regular *son-et-lumière* shows in Jackson Square to recreate the "mood" of New Orleans. Such sound-and-light displays were popular in Europe, notably at the Forum in Rome and the Acropolis in Athens. Reflecting the selective, dramatized portrayal of history typical of many commercialized attractions in the 1970s, the program was to begin with "the buzz of the mosquitoes, and the mud and the Indians," and end with the jazz music of trumpeter Louis Armstrong. The spectacle, admitted Landrieu's appointed Vieux Carré Commission director Wayne Collier, was "not designed to stimulate the imagination of a man who can look at the Pontalba Building and imagine what it was. It's more for people like me, who can't." The plan involved cutting down several ancient live oaks that would block the lighting and turning the square into a tropical garden. Landrieu also sought to use the fortress-like Washington Artillery Park viewing platform as a stadium for sound-and-light spectators.[31]

Four months after the announcement of the sound-and-light show, the French Quarter Residents Association, the Vieux Carré Property Owners and Associates, and several concerned individuals filed suit in Civil District Court to block the display. Preservationists contended that New Orleans needed no gimmicks to enhance its distinctive heritage. They charged that the shows would bring a noisy carnival-like atmosphere to a residential area. In July 1975, some one thousand New Orleanians took to the streets in protest. Undeterred by one of the thunderstorms that erupt almost daily in the semitropical heat of a New Orleans summer, they carried placards scrawled with "Spare the Square" and "Deliver Us From Doom—No Sound, No Light, No Moon." After a petition collected more than nine thousand signatures and the *Times-Picayune* ran several editorials decrying the *son-et-lumière* spectacle, Landrieu abandoned the idea. Although the indoor Mardi Gras and Jackson Square sound-and-light show schemes failed, other canned history offerings put forth by private interests reached fruition in the 1970s, including two separate private enterprises offering multimedia presentations on the city's cultural legacy in the climate-controlled Superdome and in a building situated between the historic Presbytere and Pontalba buildings facing Jackson Square. One of the gimmicks promised tourists that in "90 grand and rollicking minutes you'll see more of New Orleans than many natives encounter in a lifetime."[32]

As tourism became New Orleans's most important industry in the fifteen years after 1970, with the annual number of tourists leaping from about 2.7 million to 7.5 million and the economic impact soaring from $190 million to more than $2 billion, businesses emphasized the Creole theme that accompanied the heavily stereotyped French Quarter's transformation into a tourist area. By 1984 the Creole restaurant was ubiquitous in New Orleans, with heavy emphasis on several New Orleans dishes to the virtual exclusion of lesser-known ones. Even Kolb's, a famed downtown German restaurant since the early 1900s, found it necessary by the 1980s to divide its menu into Creole and German halves so that Crawfish Etouffée received as much attention as Wiener Schnitzel. A number of French Quarter restaurants that sprang up during the 1970s and 1980s sought to become instant traditions. The insertion of "Original" or "Old" in front of a name lent prestige when courting unsuspecting tourists. Hence, it mattered little that Tony Moran's Original Old Absinthe House Restaurant at 240 Bourbon Street claimed to occupy the Old Absinthe House, which was actually located at 400 Bourbon, though its bar had been moved two blocks away. Restaurant advertisements used similar language—"traditional" or "world famous"—or claimed to serve "the food that made New Orleans famous." Even Cajun themes became hopelessly entwined with Creole themes in the tourist mind as marketers misappropriated the Acadian French culture of rural southern Louisiana to the French Quarter.[33]

The effort to court mass tourism not only eroded the French Quarter's role as a residential neighborhood, it also destroyed much of one of the South's most historic African American communities—Faubourg Tremé—which lay adjacent to the French Quarter and encompassed the site of the Storyville red-light district. If the French Quarter was the cradle of the city, Tremé was the cradle of the black community. Tremé, whose architecture rivaled that of the French Quarter, had for more than two centuries served as a racially integrated, though predominantly black, working-class neighborhood. Many of the city's black jazz musicians got their start in Tremé, an area that nurtured the evolution of a distinctive brass band culture built around street parades and the funeral processions of mutual benefit societies.

Nevertheless, when the city's tourist industry was beginning to expand after World War II, white city leaders cared little for marketing New Orleans to black travelers, who were few in number and generally had less purchasing power than their white counterparts. Nor did tourism promoters care (or dare) to defy Jim Crow proscriptions against white patronage of black businesses by encouraging white tourists to venture into Tremé, where they would have seen more jazz music than could be found in the Quarter at that time. For white leaders, Tremé represented a source of consternation as they tried to tame the peculiarities and reduce the unpredictability of the inner city in their appeal to suburbanites, both local and tourist.

Beginning in the 1950s, City Hall waged a dirty war against Tremé in a transparent effort to insulate the French Quarter from blacks. The initiative, which closely paralleled similar actions in other southern cities at mid-century, involved routing major traffic arteries through the neighborhood and redeveloping densely populated blocks with a super-block of civic facili-ties and park space. New Orleans's urban renewal efforts—locally funded be-cause before 1968 state law prohibited the acceptance of federal urban re-newal dollars—succeeded in driving African Americans farther from the French Quarter as rents there were too high for most blacks.[34]

The redevelopment of Tremé began with the Cultural Center plan hatched during the latter years of the Morrison administration. Over the next ten years, more than one thousand African Americans lost their homes to the bulldozers. Fragmented in the 1950s and 1960s while the City was acquiring land for "slum clearance," Tremé became politically organized by the early 1970s under the auspices of the Tremé Community Improvement Associa-tion (TCIA). As pressure mounted in the black community, Mayor Landrieu decided in 1972, several months after Louis Armstrong died, to create a Louis Armstrong Park instead. Clearly, the mayor hoped to use the park as a political reparation for disgruntled blacks as well as for a new tourist attrac-tion. The situation was fraught with ironies. First, City Hall bulldozed a cul-turally rich historic black neighborhood that had been a crucible of black music to build a "Cultural Center" where whites would go to view sympho-nies and operas. Similarly ironic was Landrieu's about-face when Tremé dis-puted the plan. His scheme to name the park for Armstrong came just a few years after City Hall had allowed Satchmo's birthplace to be demolished for a new police department complex. Clearly, the mayor had little concern for the preservation of culture.[35]

City Hall's plans for Armstrong Park had little to do with providing a service to residents and everything to do with creating a new tourist attrac-tion for a suburban white clientele. After HUD announced a $1 million grant for the Armstrong Park, City Hall commissioned San Francisco–based urban design firm Lawrence Halprin and Associates to devise a master plan. The resulting plan, inspired by Tivoli Gardens in Copenhagen, Denmark, featured lagoons, amusement rides, restaurants, and a casino. Many people decried the plan's Disneyland-like "ersatz" image, and one local architect said it was a transparent scheme to create a New Orleans in microcosm when the real thing existed just across the street. Another critic dismissed the design as "an outrageous spectacle." Still others complained that the failure to build the New Orleans version of New York's Lincoln Center, as had been prom-ised, circumvented the will of Orleans Parish voters who in 1968 approved a $4.6 million bond issue for such a project. A black spokesman from the St. Bernard Housing Project remarked that Armstrong Park was supposed to pay tribute to a great trumpeter, but instead, as a theme park, "it sounds like literally paying tribute—money."[36]

Although community protests resulted in City Hall's downsizing the park as well as delaying its intended dedication on Independence Day in 1976, Armstrong Park finally opened on April 15, 1980. The rape of Tremé in the interest of tourism-oriented urban revitalization demonstrated not only the limited capacity of tourism to revive the inner city but also leaders' skewed priorities, in which a black neighborhood was deemed unworthy of preservation and forced to serve as an adjunct to a white tourist area. Armstrong Park immediately became a white elephant, its opening-day crowds replaced by a trickle of visitors. The financially strapped city government, utterly incapable of maintaining the park, began looking for a private developer to save the venue from decay. A number of subsequent plans to operate the park as a theme park fell through, but the efforts reflected the ascendancy of kitsch in heritage packaging, which would reach its zenith in the 1984 Louisiana World Exposition.[37]

The New Orleans experience reflects larger trends in the postwar southern city. Throughout the South, cities benefited from massive federal largesse during World War II, which in turn jumpstarted their economies and began to close the development gap with northern cities. However, in the process many older southern cities along the coast fell behind as dynamic inland cities surpassed them. In cities such as New Orleans, Richmond, Charleston, Savannah, and Mobile, which tended to have deeper cultural roots than their inland counterparts, heritage gradually became a lucrative commodity as American nostalgia and the modern tourism industry soared. New Orleans illustrates the gradual shift other southern cities underwent in packaging themselves as tourist commodities. Like other cities in the region, the Crescent City emphasized the dichotomy of progressive present and romantic past. Into the 1960s this construction of a marketable image encompassed stereotyped notions about the historic role of African Americans in society and culture. Only when national conventions and sporting events foreswore southern cities did tourism leaders recognize the economic incentive of integration.

New Orleans in the 1960s and especially the 1970s and 1980s also exemplified a regional and national trend toward creating tidy, controlled tourist venues that distilled their cities' heritage into simplistic representations intended to appeal to the broadest possible range of visitors. It did so both by looking to attractions outside the region, such as Disneyland in California, and by serving as a model of cultural uniqueness for cities lacking a readily identifiable image. The French Quarter's fame influenced other southern cities tremendously. Atlanta created instant heritage by manufacturing an old underground city beneath its downtown viaducts, while Tampa discovered the tourist potential of Ybor City, an authentic ethnic neighborhood that bore more than a passing resemblance to the Vieux Carré. Throughout the South, from Norfolk to New Orleans, cities opened tourist attractions such as festival marketplaces, re-created cultural sites, and reenacted history through flashy multimedia shows.

Only in the 1980s and 1990s did southern cities clearly begin to embrace the nuances of their heritage, encouraging multicultural tourist interests instead of catering to the statistically typical American. While New Orleans slid from the nation's third largest city in 1840 to the forty-second on the eve of the twenty-first century, it took advantage of its economic slump to preserve and package a cultural image that in many ways galvanized dozens of southern cities to follow its lead in embracing heritage tourism in the latter half of the twentieth century.

6
Creating a "Variety Vacationland"
Tourism Development in North Carolina,
1930–1990

Richard D. Starnes

"Ya'll come to see us" is an expression a southerner might use to express endearment, hospitality, and to reinforce the bonds of friendship. During the twentieth century, this traditional southern expression took on a larger social and economic importance. Tourism is one of the most important aspects of the society and culture of the modern South. Each year, millions of visitors flock to the region, drawn by a complex mix of climate, geography, entertainment, and culture. Tourism is also one of the fastest growing aspects of the regional economy, generating billions of dollars in economic impact. Businesses large and small attempt to meet tourist demands for goods and services. States, localities, and individual attractions compete fiercely with one another for a larger share of tourist traffic. Often whole communities are transformed or created outright to serve the needs of visitors. Tourism therefore is more than an economic activity. It is a force that shapes society and culture at all levels of southern life.[1]

Although some southern resorts enjoy more notoriety than others, North Carolina provides an excellent case study of state-level southern tourism development. By the 1930s, North Carolina's political and business leaders recognized that tourism was a promising component of the state's economy and promoted tourism as a catalyst for general economic development. Economic and political leaders across the state united to create the foundations of a successful tourism industry: an appealing image and a viable, hospitable tourism infrastructure. The resulting advertising campaigns, public and private construction projects, and increases in visitor traffic established tourism as a key element of the state's economy. But this "Variety Vacationland" of booster visions was not without costs. Because of its reliance on geography, hospitality, and culture, tourism exposed important social and economic rifts across the Old North State. In short, the course of North Carolina's tourism development yields important insight into this little-explored aspect of southern social and economic history.

Tourism existed in some areas of North Carolina during the nineteenth century, but it did not play a serious role in the state's economy until after World War I. North Carolina boasted many natural advantages that made it an attractive tourist destination. With a scenic coastline in the east, breathtaking mountains in the west, and a mild climate, the state had a landscape on which to build a successful tourist economy. After World War I, state-published guides touted the advantages of mountain and seaside resorts and welcomed the emerging golf mecca at Pinehurst. State economists predicted a larger role for tourism in North Carolina's economic future. Moreover, the state government, dominated by "business progressives," laid the foundation for tourism development with the establishment of a state park system and an excellent state-maintained highway network. Governor Angus McLean told an audience at the 1925 Toe River Fair in Mitchell County that "Western North Carolina already rivals Florida as a resort section. Your mountains are alive with tourists and visitors, intrigued by good roads, claimed by beauty, invited in many instances to remain citizens to take advantages of wide-spread opportunity."[2] However, little official effort was invested in developing the state as a tourist attraction until O. Max Gardner came to the governor's office in 1928.

The deepening financial crisis of the 1920s led state planners to embrace tourism as a partial solution to North Carolina's economic woes, a campaign Gardner himself led personally. In an advertisement in a special travel edition of the *New York Evening Post*, he reminded readers of North Carolina's attractions. "Our resorts," he noted, "climatically are ideal for both winter and summer sojourns, with the lofty and majestic mountain peaks of Eastern America in the western section, a distinct pineland retreat in the center, and a balmy seacoast on the east." Visitors would find North Carolina "a prototype of the New South" and "will not be able to resist the temptation to prolong your stay." State officials also recognized that large federal public works projects would increase tourist traffic. As early as 1929, Gardner praised efforts to establish the Great Smoky Mountains National Park so "this wonder-land of our mountain region may be saved for the enjoyment of our own people and the nation," and he campaigned actively for the establishment of the Cape Hatteras National Seashore.[3] These were large, publicly owned scenic attractions that bolstered the state's tourist appeal. The governor proposed to make the most of such attractions to draw more visitors and their money to North Carolina.

Official efforts to promote the state's tourism industry received private assistance after 1934 from a new group called The Carolinas, Inc. Envisioned as an organization "to build tourist travel, to encourage additional industries, to attract farmers and capital, and to encourage the development of the natural resources of this section," these businessmen from both North and South Carolina were boosters who would make nineteenth-century New South booster Henry W. Grady proud. Led by North Carolina resort owners L. B. Moore and Coleman W. Roberts, the organization served as a clearinghouse for visitor information and as a lobbying group for the tourism industry. According to members, tourism could bring over $50 million annually to North Carolina alone, a phenomenal boost to the state's economy during the 1930s. Like Gardner, The Carolinas believed that tourism could help the state weather economic hardship at all levels. Coleman Roberts argued that "a large travel market . . . will help every community whether it be a resort center or a sleepy rural village, and it will help every individual, whether it be a hotel proprietor or a store clerk." The organization viewed tourism as a component of a comprehensive economic vision. By increasing "our portion of the [national] tourist business, now estimated to be worth five billion dollars a year," North Carolina would reap enormous important benefits. Tourism would "not only bring about greater local consumption of products and provide greater local employment" but would enhance the state's overall economic future as "the travelers themselves become residents, investors, [and] manufacturers." In short, tourism could be catalyst for all forms of economic development.[4] This growing consciousness and cooperation on the part of business owners and state leaders laid the foundation for tremendous tourist growth following World War II.

Efforts by The Carolinas, Inc., convinced state officials that North Carolina should improve tourism advertising. Lobbying by Governors Gardner and J. C. B. Ehringhaus, the Carolina Motor Club, and other travel-related groups convinced the legislature in 1937 to create a Division of State Advertising within the Department of Conservation and Development. Economic development advocates praised this move. R. Bruce Etheridge, director of Conservation and Development, spoke for many when he noted that "this campaign, we believe, will be one of the soundest investments made by the state in some time."[5] With a $125,000 appropriation, the Division published a full-color tourist guide titled *North Carolina, A Variety Vacationland*, specific brochures on golf, hunting, and fishing, and took out advertising in leading national magazines and newspapers. Tobacco magnate R. J. Reynolds funded a documentary film to accompany this campaign. Governor Clyde Hoey, who took office in 1938, assisted these efforts by creating a Governor's Hospitality Committee to correspond with tourists and place them in contact with members in areas they wished to visit. State officials also realized that federal projects such as the Works Progress Administration's *Guide to the Old North State* would attract new visitors.[6]

These promotional efforts met with considerable success. A survey conducted at Newfound Gap in the Great Smoky Mountains National Park on one day in 1938 indicated that seventeen of the twenty-four families interviewed requested and received promotional materials from the Division of State Advertising. During the first six months of 1938, 21,050 potential visitors requested tourist information. Officials expected tourist expenditures in 1938 to exceed $50 million, "which amounts to more than the entire return of the cotton crop and about one third the value of the tobacco crop," an increase they attributed to state advertising campaigns. Such spending resulted from the variety of attractions North Carolina offered visitors, and officials did their best to promote the different regions equally. Despite such efforts, state advertising elicited no small degree of jealousy among resort communities. In 1940, shortly before the agency was taken over to support military mobilization, news bureau manager Robert L. Thompson noted the difficulties of promoting such a large and diverse tourism industry. "Our job is to publicize the whole state," and despite its best efforts, the division "ran afoul of resort competition every day." A frustrated Thompson lamented that "the coast says we are doing too much for the mountains, and the mountains say the same about the coast."[7] Despite such problems, tourism was poised to play a greater role in the state's economy. Together, federal and state efforts added to North Carolina's tourism infrastructure, made potential visitors more aware of available attractions and amenities, and integrated tourism as a component of the state's economy.

The Second World War interrupted tourism development, but afterwards tourism assumed a larger role in the state's economy with an annual impact of nearly $100 million by the 1950s. As one booster put it, since 1945 "the tourist industry has become such an important economic factor in our State that it must be continued in healthy volume, or there would be ill effect upon the economy of the State as a whole, and disasterous [sic] effect upon some of its regions are—like Dare County, almost wholly dependent upon the tourist industry." State leaders continued to recognize tourism's economic potential. Governor Robert L. Cherry reinstituted the Division of State Advertising after the war, lobbied federal officials for larger appropriations to North Carolina's national parks and forests, and urged "our resort centers [to] pay increasing attention to appearances, service, food, fair prices, and recreational facilities." "Vacationists," Cherry noted, "want to go to a pleasant place, be comfortable, be treated courteously, fed well, and have fun." Relative prosperity, improved highway networks, and the democratization of travel in the form of motels and other moderately priced tourism-related businesses brought more visitors to the South generally and North Carolina specifically. Tourists took to the roads, and entrepreneurs built motels, restaurants, souvenir stores, and other businesses to accommodate them.[8]

One of the most important postwar milestones for North Carolina's tourism industry was the genesis of a collective consciousness on the part of tourism business owners. The Carolinas, Inc., had acted as a voice for tourism in the halls of government and was highly successful as a lobbying group, but it was a casualty of the war. The North Carolina Travel Council, formed in 1955 during the administration of Governor Luther H. Hodges, replaced the earlier agency as a lobbying and promotional arm for the industry within the state and reflected tourism's new economic importance. But the most important issue the Travel Council faced remained what one editorialist termed "the all-state viewpoint," promoting all parts of the "Variety Vacationland" equally. Although tourism business owners shared many of the same problems and perspectives, they remained competitors, a tension that grew more intense as tourism grew economically more important.[9]

State promotional efforts created a marketable image and drew thousands of new visitors to North Carolina, but individual business owners and local politicians began to feel that the state was too large and diverse to promote as a whole. They appreciated state efforts and recognized the importance of state- and federally owned attractions, but boosters believed that the best way to make tourism work for their local communities was to organize at the grassroots. As one tourism promoter put it in 1955, tourism offered not only "incidental support to industrial development but, for many communities, tourism offers the best or only means for increasing local income."[10]

An early such organization was the Western North Carolina Associated Communities (WNCAC), formed in 1946 "to organize all counties and communities west of Asheville for mutual benefit on matters pertaining to individual expansion, tourist business, game and fish and roads [sic]."[11] From the outset, tourism was the key element in the organization's development efforts. WNCAC members realized regional tourism relied heavily on government spending and facilities and invited federal officials from the Tennessee Valley Authority (TVA), Great Smoky Mountains National Park (GSMNP), and the Blue Ridge Parkway to meet and brief members concerning recreation development undertaken by their respective agencies. Members pushed for additional development on the North Carolina side of the GSMNP, including a museum, additional access roads, and improved visitor facilities. The organization lobbied for the completion of the Blue Ridge Parkway, for improvements to overlooks, and for more cooperation between parkway officials and local business owners. WNCAC leaders and TVA officials worked together on a survey of regional recreational facilities and on several development projects, but that did not mean the agency was beyond criticism. WNCAC admonished TVA officials for allowing the level of Fontana, Hiwasse, and other mountain lakes to fall below a level that allowed recreational use. In short, the organization emerged as an advocate for regional tourism and a liaison between local businesses and government officials.[12]

These tourism boosters increasingly recognized their reliance on one another. An early WNCAC report put it best, stating, "Murphy's tourist on Monday night might well be Bryson City's on Tuesday night, and Asheville's on Wednesday night." Therefore, "the treatment of any tourist by a tourist facility operator was the business of all tourist facility operators."[13] WNCAC set standards for cleanliness, amenities, and service for all members as a way to safeguard the region's share of the tourism market. As one member put it, "at long last the people who are in this business get together, drive out the racketeers, and have a real professional organization which will protect and further a business of inestimable value to [the] area and to North Carolina."[14] Organizations similar to the WNCAC emerged in Southern Pines, Wilmington, the Outer Banks, and other tourist areas, promoting local images and attractions and building tourism infrastructure at the local level.

But carving out a larger share of the South's tourism market required more than promotional campaigns and booster groups. Competition from Florida, South Carolina, and Virginia pushed tourism business owners in North Carolina to become more creative in the tourist experiences they offered to visitors. Scenic tourism remained important. Depression-era federal investments in the Blue Ridge Parkway, the Great Smoky Mountains National Park, Cape Hatteras National Seashore, and other projects continued to pay rich dividends. But, as tourism developers attempted to garner a larger share of the southern tourism industry, new types of recreational and cultural attractions emerged to supplement scenic tourism throughout the state. Post–World War II visitors demanded fresh attractions and North Carolina developers scrambled to provide them.

The first attempts to build new attractions depended heavily on scenery. In 1952, Hugh McCrae Morton purchased Grandfather Mountain near Linville and set about developing it as a private scenic park. Similar efforts at Chimney Rock in Polk County and at nearby Little Switzerland during the 1920s and 1930s had shown Morton the economic potential of such endeavors. He erected a "Mile-High Swinging Bridge" later that year to give visitors the opportunity to enjoy the mountain vistas. He also set aside the majority of the property as a nature preserve, inviting tourists to observe black bears, deer, golden and bald eagles, and other forms of indigenous wildlife in their natural habitats. Morton also used scenic and natural attractions as a springboard into other ventures. His most successful addition, the Highland Games, was designed to "foster and restore interest in traditional dancing, piping, and athletic achievement, and the Gaelic culture." Although Highland Scots settled elsewhere in North Carolina, Morton's fascination with his roots and the majestic mountain backdrop made this annual event popular, drawing visitors from across America to hear bagpipe music, eat Scottish food, and watch burly men in kilts toss the caber. Because of Grandfather Mountain's success, Morton emerged as one of the leading voices for the tourism industry in the state, calling for resorts to cooperate more with one another in development efforts.[15]

Although not a theme park in the traditional sense, Grandfather Mountain helped establish large, privately owned attractions as key components of the tourism infrastructure. By the 1950s, other theme parks attempted to give vacationing families an alternative to outdoor recreation. Tweetsie Railroad was one of the earliest theme parks. Built by Blowing Rock native Grover Robbins, Jr., the park blended mountain scenery, the lure of the railroad, and the cultural popularity of the wild West. Train rides, staged gunfights, and saloon variety shows entertained Tweetsie visitors. By 1963, Tweetsie claimed to attract over three hundred thousand vacationers annually. Maggie Valley's Ghost Town in the Sky and Cherokee's Frontier Land also exploited western themes. Ghost Town claimed the highest (in terms of elevation) roller coaster in the United States and during the 1964 season drew over five thousand visitors a day. Tweetsie's success led Robbins to build two other theme parks, The Land of Oz on Beech Mountain and Rebel Railroad in Pigeon Forge, Tennessee. The Land of Oz was a strange but somewhat successful blend of scenery, fantasy, and popular culture. Dorothy, the Tin Man, and other Oz characters, together with related rides and amusements, entertained guests against a mountain backdrop. Santa's Land in Cherokee offered visitors an opportunity unique for the summer tourist season. Vacationers talked with Santa, visited elves in the toy workshop, and rode a series of Christmas theme rides. How parents explained (and continue to explain) the presence of the jolly old elf in the North Carolina mountains remains a mystery. Carowinds, built in 1969 near Charlotte on the North Carolina-South Carolina line, was the largest and most profitable of these attractions. Theme parks broadened the state's tourism infrastructure, allowing visitors to experience fantasy, entertainment, and carnival rides at an affordable price.[16]

Morton's efforts also invigorated interest in cultural and heritage tourism and emerged as a way for communities to offer new attractions and a wider variety of entertainment. Attractions such as Bascom Lamar Lunsford's Mountain Dance and Folk Festival, Roanoke Island's outdoor drama "The Lost Colony," and state and federal historic sites drew numerous visitors before World War II, yet localities did not view local history and culture as marketable commodities until after 1945. Bath, Edenton, New Bern, and other municipalities began to market their histories' attractions but at no place was the junction of heritage and tourism more clear and controversial than in Cherokee.[17]

In 1947, members of the Western North Carolina Associated Communities organized the Cherokee Historical Association (CHA). Dominated by white tourism business owners from outside the reservation, the group hoped to use the historical experience of the Cherokee as a route for regional and tribal economic development. Drawing on earlier tribal efforts, the CHA raised funds to stage an outdoor drama based on the "Trail of Tears," the wrenching removal of the tribe from its native lands in 1838.[18] Called "Unto These Hills," the drama—better theater than history—staged its premiere on July 1, 1950. Tourism promoters responded enthusiastically. State officials, local government leaders, tourism business owners from across the state, and even Francis Cardinal Spellman praised the drama as both a fresh attraction and an educational endeavor. Tourism business leaders were more interested in profits than lessons but seemed satisfied with the initial season's attendance of over 107,000 people. The CHA netted a $70,000 profit and established the state's single largest heritage attraction.[19]

The drama's success led CHA and tribal officials to explore other ways to use the tribe's historical experience as an attraction. The Oconaluftee Indian Village was another CHA-sponsored project that marketed Cherokee culture to tourists. While "Unto These Hills" presented a romantic historical interpretation, the village itself attempted to depict the everyday life of an eighteenth-century Cherokee village. Constructed in 1952, the village included a period home, gardens, and a tribal lodge. Cherokee crafters in period dress demonstrated basketry, stonework, canoe making, pottery, and other traditional crafts while a trained docent placed the activities in historical context. By reenacting tribal social history, the village entertained and educated visitors and pumped much-needed revenue into the reservation's economy. Interestingly, some of the arrowheads and baskets found their way to souvenir shops where their provenance gave them additional authenticity and a higher market value.[20]

"Chiefing" was the most controversial aspect of heritage tourism in Cherokee. By the 1940s, Cherokee men were donning the elaborate headdresses of the Plains Indians and standing beside teepees strategically positioned near souvenir shops, allowing tourists to have pictures taken with them. Cherokee "chiefs" soon realized that their income was tied to their exotic appearance. Henry Lambert, a long-time "chief," understood the difference between historic authenticity and a profitable tourist attraction. "If you are going into show business," he said, "dress for it." Other "chiefs" experimented with wearing the traditional Cherokee buckskins, only to find that tourists were more interested in finding their own image of Indian culture than in viewing a historical reality. The "chiefing" trade was quite lucrative, and after twenty-five years Lambert hoped "to be doing this until I'm 99." But he also hoped his grandson would go to college and find a more lucrative, permanent, and less exploitative way to make a living.[21]

This type of heritage tourism stirred controversy between both visitors and the Cherokee themselves. Writing to the *Cherokee One Feather* in 1979, R. F. Stamper, home on leave from the Navy, noted that his son had come to embrace the "chiefs" with their elaborate headdresses and teepees as the embodiment of Indian identity. Stamper's son called to the "chiefs" enthusiastically, waving his arms out the window. When reminded that he was also a Native American, the boy replied, "Yes, but not that kind." Stamper lamented, "I guess when I get back home I will have to buy him an outfit so

Ramsey Walkingstick "chiefing" in Cherokee in 1956. (Courtesy of the North Carolina Collection, University of North Carolina at Chapel Hill.)

he can become that kind of Indian."[22] Tourism did not force all Cherokee to become "that kind of Indian," but it led some to question the exploitation of Cherokee culture by white tourism entrepreneurs. Many tribal members resented the Cherokee Historical Association for using native culture as a tourist attraction. Former Vice-Chief Fred Bauer noted that CHA projects like "Unto These Hills" had caused many Cherokee to embrace a counterfactual version of their own history and culture. "Little Indian children are in the cast, and a generation has grown up to adulthood impressed with the Drama as their history," he wrote. "The myth comes at the Indians from all sides; it has completely supplanted the history, and the true origin of the Eastern Band is not to be found." Sociologist Larry French issued one of the most scathing indictments against cultural tourism on the reservation. He condemned CHA, arguing that it was "long recognized as the 'hidden government' of the Eastern Band of the Cherokee Indian." The organization's efforts, French argued, amounted "to nothing less than 'cultural genocide,' clearly one of the most despicable forms of human interaction."[23] Yet visitors packed Cherokee each summer, visiting the local attractions, and leaving with tomahawks, headdresses, and, often, with a misunderstanding of the culture and history of the Cherokee people.

Even as tourism grew more important, public and private boosters continued to market North Carolina to white, almost exclusively middle-class visitors. The harsh realities of segregation defined tourism as much as any other segment of southern society. Although African Americans did visit North Carolina for leisure, they were forced by law and custom to vacation separately from whites. Black visitors could not patronize most roadside restaurants except to place take-out orders and were barred from segregated hotels and motels and excluded from premier resorts across the state except as employees. As elsewhere, small numbers of black-owned businesses catered to African American tourists. Segregation led state officials to designate at least one state park for use by blacks, and city ordinances in coastal towns such as Atlantic Beach and New Bern set aside part of the public beach for black use.[24]

African Americans were not the only groups to suffer discrimination from North Carolina resorts. In 1955, Robert Liverman, the president of the North Carolina B'nai B'rith Association, wrote Governor Hodges complaining that resorts, particularly those near Southern Pines, practiced severe discrimination against Jewish tourists. Guests, usually from the North, were routinely denied accommodations, even if they had made previous reservations. A survey conducted by the association found that 38 percent of all North Carolina resorts admitted to discrimination against Jewish visitors. Liverman called on the governor to pressure resort owners to end such practices in the name of justice and economics. "It is unnecessary for me to point out," he wrote, "that the practice of resort religious discrimination is not only cause for embarrassment to many fine North Carolinians who have contributed much to the well being of our state but is contrary to the democratic traditions of our state and nation."[25] Nevertheless, representatives from the governor's office reminded Liverman that private establishments could select their own guests.

The civil rights movement presented unique challenges to North Carolina's tourism business owners who wanted to attract white tourists but realized the more overtly racist images sweeping the South were distasteful to many potential visitors, including those from outside the region. When signs stating "Negro Not Wanted" appeared along major highways near Rocky Mount in 1957, the local chamber of commerce realized that such signs could harm the state's hospitality businesses. R. Graham Dozier wrote the governor's office that "it would appear to me that if at all possible something should be done to have signs of this type removed before adverse publicity to North Carolina is spread on the pages of some newspapers in larger cities."[26] Tourism business leaders willingly excluded African Americans from their accommodations in an effort to maintain the segregation preferred by their white clientele, but they realized that visible and vocal segregationist stands could undermine tourism promotional campaigns.

The Civil Rights Act of 1964 integrated tourism in the South, a move that theoretically opened more North Carolina resorts and attractions to black citizens. But many white business owners chose to continue to close their doors to black visitors until court challenges, as well as social and economic pressures, broke down old barriers. By the 1980s, state-published guides and locally published brochures featured more black families enjoying the state's attractions, but they remained few in number. The state did not spend considerable effort marketing North Carolina to black visitors until the late 1990s. Even the black historical experience emerged as an important attraction. In 1986, Dorothy Spruill Redford organized "Somerset Homecoming," a reunion of descendants of slaves and slave owners at Somerset Place, a state historic site that was once the largest plantation in North Carolina. State officials then committed to interpreting the slave experience, as well as that of the slave owner, at Somerset Place, using heritage tourism as a conduit for education and racial healing. By the 1990s, Princeville, the oldest town founded by African Americans in the country, began a successful promotional campaign to market the town's unique history to build the local economy. Once excluded from tourism, African Americans in North Carolina came to embrace tourism as a route to local prosperity and cultural understanding.[27]

Like leaders in Princeville, business owners and politicians across North Carolina understood tourism's most powerful effect. In 1960, visitors spent $245 million in North Carolina, and the tourism industry employed 72,340 workers. Four years later, Governor Terry Sanford noted that tourism had a total economic impact of over one billion dollars annually. By 1999, that figure had increased to $11.9 billion and the workforce swelled to 198,200 workers, making tourism the state's second largest industry. By the 1990s, the state government spent over ten million dollars each year, in addition to the advertising of local governments and individual attractions, attempting to draw more visitors to the state. New attractions emerged, including a larger outdoor recreation industry, a number of popular ski resorts, and numerous local festivals, museums, and events designed to draw visitors. By the 1990s, tourists also generated nearly one billion dollars in state and local tax revenue, a fact government leaders at all levels could not ignore.[28] Tourism is big business in North Carolina, and some forecasters argue that it will replace agriculture as the state's leading economic activity in the twenty-first century.

For business owners, tourism can be highly profitable, but for workers, the hard, often demeaning work and long hours elicited small financial rewards. Waiters, waitresses, bellmen, and porters often worked for a small base salary, and in many cases, for tips alone. Wages for tourism-related jobs remained low. In fact, business organizations such as the Western North Carolina Tourist Association lobbied state and local officials to exempt seasonal service workers from minimum wage regulations. Labor statistics show that tourism workers were among the lowest paid in the state. In 1948, service workers in western counties made between nineteen and thirty-seven cents per hour, with blacks earning less than whites in the same job. Ten years later hotel and motel workers made an average of $26.67 per week across North Carolina; the average manufacturing weekly wage was $61.65.[29]

Not only did tourism workers draw low wages, but the work was seasonal as well. In the 1970s, summer month unemployment on the Cherokee Indian Reservation dropped as low as 1 percent, but after the tourist season, it rose as high as 25 percent. In other resort communities, tourism workers were also locked into a seasonal employment cycle that prevented any true economic progress. African Americans and white women filled most of the state's tourism jobs in North Carolina, exacerbating poverty in many resort communities. Few workers managed to move beyond menial service jobs. By the 1960s, some community colleges began to offer diploma and degree programs in hospitality management, giving graduates a tangible credential that could increase responsibility and income. But most employees simply labored for low pay and few benefits. Tourism operators, not workers, reaped the lion's share of tourism's profits.[30]

Tourism also changed local landownership patterns across North Carolina, as resort developers, second-home owners, and retirees entered local real estate markets in the mountains, the piedmont, and along the coast. Critics of this process, such as staff members at the Highlander Folk School, pointed to unscrupulous methods used by some land speculators. One family reportedly sold a large tract of farmland to resort developers for a new roof on their farmhouse. However, some sold their land willingly and worked with outside interests to purchase resort tracts. Mack Higgins, a farmer in the Little Laurel Valley, refused to sell his land to a Florida tourist but noted his neighbor's complicity. "Our mountains are just being ruined," he said. "And we let 'em do it." The North Carolina Public Interest Research Group noted that between 1968 and 1973 the number of acres held by local residents in ten mountain counties dropped by 10 percent. By 1981, another survey of landownership in twelve mountain counties revealed that persons outside the respective counties owned 82 percent of land in western North Carolina, and 45 percent was owned by residents outside the state. On Hawker's Island, a small community of 1,600 on the Outer Banks, second-home owners bought up large tracts of land in the 1970s, changing the nature of the community. Gone were the days when islanders could beach their boats anywhere along the coastline and cross property lines on their way to fish or shop. New owners fenced their property, took native islanders to court for trespassing, and even threatened to shoot children who trespassed. Faced with skyrocketing property costs, many islanders moved elsewhere. By 1987, the local principal wondered if there would be enough children left on the island to maintain a school.[31]

Larger numbers of visitors, and a larger economic role for tourism, created serious environmental issues such as declining air quality, widespread pesticide use at resort golf courses, erosion, and increased demands for water and sewer services. Viewed as a clean industry, tourism had pronounced, though often localized, environmental effects. As a federal land use report noted in 1982: "the very features and characteristics which have made the mountains a very special place to live, and which also attract thousands of vacationers each year . . . are being eroded away by unregulated, uncontrolled development."[32] In 1983, the U.S. Capital Corporation began construction on a ten-story resort complex on Avery County's Little Sugar Mountain. Leveling the mountaintop to make room for the project, the developers raised the ire of local residents who felt outside interests were exploiting their land. State representatives took notice and passed the Mountain Ridge Protection Act, which prevented the construction of buildings over forty feet high on ridge tops in twenty-four mountain counties. Still, few privately owned mountainsides remained in their natural state. Along the coast, ordinances to prevent beach erosion and other environmental damage seemed inadequate given the increasing number of homes, condominiums, and hotels found along the state's beaches.[33]

Resort communities across the state felt the effects of tourism development to greater or lesser degrees. Maggie Valley in Haywood County is a case study of continued reliance on tourism as a community development strategy. Chartered in 1974, the town was an outgrowth of post–World War II tourism development. As early as 1953, visitors recognized the initial stages of tourism-related growth. The number of motels and craft stores increased, and land for resort homes had begun to sell. In 1972, the town claimed twenty-six motels, as well as several other types of tourist lodging, offering accommodations for four thousand visitors, four times the native population. A 1977 planning report noted that "no industry exists in Maggie Valley, and, very likely, none will ever situate in the town." Instead, the town relied on a theme park, a ski resort, and retail stores catering to tourists. Almost half of the community's businesses closed their doors during the winter months, and most residents worked at least part of the year in jobs located elsewhere in the region. Maggie Valley's leadership realized that tourism was the community's reason for existence, and little could be done to alter that fundamental fact.[34]

The commodification of culture, low-wage tourism jobs, inflated land prices, and negative personal experiences bred no small degree of animosity among some residents toward visitors. Part of this was a resistance to being viewed variously as a servant, a display, or an attraction. One scholar noted that on Hawker's Island "a strong sense of loss and resentment permeates when islanders talk about the tourists. Islanders believe that they are economically caught in a losing battle." An Ashe County resident argued in 1988 that the economic benefits of tourism amounted to economic and cultural colonialism. "The tourists always want to spend money," she said. "They want local people to provide things for them to spend money on, and that's the beginning of dependency. The spiral begins, and you begin to wait for the tourist, although you don't like them. . . . Catering to people is something you don't like to do, a certain amount of self-respect is lost."[35] Stereotypes in tourists' minds often affect relations between hosts and guests. One tourist asked a Blowing Rock resident where he could find "a real, honest-to-God hillbilly . . . like Li'l Abner or Snuffy Smith—like those mountaineers in that movie Deliverance." Another Blowing Rock woman felt that "when visitors hear my accent, they look down on me, or at least become patronizing."[36] Still, locals must often hold their tongues. Tourism depends on hospitality, even in the face of rudeness and insults aimed at local culture. Natives walk a fine line between asserting their displeasure at visitor attitudes and economic preservation.

By the 1990s, the "Variety Vacationland" of booster visions was thriving and had been for nearly thirty years. Tourism had emerged as one of North Carolina's leading economic endeavors, a catalyst for social and demographic change, a medium of cultural interaction, and a defining force in many communities. Yet, tourism within the state and region has received scant scholarly attention. The history of tourism is the history of boosterism and image making, of workers and business owners, of the landscape and the environment, and of society and culture. North Carolina's experience with tourism offers lessons about the nature of southern tourism, its economic and social effects, and its role as an agent of change. By exploring the themes, scholars may better grasp the significance of this powerful but little explored force that shaped so many aspects of the modern South.

7
From Millionaires to the Masses
Tourism at Jekyll Island, Georgia

C. Brenden Martin and June Hall McCash

On an early summer afternoon in 1962, Bruyan Deneroy and his wife were driving through Georgia on their way to Florida. Keenly aware that certain south Georgia towns were notorious for speed traps, the couple from Newburgh, New York, stayed well within the speed limit. Suddenly the flashing lights and siren of a Brunswick police car beckoned them to pull over. Mr. Deneroy could hardly believe it, but he grudgingly pulled the car to the side of U.S. Highway 17. When the officer approached the car, he looked at them and asked, "You folks on vacation?" Hoping it would make a difference, Mr. Deneroy confirmed that they were indeed tourists. "Will y'all come along with me?" The patrol car escorted them not to the city hall or jail, but instead to the Chamber of Commerce building, where a committee of local boosters greeted them warmly. "How'd you like to spend the night with us?" one of them asked. Still not sure what was going on, Deneroy responded cautiously, "Where, in jail?" The men burst into laughter and finally told them that they were in the midst of a major campaign to promote Jekyll Island, off the Brunswick coast, as a resort. To boost word-of-mouth publicity, they were hauling in out-of-state motorists and offering them a free overnight stay at Jekyll.[1]

The Deneroys' "tourist trap" experience is indicative of the remarkable changes Jekyll Island underwent in its evolution as a tourist resort. A few decades earlier, Jekyll had been a retreat for one of the wealthiest and most exclusive private clubs in the world, and a visit would have required an invitation from a club member such as J. P. Morgan or Marshall Field. Now a state park for the masses and accessible by automobile, local boosters were going to great lengths to divert the Florida-bound traffic to the island, something that would have been unthinkable during the club era.

The story of the island's transition is an amazing tale of southern politics at its worst, sometimes its best, and certainly its most colorful. Although replete with rumors of political corruption and influence peddling, it also contains critical moments of individual integrity and caring that would profoundly affect Jekyll's future. In the end, despite trial-and-error methods of development, incessant criticism, and periodic reorganization, the administrators of Jekyll Island succeeded in creating Georgia's first coastal state park with an appeal for a true cross-section of citizens. The Jekyll experience holds many lessons for other states wishing to develop similar "playgrounds" for their people. While Jekyll's evolution is in many ways unique, in other respects it was shaped by the larger trends of tourism and resort development in the South. It all began many years before the state acquired the island.

Jekyll's early history is one of Native American tribes, notably the Guales and Timucuas, Spanish missionaries, English colonists, enslaved Africans, and French planters. Prior to the Civil War, the du Bignon family, members of the Breton merchant nobility, emigrated from France to escape the upheavals of the French Revolution and eventually settled on the island to cultivate sea island cotton, an undertaking for which they, like other coastal planters, employed slave labor. However, in the difficult times following the Civil War and the shift away from a plantation economy, most of the island was sold in parcels. One member of the family, John Eugene du Bignon, a great-grandson of the first du Bignon in America, was intent on repurchasing the entire island to resell for profit. With his brother-in-law Newton S. Finney, who was by 1884 living in New York, he conceived the scheme of selling the entire island to a club composed of wealthy men, which Finney, a member of the city's elite Union Club, the so-called "mother of clubs," decided to organize.[2]

The move to sell the island as a retreat for affluent northerners was part of a much larger development of coastal tourism in the South. As railroads opened accessibility and increased capital, resorts catering to the new industrial elite began to flourish along the southern coasts. The sale of Jekyll and the creation of the club were made even easier, perhaps, by the fact that in 1881 Thomas Carnegie, brother of Andrew Carnegie, had purchased large portions of adjacent Cumberland Island, where he built a magnificent estate, Dungeness.[3] Carnegie was among the first of many wealthy capitalists, among them Henry Ford, Howard Coffin, and R. J. Reynolds, who discovered the beauty of coastal Georgia and established homes there within the next several decades.

The city of Brunswick, still seeking full economic recovery from the war years, did its part, and the local *Advertiser and Appeal* in 1885 printed a pamphlet called *Brunswick—The City by the Sea*, probably the first ever published in the city to solicit the tourist trade. It touted Glynn County's attractions as a tourist resort and sought to allay some of the understandable fears about the miasmic climate of the area, where malaria and yellow fever had periodically ravaged the population. It boasted for the area a climate "as pleasant . . . as can be found" and claimed that, while the winters "are never severe, snow being almost unknown and ice a rarity," the summers are also rendered "quite pleasant by constant refreshing breezes."[4]

In fact, John Eugene du Bignon, a New South entrepreneur of the first order, was most likely the primary instigator of the pamphlet. He recognized the potential for tourism in the area and became a major promoter of both Brunswick and Jekyll. Not only was he involved in the management of various newspapers and publishing companies, among them the Brunswick *Times Advertiser* and later the *Brunswick News*, he was also the principal owner of Brunswick's Oglethorpe Hotel. His other tourism-related businesses included a steamboat company, a transit company, and a railroad. Such interests clearly reflect his awareness of the possibilities of tourism in the area, the importance of promotion, and tourists' needs for lodging and transportation.[5] He also perceived a growing need on the part of northern businessmen for rest and relaxation. As a consequence, he busied himself in preparing Jekyll Island to receive them, stocking it with abundant game, and readying his newly constructed house to serve as temporary living quarters for potential buyers.

While his du Bignon brother-in-law made the island ready for visitors from New York, Newton Finney set about to interest fellow Union Club members in the new organization, founded in 1886, that he planned to call the Jekyll Island Club. To say that he was successful in his salesmanship is to put it mildly. Henry Hyde, president of the Equitable Life Assurance Corporation, after reading the club's prospectus, which underscored the island's natural beauty, said it sounded like "a fairy tale" and quickly added, "I will be happy to join."[6] Before it was over, Finney had enlisted in his club what the *New York Times* would call the crème de la crème of New York and

Chicago society.[7] Founding members included names that were virtually synonymous with wealth in America, like J. P. Morgan, William Rockefeller, William K. Vanderbilt, Joseph Pulitzer, Pierre Lorillard, and Marshall Field. Indeed, estimates suggest that members of the Jekyll Island Club once represented one-sixth of the world's wealth, and in 1904 *Munsey's Magazine* called Jekyll "the richest, the most exclusive, the most inaccessible" club in the world.[8]

It took a great deal of work to get the island ready for its opening season in 1888. Club officers hired a Chicago architect, Charles A. Alexander, to build a magnificent clubhouse, while landscape architect William Horace Shaler Cleveland laid out the grounds. Recognizing from the outset that Jekyll's environment was its chief asset, Cleveland sought to disturb its unspoiled areas as little as possible. Club officers adopted a strict philosophy of simplicity to take advantage of but not compete with the natural setting of the island. From 1888 to 1928 members constructed "cottages" on the island that were, for the most part, in keeping with this adherence to simplicity. Unpretentious (though undeniably large by ordinary standards) Queen Anne and shingle styles prevailed in the early years, while later cottages would reflect architectural trends of Italian Renaissance and Spanish eclectic styles. Some of the nation's most prestigious architects designed cottages for Jekyll members, among them David Adler, Charles Alling Gifford, John Russell Pope, and Carrère and Hastings. In all, club members would construct fourteen cottages on the island, in addition to the one that had been built in 1884 by John Eugene du Bignon. In 1896 the Sans Souci, a complex of six apartments, was begun, with club members William Rockefeller (who also owned a cottage) and J. P. Morgan among the original apartment owners. Finally, in 1901 an annex of eight privately owned apartments was attached to the clubhouse, with owners including Cornelius Bliss and Edmund Hayes.

The Jekyll Island Club operated only in the months from January to April, when members and guests sought refuge from the icy northern winters and the harried business world as well as leisure time with their social peers. The seasonal nature of the club necessitated both a year-round staff and seasonal employees. For the most part, year-round employees were local residents, many of them black, who attended to construction, caretaking, landscaping, and road maintenance duties. Seasonal laborers, including the chef, waiters, and specialty cooks, as well as a large contingent of chambermaids, many of them recent immigrants to the United States, were brought in from

New York in late December or early January. In addition, club members and their families arrived with their own bevy of servants—maids, butlers, secretaries, and tutors.

While it took a small army of workers to meet the needs of the millionaires, the primary occupation for the club members themselves was relaxation. Leisure activities varied for the millionaires throughout the club's fifty-four active years from 1888 to 1942, as its members followed the whims of national trends. Jekyll was established initially as a hunting club, to take advantage of the island's abundant game of deer, quail, pheasant, ducks, marsh hens, doves, wild hogs, and even an occasional alligator.[9] Although hunting, enjoyed by both men and women, always remained a Jekyll pastime, it would soon be rivaled in popularity with bicycle riding during the Great Bicycle Craze of the 1890s. Other activities included horseback riding, carriage driving, and eventually golf. Swimming was not initially a particularly popular sport among club members in light of the fact that they were on the island during the winter months when ocean waters were chilly. However, in 1927 when the club opened its swimming pool in front of the clubhouse on the leeward side of the island, well protected from the cool sea breezes, it was an instant hit with the younger members, both male and female, whom it sought to attract.[10]

From the outset, the club was conceived as a family resort, and the first article that announced its formation noted that it was not intended to be "a selfish and exclusive man's club" but that "ladies . . . will be freely admitted to all the privileges."[11] Although all the founding members were male, in 1893 the first woman joined the membership ranks, and by the end of the 1930s, approximately 25 percent of club members were female. Admission to the club was never easy, and most of the members after 1886 had a family or business connection with another member, who would nominate them for membership. Only once in the 1920s did the club accept a full contingent of one hundred members.

The coming of the Great Depression, however, would make membership in such an exclusive and expensive club difficult. Membership rosters began to decline dramatically in the early 1930s, 34 percent in only two years, despite the fact that J. P. Morgan, Jr., was serving as president, thus guaranteeing that the club's prestige remained intact. In earlier years, the club had kept itself afloat financially with annual assessments and large donations from individual club members, who were less eager to provide such support during the depression years. At the end of the 1932 season, the club treasurer reported a deficit of $28,000. Alarmed at the growing deficit and declining number of members, club officers in 1933 inaugurated "associate memberships" in an effort to raise revenues and attract a new generation to the club. These associate memberships would allow the club to add up to 150 members to the club rosters. Associates could join for a fraction of the cost of what they now called Founders' memberships. Dues for Founders stood at $700 in 1933, while Associates paid only $150.[12]

While the increased participation and revenue that resulted from new memberships kept the club afloat for the next nine years, the depression took its toll. So too did changes in club management. In March 1930, Ernest Gilbert Grob, club superintendent who had for forty-two years attended to the club members' needs with gracious, old-world charm, retired. The hiring of a new, and largely absentee, superintendent with more "modern" managerial techniques, exacerbated the problem. By this time most of the original members were either dead or too old to make the journey to Jekyll.[13] Further, the club's Victorian atmosphere, while popular with today's visitors, in the 1930s seemed out-of-date. The northern elite preferred faster-paced and more stylish vacation spots in Florida or on the French Riviera to old-fashioned Gilded Age resorts like Jekyll Island.

World War II would finally bring an end to the club era and, in its wake, epochal changes in tourism in general. Jekyll's last club season was 1942, when in April of that year it closed its doors forever. Club officers considered reopening for the following year "on a very limited scale," but fuel, supplies, labor, and transportation had been largely diverted to the war effort.[14] Although submarine activity off the coast of Georgia has been blamed for the closing of the Jekyll Island Club, the earliest news reports about such activity occurred only after the season's end, and club officers never mention any such activity or danger in their correspondence.

During the war years, however, the United States military, with full cooperation of club officials, occupied the island. In the meantime, Bernon Prentice, Jekyll president at the end of the club era, explored the possibility of reopening after the war, though on a somewhat different and more modern basis that would allow them to compete more effectively with newer resorts. He envisaged "intelligent changes," including "a Casino on the beach," another golf course, and helicopter access to the island.[15] Considering the formation of a syndicate to buy the island and make it into a more commercial resort, he discussed the idea with Alfred W. ("Bill") Jones, whose Sea Island Company had overseen the Jekyll properties during the war years. The greatest obstacle to such a scheme was, of course, money, and Jones was pessimistic that it could be found, although he was willing to canvass various possibilities. However, when Frank Miller Gould, the grandson of millionaire Jay Gould and the only remaining club member with sufficient funds to bankroll such a plan, also expressed an interest in the syndicate, they began in earnest trying to buy up members' shares and outstanding bonds. But Frank Gould's unexpected death on January 14, 1945, at the age of forty-five, dashed their hopes.

Uncertainty loomed once more over the future of Jekyll Island. Prentice, confronting declining interest on the part of its few remaining members and the loss of its key benefactor, turned to Sea Island associates Bill Jones and James D. Compton for guidance through the difficult postwar transition. Jones and Compton, respectively the chairman and president of the Sea Island Company, drew their considerable experience from administering the Cloister, a luxury resort on nearby Sea Island that their predecessor, Hudson automobile tycoon Howard Coffin, had opened in 1928. Sensitive to the implications of Jekyll's postwar development on their own resort, they feared that it might "fall into the hands of strangers" whose "character of operation and development would be unpredictable and might indeed be highly undesirable and even damaging to the Sea Island Company."[16]

They briefly considered buying Jekyll Island themselves, but, after conducting a feasibility study, they were not optimistic about its prospects. Jones clearly understood that the rise of automobile travel was altering the nature of tourism. "In the old days . . . families went to a vacation spot and settled down for one, two or three months. The automobile has basically changed this. Though there are some people who spend the entire winter at the Cloister the average length of stay is less than ten days." He believed that a causeway and bridge for automobile accessibility was the key to Jekyll's future and suggested that it would have to be financed with private capital, because government funding would not come "for a long long time." Jones also considered the island's entire utility infrastructure outdated. Outlining the staggering costs of modernizing the resort, he asserted that "successful operation of the present club facilities . . . would be practically impossible unless some fairy godfather could make up operating deficits."[17] By mid-1946, even the normally optimistic club president Bernon Prentice lamented that "there is no way that I know of for the club to go as it has been."[18] They began to discuss quietly among themselves the possibility of selling the island.

At this most uncertain time, the state of Georgia stepped in. In August

1946, Revenue Commissioner Melvin E. Thompson was actively looking for a Georgia coastal island for the state to acquire as a public park. After inquiring about St. Simons, Blackbeard, and Ossabaw Islands, Thompson and a special beach park commission appointed by Governor Ellis Arnall began investigating the prospects for purchasing Jekyll Island from the struggling private club.[19] Although club officials coyly insisted they still intended to open for the 1947 season and that the island was not for sale, Thompson moved quickly to propose its acquisition. Two of the remaining cottage owners bitterly resisted relinquishing their Jekyll property, but club officials seemed resigned to the state's acquisition of the island and pledged that "the club will cooperate . . . to provide a public beach for the people of Georgia."[20]

Adding further confusion to an already uncertain situation, the Georgia state government was thrown into chaos following the death of governor-elect Eugene Talmadge in December 1946, prior to his inauguration. With no clear guidance from the state constitution about who should assume executive powers when a governor-elect died before being sworn in, a highly partisan political battle erupted that halted governmental action on Jekyll for more than two months. The succession controversy pitted M. E. Thompson, who had been elected lieutenant governor, against Talmadge's son, Herman, who proclaimed victory through a questionable campaign of write-in votes. The pro-Talmadge state legislature, determined to settle the matter in Herman's favor, boldly elected him as governor. Governor Arnall, however, supported Thompson's claim as his rightful successor and declared that the courts must settle the matter. When Arnall refused to give up the governor's seat to anyone but Thompson, Talmadge's supporters physically removed him from the executive mansion. Thus, Talmadge operated as governor in the executive mansion, while Thompson acted as governor-in-exile at a downtown Atlanta office building. This dual governorship continued until March 19, 1947, when the Georgia state Supreme Court upheld Thompson's claim.[21]

Within days after this court decision, Thompson resumed his move for state acquisition of Jekyll Island, this time acting in the capacity of governor rather than revenue commissioner. When negotiations for an outright purchase of Jekyll reached an impasse, Thompson initiated condemnation proceedings on June 3, to acquire the island by right of eminent domain. Talmadge, still chafing at the outcome of the succession crisis, loudly protested "Thompson's Folly," insisting that his cronies wanted an island "where they can go to hide from the people and scheme to spend the state's money for the favored few."[22] Thompson, however, dreamed of a much different future

Isle of Golden Schemes

Governor M. E. Thompson's dream of a public beach for "the plain people of Georgia" drew criticism over the role of politics and favoritism in Jekyll Island's development. (© 2002 The Atlanta Journal-Constitution. Reprinted with permission from The Atlanta Journal-Constitution.)

for Jekyll. Trying to whip up support for the Jekyll purchase in the face of unrelenting criticism from Talmadge, Thompson insisted he merely wanted "to convert Jekyll Island . . . into a state park for the plain people of Georgia."[23] He, like many others, recognized that the automobile had democratized tourism and made the coastal areas accessible to a greater number of people. A larger middle-class population in the postwar years created a need for affordable tourist accommodations. He contended that he was merely "thinking of the poor farmers' sons" in considering the acquisition of the island.[24] While some editorials denounced it, most news writers supported Thompson's proposed takeover of Jekyll, which they envisioned as "a southern version of New York's Great Jones Beach" or a "new Coney Island."[25]

With a series of legal maneuvers in the summer of 1947, the state of Georgia quickly settled disputing claims and acquired the island through condemnation, compensating the former property owners in the amount of $675,000. The state took possession of Jekyll Island on October 7, 1947, thus ending Jekyll's period of splendid isolation as a millionaires' retreat and beginning its era as a state park for the masses. This transaction was symbolic of larger postwar changes in southern tourism. Not only does it reflect the democratization of tourism and the rapid rise of middle-class resorts, it also illustrates the increased role of state governments in promoting and financing the growth of tourism after World War II. Although a small number of cottage owners, still clinging to the vanishing elitist traditions, were greatly distressed by the course of events, Bill Jones declared it to be "a good solution to a difficult problem."[26]

Still under attack by Talmadge, Thompson moved quickly to prove the worth of his purchase before the special gubernatorial election to be held in 1948. After consulting with Jones throughout the entire acquisition process, Thompson was also persuaded of the need to bring automobile accessibility to Jekyll Island. Hoping to lure some of the millions of tourists who traveled by car through Georgia every year en route to Florida, he immediately unveiled a plan for a multi-million-dollar project to build a state-financed causeway and bridge to Jekyll.[27] Thompson predicted that the road-building project would be completed within a year, but it would, in fact, be another seven years before Jekyll Island was finally accessible by automobile.

Meanwhile at Jekyll Island, Georgia State Parks administrators contracted with private hotel managers (Thomas S. Briggs, 1948; Barney Whitaker, 1949–51) to open the former Jekyll Island clubhouse as a hotel for tourists. The Brunswick Chamber of Commerce, eager to promote the tourist trade to cushion the economic blow from a recent wave of postwar closings of factories and shipyards, even offered to provide free boat transportation to tourists. Nevertheless, still without convenient automobile access, few visitors ventured out to Jekyll Island.[28]

To make matters worse, the political prospects for Thompson's plan to build roads and develop Jekyll Island plummeted after Herman Talmadge was elected governor in 1948. Still nominally opposed to state ownership of Jekyll Island, Governor Talmadge decided in 1949 to lease the island's facilities to private enterprise for the remainder of his term, and he requested that state legislators create a Jekyll Island State Park Authority to administer the leases.[29] Established in February 1950, the Jekyll Island Authority, as it is now called (and henceforth referred to as JIA), is a quasi-public corporation that has broad powers to develop, administer, and promote the island as a tourist attraction. Consisting originally of five members appointed by Governor Talmadge, the Authority was obligated by its charter to permit development on "not more than one-half of the land area of Jekyll Island, which lies above water at mean high tide," and to create a vacation spot "at the lowest rates reasonable and possible for the benefit of the people of Georgia."[30]

As the legislature deliberated the bill, Talmadge offered to let Glynn County representative Charles Gowen name one of the authority members in exchange for his support. Gowen, who had worked with Governor Thompson in smoothing the way for the acquisition of Jekyll, made the fortunate, and as it turned out, critical choice of the Sea Island Company's president, J. D. ("Jim") Compton. Compton brought not only experience and understanding of the coastal landscape and its attraction to tourists but also a sense of integrity to an otherwise inexperienced and politicized body. Few knew the island better than Compton, who had helped to oversee Jekyll facilities from 1942 to 1947 and had administered the Sea Island Company's feasibility study a few years earlier. Deliberations recorded in JIA Minutes indicate that Compton, above all others, underscored the need for careful planning of Jekyll's development, while being ever mindful of the Authority's mandate to make the island accessible to all Georgians.[31]

Compton persuaded the JIA to hire Robert and Company, Associates, a nationally known Atlanta-based engineering firm, to draft the master plan that would become the basic blueprint for the next half-century of development on Jekyll Island. The chief architect of the plan, Robert and Company's engineer Andrew Steiner, credits Compton for the Authority's approval of his "natural beauty" plan over a competing designer's layout for "another Daytona," which some JIA members preferred. Steiner spent six months studying the island in consultation with Compton and planning its future layout, to include a network of roads, residential subdivisions, a shopping center, a small airport, golf courses, and beachfront development of motels, condominiums, and amusement parks.[32] Perhaps most notably, the master plan called for going beyond the state requirement and leaving approximately two-thirds of the island undeveloped and in its natural state—one of the most treasured qualities of Jekyll Island to this day.

While the plan was being drafted, Authority members addressed several more immediate concerns. Most problematic was the continued lack of automobile access to the island. By early 1950, the causeway to Jekyll was complete, but construction had not yet begun on a bridge over Jekyll Creek. Although JIA members and Glynn County commissioners pressed for "the prompt completion of an access highway by the bridging of Jekyll Creek," both political foot dragging and the federal government's need for steel during the Korean War delayed construction of the bridge for another four years. Consequently, the Authority decided "that the Island Facilities shall close on January 15, 1951."[33] Although the island was open on a limited basis to visitors by way of a ferry from Brunswick, Jekyll would not fully reopen to the public until December 1954, prompting some journalists and politicians to complain about inefficient administration on "Georgia's Padlocked Island."[34]

In reality, the Authority made significant progress during those years, and, in fact, the state legislature would pass a resolution in March 1953 commending the Authority "on its devotion to duty and the progress it had made." Not only did they carefully craft and approve the master plan, they also initiated "improvements" on the island, using convict labor to build roads and clear lots for residential use. In April 1951, the JIA hired the park's first superintendent, Hoke Smith, to oversee the facilities and to guide the work of convict labor.[35] Additionally, like administrators at other southern resorts, the Authority was compelled to confront the issue of developing a state park for all Georgians within the framework of the state's Jim Crow laws. According to newspaper accounts in the 1950s, Jekyll Island possessed the only public beaches in Georgia accessible to African Americans. Not surprisingly, local black citizens made it clear as early as 1947 that "[N]egroes are just as much interested in the development of the resort as whites."[36] Likewise, shortly after the JIA announced it would lease residential lots on the island, they received a letter from black leaders in Savannah "inquiring about the status of a [N]egro development on Jekyll Island." Replying that "the Authority has given careful consideration to the needs of the [N]egro citizens of Georgia," the JIA set aside for African Americans the remote south end of the island, the area least developed and the farthest away from the historic millionaires' village.[37]

The JIA intended to develop the segregated black section of Jekyll Island, which they named St. Andrews Subdivision for the sound that lay between Jekyll and Cumberland, along lines similar to the all-white northern end of the island. Thus, plans for St. Andrews included beach facilities, a bathhouse, a picnic pavilion, a hotel, a restaurant, and a residential subdivision, which was officially opened on September 24, 1955. Although the pricing of leases on these lots was "exactly comparable to white subdivision lots," as was usually the case in the Jim Crow South, the facilities for blacks at Jekyll were separate but unequal.[38]

As the JIA began implementation of its plan, Georgia politics entered the picture once again, ushering in a troubled period of what many journalists judged to be one of corruption and political favoritism. In January 1954, the state Highway Department awarded a $207,893 paving contract for the Jekyll Island causeway to Acme Construction Company, owned by state senator James ("Jimmy") Dykes from Cochran, Georgia.[39] Dykes was also reportedly a good friend of Governor Herman Talmadge, future governor Marvin Griffin, state Highway Department chairman James Gillis, and JIA chairman D. B. Blalock, who himself owned two businesses that sold road paving equipment. These political connections were vital in Dykes's ultimate control, direct or indirect, of almost all business activities on the island.

After the Jekyll Creek Bridge finally opened on December 11, 1954, Dykes's influence grew rapidly. By the end of 1955, he had acquired exclusive leases on paving projects, building supplies, hotel properties, concessions, a gas station, and general contracting. In fairness to Dykes, he was sometimes the only bidder on the various projects. On the other hand, he clearly had an advantage in that he often had prior knowledge about the call for bids, which, after the posting in newspaper announcements, usually gave bidders only two weeks to submit. Ever since he had acquired the lease to open the island's first business, the Bonded Building and Supply Company, he had the additional financial advantage of having crew and materials already on the island. As a consequence, for a time Dykes would have a virtual monopoly on the construction and contracting business on Jekyll.[40]

In late May 1955, the Authority leased the Jekyll Island Clubhouse as a hotel to a firm from Cochran, Georgia, after Dykes had assured JIA that he had no connection with the company. After the lease was granted, however, it was revealed that not only was Dykes a principal stockholder, he was also designated as the operator of the Jekyll property. Although JIA chair Senator D. B. Blalock insisted that "it was two months before we ever had any inkling that Jimmy was connected with it," he seems to have benefited financially as well from Dykes's operations.[41] An audit in 1955 showed that Blalock's firms had sold more than $85,000 worth of road building machinery and parts to the state for use at Jekyll. It also revealed that Dykes was in arrears in the rent on his leased properties. Even after these conflicts of interest and lease violations were discovered, the JIA negotiated an additional $218,000 paving contract with Dykes and his brother-in-law and allowed him to open the Jekyll Insurance Corporation, which also dealt in real estate and cottage rentals on the island.[42]

These shady dealings did not go unnoticed. Jim Compton, who oversaw JIA purchases, began to question requisitions and invoices related to Dykes. On June 17, 1955, he complained to Blalock that "I am opposed to the very sloppy way in which materials and equipment are being ordered. . . . I don't think anyone can tell what has been ordered, what it cost, and who authorized the [purchase]. I do not care to be involved in the controversy which is very likely to arise over the placing and payment of these orders." Six weeks later, on July 30, Compton stunned Authority members by tendering his resignation, ostensibly for reasons that "have to do with my business and my health." However, in a private letter to Blalock, he begged: "Please don't let any one individual or group get control of all the island's best facilities, as has been the tendency during the past eight to ten months, for it will hurt the further development of the island and bring great criticism down on the authority."[43]

Compton's words were prophetic, for within a few weeks of his resignation, the state's Legislative Economy Committee launched an investigation of the Jekyll Island Authority. The committee's controversial hearings resulted in a 78-page report that severely criticized the Authority for sloppy bookkeeping and recommended dissolving JIA and turning the island over to the state Parks Department or selling it altogether.[44] This report was released amid an avalanche of criticism from politicians and journalists, directed at the high prices at Jekyll Island and the Authority's policy of leasing residential lots. Throughout the mid-1950s, many people complained that the cost for accommodations at Jekyll "is far out of reach of the average Georgian" and urged the Authority to build low-cost housing and motels "so the average man could take his family there for a summer vacation."[45] More importantly, the residential leasing policy came under heavy scrutiny after lessees had difficulties securing mortgage loans on leased property and a Georgia Supreme Court ruling apparently cleared the way for Glynn County to tax Jekyll properties. Asserting that the leasing policy inhibited development of the island, some legislators viewed it as "out of step with the way America does things" by putting the state in competition with private developers.[46]

Governor Marvin Griffin, asserting, "I'm a free enterprise man myself," indicated he was in favor of selling residential lots outright or perhaps swapping the entire island for a nuclear reactor. To study the matter he created a special legislative commission that recommended the state keep Jekyll Island as a state park and even spend another $397,731, most of it earmarked for properties leased by Jimmy Dykes.[47] Governor Griffin acquiesced to the committee's recommendations, and the controversy over Jekyll Island temporarily waned. However, in July 1956, shortly after the opening of the $10 million bridge linking the Jekyll causeway to Brunswick, all hell broke loose. First, Dykes was accused of selling beer on the island without a liquor license; then the *Atlanta Constitution* published a series of scathing articles that charged the JIA with corruption. In response, Griffin announced that he wanted "to dispose of this 'white elephant,'" and he froze all further spending on Jekyll.[48]

In the wake of such publicity, tourists flocked to the island "to see what the ruckus was all about." Overall they were pleasantly surprised by what they found. One Atlanta visitor commented: "I went down expecting, from newspaper reports, to find a jumble of inefficiency and beer joints, but I found neither. . . . In fact, I have never seen a more beautiful, natural or better-run place."[49] Nonetheless, after nearly a year of negative publicity, there was still strong sentiment in the state to shake up the Authority or sell the island. In the legislature, a compromise eventually emerged that rejected the notion of selling Jekyll and instead created a newly constituted Authority comprising high-ranking officials, including the secretary of state, the public service commissioner, the state auditor, the attorney general, and the director of the Department of State Parks.[50]

Established in March 1957, a restructured Jekyll Island Authority ushered in a prolonged period of rapid development and political stability. The recently appointed members had clear ideas about how they wanted to develop Jekyll. State auditor B. E. Thrasher, who served as JIA's secretary and treasurer, commented: "I like the idea at Daytona Beach with its great expanses of attractive motels and small apartments. . . . I lean that way for Jekyll." The new Authority chairperson, Secretary of State Ben Fortson, also surmised that "people mostly come to Jekyll to go to the beach."[51] As a consequence, the Authority sped up beach area development, and within two years, Jekyll's beachfront boasted a shopping center, two motels, concession stands, a two-mile concrete boardwalk, acres of paved parking lots, and several new homes.

The JIA also leased properties for a campground and an amusement park and initiated plans for a convention center and an indoor pool beside the beach. Fortunately, all of these developments took place within the framework of Robert and Company's original master plan, which the new Authority members pledged to follow.[52]

Although the legislative act that reorganized the Authority empowered JIA to sell commercial and residential lots, some members were adamantly opposed to turning over state property to private enterprise. Before he was named to the Authority, Thrasher, who was very reluctant to join JIA in light of recent controversies, made it clear that "if it was their idea to make a real estate development out of the island, they had better leave me off the board." Both he and Fortson believed that if Jekyll were to live up to its promise as a resort for all Georgians, then the state must maintain the leasing system and finance the construction of motels and other inexpensive accommodations. When the Authority undertook a legal study of the leasing system on Jekyll, they concluded that they could not break the leases "without bringing them into court." As a consequence, they opted not to exercise their right to sell lots.[53]

Nevertheless, the JIA moved quickly to address Jekyll's greatest source of embarrassment for the last few years—Jimmy Dykes. They ordered an examination of his leases and found that he had defaulted on several provisions, including nonpayment of rent and the failure to have proper amounts of insurance. Although he paid his back rents, they still brought legal action to strip him of his leases, against which Dykes fought and prevailed in the courts. However, still under pressure, Dykes finally signed a quit claim deed relinquishing all his business leases on January 22, 1960, and by 1963, he had severed all his ties at Jekyll.[54] In spite of the crackdown on Dykes, rumors of political influence peddling on Jekyll Island persisted, with the most common charge being that legislators and political bureaucrats received preferential treatment in receiving residential lots on Jekyll Island. The *Atlanta Constitution* undertook an investigative probe in 1964 to look into the matter and discovered that, out of 326 houses that had been built by 1964, only fifteen belonged to present or former state legislators, state officials, or their family members. There is no question that the Authority did grant leases to former legislators to build beachside condominiums and apartments, but the rumors of influence peddling appear to have been somewhat exaggerated.[55]

During the 1960s, Jekyll Island enjoyed a welcome period of sustained growth and stability. Few officials talked of selling the island anymore; to the

contrary, journalists and politicians all over Georgia praised the work being done at Jekyll and hailed it as the state's finest beach resort. Furthermore,
the state of Georgia launched a concerted effort to promote tourism by eliminating speed traps, lifting tolls, and boosting the state's image. Governors
Ernest Vandiver and Carl Sanders in particular set out to compete with
Florida for a greater share of the tourist trade. Vandiver's efforts led to the
creation of tourist welcome centers, the establishment of a tourism division
within the Commerce Department, and an increased budget for tourism promotion, while Sanders, who also vowed to give Florida resorts a "run for their
money," endorsed the state's "Stay and See Georgia" campaign. These efforts, combined with local promotional campaigns, paid huge dividends as
tourist spending in Georgia grew to nearly $400 million by the mid-1960s.
By 1965, Jekyll Island had moved out of the red and into the black, generating $600,000 of revenue for the state.[56]

Even during this boom period, however, Jekyll was wrestling with the
South's traditional moral dilemmas of alcohol and race relations. During the
term of Governor Vandiver (1959–63), who threatened once again to sell
Georgia's state parks if segregation could not be maintained, the Authority
stayed faithful to Jim Crow, providing often-inferior facilities to black visitors. Typical of such efforts was the new Aquarama, a large indoor swimming
pool within an architecturally dramatic and modernistic structure, unveiled
by the Authority in 1961; three years later, for the African American tourists
on the south end, they built a much smaller pool inside a building that resembled a big tin box. Whether it was for lack of promotion, lack of investment, lack of equal facilities, or lack of interest, the St. Andrews development rarely drew large crowds of black visitors and, thus, the plan for a
separate residential and commercial district never fully materialized. The
"for-blacks-only" Dolphin Motel struggled under several different managers,
never making a profit. It was 1963 before the first black-owned house was
built at the St. Andrews subdivision. In fact, during the 1960s only four
black families built houses on the south end of the island before St. Andrews
was later opened to white lessees.[57]

The first public stirrings to desegregate Jekyll Island came in May 1960,
after the NAACP announced its plans to integrate public beaches along the
southern coast. Attorney general and JIA member Eugene Cook responded
by issuing a prepared statement calling on the governor to declare mar-
tial law on Jekyll if integration were attempted. Other Authority members,

namely Fortson and Thrasher, did not support Cook's proposed course of action. Thrasher publicly stated that JIA probably could not close the resort and that he, for one, did not want to.[58] The issue came up again in March 1963, when the biracial Georgia Council on Human Relations asked the Authority to voluntarily desegregate Jekyll Island or face court action. Fortson responded that "a majority of white people won't accept integration" and, "as custodians of the island, we must do what is best for the majority of people." Nonetheless, he pledged to confer with other Authority members before taking any action. A few days later, NAACP leaders from Savannah and Brunswick tested the segregated facilities at Jekyll Island, visiting the amusement park, beach houses, cafeteria, indoor swimming pool, picnic areas, motels, and golf course. A spokesperson announced: "We were denied entrance to all these places except the drug store, where two of our group ate lunch at the counter."[59]

As a result, in September 1963, state and local NAACP leaders filed a class action suit against the Jekyll Island Authority, arguing that segregated facilities violated the Fourteenth Amendment rights of black citizens. Governor Carl Sanders vowed to fight the suit, but seven months later a federal district judge ordered the Authority to desegregate all state-operated facilities and later decreed that all future leases "must require that the lessees operate without discrimination as to race or color."[60] In the aftermath of these rulings, Jekyll Island integrated peacefully and quietly. As most black tourists began to use motels and recreation facilities elsewhere on the island, occupancy at the Dolphin Motel plummeted, forcing it to close in 1965. The Authority later converted the Dolphin into a facility for youth groups.[61]

Throughout the 1960s, Jekyll Island also struggled over the issue of liquor. Although Glynn County was "wet," most people assumed that selling liquor on state property was illegal. Nevertheless, it was widely known that several Jekyll facilities served alcohol. In the 1950s and 1960s, motel operators fought in vain to acquire liquor licenses, but politics kept getting in the way. After the state attorney general announced in 1965 that he knew of no law prohibiting the sale of liquor on state property, the Glynn County Commission promptly granted liquor licenses to several Jekyll motels. But Governor Sanders, under pressure from such people as Dr. Louie Newton, a Baptist preacher and longtime crusader against "the blight of liquor," ordered the state revenue commissioner to deny the necessary state licenses in order to block liquor sales on Jekyll. The matter was finally decided by a May 1971 referendum in which Jekyll residents voted 223 to 96 to allow the sale of liquor. Although one local politician threatened a court challenge, the liquor wars ended a month later when the state gave its final approval.[62]

Over the last thirty years of the twentieth century and into the twenty-first, the most critical issues at Jekyll have concerned environmental and historical preservation. Maintaining the historic clubhouse and cottages has been a continuous struggle against the island's damp and salty climate. The earliest efforts at historic preservation had come in the Jekyll Island Club era when in 1898 several club members led a campaign to save the endangered Horton House, a colonial tabby structure at the north end of the island. In the early state era, however, historic preservation was not a high priority. In fact, until they began to realize that the historic homes of the island could serve as a valuable draw for tourists, early administrators made the unfortunate mistake of demolishing several of the club members' cottages.[63] Most, however, were left standing, and focused efforts to preserve the club's history began in 1954 when the Authority leased the Rockefeller home, Indian Mound, to a woman named Tallu Fish, who opened the house to the public as a museum, becoming both its curator and publicist.[64]

Not all state officials recognized the importance of the island's historic structures, however, and state auditor Thrasher once remarked that the hotel and cottages were "a rathole to throw money down the drain." Fortunately such viewpoints did not prevail, and during the 1960s administrative support for historic preservation was boosted during the successive terms of JIA directors Judge A. J. Hartley (whose official title was executive secretary) and Horace Caldwell. As early as 1963, Hartley, a former assistant attorney general and administrative aide to two governors, envisaged the restored historic district as "a sort of little Williamsburg." By December 1965 preservation work had begun, with the newspapers announcing that the "entire village" was being restored at a cost of $50,000.[65] The following June, the Authority commissioned J. Everette Fauber, Jr., who had worked at Colonial Williamsburg, to draft preliminary plans for restoring the "Millionaires' Village." Approximately two years later, the JIA employed its first full-time preservationist, Roger Beedle, who spent the next six years studying and stabilizing the structures. Landscape architect Clermont Lee was also brought in to help formulate plans to restore the district to its former splendor. However, a lack of adequate funding hampered the project, and by 1972 Caldwell was lamenting that, though the work continued, the historic structures had "deteriorated to the point that restoration is almost prohibitively costly."[66]

The Jekyll Island Club hotel closed its doors in the early 1970s, to sit empty and deteriorating for more than a decade, while the restoration project died for lack of funding. The issue of historic preservation would not come to the forefront again until 1983 when the JIA established once again among its priorities the "restoration of Millionaire's Village and opening of Jekyll Club."[67] Nothing was done, however, until 1984 when a young Brunswick architect named Larry Evans persuaded a friend, Vance Hughes, to join him in an ambitious project to restore the deteriorating clubhouse. Evans and Hughes had been looking at the club district for several years without taking action, but they decided it was now or never. Generous tax incentives and federal grants for the restoration of historic buildings were set to expire at the end of 1986. Thus, once the JIA finally approved their proposal in February 1985, Evans and his partner worked quickly to get their financing in place, restore, and reopen the hotel by December 1986. In an amazing and determined effort, once the required $20 million funding was finally assured, Evans and Hughes, both passionately dedicated to the project, quit their regular jobs to see it through. Working frantically, both day and night toward the end, they managed to meet the deadline and complete the extensive restoration in only nine months. The result was a marvel, bringing renewed life and vigor to a languishing historic district and sparking even greater interest in restoration. The same year that the Jekyll Island Club hotel reopened, the JIA hired a young man named Warren Murphey to oversee its preservation efforts on the various cottages. Ten years later Murphey became Director of the Jekyll Island Museum and eventually Director of Museums and Operations. Since 1986, when the preservation budget was only $200,000 for the restoration of four structures, the historic district has become a major focus of JIA efforts, with a budgetary appropriation from the state in 1999 of $2.5 million. All in all, Judge Hartley's dream of making the Jekyll Island historic district "a sort of little Williamsburg" seems to be coming to fruition.[68]

Environmental issues have been another major concern in recent decades. A primary problem has been the issue of beach erosion, a matter of concern even during the Jekyll Island Club era.[69] The ever-shifting contours of beaches are part of the natural life cycle of barrier islands, but at Jekyll human actions have compounded the problem. First, the repeated dredging of St. Simon's Sound north of Jekyll Island has had the unintended consequence of denying beaches to the south the replenishing sands that normally washed up on Jekyll's shores, diverting them instead to fill in the dredged channel. Second, during the 1950s, the Authority, apparently unaware of

Bulldozers on the Beach. As the popularity of Jekyll Island grew, the conflict between preservation and development grew more pronounced.(Courtesy of Jekyll Island Museum and Archives.)

the fragility and importance of beach flora and dunes, ordered a number of major dunes to be bulldozed to clear sites for motels and to improve visibility. Newspapers also reported that island workers hauled more than 100,000 cubic yards of sand from the beachfront dunes to shore up roads, bridges, and other development sites. The consequent erosion led the JIA to reinforce the demolished dunes in certain areas near the island's business district with sea walls in 1962. Just two years later, after the storm surge of Hurricane Dora destroyed beachfront facilities (including the island's amusement park Peppermint Land) and caused major erosion problems, the Authority decided to try to halt the encroaching tides with additional revetments—large chunks of granite placed on the beach to stabilize the shoreline.[70] Revetments, however, only exacerbated the problem, resulting in even more severe beach erosion of the island's north end.

Another major environmental battle at Jekyll Island in recent decades concerned imposing limitations on development. In the late 1960s, as the Authority approached the complete implementation of Steiner's original master plan, economic pressures mounted to develop larger and more lucrative tourist attractions. Mindful of a state legislative mandate that Jekyll Island must be economically self-sufficient by 1972, the Authority gave its approval in 1970 for the construction of Sea Circus, proposed as a smaller version of Florida's Sea World and "a major year-round commercial tourist attraction." Si Fryer, a Jekyll resident originally from Arizona, mobilized a group of island citizens to prevent development on the six-acre beachfront site on the island's south end. The controversy over the proposed development of Sea Circus prompted state representative Michael Egan to draft and shepherd through the state legislature a bill that legally limited development to 35 percent of the island's land area, leaving 65 percent undeveloped. It was a provision that had from the outset been part of the Steiner master plan, but Egan's effort incorporated it into law.[71]

This legislation, however, did not strictly define what constituted "development," leaving an inadvertent loophole for further encroachment on the island's natural areas. For instance, some planning consultants for the JIA argued that golf courses were not really development, but rather "wildlife habitat." This debate came to a head in 1995, when the Authority incurred the wrath of island residents and environmentalists by beginning construction on a new golf course before obtaining the proper permits. Jean and Leonard Poleszak, leaders in the Jekyll Island Citizens Association, rallied island residents and regional conservationists, who convinced the state Environmental Protection Department to halt development of the golf course. This controversy prompted the resignations of George Chambliss and John McTier, respectively executive director and chair of the JIA, who had guided the island through more than a decade of self-sufficient growth. It also sparked further legislative action to cap development of Jekyll strictly at 35 percent and to require the drafting of a new master plan to guide the island's future. Upon signing the bill into law, Governor Zell Miller announced: "While we are going to continue to promote Jekyll Island as one of our great tourism destination sites . . . we are not going to ever overdevelop this environmentally sensitive island."[72]

The story of Jekyll is yet unfinished. The JIA's charter and all leases on the island are set to expire in the year 2049, creating major questions about its future. Will the state continue the "trustworthy stewardship" of the island called for by the Authority's current mission statement? Will it turn Jekyll over to private development? Those who will ultimately decide these questions should be cognizant of the issues surrounding Jekyll Island's history as a resort. Throughout its evolution from millionaires to the masses, the natural beauty of the island has always been its biggest draw, and, at the dawn of a new millennium, it attracts approximately 1.4 million visitors a year. Today, the Authority maintains a delicate balance between free enterprise and state control through partnerships with private investors. Governor M. E. Thompson's dream of a public beach for "the plain people of Georgia," nearly derailed by political machinations, has been fulfilled thanks to those who carefully planned and nurtured the island's development to complement its natural beauty and historical significance. Visitor surveys, interviews with island residents and administrators, and the most recent master plan (1996) all concur that Jekyll Island's preservation of "an unspoiled microcosm of the coastal environment" is what makes it a unique and enchanted place. Put simply, Jekyll's future as a tourist destination depends on the preservation of its natural and historical amenities. Will it be done? "The longer it remains the way it is . . . it becomes more and more priceless," says one resident. But looking out his window over the beautiful Marshes of Glynn, he worries that over-development may one day ruin it. "It would be a travesty if that happens."[73]

8

Astride the Plantation Gates

Tourism, Racial Politics, and the Development of Hilton Head Island

Margaret A. Shannon with Stephen W. Taylor

Few sections of the South developed more rapidly than Hilton Head Island, South Carolina.[1] From a population of five hundred in 1960, the foot-shaped island at the southern end of Beaufort County reached thirty thousand full-time residents less than forty years later. Completion of the James F. Byrnes Memorial Bridge in 1956 opened the previously isolated island for large-scale high-end resort development and the construction of second homes for wealthy whites. South Carolina industrialists Charles Fraser and Fred Hack led the charge toward this development, and later investors would complement the expensive early developments with more modest facilities aimed at middle-class tourists. By the 1970s, the instantly recognizable Harbour Town lighthouse and its accompanying array of gift shops and restaurants overlooked one of more than twenty golf courses on the island. In the peak week of the 1999 tourist season, the island housed more than a quarter million people at a time, and tourist-oriented development had spread to the mainland as well.

The transformation of the island was remarkable. Almost entirely black in 1950, the population by 1980 was overwhelmingly white. Once among South Carolina's poorest communities, it grew to serve as home to elite residences, golf and tennis tournaments, expensive retail shops, and more. Purveyors of Mercedes-Benz, BMW, and Rolls Royce automobiles moved into land once farmed for subsistence by some of the South's few black landowners.

Attempts to understand the racial dynamics of southern economic development have too often fallen victim to the fallacy that African Americans have never participated in the course of that development, and observers of

Hilton Head have thus far neglected or oversimplified the role of African Americans in the quest for tourist dollars.[2] This essay is a first step toward analyzing a more complex set of relationships—between white and black islanders, between islanders and the rest of Beaufort County, between residents and tourists, and between longtime residents and newcomers. This case study also illustrates the broader principle that economic identity, not racial identity alone, creates political coalitions, and it is these economic issues that determine the course of industrial development in general, and tourist development in particular—demand by consumers of tourist goods and services is fairly elastic, the market for such goods and services is rather crowded, and the tourist industry is incompatible with most other industries.

Tourism was not the only choice available for Hilton Head's development. Beaufort County, like many southern counties and municipalities, had been striving to attract industry to the area since the 1930s. County boosters offered cheap land, low-wage non-union labor, favorable tax conditions, and indifference toward pollution. In return, the county would get more jobs and economic growth, albeit at a high price. County leaders believed they had "hit the jackpot" when the German company Badische Anilin Soda Fabrik (BASF) announced its intention to locate a chemical plant in the county. The proposed site was at Victoria Bluff, overlooking the Broad River just upstream from Hilton Head.[3]

The controversy divided Beaufort County between those who believed the plant's economic advantages would outweigh any potential environmental cost and those who feared that pollution from BASF would ruin the explosive growth of tourism at Hilton Head. Residents of the northern half of the county, upstream of the proposed site, generally supported the construction of the plant. Desiring the county's improved economy for the enrichment of both haves and have-nots in the area, they had suffered several near misses in the past quest for industrial salvation, and these had often been related to pollution concerns. Additionally, by the late 1960s, many began to worry that cutbacks in military spending would reduce the forces at Parris Island, upon which the county still depended heavily for economic survival. Thus they were even more desperate to hang on to the BASF proposal, especially since this company, unlike past ones, was at least publicly committed to satisfying environmental concerns.[4] Shortly after the BASF announcement, the Beaufort *Gazette* published an editorial on December 11, 1969, that stirred controversy by arguing that South Carolina's anti-pollution laws should be strengthened. Under stricter legislation, the lowcountry would have the opportunity to experience the kind of economic prosperity that the textile industry had brought to South Carolina's upstate.[5]

Downstream of the Victoria Bluff site, and especially at Hilton Head, most residents opposed the plant for environmental reasons. The Hilton Head residents at the forefront of opposition to the BASF plant fell into two groups: developers and fishermen. The largest developers were all white, though there were some black business owners who saw potential for expansion threatened by the proposed plant. The fishermen were mostly black and were divided between those who worked on white-owned boats and those who were members of the black-controlled Hilton Head Fishing Cooperative. Of the fishing companies, the Hilton Head Fishing Cooperative was most vocal and most successful in calling attention to the potential environmental costs of the plant. A petition drive and a massive public relations campaign involving the shrimper *Captain Dave* attracted federal involvement in the controversy. Soon the Cooperative and several local fishing companies filed lawsuits as well.[6]

At this point a different group, developers with their eyes on the tourist dollar, entered the dispute over BASF. The Hilton Head Company, the Island Development Corporation, and the Port Royal Plantation Corporation quickly added their own lawsuits to that of the fishing companies. As with the case of the fishing companies, this second group of lawsuits called for an injunction against BASF, alleging that the island companies would suffer irreparable harm if the chemical company were allowed to locate in Beaufort County. Black and white lawsuits asked for the same remedy, based on the same fears that the plant's pollution would damage their businesses. The owners of all three development companies were white but shared the same concern for the island's economic future as the black fishermen.[7]

The strong opposition of Hilton Headers to the BASF plant began to cause doubts in the minds of Beaufort County residents that the plant would ever be built. They wondered what they would do in the absence of such an industry to improve the county's economy. Hilton Head developers Charles Fraser and Fred Hack suggested an alternative: a tourist center could be built at the Victoria Bluff site, bought and financed by their companies. The center Fraser and Hack proposed would be modeled after Six Flags over Georgia and would be worth $50 million. Fraser hypothesized that such a tourist center would create considerable job opportunities and ancillary businesses and would attract as many as five thousand visitors per month to the area. The kind of development Fraser and Hack proposed in Beaufort County would directly benefit their preexisting investments by complementing what they'd already begun, without jeopardizing the fishing and tourist industries or compromising the quality of life in the "plantations" they had already constructed.[8]

In early 1971, embarrassed by the controversy and forced into reassessing their entire North American operations, BASF announced plans to pull out of Beaufort County completely. As BASF made that decision, a Clemson University committee released a preliminary draft of a report commissioned by Governor Robert E. McNair on the economic choices for Beaufort County. This report, by a team composed of members of the departments of Agricultural Economics and Rural Sociology as well as the Water Resources Research Institute, concluded that an industrial facility such as BASF would raise per-capita income 7 percent and create many high-paying jobs that would initially employ non-Beaufort residents and over time would employ increasing numbers of natives. Moreover, they expected the plant to create satellite businesses that would immediately offer job opportunities to natives.[9] Just as the Clemson committee reached its conclusions on the profitability of the plant, Governor McNair was blaming "anti-pollution frenzy and individual selfishness" for BASF's decision to abandon the project completely, thus robbing the state of the "fattest industrial prize" ever. BASF agreed to sell the land back on a no profit, no loss basis.[10]

In the absence of BASF, the committee members believed the resort industry would have to double in size in order to compensate for the loss of the plant. They did not see this as an impossible scenario. Additionally, locals would immediately qualify for such jobs without extensive technical training. But the committee did warn that such development would increase the region's dependence on low-paying seasonal work.[11]

The committee found the greatest economic difference between the two plans to be in tax revenue. During the initial period in which the plant would enjoy state and local tax breaks, the plant would produce $675,000 more in yearly revenue than an expanded tourist economy could. Of this amount, $525,000 would go to Beaufort County. After the tax break years, the plant would out-earn tourism by $950,000 annually.[12]

During the fight over the proposed plant, developer Fred Hack's Hilton Head Company had commissioned a study by the firm of Skidmore, Owings & Merrill, of Washington, D.C., to examine possibilities for industrial development that would complement or at least not affect the environment of the area while providing jobs. Released in June 1972 after BASF had withdrawn,

the report concluded that full development of the island (exclusive of mainland Beaufort County) could mean the creation of ten to twenty thousand new jobs through a combination of tourism, agriculture (including seafood industries such as crab farming), and light industry, as well as some
heavy industry. Zoning laws would confine heavy industry inland along
Interstate 95, and light industry between I-95 and the coast, leaving the
coast unindustrialized. Still, employment increases in this study were expected to be mostly in the services sector: such jobs made up 60 percent of
all jobs at the time of the study, and that number was expected to go higher.
So the conclusions of the Hilton Head report coincided with the findings of
the Clemson committee, with this difference: by 1972, having successfully
defeated BASF, Hilton Head residents were in a position to get their way.
The question was no longer what was best for Beaufort County, but what was
best for Hilton Head.[13]

Later industrial proposals failed as well, due to opposition posed by both
black and white Hilton Headers. In 1973 the Chicago Bridge and Iron Company proposed to build liquefied gas containers at Victoria Bluff. As was the
case three years before, extremes of poverty and wealth clashed in Beaufort
County. Proposed industrialization would benefit the poor, but the compara-
tively affluent and those who depended on tourism for their income worried
about their lifestyles. And, as the Palm Beach (Florida) *Post-Times* pointed
out, many of Hilton Head's retirees were former executives who were experienced in similar environment versus industry fights—from the other side.
Hilton Head's power in such fights was increasing.[14]

The BASF controversy damaged black political empowerment at the
county level by dividing the black community. African Americans north of
Victoria Bluff stood to gain much from the BASF plant; most importantly,
they would receive relatively high-paying year-round jobs rather than the
low-paying seasonal jobs offered in the tourist industry at Hilton Head. Their
counterparts south of the site depended more heavily on the environmentally
sensitive fishing and tourism-centered economy and resisted the plant. African Americans in Beaufort County possessed most of the ingredients necessary for political empowerment: they lived in a relatively mild racial climate, they were a significant portion of the population, they had strong
leaders and resources independent of local white control (federal protection
of jobs at military bases, work in their own jobs like the shrimp co-op, and
the presence of the Penn Center), and they were able to see a very clear ma-

terial benefit to unity in the effort to secure a better economy in Beaufort County.[15] But the disunity arising from the BASF controversy undermined this empowerment and led to the entrenchment of African Americans in low-paying seasonal jobs, as defeat for BASF reinforced the importance of the tourist industry and further promoted rapid growth at Hilton Head.

The failure of the BASF initiative left Hilton Head firmly in control of the county's economy and made possible the tremendous boom of the 1970s, which attracted both tourists and year-round residents. Most of the new arrivals were white and wealthy, and many were attracted by the romantic image conveyed by the marketing of the lowcountry "plantations."[16] With the tourist boom and the accompanying development at Hilton Head, black land-ownership fell, both in absolute acreage and in number of individuals, as well as in proportion to the island's white population. Scholars and activists attribute this decline to economic change, ignorance, traditional inheritance patterns, and outright fraud. In this respect, Beaufort County and Hilton Head are just small examples of a larger southern problem.

People who own their own land tend to be more independent and self-sufficient, according to authors Leo McGee and Robert Boone and others. They are more likely to register and vote, they are more likely to run for office, and they have more personal and public dignity. Black landowners have more political power than landless blacks, and they also seem to have a better image of themselves. Declining black landownership deprives African Americans of a base of political power and restricts their political autonomy.[17]

While landownership had been difficult to achieve for most blacks in the South, many of Hilton Head's black families had owned their land since the Civil War. After the Civil War, African Americans either bought or assumed ownership of subdivided, abandoned, and confiscated plantations. On these lands, subsistence farming and fishing provided the residents of Hilton Head with a simple but sustainable livelihood. They also kept land values low. In the 1950s, when developers began to buy land on the island with an eye toward residential and tourist development, land values began to rise. Initial development of the island took the form of lumbering operations that briefly served as a source of income for residents of the island. After the construction of the James F. Byrnes Bridge brought tourists to the island for the first time in 1956, land values increased dramatically. This increase in the value of land led to a rise in land speculation, and these factors, along with the problem of "heirs property," rising property taxes, and the decreasing availability of jobs outside the tourist economy, contributed to the decline of black landownership at Hilton Head.[18]

Migration of African Americans from the South aggravated the problem of "heirs property." Many black landowners failed to make wills specifying who should inherit their land. Thus, titles to black lands often remained in the name of a long-deceased ancestor, with multiple living heirs, siblings, and cousins each holding varying percentage shares in the entire plot. These shares sometimes became so numerous as to make any division of the land impractical. Selling the land and giving each heir a portion of the proceeds consistent with the share held became the only way to clear the title under such conditions. According to the Black Economic Research Center, this situation invited fraud, in which a developer with access to cash bought out one heir's share, usually someone who had moved away and no longer cared about the land but did want the cash. Having bought an heir's share, the developer could then sue to have the title cleared. This action would force an auction, at which the developer would offer the highest bid. Thus many black families were legally deprived of their land, clearing the way for the construction of hotels, condominiums, and shopping malls.[19]

Another problem leading to the decline of black landownership is the difficulty African Americans had in obtaining mortgages, either because of racism or because of unclear titles. This precluded initial purchase as well as the construction of tourist-related improvements that would make the land more profitable. Unable to increase the profitability of their land, but faced with rising land values, many African Americans in developing areas found themselves increasingly pinched by limited incomes and rising property taxes. Frequently, this situation resulted in loss of land at tax auction.[20]

In Beaufort County, the Penn Center played an instrumental role in helping blacks retain their land. The Penn Center's project, Black Land Services (a joint venture with the Black Economic Research Center), found that the greatest threat to black landownership was the problem of intestate property. In South Carolina, heirs' property could not be improved and could not be used to secure a mortgage. In a report, the Penn Center obliquely charged Hilton Head developers with exploiting this situation: "A great deal of the intestate property has become valuable due to the development of large nationally known, 'plush' resorts. Developers have begun the quieting title process which frees the land from the claims of the heirs."[21]

The Penn Center produced a booklet aimed at publicizing this problem. Intended for legal professionals such as paralegals and lawyers, the *Black Land*

Manual outlined the ways in which black landownership was threatened and explained South Carolina law on each point, citing strategies to save the land. It also contained a stinging indictment of Hilton Head developers:

> Hilton Head, which developers bill as the "Western Hemisphere's Riviera," was at one time owned by Blacks. The white, sandy beaches make the island "ideal" as a recreation and resort location. Speculators moved in and started land grabbing operations. Just recently, speculators offered the Black heirs to a particularly attractive portion of realty $1200 per acre for title to the property. Some of the vendors sold at the offered price. With the aid and assistance of personnel from Project Black Land, other property owners in the vicinity are receiving offers upward of $30,000 per acre. The speculators who have purchased the land in the area have been able to sell the land at up to $100 per square inch.[22]

In later years, African Americans on Hilton Head would call themselves an "endangered species" driven out by economic development of the island as a rich man's paradise. Where once African Americans owned their own homes and operated their own small farms and lived independently, new-style gated subdivisions called "plantations" sprang up.

Over time, the decline of black landownership would make itself felt in other ways. Hotels organized buses to pick up African Americans who had been driven off the island to the mainland and carry these workers on one- and two-hour one-way commutes to scrub toilets for the tourists. Young people attracted to the relatively high-paying menial work in the resort industry on the island tended to drop out of school early. The decline in black landownership caused a loss of independence as small, autonomous enterprises such as farms and fishing operations disappeared, leaving behind a dependent black underclass serving the needs of Hilton Head's tourists.[23]

In addition to the problems created for the black community by the loss of their land, there was the problem of how land remaining in black hands could be used. Newcomers valued the island for its environmental qualities and as a residence or vacation destination. On the other hand, native islanders saw the island as their ancestral home and a location for their livelihood—be it fishing, farming, or some other occupation. As newcomers grew to dominate island politics and control the island's destiny, native islanders found their freedom to develop their land as they chose threatened.

Thus, white newcomers' attempts to control the environment and make it more attractive for tourists also served to cut black landowners off from the one remaining economic opportunity they had.

A 1972 effort by Beaufort County to zone a corridor along Highways 278 and 46 as forest-agricultural drew fire from island blacks who resented being cut out of the growing economic opportunities of the island's development. Highway 278 formed the spine of the island's road system and was the only route to the mainland. Highway 46 was a major feeder route from the interstate highway system to the bridge. Both highways were excellent locations for business, and at that time land owned by African Americans accounted for much of the road frontage.[24]

Such zoning efforts compounded black Hilton Headers' land problems. In order to retain their land, they needed to develop it profitably. Hilton Head's developing tourist industry offered many lucrative opportunities, but the zoning proposal fenced many away from a chance to take advantage of those opportunities. At a community meeting called to deal with the issue, George Peyton, a Charleston attorney representing the island's NAACP chapter, pointed to a 15-acre tract near Singleton Beach on which owners hoped to build a mini-mall. As part of the Highway 278 corridor it was zoned agricultural and the owners were prevented from developing. Similar examples abounded, both on the island and on the feeder routes to it.[25]

The island's aesthetic appeal was its major asset in the quest for tourist dollars. But efforts to preserve that aesthetic appeal often formed the basis for restrictions on how the island's native residents could use their own land. In 1978, faced with the arrival of new corporate developers who refused to abide by earlier "gentlemen's agreements" on the island's appearance, the Beaufort County Joint Planning Commission proposed a set of stringent land-use guidelines. These guidelines specifically excluded the "plantations," because they had land-use restrictions of their own in deed covenants. Thus, the new restrictions targeted non-plantation land, where most of the island's native black population lived. Black islanders protested that these provisions unfairly restricted their ability to make money out of their land. "We do not intend to stand idly by while poor people are indirectly robbed of their land," the island's NAACP leadership warned.[26]

Responding to such charges, chairman of the Beaufort County Joint Planning Commission Peter Hyzer pointed out that the proposed codes would not prevent, for example, the location of a junkyard along U.S. 278; the codes would merely insist on the construction of a concealing fence. The island's black residents considered this to be a "slippery slope" provision adding increasing financial burdens on black entrepreneurship until African Americans were driven out.[27]

By the early 1980s, developers and "plantation" residents began development of a long-range land-use plan, in an effort to forecast sewer, water, garbage, and road needs for the island. Long-range planning seemed the most efficient means of providing for the island's infrastructure. However, this kind of planning was met with skepticism by the island's native population, who again considered it just another effort by whites to control blacks' land. According to Chris Porter, a reporter for the Hilton Head Island Packet, "the truth as far as many black property owners are concerned is that [tourist-centered] development is going on all around them, and it's serving only to raise their own property taxes to a point where they either have to sell or develop."[28]

For most African American families, however, development was not a real option. In 1983, the Penn Center newsletter opined, "Decisions regarding development standards will have a major impact on Black landowners since, in most cases, Blacks lack capital for high quality development." Moreover, many island residents were concerned that giving the Beaufort County Joint Planning Commission any information about their plans for their land would hamstring them later if their development plans changed.[29]

Black Hilton Headers were often accused of opposing controlled development, but the truth is subtler. Most did not oppose controlled development on the island, nor did they oppose the aesthetic goals articulated by developers like Charles Fraser. They merely wanted to preserve their own self-determination. Black Hilton Head resident Morris Campbell, a political activist and county councilman, proposed a moratorium on construction at Hilton Head in February of 1982. He noted that the council was reviewing forty-seven new projects, of which thirty-six were at Hilton Head. The moratorium on building permits for ninety days would permit the council to "catch up" and control development at Hilton Head along appropriate lines. Campbell's leadership role in the island NAACP placed him in touch with the currents of activist thought in the area, so his position on development is noteworthy. Although the measure failed, it shows that black Hilton Headers did not necessarily oppose the principle of controlled development.[30] Campbell kept up his fight for a moratorium on multi-family dwellings, which islanders derisively called "stack-a-shacks." Later, after reducing his measure from ninety days to sixty, he gained the support of the Joint Planning Com-

The gates at a Hilton Head resort reflect the barrier between elite newcomers and the island's native-born black population. (Photograph by the authors.)

mission chairman, but in a second try the measure failed again in a vote of four to two. Eventually Campbell's proposal, in spirit at least, won out when the Joint Planning Commission voted not to consider for forty-five days any developments proposing to construct with a density of more than eight units per acre, a moratorium that would undoubtedly include most tourist-centered facilities.[31]

Another complaint by African Americans about the use of land at Hilton Head centered on the gated "plantations" that formed the luxurious residential communities on the island. Before development began, the island's native residents could go anywhere on the island they wanted. After development, access was restricted to residents or people with residents' permission, such as workers or guests. In the case of Sea Pines Plantation, non-residents could gain admittance by paying a $3 fee.[32] In part, African Americans were offended by the very existence of gates intended to keep them out except when admitted by permission. The gates, and the use of the "plantation" label, served as uncomfortable reminders of the legacy of slavery. "I find it very offensive that more than half the island I grew up on is behind gates," one islander complained. But newcomers did not seem to understand the concerns of the African Americans who had lived on Hilton Head all their lives. "There are lots of private areas all over the country. . . . If they want to fence off their property, nobody is stopping them," said one Sea Pines resident.[33] Implicit in this view is also an indifference to (or unawareness of) the negative connotations of the word "plantation" for the descendants of slaves.

Some saw this approach to development as a blatantly racist attempt by whites to recreate the Jim Crow South, a perception no doubt strengthened through the use of the term "plantations" by developers to refer to the gated, mostly white neighborhoods. Emory Campbell, Morris Campbell's brother, recalled welcoming the bridge in 1956, thinking it would make traveling to Savannah to shop easier. But development followed the bridge, and development brought problems native islanders had never before faced. In 1960, Campbell and some friends were on their way home from work as caddies when a white deputy pulled them over, inquiring, "What are you boys doing up here anyway?" Twenty-eight years later, Campbell recalled, "That was the first time that I knew there were places on Hilton Head or places anywhere in this world that I couldn't go because I was black."[34]

Even more infuriating, African Americans found themselves shut away from family cemeteries when the "plantations" developed around these sites, and they resented paying the fee to visit their ancestors, who, after all, had been there first. Charles Fraser refuted these charges:

> They complain about the gates. My guess is, if those gates had not been installed the amount of jobs on Hilton Head today would be 10 percent of what it is and their land would be worth about $1,500 an acre instead of $50,000.
>
> Did they tell you about the cemetery? It's their favorite gambit with the media. "Oh they won't let me visit old granddaddy's burial place." That's absolute hogwash! The road to it was impassable when we bought the property and there have been more burials since we took over than in the previous 50 years. From Day One, there have been orders if anyone wants to visit or bury someone, let 'em through.[35]

Because of the boom built around tourism, black and white Hilton Head residents found it increasingly difficult to see eye to eye on the issue of land-ownership and use. What looked like positives to whites, such as rising land values, were negatives to blacks because each group had different goals. Those gates, which Charles Fraser said contributed to rising land values on the is-land, symbolized what Emory Campbell was talking about when he said that it was in 1960 that he first experienced racial segregation.

In sum, control over land was the defining issue in the struggle for black political empowerment at Hilton Head. As Hilton Head's development pro-gressed, fraud, rising taxes, land-use restrictions, and the inaccessibility of development loans threatened black landownership. African Americans, however, were not just concerned with ownership of their own land as a res-ervoir of political power. As the island's longest residents, they deeply re-sented newcomers dictating land-use laws to them. Similarly, they hated the gated "plantations" which denied the island's native residents free access to areas previously available. Finally, because whites and blacks at Hilton Head had differing values and goals for the land itself, the dispute over land at Hilton Head became a divisive force socially, creating misunderstanding and resentment between the communities. Because of their greater numbers, newcomers' goals for the island overcame natives' objections, ultimately con-tributing to the decline of black political power at Hilton Head. However, because African Americans did fight, they were able to maintain some voice in the decisions about changes that took place on the island and were able to prevent their total political disappearance.

The racially and economically divisive fight over municipal incorporation helped to define the island's politics in more explicitly racial terms. The dra-matic growth the island experienced in the 1970s caused problems that raised the issue of island self-government. Increasing population put greater and greater strain on the island's water supply, roadways, police, and fire pro-tection. High-density construction led to increasing visual blight. Waste clogged both sewage plants and landfills. Poor drainage led to flooding prob-lems, which were further complicated by the lack of an evacuation plan. These concerns forced a struggle between black natives and mostly white newcomers over control of the island's destiny. In 1973 black islanders actu-ally proposed incorporation, but in 1983 they actively opposed it. Similarly, in 1973 whites opposed incorporation but favored it ten years later. Both times, whites got their way.[36]

During the 1970s Hilton Head acquired the image it has today, of a sun-soaked leisured isle of beautiful people and relaxed living. The Heritage Golf Classic arrived at Hilton Head in 1969, and the first Family Circle Tennis Cup tournament was held in 1973. By 1975, the island grew large enough to support its own hospital, and by the late 1970s its first public housing

The Hilton Head community's attempt to prevent unbridled development on the island. (Photograph by the authors.)

project was built. While the island attracted more and more tourists, it also began attracting middle-class and wealthy year-round residents, many of them drawn by the island's apparent isolation and concerned by its rapid growth. As early as 1973, the island's explosive growth and developing tourist trade already showed signs of uncontrolled expansion. Plantation residents expressed concern about preserving the island's aesthetics as well as controlling growth, but they also wanted to preserve high property values and the profitability of tourism. The rapid growth meant that Hilton Head's economic and social life were growing more distant from the rest of Beaufort County, and the county's inability to respond effectively to the island's rapidly changing needs created sentiment in favor of some sort of self-government. Complicating Hilton Head's relationship with county government, development fragmented Hilton Head between haves and have nots, making the island unable to speak with one voice politically.[37]

The gated, lavish residential neighborhoods, which comprised over 50 percent of the island, symbolized the community's fragmentation. Behind these gates lay manicured lawns, gracious houses, rolling golf courses, private beaches, and winding lanes. Outside the gates were most of the resorts, businesses, and the island's black neighborhoods. These last often had poor roads, minimal water and sewage services, and minimal garbage pickup, while inside the plantations the level of services provided was much higher and included neighborhood pools and garbage pickup by quiet miniature electric garbage trucks paid for through neighborhood association dues. With different demands emerging from Hilton Head, the county did not know to whom to respond, or how.[38]

Responding to this fragmentation and the growing political crisis resulting from it, in 1973 the Hilton Head Community Association hired Clemson political scientist Horace Fleming, Jr., to advise them on their options. Fleming's report, released in 1974, outlined three possible ways Hilton Head residents could gain some self-determination and therefore gain greater control over the island economy. Reminding islanders that Hilton Head contributed over 50 percent of the county's tax revenue, Fleming suggested that Hilton Head could "secede" from Beaufort County, forming its own county; it could "secede" and join Jasper County (a poorer county Hilton Headers might more easily dominate politically), or Hilton Head could form a municipality.[39]

To cope with the increased demands placed by the growing tourist industry on the island's infrastructure, in 1973 those who were most heavily invested in the tourist industry supported the creation of a Public Service Association (PSA). The island's black residents generally opposed the Public Service Association proposal because they believed it would ignore their interests, noting that the PSA districts as drawn explicitly excluded those areas of the island where the island's African American population was most dense. Demographic superiority guaranteed white victory in the ensuing referendum.[40]

Despite high hopes, the new Public Service Association quickly proved inadequate; both tourist development and the growth of the residential "plantations" continued to strain the island's infrastructure, and visual blight resulting from the construction of high-density housing persisted. In late 1974, many white Hilton Headers backed yet another referendum, which would create a unique governmental body to study Hilton Head's needs and report to the Beaufort County Council and to the county Joint Planning Commission, enabling the island to speak to the county with one voice.[41] Since the new body would be funded by additional taxes, the NAACP opposed the referendum as too burdensome on the poor community.[42]

This second referendum passed, but with such a slim margin of victory that many worried the county council might reject the commission as lacking a mandate.[43] While the Beaufort County Council met to discuss the commission referendum and to decide whether to allow the creation of the Hilton Head Commission, the Hilton Head NAACP continued to fight the commission proposal.[44]

A few weeks after the white victory in the second referendum, the county council appointed Perry White, executive secretary of the Hilton Head NAACP, to the Beaufort County Joint Planning Commission in an attempt to ease black fears. He joined Peter Hyzer, the white Hilton Header who was appointed in the days after the referendum. White's appointment began a shift in the position of many black residents toward incorporation. With White on the commission, worries that the county government would ignore the concerns of black islanders began to fade. Hilton Head was gaining a voice in county government after all, and African Americans obtained some representation of their concerns as part of the bargain.[45]

As Hilton Head's white population in the "plantations" grew, the black community was growing proportionately smaller and their voice in Hilton Head politics was becoming increasingly weak.[46] However, in countywide government, where the black population was larger and more unified, African Americans had been able to gain positions. Because of the dilution of their numbers at Hilton Head, black islanders turned to county government for assurance their interests would be respected. In 1973, three African Americans held county council positions. By 1982, that number had increased to seven.[47]

In a successful February 1982 referendum, the island finally got its unique governmental body, the Hilton Head Island Commission. Of 7,177 registered voters, only 2,457 actually voted. The vote was overwhelmingly in favor of the commission, with only forty-six no votes, thus overcoming earlier concerns that the idea lacked a mandate. Initially, county council appointed a black man, Tom Barnwell, to the commission, but he declined to serve, leaving the commission all white. Black councilman Morris Campbell then proposed an amendment to the county's Advisory Commission Ordinance, which had provided that members of any special commission would be chosen by county council. Campbell's amendment provided that commissions be created "according to demographics in order to guarantee the fairest representation of all the people." Implicit in Campbell's words was the ominous assumption that black and white interests would never coincide. Campbell's proposal never gained sincere attention.[48]

By 1982, some island services, particularly fire and medical services, looked as though they would serve adequately despite the anticipated growth of the island through the 1980s. However, the increasing population and increasing influx of tourists caused worry about the adequacy of police protection, maintenance of recreation areas, "control of island growth and development (planning, zoning and land use), transportation and traffic control, water and sewer service, and environmental protection services." Moreover, deed covenants were proving inadequate to protect the island from visual blight, as new investors built on land not subject to deed covenants and ignored old gentlemen's agreements with respect to types of construction and density requirements.[49] Incorporation seemed to offer white Hilton Head a better chance to control its own destiny and preserve the "rustic appearance" that so attracted the tourists and their money. But the African American community saw incorporation as a further tightening of the noose around what remained of their power to share in the island's prosperity and to direct the island's destiny.

Cognizant of African Americans' concerns and mindful of the continuing problems with infrastructure, Horace Fleming and colleague Michael L. M. Jordan developed a new plan for field research into islanders' needs and sentiments regarding government reorganization.[50] Jordan and Fleming found that black Hilton Headers were not always cooperative with their efforts and were very suspicious of whites' motives behind incorporation. Black residents shared their views on the issue at a meeting at the First African Baptist Church on Valentine's Day 1983, pointing out the inequity in services, fearing incorporation would lead to higher taxes but not better services.[51]

The community was so heterogeneous—African Americans, southern whites, northern whites, newcomers and natives, developers and retirees, rich and poor, farmers, fishermen, and businessmen—that getting a consensus was nearly impossible.[52] African Americans feared that, in contrast to their earlier support for incorporation as a means of preserving their voice, this time and in this format incorporation would mean paying more and getting less, trading good county-level representation for an uncertain future. Blacks on the island had many more concerns for the future than whites did, and whites seemed not to notice this. In the *Islander* magazine, a kind of local

Southern Living extolling wealth, beauty, and the good life, a January 1979 article titled "A General Air of Optimism" contained photographs of local businessmen and their predictions for the future. Whites expressed optimism about the future, seeing increasing profits and opportunities in the year ahead. Isaac Wilborn, the black principal of the Hilton Head Elementary School, and county councilman Morris Campbell both expressed fear about the lack of opportunity for blacks to move out of dead-end minimum wage jobs on the island.[53]

The boundaries of the municipal precincts, or wards, as they existed in 1980 and were preserved in the 1983 election and formation of the town, contributed to black fears of dilution of their political power. Ward boundaries in general corresponded to the outlines of the plantations. Whites dominated all of the wards. The greatest concentration of African Americans was in Ward 5 on the north end of the island, and this had only 39 percent black population. The next greatest was Ward 4 with 30.2 percent black. The other three wards had 13 percent black or less. So African Americans could easily be outvoted in elections held either by ward or at-large. A majority African American district could have assured black Hilton Headers a voice in municipal matters, but despite repeated calls for such by the island NAACP, it was never seriously considered. Achievement of white goals for the island as a tourist and retirement destination seemed assured.[54]

The issue of incorporation finally went to the voters on May 10, 1983. With only 51.6 percent of the eligible voting population participating, the final tally was 2,405 in favor and 1,638 against incorporation. African American turnout was high. In precinct four incorporation failed, and the vote was close in precinct five; precincts four and five held the greatest concentration of black voters.[55] After the successful vote for incorporation, in response to the incorporation of the Town of Hilton Head Island, the NAACP filed a lawsuit, asking for the incorporation to be set aside. The U.S. Supreme Court eventually upheld the vote.[56]

The referendum on incorporation did not end black islanders' quest for a voice in the island's development. Black businessman Henry Driessen, who had opposed incorporation, was soon elected to fill an at-large seat on the new town council. He won by appealing to voters' desire to heal the breach caused by the dispute over incorporation, and in doing so gained strong white support as well as black. Driessen received 47 percent of his support from two nearly all-white precincts at the southern end of the island.[57]

Despite Driessen's attempt to find common cause among the increasingly divided population, white residents' goals still conflicted with the goals of many black islanders. Superficially, these goals may look like lifestyle choices, but fundamentally they are economic issues that caused division and disharmony. Behind the gates, what some called privacy was exclusion to others. When whites wanted more and better services, and voiced a willingness to pay, blacks worried about increased tax bills for what they considered unaffordable luxuries. As whites spearheaded a move to develop governmental autonomy from what they considered an unresponsive Beaufort County, blacks worried about losing their voice in matters that would have a direct impact on their lives. So African Americans spent much of the 1970s and early 1980s struggling to gain and keep their political voice. Throughout the period, African Americans united and delayed or stopped some proposed measures. In the end, however, they lost their bid to prevent incorporation, because the evolving tourist economy and the rapid growth of the white population undermined their voting strength at every turn. As the success of Campbell and Driessen attests, white Hilton Headers were willing to support black candidates when their political positions coincided with white interests. But in the end, the demographic change brought by tourism ensured both increasing racial polarization and increasing white dominance of island politics, leaving black landowners like Henry Driessen caught with one foot on each side of the plantation gates.

9

The Road to Nowhere

Tourism Development versus Environmentalism in the Great Smoky Mountains

Daniel S. Pierce

Traveling north out of Bryson City, North Carolina, on Fontana Road one encounters a rather surprising sight. As a motorist approaches the boundary of the Great Smoky Mountains National Park, a large sign looms on the left side of the road:

Welcome To
The Road to Nowhere
A Broken Promise!
1943– ?

Traveling on into the park, the point of the sign's message becomes somewhat apparent as the road abruptly ends at the beginning of a tunnel. Visitors can walk through the tunnel and see that on the other side is not a road, but a dirt trail designed for horses and foot travel. The presence of the sign and the tunnel highlight a bitter conflict between many Swain County residents and environmentalists over a 1943 promise made by the federal government to construct a road to replace North Carolina Highway 228, which was inundated when Fontana Lake was created by the Tennessee Valley Authority (TVA).[1] Swain County commissioner David Monteith, whose family once lived in the area, sees the situation clearly: "It's a legal obligation." The road "could be a real tourism boom for this county." Ted Snyder of the Sierra Club sees the issue equally clearly: "You have a huge tract of unroaded, inaccessible wild land and that's the way it should be." And so the debate has gone on for most of the forty-seven years since the initial commitment was made, with little chance of compromise or solution on the horizon.[2]

The controversy over the "Road to Nowhere" serves as an appropriate metaphor for the conflict inherent in scenic tourism. This conflict is enshrined in the enabling legislation that created the National Park Service in 1916. According to the National Park Service Act, the purpose of the national parks "is to conserve the scenery and the natural and historic objects and the wildlife therein and to provide for the enjoyment of the same in such manner as will leave them unimpaired for the enjoyment of future generations."[3] The conundrum of how one both provides access to and enjoyment of scenic areas while preserving and maintaining the scenic and ecological values that attract people in the first place is one faced by promoters of scenic tourism throughout the South. In the twentieth century, this conundrum often turned into conflict, as tourism boosters emphasized access and recreation, while rising numbers of environmentalists promoted preservation and protection.

As the most popular and economically successful scenic attraction in the South, the Great Smoky Mountains National Park—attracting more than eight million visitors and generating more than $600 million in consumer spending in the surrounding region annually—has seen more than its share of this type of conflict. Indeed, almost from the time the first visitor entered the park, boosters and environmentalists have waged an ongoing battle over land management practices in the Smokies. At the same time, the Park Service itself has waged its own internal battles over its mission, and has chosen sides in various conflicts with one or the other sides.

At the heart of these controversies in the Smokies, and at other scenic attractions, has been the construction of roads. For boosters, roads provide easy access to attractions, thereby bringing tourists and their dollars to the region. For environmentalists, these roads scar the landscape, clog waterways with silt, artificially divide ecosystems, damage wildlife habitat, and in the long-term destroy or dramatically change the attraction itself.

Since the early days of the twentieth century, southerners have attempted to use the region's beauty to attract tourists. Scenic tourism in the South can be traced to the eighteenth century with elite resort areas scattered throughout the Southern Appalachian region. Charleston's upper crust began summering in the Blue Ridge Mountains at least as early as 1782, and Virgina planters established early resort colonies in the Virginia mountains at White Sulfur Springs and other sites. Other scenic and health resorts sprang up in the eighteenth century at Montvale Springs and Monteagle in Tennessee, and Warm (now Hot) Springs and the Sulfur (Deaver's) Springs near Asheville, North Carolina.[4]

Travelers' accounts of the beauties of the region helped to attract guests

The fight over the "Road to Nowhere" symbolizes tension between two different visions of tourism development in Swain County, North Carolina. (Photograph by the author.)

to these resorts. Charles Lanman, who visited the region in 1848, waxed poetic as he looked out of his window at the Sulfur Springs: "I had a southwestern view that was eminently superb. It was near the sunset hours and the sky was flooded with a golden glow, which gave a living beauty to at least a hundred mountain peaks, from the center of which loomed high towards Mount Pisgah and Cold Mountain, richly clothed in purple. . . . Directly at my feet lay the little town of Ashville [sic], like an oddly shaped figure on a green carpet; and over the whole scene dwelt a spirit of repose, which seemed to quiet even the common throbbing of the heart."[5] The southern Appalachian scenery elicited a similar response from Frederick Law Olmstead when he visited a few years later. After climbing Richland Balsam in Haywood County, North Carolina, Olmstead observed: "The view from under the cloud was very beautiful. The grand character of the scenery is less than that of the White Mountains, but it has impressive subtlety and repose." Olmstead showed a bit of prescience when he continued: "these mountains would be more pleasurable to ramble over than the White Mountains, and will probably, when railroads are completed in this neighborhood, be much resorted to for pleasure." Indeed, scenic tourism in the region benefited greatly when railroads penetrated the area in the late nineteenth century. By the early part of the twentieth century scenic tourism came to be seen by many communities in the South as the great economic panacea that would finally bring the region into the nation's economic mainstream.[6]

No development in the region spurred scenic tourism more than the arrival of the automobile. As the price of automobiles plummeted, ownership soared in the late teens and twenties. Indeed, the number of registered automobiles in the South increased from approximately 25,000 in 1915 to 146,000 in 1920. Along with this increase motorists demanded improvements in the abysmal roads of the region. Indeed, during the 1920s good roads became one of the primary political and civic issues in the region. Historian Francis B. Simkins called good roads the "third god in the trinity of Southern progress," an issue accorded the same enthusiasm as educational and industrial projects.[7]

Scenic tourism promotion and development went hand-in-hand with the regional drive for good roads. Local, state, and regional automobile clubs promoted scenic tourism as actively as they promoted good roads. By the 1920s the "pneumatic hegira"—as historian Howard Preston has termed it—was on in the South as automobile tourists flooded the newly built or improved roads. Although many headed to Florida, which experienced the greatest boom, others sought different scenic and recreational locations.[8]

Perhaps no scenic destination in the South is more intimately connected to the automobile than the Great Smoky Mountains National Park. Park boosters firmly believed that the establishment of a national park in the region would attract hordes of tourists and bring good roads. In 1924, just as boosters began to promote the park idea, the Knoxville Sentinel argued, "With the establishment of a national park in the Appalachian region, roads would be built and maintained by the government, thus eliminating drawbacks offered motoring tourists."[9] Automobile clubs on both sides of the Smokies lined up early in support of the park movement. The East Tennessee Automobile Club (ETAC) played an especially active role in the park movement, shared office space with the principle park booster organization, the Great Smoky Mountains Conservation Association, and even had the same board of directors. Russell Hanlon, secretary-manager of the ETAC, asserted: "It was often difficult to determine which group was meeting."[10]

Park boosters were encouraged in their thinking by the National Park Service itself. Since its establishment in 1916, the Park Service had struggled for funding and recognition. The Park Service's first director, Stephen

Mather, and his chief aide, Horace Albright, believed that making the national parks as accessible as possible would increase visitation and help create
a secure place in the American consciousness for the parks. Earlier, Mather
and Albright worked with western railroads to promote visitation to the
parks through the "See America First" campaign. In the 1920s, with the increased popularity of the automobile, the Park Service actively promoted
automobile tourism to the parks and built increasing numbers of roads and
roadside attractions into the marquee parks of Yellowstone, Yosemite, and the
Grand Canyon. Indeed, these roads in the national parks helped bring the
term scenic drive into the national vocabulary. At Yosemite, the National
Park Service promoted the ultimate experience for the modern tourist: driving their automobile through the Wawona Tunnel Tree, a tunnel carved
through a living giant Sequoia. The Park Service also kept close track and
widely publicized the resultant dramatic growth in visitation and the economic benefits that accrued to surrounding communities.[11]

This message was not lost on park boosters in East Tennessee and Western
North Carolina. As a result, Knoxville and Asheville tourism boosters, who
were responsible for raising a good deal of the money to purchase park land,
developed a distinct vision for what a Great Smoky Mountains National Park
would bring to the surrounding region. Indeed, the boosters saw the preservation of the Smokies as a means to bring millions of tourists to the region,
good roads, increased publicity, and even greater industrial development.
Knoxville booster Cowan Rodgers declared during the fund-raising campaign that if a national park was established in the Great Smoky Mountains,
"millions will annually come through our gates and scatter the golden shekels
in our midst." The *Asheville Citizen* touted the potential park as a "modern
combination of Aladdin's Wonderful Lamp, the touch of Midas, the Magic
Urn, and the weaving of straw into gold by Rumpelstiltskin."[12]

The key to unlock this treasure trove for park boosters was roads, and in
the early days of development in the Smokies, boosters had the full support
of the National Park Service. Park Service director Horace Albright expressed traditional Park Service policy on roads in the Smokies in a 1931
letter: "I view my future obligations in the development of that park with a
great appreciation of the serious responsibilities involved to protect and guard
as much wilderness as possible, at the same time making it reasonably accessible for the motorist. We may have to concede it a fact that by far the greatest number of people will see what they are permitted to see of this glorious
mountain country from their motor car, and not by horseback or hiking. At

any rate we will have to plan ahead for the enjoyment of the park by those who are not as strong and agile as you and I, for they too are entitled to their inspiration and enjoyment."[13]

The Park Service also faced political pressure to build roads to provide employment, especially as emergency funds became available from the federal government through the New Deal. J. R. Eakin pointed this out to Albright in 1932 in discussing a movement launched by the Asheville Chamber of Commerce to build a skyline highway the entire length of the park. "I believe the Tennessee and North Carolina delegations in Congress will line up solidly behind this movement [road construction in the park] for things are in a bad plight in this country, as elsewhere."[14]

One of the great triumphs for park boosters came with the completion in 1930 of a transmountain highway, the so-called Indian Gap Highway (although it actually passes over Newfound Gap). Although significant portions of this highway—now U.S. Highway 441—had to be reconstructed later due to the haste with which the states of North Carolina and Tennessee pushed the road through, boosters hailed its completion. The culmination of the highway project especially provoked enthusiasm at the two gateway communities, Gatlinburg, Tennessee, and Cherokee, North Carolina.[15]

With the completion of the Indian Gap Highway, boosters now looked to the Park Service to begin construction of their dream road, a skyline drive running the length of the park east to west. The simple fact that the Park Service had already begun and had almost completed a similar scenic drive in the Smokies' sister park, Shenandoah, caused many boosters to believe such a road was theirs by right. While the Park Service made it clear that the area east of the Indian Gap Highway would remain a wilderness with no paved roads, they did not oppose the idea of a skyline drive through the western end of the park from Newfound Gap to Deals Gap. Park superintendent J. R. Eakin, in particular, was a staunch supporter of the project. Eakin believed that the construction of a skyline drive in Shenandoah had created a "precedent from which we cannot escape, even if we desired to do so."[16]

However, park boosters did not count on a new group of wilderness advocates who, though small in number, were beginning actively and vociferously to oppose such projects. Indeed, as Park Service plans to build the skyline drive became public, opposition from proponents of wilderness preservation began to mount. Harris Reynolds, Secretary of the Massachusetts Forestry Association, wrote to the Park Service warning them that "we must retain at all costs some real wilderness areas or our eastern parks will become merely enlarged municipal parks." The Executive Board of the Izaak Walton League passed a resolution against any road building in the higher elevations of the Smokies. Harlan Kelsey, a member of the Southern Appalachian National Park Commission, pleaded with Albright: "There are plenty of national parks and state parks where the herd instinct can be fully satisfied but for God's sake let's keep our national parks, so far as we can, in a truly wild state."[17]

The most vociferous and important opponent to the skyline drive, however, was Knoxville lawyer and clerk of the U.S. Circuit Court of Appeals Harvey Broome. A native of the region who had made frequent hiking and camping trips into the Smokies, Broome had recently returned to Knoxville after living in Chicago. He immediately threw himself into the park movement and the activities of the Smoky Mountains Hiking Club. However, his vision of what a national park in the Smokies would look like differed dramatically from those of his compatriots in the park movement and even in the hiking club. In 1931 Broome wrote to Horace Albright expressing his views on the skyline drive and on general park development:

> Frankly, I think the automobiles rob us of our sensitivities and powers of appreciation. People (I admit there are exceptions) who expect to see the mountains from a car have no conception of the irresistible appeal to others of a leisured walk thru these vastnesses, far from the noise and impact of the machine world. Why great areas of this region should be thus seared and blighted by roads upon the demand of those who will never know what true appreciation is, and who do not know what they ask of those who love the mountains and who love to pit their strength and emotions and souls against their challenge, I do not understand. Must we yield to the cheap, when the vision of the better thing for man is clear? Many writers are of the opinion that the machine age is but a passing phase in the movement of civilization. Do those who believe that and who are entrusted with the exploitation of one of the grandest, most exquisite and spiritually refreshing areas, trust their vision and dare to stand out against the popular clamor?[18]

Despite Broome's passion, he remained a lone local voice of opposition for a number of years, often considered a genial crank by park boosters.

The Park Service moved quickly to answer these critics. Park Service assistant director Arno Cammerer responded that those not thoroughly acquainted with the situation had stirred up rumors. Reflecting his pro-development biases, he argued that the road would not follow the crest of the mountains except to the proposed observation area at Clingman's Dome, but would be built from gap to gap and would not include the eastern part of the park. He further asserted that the Park Service sought to develop the national parks for the "health and enjoyment of the people, not only for the young and husky . . . but also that the elderly people, the infirm and growing children may enjoy the hidden wonders of the park."[19]

In late 1932 and early 1933 the Park Service plan received some important endorsements. Both the National Parks Association and the locally influential Smoky Mountains Hiking Club voiced their approval. Harvey Broome provided the only dissenting vote on the board of directors of the hiking club. Even Harlan Kelsey came to consider the skyline drive project unavoidable and even necessary. In early 1933 the construction of a skyline drive through the western part of the park seemed inevitable.[20]

In 1934, however, Harvey Broome formed an important alliance with Benton MacKaye, the father of the Appalachian Trail, who had moved from his home in Massachusetts to work for the Tennessee Valley Authority in Knoxville. The two discussed development problems in the Smokies and began to map strategy on how they could prevent the skyline drive and other "improvement" activities in the park. In October 1934, Bob Marshall, Director of Forestry for the Bureau of Indian Affairs and the strongest advocate for wilderness protection in the Department of the Interior, visited Knoxville to address a meeting of the American Forestry Association (AFA). In his speech Marshall condemned the idea of the skyline drive, "Since the forest land in this country is very limited, it is necessary to establish recreation priorities in the use of the forests so that the most precious values will not be wiped out by secondary or even trivial uses which could be enjoyed in other environments."[21]

On an outing to visit a Civilian Conservation Corps (CCC) camp in the Smokies during the AFA meeting, Marshall, MacKaye, Broome, and Bernard and Miriam Frank began an intense conversation about the importance of wilderness preservation and the dangers to wilderness that roads posed. The discussion became so intense that they pulled off the road and there on the shoulder began to outline and organize "the first national organization devoted solely to the preservation of wilderness." The roads issue in the national parks, particularly Great Smoky Mountains, became the focal point for this important new movement. The group enlisted the aid of other like-minded people, including Aldo Leopold, Harold Anderson, and Robert Sterling Yard. In January 1935, these men and women and two others came together to establish the Wilderness Society, to fight in an organized manner such projects as the skyline drive. In an article on the society, Broome explained its mission: "It is to preserve these remaining areas, where natural creation in its pure state yet be observed and its potencies felt, that the Wilderness Society is formed. It purposes to arrest the encroachment of man's world upon the natural, and to take steps to set aside areas, variant in size and use, but alike in their freedom from intrusions such as roads, radios, overdone trails, transmission lines and other manifestations of the machine age." Broome, and his Wilderness Society cohorts, had now set themselves on a collision course with tourism boosters over development in the park.[22]

Although it would take years for much of the American public to heed the call made by the Wilderness Society, Secretary of the Interior Harold Ickes became an important early convert to the cause of wilderness protection. Even though Ickes spent most of his adult life as an urban reformer in Chicago, he quickly came to develop an appreciation of the value of wilderness. On a 1934 trip to Yosemite Ickes mused: "One should get away once in a while as far as possible from human contacts. To contemplate nature, magnificently garbed as it is in this country, is to restore peace to the mind."[23]

Ickes sent Bob Marshall on a trip to investigate the skyline drive in the spring of 1935. In a memo to Ickes, Marshall argued that "a skyline drive, or additional fraction of it would be indefensible." He further reflected this new thinking on national park development by asserting "that it will be much easier to convert a wild area into a developed one in the future than wipe out development and restore wilderness."[24]

The skyline drive idea died hard, however, as Cammerer, now director of the Park Service, encouraged Ickes to visit the site of the proposed road to judge the merits of the project. Cammerer reminded Ickes that elimination of the skyline drive project would handicap the work of a number of CCC camps in the park. He further advised Ickes that the road and trail program had received the approval of the Smoky Mountains Hiking Club, the Potomac Appalachian Club, and the Appalachian Trail Conference.[25]

Cammerer's appeal went unheeded, however, as Ickes pronounced the death knell for the skyline drive venture in September 1935 at a state park authorities meeting. At the same time he helped usher in a new era for the National Park Service and its relationship to wilderness: "I am not in favor of building any more roads in the National Parks than we have to build. . . .

This is an automobile age, but I do not have much patience with people whose idea of enjoying nature is dashing along a hard road at fifty or sixty miles per hour. I am not willing that our beautiful areas ought to be opened up to people who are either too old to walk, as I am, or too lazy to walk, as a great many young people are who ought to be ashamed of themselves. I do not happen to favor the scarring of a wonderful mountainside just so we can say we have a skyline drive. It sounds poetical, but it may be an atrocity."[26]

The death of the skyline drive marked an important early victory for this new group of wilderness advocates. Their voice had been heard at the highest levels of the federal government and they succeeded in stopping a road project backed by local tourism boosters and by the National Park Service itself. The efforts of the Wilderness Society combined with the lean budget years during World War II kept road projects on the back burner in the Smokies for the next decade or so, but the push for roads in the park would not end with this one defeat.

Tourism boosters and the Park Service were stunned by the defeat. However, the early success of the Smokies in attracting tourists, the rapid growth and development of the gateway communities of Gatlinburg, Tennessee, and Cherokee, North Carolina, and the completion of construction of a portion of the skyline drive before opposition mounted—from Newfound Gap to Clingman's Dome—temporarily quieted their displeasure.

Indeed, with the completion of the Indian Gap Highway in 1932, East Tennessee and Western North Carolina stood poised to reap the economic benefits that the park boosters had promised. The two gateway communities of Gatlinburg, Tennessee, and Cherokee, North Carolina, almost immediately experienced a tourist and development boom even in the midst of the Great Depression and World War II. Gatlinburg's population increased from seventy-five residents in 1930 to nearly 1,300 in 1940. TVA reported growth from ninety-three permanent structures in the Gatlinburg town limits in 1934 to 641 in 1942. Local entrepreneur Rellie Maples, like many other Gatlinburg business promoters, prospered tremendously during the period. Maples's first successful enterprise was the Gatlinburg Inn, built in the late 1930s. He later added the Log Cabin Sandwich Shop to his empire and helped organize and became the first president of the Gatlinburg First National Bank in 1951.[27]

Although Cherokee grew at a slower pace, it too prospered as tourists flocked to the Smokies. The purchase and development of the Boundary Tree area by the Cherokee Tribal Council in the late 1940s and the opening of the outdoor drama "Unto These Hills" in 1950 brought a flood of visitors to the shops, restaurants, and motels of the reservation. Indeed, in its first season, "Unto These Hills" attracted 107,140 viewers.[28]

By the 1950s, the Smokies had become what historian Margaret Brown has called a "drive-in wilderness." The elbow grease supplied by the CCC made Highway 441 and the Little River Road—constructed along the old railroad bed of the Little River Railroad—the very models of the scenic drive in a national park. One writer declared, "lined with countless varieties of trees, shrubs, and flowers, [the roads] lead along beautiful streams with lovely waterfalls, through cool shadowed gorges, virgin forests, and fertile valleys." The addition of the Cades Cove Loop Road provided an additional motoring attraction with a pastoral setting of level open fields framed by the craggy peaks of the Smokies. The beauty of the Smokies was that one never had to leave the confines of one's car in order to experience this "nature," this "wilderness." To be sure, few strayed far from their automobiles and the numerous park overlooks as only an estimated 6 percent of park visitors actually hiked a trail. That said, the park effectively fulfilled the dreams of its booster progenitors. By 1956 the tourist attractions of Gatlinburg and Cherokee, combined with the natural beauty of the Smokies, attracted an estimated 2.5 million visitors annually.[29]

Because of the limitations on roads in the Smokies, however, other surrounding counties and towns did not experience the same benefits. Indeed, for counties such as Blount and Cocke in Tennessee, and Haywood, Swain, and Graham in North Carolina, the park often proved more of a curse than a blessing. Each of these counties lost sizable amounts of land from their tax rolls as a result of park land purchases and saw little in the way of tourist traffic or tourist money to compensate for their loss.[30]

No county was harder hit than Swain County, which received triple blows to its tax base between 1925 and 1943 when almost 75 percent of its land went into the federal domain and was lost to possible tax revenue. In 1925 Cherokee tribal lands in the county were removed from the tax rolls when the federal government assumed trusteeship over the tribe. In the 1930s the county lost almost half of its land to the Great Smoky Mountains National Park. In the 1940s the county lost another sizable chunk of its land to the Tennessee Valley Authority for the construction of the Fontana Dam and the subsequent flooding of the valley behind the dam. TVA purchased an additional 44,000 acres of Swain County land and then transferred ownership to the National Park Service when the impoundment of water flooded North

Carolina Highway 228, effectively cutting off the north shore of Fontana Lake and an estimated two thousand inhabitants. All in all, Swain County lost over 150,000 acres from its tax rolls, land valued for tax purposes in the 1940s at over $4 million.[31]

Residents of these counties, and in particular Swain County, have been vociferous in demanding new roads that they hoped would route tourists through their counties and allow them the same type of opportunities offered to Gatlinburg and Cherokee. Indeed, since the dedication of the park in 1940, hardly a year has gone by without the introduction of a new road project by local boosters or the revival of an old one. The longest lived of these ventures, the so-called North Shore Road, had its genesis in 1943 when the National Park Service and the Tennessee Valley Authority signed an agreement with Swain County, North Carolina, and the state of North Carolina. The federal government promised to build a thirty-seven-mile road replacing the inundated North Carolina Highway 228. The road, connecting Bryson City and Fontana Dam, would be built in exchange for the land between the park boundary and Fontana Lake. The Park Service promised that construction on the road would begin "as soon as funds are made available by Congress after the war."[32]

Progress on the promised road, however, proved excruciatingly slow for Swain County residents. Shortages of funds and labor during World War II prevented much work early on. By 1949, the Park Service had only completed a one-mile, dirt access road from Fontana Dam to a few cemeteries. Frustrated by the delays, Bryson City attorney T. D. Bryson and Congressman Monroe Redden demanded that the federal government either build the road immediately or return the north shore land to the county. When this failed to provoke a response, Redden introduced a bill into Congress to return the land to the county as "Congress will perhaps never appropriate that much money [an estimated $10,000,000] for this purpose; certainly not in the foreseeable future will this be done." The hopes of Swain Countians, however, flagged when the bill died in committee.[33]

In the 1950s, the North Carolina State Highway Commission improved and paved a number of existing roads in Swain and neighboring Graham County, effectively connecting Bryson City with Fontana Dam with North Carolina Highway 28 (also called the south shore road). The construction of this new road, then, fulfilled the intent of the agreement made in 1943, to replace North Carolina Highway 228 and connect Bryson City to Fontana Dam, at least from the perspective of the National Park Service. Park

Service official William Zimmer asserted in an internal memo that "the proposed Bryson City-Fontana Road is an unjustifiable extravagance, notwithstanding the existing iron-bound three-way agreement." For many opponents of the north shore road project, North Carolina Highway 28 made the "iron-bound agreement" anachronistic. Environmentalist Henry Wilson pointed this out to Secretary of the Interior Stewart Udall in a 1962 letter: "I am all for the sanctity of contract but many years ago the government agreed to maintain a cavalry troop in Bryson City to defend against Indian attacks, would it still feel compelled to do so?" In addition, Park Service officials argued that the state of North Carolina had not built a road providing access to the park boundary from Bryson City so any construction within the park would be difficult and useless until the state built such a route.[34]

Swain Countians dug in their heels, however, and continued to demand that the federal government fulfill its obligations. Although most individuals would have made little in the way of distinction between the north shore road and the south shore road, civic and business leaders in Swain County did. Most importantly, for these people, Highway 28 ran primarily through Graham County, while the promised replacement of Highway 228 would run entirely through Swain. Indeed, as historian Stephen Taylor has argued, the new road did not "satisfy the needs" of local politicians or tourist developers. Although they knew that the property in the national park alongside the north shore road could not be developed, the road "would funnel traffic around the western half of the park directly into Bryson City, where tourist development could proceed and provide a needed injection of revenue."[35]

In the late 1950s and early 1960s, Swain County and the state of North Carolina stepped up their pressure on the National Park Service to honor its commitment. The state constructed a 2-and-½-mile road from Bryson City, which ended at the Park boundary in the late 1950s, at an estimated cost of $400,000. In a scathing September 1960 letter to Secretary of the Interior Fred Seaton, North Carolina Governor Luther Hodges lambasted the Park Service and the Department of the Interior for their failure to build the road in a timely fashion. "I express the firm view that the Department of the Interior has an obligation to give more than lip service to the fulfillment of its contractual agreement." Hodges also responded to road opponents who argued that the road would "despoil a virgin or primeval wilderness," by pointing out that until 1943 the area was populated by considerable numbers of people. The governor continued by refuting the argument that Highway 28 fulfilled the intended function of the north shore road and that the road was no longer needed. Highway 28 "was not constructed nor intended to serve as a major traffic route nor as a substitute for the anticipated north shore road."[36]

In response to this pressure, the Park Service finally began construction on the road in 1960 and in August 1963 opened a 2.5-mile section. However, as construction continued, the Park Service experienced massive difficulties. The rock the roadbed was cut through regularly crumbled, requiring additional expenditures of time and money. Even when the first section of the road was completed landslides plagued the route. Assistant Secretary of the Interior Stanley Cain called attempts to build the road an "engineer's hell." Despite these problems, construction continued and an additional 2.1 miles was completed and opened in July 1965.[37]

Even as the Park Service continued work on the north shore road, National Park Service officials proposed a new idea. As part of the Park Service's "Mission 66" plan—a ten-year program to make the national parks more "user friendly" by improving existing roads, constructing new ones, and upgrading and constructing new visitor facilities—Park superintendent George Fry proposed an alternative to the north shore road. Instead, the Park Service would build a 34.7-mile transmountain highway that would rise from Monteith Branch, climb the upper reaches of Hazel Creek, cross the divide at Buckeye Gap, and descend Miry Ridge, connecting Bryson City with Townsend, Tennessee. In negotiations with Swain County officials in 1964, Fry gained an agreement to substitute the new transmountain road for the one specified in the 1943 agreement. The people of Swain County rejoiced at the prospect of becoming a major park entrance, believing that they would finally reap their fair share of tourist traffic and revenue.[38]

Support for the project quickly began to mount. The director of the National Park Service, George Hartzog, threw his support behind the project and defended the building of the road through an area many considered wilderness. "You can't just order a visitor to get out of his car," he argued, "you have to entice him out of his car. We may be able to show, through motor-nature trails, short nature walks, lookouts, outdoor exhibits, or other methods of interpretation the meaning of wilderness and what it can offer." Western North Carolina congressman Roy Taylor argued that "There is room for abundant wilderness areas and, at the same time, room for another highway to make the park more accessible and enjoyable." North Carolina governor Dan K. Moore added that "The National Park Service, in fulfilling its legal and moral obligations to construct this road, is doing something about dispersing traffic which is now cluttering the highways, and the proposed road would be the least damaging to conservationists." Governor Frank Clement of Tennessee and Knoxville U.S. representative John Duncan also supported the transmountain road and voiced their support in public hearings. Civic and regional booster groups also chimed in. Carlos Campbell, a Knoxville leader in the original park movement and the author of a history of the park's establishment, argued strongly for the road: "Any person who asks that neither road be built clearly indicates, it seems to me, that such a person is either grossly ignorant of the historic background of the controversy or he is asking the Park Service to violate a valid contract, thus asking it to take a position of sheer dishonesty." The three major newspapers in the region—the *Asheville Citizen*, the *Knoxville Sentinel*, and the *Knoxville News*—also endorsed the plan.[39]

However, road boosters had greatly underestimated the strength of the growing environmental movement. Those few individuals who had pulled off the side of the road in 1934 to make a blueprint for the Wilderness Society had spawned a movement of thousands of committed individuals locally and millions nationally. Indeed, new organizations committed to environmental and wilderness protection were cropping up every day in the wake of the publication of Rachel Carson's *Silent Spring* and the passage of the Wilderness Act in 1964. Leading the fight against the road was the familiar figure of Harvey Broome, now president of the Wilderness Society. He was joined in the fight by his friend and fellow member of the Smoky Mountains Hiking Club, Ernie Dickerman. Dickerman argued, "You can't build a road through the wilderness and still have a wilderness—the two things are incompatible."[40]

The Wilderness Society issued an S.O.S.—"Save Our Smokies"—to its 35,000 members and to the nation at large. It called on people who cared about wilderness either to attend one of the two hearings on the road or to register their opposition to Fry. At a public hearing in Gatlinburg on June 13, 1966, the Wilderness Society, Trout Unlimited, the Smoky Mountains Hiking Club, the Izaak Walton League, the National Parks Association, the Wildlife Federation, the Appalachian Trail Club, the Sierra Club, and Supreme Court Justice William O. Douglas all voiced their disfavor. Dickerman also was able to generate a substantial show of opposition two days later at a hearing in the heart of the enemy camp, Bryson City. Representatives from the Carolina Mountain Club, Carolina Bird Club, the Georgia Appalachian Trail Club, Defenders of Wildlife, and several area college professors expressed their belief that the road was a bad idea. Dr. Dan Hale—a NASA physicist from Huntsville, Alabama—called the transmountain road a "colossal boondoggle" and delineated the reasons he believed Swain County had already been compensated for their lost road. A college student who had traveled from Rochester, New York, reminded the crowd that the Great Smoky Mountains National Park "did not belong to North Carolinians or Tennesseeans but rather to all Americans." He cautioned that "the tourist dollar should not override the interests of a majority of Americans." The *New York Times* even chimed in with an editorial arguing that "Slashing and tunneling through the last mountain wilderness in the East is a destructive solution to a local economic problem."[41]

Road supporters attempted to counter the arguments of environmentalists. An editorial in the *Asheville Citizen* ridiculed their concerns: "Certainly if civilization is to salvage anything of value from its headlong extravagance, it ought to save a few places where man can go to contemplate his idiocy. But preservation for the mere sake of isolation—preservation as an idealistic concept—amounts to indulging a pointless whim." While many Swain Countians dismissed road opponents as "wilderness creeps," Velma Benton offered a more plaintive response in the "Backtalk" section of the *Citizen:* "It would be a shame if the government said 'Forget about it [the commitment to build the road], it is only a contract.' Me, I am just a widow with a 14-year-old daughter, but I have a contract with the government as my daughter and I get Social Security. I feel if the government could just up and break one contract they could break any contract." Park Superintendent Fry argued that the area of concern was not a "true wilderness" as it had been "logged over and burned over." He further asserted that environmentalists should not be concerned as the road "would largely follow natural contours and traverse the park in such a way as to avoid undue damage to superlative park values."[42]

Opponents of the road once again found a sympathetic ear in the Secretary of the Interior, this time Stewart Udall. The year before he entered office, Udall declared, "the one overriding principle of the conservation movement is that no work of man (save the bare minimum of roads, trails, and necessary public facilities in access areas) should intrude into the wonder places of the National Park System." In the Buckeye Gap area of the park, site of the proposed road, Broome discovered and documented such a wonder place, the southernmost stands of red spruce in North America. Armed with this information, Broome and Dickerman energized the local community

and wilderness proponents nationwide to voice their opposition in a protest hike. On October 23, 1966, 576 individuals, including the eighty-one-
year-old Reverend Rufus Morgan, signed in at Clingman's Dome to participate in a "Save-Our-Smokies" hike. Much to the dismay of Swain County
residents—and many in Blount County, Tennessee—Secretary Udall announced on December 10, 1967, that he would not approve construction of
the transmountain road.[43]

While the transmountain road idea had been effectively buried, the north
shore road issue, however, was far from dead and showed significant signs of
life on regular occasions. In the late 1970s Swain Countians tried a new approach to gain public support in their effort to get the road completed. A
group known as the North Shore Cemetery Association intensified pressure
on the Park Service to honor the 1943 commitment, arguing that the construction of the road was necessary to give them proper access to family and
community cemeteries on the north shore. The group found its champion in
U.S. senator Jesse Helms. Helms effectively blocked legislation on several occasions that would have designated land in the park, including the north
shore area, as federally protected wilderness. Such legislation would have prevented any additional road construction in the area. Although one part of
the legislation included an offer to pay Swain County up to $16 million to
give up its claim to the road, the county has refused. Adding a new ally in
western North Carolina's Republican congressman Charles Taylor, Helms
has introduced bills on several occasions calling for the cash settlement plus
construction of the road, even if it is only a jeep road.[44]

The bitterness of Swain County residents and the desire to get something
out of the 1943 agreement with the Park Service was understandable. This
bitterness also points to a serious class division that emerges in such controversies. As residents of one of the poorest counties in North Carolina, Swain
Countians were understandably irked by the opposition of environmentalists
—whom they often perceive as upper-middle-class outsiders—to the fulfillment of a binding and even sacred promise by the federal government. In
1984 the Reverend Clarence O. Vance explained in a guest editorial in the
Asheville Citizen the meaning of the road to many county residents: "I remember the excitement at the building of the roads [section of north shore
road built in the early 60s] in Bryson City, Swain County and over North
Carolina. The editor of the local *Smoky Mountain Times* carried many articles
and editorials of what the building of the road would mean to that area and
the state. We then would have a park entrance like that on the Tennessee

side." Vance then posed a series of pointed questions to those who opposed road construction: "What of the promises made to us years ago? What of the lonely graves of our loved ones and friends? What of the needed economy which the road would have brought to Bryson City, Swain County and all of North Carolina, and would still mean to us?"[45]

The Park Service remained determined to resist construction of the road because of both environmental and economic reasons. Environmental concerns centered on the potential exposure by road construction of acidic Anakeesta rock found in the north shore area. Park Service officials feared that exposure of this rock would leach acid and heavy metals into area streams, killing aquatic life. They were also concerned about the negative impact on wildlife, particularly bears, whose habitat would be divided and reduced by the road. The expense of building such a road also became increasingly prohibitive, especially given Park Service budget cutbacks in the 1980s and '90s. Recently the Park Service estimated the cost of completing the road at $136 million.[46]

As the new millennium dawned, the parties remained at a standoff, with neither the Park Service nor supporters of the road such as the North Shore Cemetery Association, Citizens Against Wilderness in Western North Carolina, and Senator Helms willing to budge on the issue. However, Helms and U.S. representative Charles Taylor have succeeded in keeping the pot boiling, especially during election years. In the face of a bitter fight for re-election in 2000, Taylor used his influence as a member of the appropriations committee and Helms's influence in the Senate to slip in a $16 million appropriation for the road. Once again the hopes of Swain County residents were sparked. Road supporter Linda Hogue responded to the announcement with a "Hallelujah. It's about time. I think it is wonderful."[47]

Ironically, this announcement came at a time when Swain County began to actually benefit and attract tourists based on an image that highlights the area as the antithesis of the traffic, congestion, cheap tourist traps, outlet malls, go-cart tracks, and gambling of Cherokee, Gatlinburg, and Pigeon Forge. Increasing numbers of people are attracted to the outdoor recreational opportunities that Swain County affords, such as rafting and kayaking on the Nantahala River, mountain biking on the world famous Tsali Trail, tubing on Deep Creek, fishing and water sports on Fontana Lake, and hiking and backpacking in the Great Smoky Mountains. Bryson City is also one of the principle embarkation points for the Smoky Mountains Railroad, which annually attracts thousands of tourists who take the scenic train rides through the Tuckaseegee and Nantahala River gorges. Indeed, the construction of the north shore road would likely alienate many of the very outdoor recreationalists who have become the foundation of the county's economy. An editorial in the *Asheville Citizen* recently noted, "a road that does serious damage to the park would not be a boon but a setback to a Swain economy increasingly dependent on tourism."[48]

The road controversies in the Great Smoky Mountains point to many of the quandaries faced by communities throughout the South who base their economies on scenic tourism. Places scattered throughout the South, including the Outer Banks of North Carolina, the Sea Islands of Georgia, the Florida Keys, and countless communities in the Ozarks and the Southern Appalachian region face many of the same conflicts and dilemmas.

If the history of these controversies illustrates anything it is this essential tension between tourist development and the preservation of nature. While it is important to acknowledge this tension, it is also important for both tourism boosters and environmentalists to recognize their mutual interests. Tourism boosters need to recognize that if tourism is going to be a renewable and constant economic resource, they must pay close attention to preservation of the scenery that attracts those visitors. Too much access can lead to the destruction of the resource. As environmentalist Aldo Leopold observed in his classic work *A Sand County Almanac:* "When enough have seen and fondled there is no wildness left to cherish."[49] At the same time, environmentalists must realize that the people who live in these communities, especially in the South, depend on tourist visitors for their economic survival. Environmentalists need to work with communities to help them see the economic benefits that can come to them from preservation and wise and controlled development. They also need to be cognizant of and sensitive to the class and cultural divides that often make communication between the two sides difficult. Compromise and sensitivity are essential elements if communities are going to balance and even resolve the conflict between tourist development and preservation of the environment. Communities across the South that fail to do this will find the conflict never ending and, indeed, like the folks of Swain County, will find themselves on a "road to nowhere."

10
Atlanta's Olympics and the Business of Tourism

Harvey K. Newman

In July 1996, Atlanta hosted the Centennial Summer Olympic Games, an event that was without doubt the largest undertaking in the city's history. The goal of civic leaders was to promote Atlanta's image as an international city ready to play an important role in global commerce. In hosting the Olympics, Atlanta's public- and private-sector officials used tourism as part of their global economic development strategy. Visitors from around the world were welcomed to the city as a place to come, visit, and do business. Understanding how Atlanta's leaders came to use the Olympic Games as a means of promoting urban growth must begin with a look at the business of tourism and the city's growth.

The town that came to be known as Atlanta was formed at the crossroads of a system of railroads in Georgia. As soon as the rail line connecting Augusta with the new town was completed in 1845, local residents realized the need for a hotel to serve visitors arriving by train and also railroad employees. Within two months the city's first hotel, the Washington Hall, welcomed travelers to stay in its eight bedrooms and enjoy meals served "in time for cars and stages."[1] This established the connection between transportation and the business of providing hospitality for tourists that has continued throughout the city's history.

Nothing was inevitable about Atlanta's rise from a small rail junction to a major metropolis. Simply having the technology of the intersecting rail lines in place did not guarantee that Atlanta would grow beyond a modest town with need for little more than a store and blacksmith shop. Characteristics that made Atlanta distinctive emerged repeatedly in the city's history. First, there were the aspirations of local leaders. As Bradley Rice has shown, the city's business and political leaders initially wanted Atlanta to become the most important city in the state, and by 1867 Atlanta eclipsed its older rivals to become the state capital. The next generation of leaders aspired for their town to become a major regional metropolis, and by the end of the nineteenth century Atlanta had accomplished this objective. By 1925, Atlantans set their sights on becoming a major national city, but the depression and World War II slowed down the accomplishment of this goal until the decade of the 1960s. Then, in 1971 the new agenda proclaimed by Atlanta's mayor set the city's sights on becoming "the worlds next great international city."[2] For many in Atlanta the hosting of the 1996 Centennial Olympic Games was a fulfillment of this latest claim as the city once again pushed itself up the next rung on the municipal ladder. Tourism was important in the achievement of each of these objectives as business and political leaders worked together in partnership to promote Atlanta as a good destination.

During the nineteenth century, Atlantans hosted a series of three expositions, in 1881, 1887, and 1895, that showcased the town as a place for investment in textile manufacturing. The best known of these expositions, the 1895 Cotton States and International Exposition, served notice to the nation that Atlanta wished to be at the center of a New South. The vision of the city's leaders included a recognition that Northern investment capital was needed to bring factories to the region and reduce the dependence on cotton production as the staple crop on which the southern economy depended. To accomplish this objective the organizers of the exposition tried to show that Atlanta was different from other places in the South. First, they wanted to proclaim an end to the sectional rivalries that had divided North and South. States such as New York, Pennsylvania, and Massachusetts, which had once been regarded as enemy territory, were welcomed to the exposition as they provided buildings with exhibits promoting commerce between the regions. Next, the 1895 exposition also included a Negro Building with exhibits designed to highlight the progress of blacks in the New South. Another bold step was to have Dr. Booker T. Washington give an address at the opening ceremony of the exposition. Although other black leaders such as W. E. B. Du Bois criticized Washington's remarks as he accepted segregation in return for economic progress, the mere presence of the "Sage of Tuskeegee" as an exposition speaker served to highlight differences between Atlanta and other cities in the South. Finally, the 1895 exposition showed that Atlantans were willing to embrace business and commerce rather than continue the reliance on agriculture characteristic of the antebellum South. In hosting the exposition, Atlanta showed its desire to imitate Chicago and the success of its 1893 Columbian Exposition. As Chicago showed the world it had recovered from the devastation of the 1871 fire, Atlanta also demonstrated that, like its official symbol the phoenix, the city had risen in splendor from its ashes. The Cotton States and International Exposition was an important nineteenth-century example of Atlantans using tourism to promote the growth of their city.

Atlanta's business and political leaders also used the convention business to promote the city. As early as 1885, the city hosted its first national convention. With its convenient rail access, businessmen such as Ivan Allen, Sr., recognized the potential for this form of tourism as a means of economic development. As an early-twentieth-century head of the Chamber of Commerce, Allen organized the Atlanta Convention Bureau in 1912, making it among the oldest in the nation. From the outset, the business of hosting conventions reflected a partnership between the public and private sectors. Business leaders from the Chamber would identify organizations that were looking for a site for their meetings. The name of the group was given to the governor and the mayor who would write letters of invitation to the organization promising the warmth of southern hospitality in the city. The public sector contributed in several other important ways by providing an early version of a convention center in the city's municipal auditorium that opened in 1909. With a recommendation from the city council's standing Committee on Auditorium and Conventions, the city government gave financial support to host large conventions that were likely to have a sizable economic impact. The council also provided funds to illuminate Peachtree Street at night to form the "Great White Way" for convention visitors and residents to stroll and shop along the city's most important commercial street. The hotels, restaurants, theaters, and shops along Peachtree formed a separate tourist space that would continue to be important for the city throughout the twentieth century. This designation of a segregated space for tourist activity had both class and racial implications. It was designed to appeal to middle- and upper-class whites, leaving out African Americans and working-class whites.

During the nineteenth century, Atlanta and other southern cities enforced segregation of the races by custom, and early in the twentieth century this pattern was reenforced by law. Local laws passed during the first decade of the new century required restaurants, hotels, bars, and amusements to post signs declaring which race they served. While Peachtree Street was the major commercial area for whites, blacks were increasingly segregated into small commercial areas located near residential concentrations along Auburn Avenue, Decatur Street, and on the city's west side near Atlanta University Center. Restricted by Jim Crow laws, enterprising blacks developed a separate set of tourist businesses serving not only African American business travelers but also an increasingly important black convention business. Auburn Avenue had the largest concentration of black businesses; it featured hotels, clubs, restaurants, theaters, and other amusements that catered to a generally more well-to-do class of African Americans than the Decatur Street area, which served a working-class black clientele. Even though Atlanta was the headquarters of the Ku Klux Klan following its revival in 1915, the city's African American tourism businesses recruited conventions with the same fervor as their white counterparts. For example, in 1920, the local chapter of the National Association for the Advancement of Colored People (NAACP) hosted the national meeting of the organization with W. E. B. Du Bois as the featured speaker. The city's white officials would welcome black conventions to Atlanta and on occasion even desegregate public parks that were restricted for use only by whites, allowing African American convention visitors to use the facilities before closing them to blacks after the group left town.

The pattern of segregation in the city's convention business continued until challenged as part of the struggles of the civil rights movement of the 1960s. Following the example of students in Greensboro, North Carolina, a small group from the Atlanta University Center began to test Atlanta's Jim Crow segregation laws by "sitting in" at lunch counters in downtown. After more than a year of these peaceful demonstrations, the students, political leaders, and business owners reached an agreement to desegregate restaurants and lunch counters in September 1961. Atlanta was the first southern city to take this step toward ending segregation in its tourism businesses. This voluntary agreement did not end all segregation in the city's restaurants, but it showed that Atlanta was attempting to live up to the slogan proclaimed by Mayor William B. Hartsfield that it was "the city too busy to hate."

Atlanta's Convention Bureau officials were in the awkward position of trying to attract national conventions that included both black and white delegates to hotels that were segregated. In November 1961, the local chapter of the NAACP issued a call for the integration of Atlanta's hotels. The Atlanta University Center students were again eager to challenge the status quo, and in March of the following year, staged a "sleep-in." The students made reservations at the Henry Grady Hotel by mail, and when they arrived and were refused rooms, the students announced their intention to sleep in the lobby until the desegregation of the hotel. Faced with this kind of pressure, the Chamber of Commerce issued an appeal to all businesses in the city to integrate so that Atlanta could maintain its healthy climate for business. Eighteen hotels and thirty restaurants responded with a voluntary agreement to end racial segregation in their businesses. While the voluntary agreement was an important step for a southern city, it did not stop some hotels, motels, and restaurants from continuing to discriminate against African Americans. This prompted Atlanta's mayor, Ivan Allen, Jr., to go to Washington, D.C., in the summer of 1963 to testify in support of the proposed federal Civil Rights Act that would require the integration of all public accommodations.

When the Civil Rights Act became the law of the land in 1964, the test cases for the desegregation of both hotels and restaurants came from Atlanta. In both instances federal marshals backed the efforts of the Atlanta University Center students in their attempts to integrate these public accommodations. Hotels, restaurants, amusements, and other convention businesses were now required to serve blacks and whites on equal terms. This was an advantage to the convention industry in Atlanta that had quietly supported voluntary efforts at desegregation. However, an unforeseen consequence of the civil rights act was the end of many African American tourism businesses. As one black community leader expressed it, "We were now free to eat and sleep in their places, but they (whites) did not eat and sleep in ours."[3] Integration had the unintended effect of contributing to the steady decline of the small black-owned hotels, restaurants, and clubs on Decatur Street and Auburn Avenue.

Atlanta's convention-oriented businesses were also changing during the decade of the 1960s. Prior to this decade, most of the city's hospitality businesses were locally owned. With Atlanta able to desegregate its businesses and schools much more peacefully than many other cities in the South, it became an attractive market for national corporate investments. Hotel chains such as Marriott and Holiday Inn invested in downtown properties often located on land cleared by the urban renewal program. In 1967, local architect and developer John Portman opened the Hyatt Regency Hotel as part of his Peachtree Center complex. The revolving blue glass bubble of the Hyatt's cocktail lounge became a landmark on the city's skyline as well as a symbol of the sleek modern image Atlanta's leaders sought to project.

Other signs of national city status also arrived in the form of new sports stadiums and major league franchises in baseball, football, basketball, and hockey. By the end of the decade Mayor Allen declared that Atlanta was more than a regional capital; the city was now a place of national importance. The mayor could point to other important components of the city's tourism industry, such as a new jet-age airport, a new convention center, approval of a referendum for liquor-by-the-drink sales, and plans under way for a rapid transit system. Atlanta's best-known tourist attraction was an area near the railroad tracks under the city's viaducts where residents and visitors alike enjoyed a unique set of shops, restaurants, and clubs known as Underground Atlanta. With these amenities, plus a doubling of the number of hotel rooms in the downtown area since the end of World War II, Atlanta's leaders felt that the city was at last a major league city on a national scale. Tourism played an important part in promoting this growth. In 1960, the city hosted 251 conventions attended by 120,000 participants. Ten years later, Atlanta ranked third, behind New York and Chicago, with the number of conventions hosted at 525, while attendance grew to 420,000.[4] But, with the goal of national prominence achieved, Atlanta's leaders were ready to raise their sights to an even higher rung on the municipal ladder.

The challenge was announced by the newly elected mayor of the city, Sam Massell, who in 1971 proclaimed that Atlanta would be "the next great international city." At the time, the city's claims to international status were modest at best. The name of the airport was changed to Hartsfield International to recognize the single flight to Mexico City, and the city's new convention center was dubbed the Georgia World Congress Center since the facility featured simultaneous translation capability to host international visitors attending such events as the annual textile equipment exhibit known as the Bobbin Show. However, Atlanta's growth as a city was not based on slogans and boosterism alone. It also depended on the hard work of business and political leaders working together in a partnership that has been described as a regime.[5] This traditional partnership was threatened during the decade of the 1970s when Atlanta became a majority African American population and elected its first black mayor, Maynard H. Jackson, in 1973. The mayor angered business leaders during his first term by requiring affirmative action in hiring and minority participation by firms having contracts with the city. After some notable public conflicts, the two sides formed a working relationship during Jackson's second term in office, and the city's new Hartsfield International Airport was completed on time and under budget.

The partnership between business leaders and public officials was renewed by Jackson's successor, former United Nations Ambassador Andrew Young, who was elected in 1981. Learning from Jackson's often-confrontational relationship with Atlanta's mostly white business leaders, Young smoothed relationships with them and used his contacts to promote overseas investment in Atlanta. His globe-trotting style was effective in promoting international investment primarily in real estate. Many of the city's hotels were bought or built with foreign capital during Young's tenure as mayor. Saudi, French, German, Swedish, Swiss, British, and Japanese companies invested in Atlanta hotel properties as a result of the mayor's promotional efforts. Prior to the 1960s, small local companies owned most of the hotels in the city. During the 1960s, national hotel chains established a dominant position in Atlanta's hotel market. Since the 1980s, investments by multinational corporations are increasingly important to all aspects of the city's tourism businesses.

At the urging of the Atlanta Convention and Visitors Bureau (ACVB) and the city's hospitality industry, Mayor Young supported the redevelopment of Underground Atlanta as a festival marketplace. The familiar partnership of business leaders and city hall brought in the Rouse Corporation that had developed and managed similar projects such as Faneuil Hall in Boston and Harborplace in Baltimore. Hospitality industry leaders insisted that the redevelopment of Underground Atlanta was essential to provide evening entertainment for out-of-town visitors. When the project reopened in 1989, more than 80 percent of the $144 million investment came from a variety of public sources representing a substantial public sector contribution to Atlanta's tourism infrastructure. Another major public sector investment to support the city's hospitality businesses was the construction of the Georgia Dome, an enclosed stadium built for the Atlanta Falcons of the National Football League. Young supported the Dome and led the city to join with the county and state governments to acquire land for the stadium even though the project required displacing a low-income black neighborhood and several churches. Opponents of the project were successful in securing relocation assistance for the residents and churches, but the Georgia Dome reminded many city residents of the dislocation caused by urban renewal and expressway construction.

As mayor, Andrew Young used his considerable diplomatic skills to boost the reputation of the city. He helped the ACVB raise $2.5 million to promote Atlanta's convention business with the slogan "Look at Atlanta Now."[6] Of even more significance was the success of the partnership with business leaders in securing high-profile events for the city such as the 1988 Democratic National Convention. The convention focused national and international media coverage on Atlanta as reporters described things about the city as diverse as barbecue and collard greens to strip clubs. The Democratic National Convention also showed how Atlantans continued to use the business of tourism to promote the growth of their city. Preparations for the arrival of the Democrats also gave Atlanta's business and political leaders a rehearsal for an even larger and more important international event.

In 1987, a local real estate attorney and former University of Georgia football player, Billy Payne, conceived the idea of hosting the 1996 Summer Olympic Games. Mayor Young was among the first to join Payne in the quest to develop a bid and to sell the proposal to local business leaders, the U.S. Olympic Committee (USOC), and the members of the International Olympic Committee (IOC), who would eventually make the decision on which city would host the games. None of these audiences proved easy to convince that Atlanta would be the best choice for the event. Even the Coca-Cola Company, with its headquarters in the city and a long-standing tradition of corporate support for the Olympics, was initially reluctant to support Payne and Young's Atlanta bid. However, Payne, who is described as "the hero of the hard sell," joined Young and a handful of other volunteers in winning commitments inside the boardrooms of local corporations and other institutions, so that by April 1988 Atlanta won the approval of the USOC, putting the city into the international competition for the games.[7]

After the success of the 1984 Los Angeles Olympic Games that generated a surplus of $225 million and focused the attention of a global audience estimated at 2.5 billion television viewers on that city, other municipalities have come to see the Olympics as a major stimulus to economic development. For Atlanta's leaders the games offered the opportunity to draw attention to a place with aspirations to be taken seriously as a world city. The Olympics are so large that hosting the event has the potential to reshape a city and its reputation in the world. Such a prize naturally attracts intense competition among localities wishing to host the games. In 1988, there were five other cities vying for the designation as host of the 1996 games, which would be the 100th anniversary of the modern revival of the Olympics. The official bid document for Atlanta consisted of two volumes outlining the city's plans for the venues for the sporting events, financial support, and accommodations for Olympic visitors. Major selling points of the documents were the warmth of southern hospitality and the city's unique heritage as the birthplace of Dr. Martin Luther King, Jr., and as a major center in the civil rights struggle.

The nature and extent of the Atlanta Organizing Committee's informal efforts to win the support of the IOC delegates were not made clear at the time. Billy Payne, Andrew Young, and a small group of volunteers that formed the Organizing Committee traveled the globe to promote the city's bid among the IOC delegates. After individual relationships were formed, IOC members were invited to Atlanta, where they received not only a cordial welcome but also gifts and favors such as playing golf at the home of the Masters tournament in Augusta and shopping trips paid for by the Atlanta Organizing Committee. Atlantans were not alone in attempting to influence the votes of IOC delegates in order to win the rich prize of hosting the Olympics. All together, the six cities competing for the 1996 games are reported to have spent in excess of $100 million to win the prize, with the Atlanta committee spending around $12 million.[8] Mayor Young's influence with the African IOC delegates was considered especially important in winning their support for the city's bid. To do this, Young provided athletic equipment, distributed fifty-six tons of food among thirteen African nations, and promised a training facility in Georgia for African athletes. Many of these gifts were distributed to an influential IOC representative from the Congo who was later expelled after allegations that he accepted bribes in return for his support of Salt Lake City as host of the 2002 winter games.[9]

Other members of the Atlanta bid committee provided favors to IOC delegates that appear, in hindsight, to be illegal or unethical at best. For example, Charlie Battle, an attorney with one of the city's most prestigious law firms, carried a suitcase filled with cash into the United States at the request of a Jamaican IOC delegate.[10] Whether these were favors, gifts, or bribes, the attempt to win IOC votes through lavish gift-giving and entertainment certainly appears to have been the norm among all the cities seeking to host the 1996 Olympics as well as subsequent games. After Atlanta's selection in September 1990, rumors circulated that the city used excessive gifts to influence the favorable vote, but no evidence came to light until documents were released as part of a 1999 congressional investigation into Olympic bidding in the wake of the Salt Lake City scandal.

Following the vote to hold the Olympics in Atlanta, the director of the successful bid effort, Billy Payne, assumed control of the new organization called the Atlanta Committee for the Olympic Games (ACOG) that would prepare for the games. In other Olympic host cities the leadership of the bid committee gave way to a different person in charge of preparing for the event and managing the games. Payne, however, was determined to retain control over the games in spite of efforts by the re-elected Mayor Maynard Jackson to assume leadership. This conflict between two powerful figures was conducted behind closed doors while Jackson and Payne maintained a public display of unity. Payne recognized that the games would not be staged just within the City of Atlanta, but would be a metropolitan and, eventually, a regional event. The white business leadership supported Payne, isolating the city's mayor from trying to use the games as an economic development strategy to help Atlanta's largely black low-income residents. Rather than benefit from the Olympics, many of the decisions made in preparation for the games repeated the patterns of urban renewal: expressway and sports facilities construction sacrificed the interests of Atlanta's low-income neighborhoods.

ACOG insisted that its mandate was to put on the games and not to address the serious social and economic conditions that existed in the city. The organizing committee promised that they would follow the model of the Los Angeles games, which were financed by private corporate support and hence avoided the massive public debt incurred by Montreal in hosting the 1976 Olympics. Unlike Los Angeles, ACOG faced the task of raising money and constructing almost all the venues that would be needed for the 1996 games. The result was an enormous development task that would cost more than $650 million in Olympic-related construction in Atlanta between 1990 and 1996.[11] In spite of repeated assurances that the games would be financed without public support, in fact, the total cost of the Atlanta Olympics from all public sources has been estimated at $1,050,970,000. When the dollars from all sources related to the city's preparations for the games are added together, the estimated impact on the state's economy was $5.14 billion.[12] This massive level of spending would have enormous consequences for the development of the central city and the entire metropolitan area. There were two quite different reactions to ACOG's development plans. Large institutions, such as Georgia Tech, the Atlanta University Center, the University of Georgia, and Stone Mountain State Park, were receptive to Olympic proposals and formed partnerships with Olympic planners to serve their interests as well as ACOG's. In contrast, projects that affected local residents, such as construction of the Olympic Stadium, Centennial Olympic Park, and the Olympic Village, sparked opposition that revived long-standing tensions involving issues of race and class.[13] For instance, ACOG announced its intention to build the Olympic Stadium in the low-income black neighborhood known as Summerhill next to Atlanta-Fulton County Stadium. This neighborhood had already been disrupted by the building of the old stadium on urban renewal land and by the construction of two interstate highways. When the neighborhood protested the location of a second stadium in their community, ACOG refused to change the location but did promise to demolish Atlanta-Fulton County Stadium after the games and reconfigure the Olympic Stadium for the use of the Atlanta Braves baseball team.

Likewise, the Atlanta Housing Authority agreed to the demolition of the Techwood Homes public housing project in order for a portion of the site to be used for construction of the Olympic Village to house athletes during the games. In 1990, when Atlanta was selected to host the games, more than a thousand residents lived in Techwood Homes. Eight years later when a new mixed-income community known as Centennial Place replaced Techwood Homes, fewer than one hundred former tenants were allowed to return. The rest were forced to find other housing located far from downtown and its access to transportation, employment, health care, and other benefits.[14] The Housing Authority also created an Olympic Legacy Program that would convert thirteen other public housing projects into mixed-income communities, greatly reducing the concentration of public housing residents in the city of Atlanta.

But public housing residents were not the only low-income residents affected by Olympic construction. The cleanup of areas around venue sites resulted in the demolition of more than 3,400 substandard houses. While these residents received relocation assistance, most resented the disruptions of moving since they would not be able to return to their old neighborhoods after the games. Some of these losses were offset by the construction of 336 new homes and the rehabilitation of 212 others in six low-income neighborhoods prior to the games.[15] The net loss of homes increased resentment among the city's low-income residents, who saw little benefit from Atlanta's hosting of the Olympics.

Not all of the losses caused by Olympic construction were felt in residential areas. The decision to build Centennial Olympic Park affected an area of warehouses, a few small businesses, and several shelters for the homeless just west of downtown between the Georgia World Congress Center and the headquarters of the Coca-Cola Company. While this was not a venue associated with the games, the clearing of the park land was a benefit to several major corporate sponsors. The city government also hoped that development of the park would spur investment in the area following the Olympics. Centennial Olympic Park proved a popular gathering place for spectators during the games as Coca-Cola, AT&T, and several other corporate sponsors built temporary attractions in the area. Unlike the competition venues, there was no price for admission to the park, so thousands jammed the area during the games, from its opening in the mornings until late at night. ACOG built an Olympic "Fountain of Rings" whose jets of water were choreographed to lights and music. The park's fountain was popular with children and adults as a place to splash and cool off during the hot summer days and nights of the games. AT&T constructed a temporary stage and amphitheater in Centennial Olympic Park for concerts, while other vendors set up a ferris wheel and other rides nearby. The city of Atlanta enhanced the carnival atmosphere by leasing space along sidewalks nearby to vendors in plywood booths selling food, tee-shirts, and trading pins to crowds of Olympic visitors.

ACOG worked with colleges and universities throughout the area to provide sites for the location of many of the competition venues. Georgia Tech received a natatorium for swimming and diving events and had its basketball coliseum enlarged and air conditioned to host boxing matches. The University of Georgia in Athens received an indoor training facility for the volleyball competition and enlarged its football stadium for the Olympic soccer games. At the Atlanta University Center complex, Morris Brown College received a new stadium for field hockey, Morehouse College got a new gymnasium for Olympic basketball, and Clark-Atlanta University had its football stadium renovated for field hockey. Georgia State University received an expansion of its gymnasium to host the badminton event. Georgia State and Georgia Tech also shared use of the Olympic Village as housing constructed for the athletes became dormitories for the two institutions following the games.

Visiting journalists and architects heaped considerable criticism on ACOG for the design of the Olympic venues. The demands of raising money to finance the construction of the needed facilities left little room for architectural virtuosity. ACOG defended its building program, saying that its venues met the program requirements for Olympic competition and were designed for their adaptation for subsequent use. This business-like approach to venue construction was in sharp contrast to the 1992 games in Barcelona, which used its investment in new facilities to build an impressive array of well-designed competition sites.

While ACOG prepared the city for the games, hospitality businesses eagerly awaited the anticipated bonanza from the crowds of Olympic visitors. As a major convention city with a busy airport and the intersection of three interstate highways, Atlanta's bid for the games could boast of the availability of more than fifty thousand hotel rooms in the metropolitan area in 1990. By the time of the games, this number increased to nearly sixty thousand as new hotels opened hoping to attract Olympic guests. More than 80 percent of this hotel capacity was reserved by ACOG for the use of IOC delegates, representatives of the various international sports federations, members of the various national Olympic committees, corporate sponsors, and other dignitaries. Other spaces at a considerable distance from downtown, such as the dormitories at Emory University, were reserved for members of the international press corps. The few remaining hotel rooms were quickly reserved by tour operators and real estate companies. A state law passed in 1994 attempted to prevent price gouging during the games. ACOG arranged for additional accommodations in private homes by establishing a listing service for homeowners to rent their homes to visitors during the Olympics. Many homeowners and some unscrupulous apartment owners fixed up their properties in anticipation of extra income from Olympic visitors, but there was not great demand for rented houses and apartments. Just weeks before the games began, ACOG released some of its reserved hotel rooms, creating an available supply of rooms at the last moment. Throughout the event, ACOG provided accommodations for more than 238,000 guests who stayed over 809,000 room nights in the city during the games.[16]

Other types of tourism businesses also scrambled to open in time for the Olympics. New restaurants were built along Peachtree Street from downtown to Buckhead. Among these were new "themed restaurants" such as the Hard Rock Cafe, Planet Hollywood, and a country-and-western-themed eatery and dance hall. National restaurant chains did not want to miss the opportunity to be in Atlanta in 1996. The more than forty strip clubs in the city also made extensive preparations for the games. While these clubs normally serve the regular convention trade and other visitors to Atlanta, the Olympics would bring large numbers of well-to-do patrons to swell the estimated $200 million annual economic impact of these establishments. While there are normally around four thousand exotic dancers in the city, the possibilities of around-the-clock crowds of Olympic tourists caused club owners to add more performers.[17] The week before the start of the games, lines stretched as long as two blocks around police headquarters as out-of-town dancers sought licenses to perform in the city's clubs. Owners of other amusements also anticipated an enormous economic impact from the Olympic visitors.

On Friday afternoon, July 19, 1996, city paving trucks finished laying a new asphalt surface on part of Peachtree Street in downtown just hours before the opening ceremony was held in the Olympic Stadium. Like a house-hold getting ready to have company, everything possible had been done to fix up Atlanta for the arrival of Olympic visitors. While efforts to solve the prob-lems of low-income neighborhoods fell short, the streets and sidewalks of downtown and the areas connecting venues received an extensive makeover. More than $76 million from the federal government was spent replacing side-walks, installing pedestrian signs, planting street trees, putting up new street lighting, and installing public art. This was a significant investment as well as a policy shift for a city that had permitted architect-developer John Port-man to build a system of skywalks connecting the buildings in his Peachtree Center so that visitors would not have to walk on downtown streets. For the crowds of Olympic visitors streets were fixed up so that pedestrians could en-joy walking around in the downtown area.

At the same time the street environment was being readied for the games, an entrepreneur and close friend of Mayor Bill Campbell convinced city gov-ernment that the Olympics provided an opportunity to make money from sales in tents, stalls, and vending carts on city property. Under the contract with the city, the rental from these temporary vendors would pay the city a guaranteed $2.5 million. While some see the relationship between large cor-porations and local elected public officials as a unified "growth machine," the city's vending program provoked a storm of controversy reflecting conflict be-tween local government and corporate officials.[18] ACOG criticized the pro-gram as it offered the potential for "ambush marketing" by competitors of the companies that had already paid sponsorship fees to ACOG. Officials at Coca-Cola worried that its rival Pepsi might use the stalls and pushcarts as a way to sell their products near the Olympics in spite of the fact that Coke had paid millions to ACOG to receive the designation of the official soft drink of the games. The controversial vending program lined the newly in-stalled sidewalks with booths selling fast food, tee-shirts, and other Olympic trinkets, creating a carnival atmosphere throughout downtown. Officials at ACOG complained about the "embarrassing display of tacky shacks block-ing sidewalks and impeding traffic flow," but Mayor Bill Campbell supported the vending program.[19]

ACOG estimated that it spent nearly $1.7 billion to stage the games. While broadcast rights raised $560 million and ticket sales generated $422 million, most of the remainder came from a partnership between ACOG and businesses that wished to use the Olympic theme in their advertising. The chief Olympic salesman, Billy Payne, hoped to market ten exclusive sponsorships for $40 million each. By the summer of 1993, only five companies had signed on as "Olympic Partners," creating a revenue shortfall that caused Payne to reduce the exclusivity of the program and sell sponsorships at a reduced price. This "fire sale" upset the initial group of sponsors, who complained to the IOC that ACOG was diluting their exclusive marketing agreements.[20] In spite of the criticism, ACOG granted an array of sponsorship and official licenses to 110 companies for products ranging from imported cars (BMW and Nissan), domestic cars (General Motors), watches (Swatch), salad dressing (Vidalia Onion Vinaigrette), clothing, sports equipment, and game shows (*Jeopardy* and *Wheel of Fortune*). The intensive marketing by ACOG was criticized by the initial sponsors and also by the local newspaper, which suggested that the marketing of the 1996 Olympics was the "greatest commercial orgy in history."[21] While this may have slightly overstated the case, nevertheless, by the opening of the Olympics no one could miss the dominance of local soft-drink maker Coca-Cola, which may have spent up to $250 million in marketing related to the games. These marketing dollars provided what seemed like a vending cart on every block in the city in addition to carts in the twelve-acre amusement area beside Centennial Olympic Park, sponsorship of the Olympic torch relay, and even a display of Coke bottles as art objects from each of the 135 nations where the product was sold.

When the opening ceremony began in Olympic Stadium, a capacity crowd of eighty-three thousand witnessed a display honoring the 100th anniversary of the modern Olympic movement and southern culture. The show featured the diversity of the region's music and dance performed by blacks and whites and climaxed with a tribute to Dr. Martin Luther King, Jr., and the lighting of the flame caldron by Louisville, Kentucky, native and former Olympic gold medal boxer Muhammad Ali. The artistically successful opening ceremonies showcased a South unified by symbols of blacks and whites contributing to a shared culture of athletics, music, and dance. However, when the sun rose the next morning and athletic competitions began, a multitude of problems began. The members of the international press corps were housed in scattered locations away from downtown where most events and press facilities were located. ACOG arranged for buses and drivers from transit systems across the country to provide transportation for the visiting journalists. Many of the buses broke down and others got lost as drivers were not familiar with the Atlanta area. Busloads of journalists were stranded by the roadside or arrived late at competition venues because of the transportation problems.

Opening Ceremony. Whereas some Olympic events reflected regional culture, the opening ceremony remained a grand parade of nations. (Courtesy of the Atlanta History Center.)

There were similar difficulties getting some athletes from the Olympic Village to competition sites.

The failure of a state-of-the-art IBM computer system further inconvenienced members of the press corps when results of athletic events were not readily available. The IBM Company was a major corporate sponsor of the games and was to provide instant reporting of data from the competitions. When the system failed, results were hand delivered to journalists, causing delays in meeting deadlines. Newspapers carried headlines such as "A big mess," "A disgrace," and "Incredibly mediocre" to describe the Atlanta Olympics.[22] For months afterward, international press reporters asked, "what became of southern hospitality?" Although most of their anger was directed toward ACOG and its president Billy Payne, the journalists also found much to criticize about Atlanta. They decried the excessive commercialization of the event and felt that the city looked like a cheap carnival with so many vendors selling their wares on the streets.

Atlanta was a city whose tourism industry was built around the business of hosting conventions. It had the airport, the hotels, and the facilities to host all kinds of meetings but lacked the amenities of a resort destination. Atlanta also lacked the centuries of architectural heritage that made a city such as Barcelona, the site of the 1992 Olympics, attractive to journalists. For those at the top of the Olympic hierarchy—corporate sponsors, IOC and national Olympic officials, and sports federation executives—the city offered the warmest hospitality that ACOG could provide. Most of these guests stayed in the official "Olympic Family Hotel," the Marriott Marquis, and other downtown luxury hotels. ACOG's staff included "guides" assigned to escort VIPs during their stay in Atlanta, as well as uniformed volunteer drivers assigned to motor pools near hotels and venues. These drivers were part of an army of more than forty-two thousand volunteers helping to stage the games. ACOG recruited volunteers to provide greetings and information, medical assistance, ticket taking, security, translating, help in athletic venues, and a variety of other tasks. Each volunteer received training, credentials, and uniforms, and in spite of heat, crowds of visitors, and traffic jams, the volunteers were praised for providing "gobs of southern hospitality throughout the games."[23] The volunteers were joined by thousands of temporary ACOG employees to make up an Olympic staff of almost ninety thousand.

In spite of media criticism, the Olympic athletes competed before record crowds of spectators. Most visitors and locals used the city's rapid rail system during the games, packing the train cars with riders around the clock. Thousands of tourists flocked downtown to the venues located nearby, to Centennial Olympic Park, and to other attractions such as Underground Atlanta. Contrary to the experience of the international press corps, most spectators seemed to enjoy the games and Atlanta as they filled the downtown with activity throughout the days and long into the nights. The pleasant mood of the Olympics changed suddenly in the early morning of July 27, the ninth day of the games. As crowds listened to a concert in the AT&T amphitheater in Centennial Olympic Park, a pipe bomb exploded, spraying shrapnel that caused two deaths and injured more than a hundred spectators. The mood of the games changed from a joyful festival atmosphere to fear as visitors recalled memories of the terrorist attack on the 1972 Olympics in Munich. The athletic competitions continued the following day, but the park remained closed for three days. On reopening, tighter security checks for people entering both the park and all Olympic events were enforced.

During the two weeks of the games, an estimated two million people visited Atlanta. Those who came to watch the athletic competitions were not disappointed. Record numbers of athletes (almost eleven thousand) and participating nations (197) assured fan interest in the twenty-six sports that were included in the program of events. Spectators were treated to excellent

Fountain at Centennial Olympic Park. Olympic visitors enjoying the southern summer night. (Courtesy of the Atlanta History Center.)

individual and team-sport performances, with athletes from seventy-nine nations winning medals. While American fans cheered for the 101 U.S. medal winners, visitors from smaller nations celebrated victories such as the Tongan super heavyweight boxer who won the first Olympic medal in his nation's history. Women's sports were also prominent in the games with almost four thousand female athletes participating. In addition to the tourists who came to Atlanta, the city received the added bonus of a global television audience estimated at 3.5 billion (almost 70 percent of the world's population).

While the two weeks of the games filled the city's hotels with visitors, not all the tourism businesses profited from the crowds. Many temporary vendors in their rented stalls and carts did well selling fast food that was convenient for people on the go. Other vendors on streets such as Auburn Avenue failed to attract crowds as people jammed Olympic Centennial Park and the streets near venue sites. Meanwhile, many of the city's upscale restaurants were practically empty as tourists did not take time for fine dining and local patrons stayed away. A few restaurants were rented for private parties and some accepted offers from national sports federations to rent their facilities. This helped to soften the blow of two weeks of lower than normal business. Four of the national chain restaurants that opened for the Olympics closed after the games as they failed to win customers among locals or visitors.

The Olympics also attracted a variety of cultural activities to Atlanta. Many of these were staged as part of the city's Cultural Olympiad and took place prior to the two weeks of the games. Others, such as the installation of folk art on sidewalks and the "Rings: Five Passions in World Art" exhibit at the High Museum of Art, proved popular with visitors. Theater groups suffered from poor attendance, but cultural attractions of a different sort at Underground Atlanta, Centennial Olympic Park, and the "House of Blues," which opened in the Tabernacle Baptist Church, were packed. Even President Clinton and his family visited the House of Blues to hear a performance by Georgia native James Brown.

On Sunday evening, August 4, the closing ceremony took place in the Olympic Stadium, bringing the games to an end. A capacity crowd and a global television audience watched the "Southern Jamboree" of music from the region, highlighted by "Little Richard" Penniman of Macon, Georgia. As the ceremony neared its close, the President of the IOC, Juan Antonio Samaranch, addressed the crowd. He proclaimed, "Well done, Atlanta!" and added that the games were "most exceptional." In closing the four previous Olympics, Samaranch had declared each of them to be the best ever. His faint praise of Atlanta's Olympic Games stunned Billy Payne as well as most local residents who expected the highest praise for their efforts to host the event. Samaranch's comments were merely the first round in the mixed assessments of the Atlanta Olympics that would follow.

Surveys of American visitors showed that most were impressed by the city's efforts to host the games and especially by the friendliness of local residents. Most surveyed said they had a more favorable opinion of the city after the Olympics than before the games. They regarded Atlanta as a progressive city and a birthplace of civil rights.[24] On the other hand, members of the IOC remained critical of the commercialism surrounding the Atlanta games as well as problems such as the transportation for journalists and the computer system for reporting competition results. The members of the IOC did recognize that the athletic competition was well done, attendance at the games was at an all-time high, and television coverage throughout the world was well regarded by viewers.[25]

Billy Payne and ACOG had managed to raise enough revenue to avoid the massive public debt that haunted Montreal after it hosted the games. At the same time, there was no windfall surplus of revenue such as Los Angeles received after its Olympics. The small surplus of $10 million dollars remaining in ACOG's budget was divided between the IOC, the USOC, and a planned museum in Centennial Olympic Park. Olympic-related construction also left a positive impact in some areas. Both public and private academic institutions in the state received new or improved athletic and student housing facilities. ACOG also paid for the reconfiguration of the Olympic Stadium as it was turned over to the city and county recreation authorities. The new stadium was then leased to the Atlanta Braves baseball team and renamed Turner Field in honor of local communications entrepreneur and team owner, Ted Turner. ACOG kept its agreement with the surrounding neighborhood and demolished the old Atlanta-Fulton County Stadium next to Turner Field. To enhance the view of the downtown skyline from Turner Field, the Olympic flame cauldron was relocated one block away, where it remains as a legacy of the games.

Another important legacy of the games was the Centennial Olympic Park. With its location next to the Georgia Dome and the World Congress Center, the Park was placed under the management of a state government authority. Both public and private leaders hoped the new Park would serve as a catalyst for investment in a previously rather run-down area. Their hopes were slowly realized as a hotel and restaurant located across from the Park and plans developed for luxury high-rise condominiums in the area. Additional investments were also made in existing structures in the area of Centennial Olympic Park. While the House of Blues closed after the games, the Tabernacle Baptist Church property reopened as a concert hall. An adjacent office building was renovated and construction started to double the room capacity of the Omni Hotel across Marietta Street from the Park. In 1999, the new indoor sports facility known as Philips Arena opened nearby as the home for the Hawks basketball team and the new National Hockey League franchise the Atlanta Thrashers. Three new office towers were announced for the area around Philips Arena and Centennial Olympic Park by AOL Time Warner, which also owns CNN Center and the Turner Sports teams. The planned Olympic museum was not built in the Park, but the site remained popular with visitors and locals with its skyline views, the Rings fountain, Light Towers, and other features. The green space provided by the Park also served as a gathering place for a variety of public events as well as private parties for convention groups.

The Olympic Games provided other tangible legacies for the city. Downtown Atlanta became an improved pedestrian environment because of the investment in street lighting, sidewalk paving, signage, tree planting, and public art. While these improvements did not attract businesses to parts of downtown such as Auburn Avenue, the downtown area as a whole did benefit from the preparations for the games. For many decades civic leaders tried to promote housing in downtown. The opportunity to lease residential space for the Olympics spurred both the construction of new apartments and the conversion of existing buildings into lofts. In the area around Woodruff Park developers renovated more than five hundred units of housing from commercial and office buildings. The city government leased a block-sized parking lot across from City Hall for construction of a new 100-unit apartment complex known as City Plaza. This project also featured a mix of commercial space on the street level that attracted a grocery store, an upscale soul food restaurant, and a fast food business. The success of these efforts spurred other loft conversions throughout the central city and moved Atlanta toward the goal of having a resident population downtown around the clock. As strictly a business district, many convention visitors had complained that the city looked deserted at night. This began to change with the increased numbers of downtown residents making the area more attractive and safer for themselves and visitors. These investments provided many benefits for Atlanta, such as the increased value of property, the generation of additional property taxes, and a reversal of the declining population in the central city.

There was also more gentrification in neighborhoods surrounding downtown as individual homeowners and developers invested in older single-family residences. While this process had advantages for the city, it also displaced low-income residents from their homes. Neighborhoods near downtown that experienced the influx of higher-income residents included East Atlanta, Ormwood Park, Summerhill, and Kirkwood. Tensions between the older residents and newcomers were especially high in the Kirkwood neighborhood. Displacement of low-income African Americans from their neighborhoods continued the problems that characterized the Olympic preparations as the supply of moderately priced housing in the city was reduced. The city's Housing Authority added to the problem with its "Olympic Legacy" program that demolished not only the Techwood housing project, but several others as well. These projects were replaced with "mixed-income communities" that provided a better quality residential environment for some former tenants but caused many to relocate. The result was a deconcentration of Atlanta's poverty population that scholars have observed in other cities as well.[26] The hosting of a mega-event such as the Olympics provided few benefits for large numbers of the city's poor residents. While more low-skill, low-wage jobs were created by the building boom in hotels and restaurants, the games themselves did little except contribute to problems finding affordable housing.

Atlanta's hospitality businesses also experienced mixed results from the Olympics. There were more than two million visitors to the city during the games. Hotel operators were generally happy, as they had high occupancy rates and were able to charge rates that insured profitability. Many amusements did not share in the benefits of the games. With the discretionary spending of residents and visitors going toward Olympic tickets and souvenirs, attendance at other types of amusements suffered throughout 1996. With so much attention focused on the Olympics, fewer people attended concerts, theme parks, and sporting events. For example, the Lakewood Amphitheatre lost money during the year as it hosted fewer concerts and suffered from lower attendance. Theme parks such as Six Flags over Georgia and Whitewater Park also failed to attract as many patrons as usual during the summer season. In spite of an excellent team that returned to the World Series in 1996, the Atlanta Braves failed to sell out most of their games during the season. Even Stone Mountain Park, which served as the site of Olympic competition in archery, cycling, and tennis, suffered a 15 percent drop in attendance for the year and a substantial drop in revenues.[27] While these were temporary losses, they indicate that not all the city's tourism businesses shared equally in the financial benefits of the Olympics.

The city's convention business thrived as a result of the attention focused on the Olympics in Atlanta. According to ACVB officials, there were more than nineteen million visitors to the city during 1996. While some economists predicted a slowing of the city's economic growth after the games, the strong national economy and continued promotional efforts by local leaders increased Atlanta's convention business each year during 1997 through 2000. Increased numbers of visitors encouraged more hotel building in the years following the games. At the end of 1997, there were almost sixty-seven thousand hotel rooms in Atlanta with construction booming to add to the supply. The result was a drop in the occupancy rate, but not below the levels considered profitable by the industry.[28] By December 2000, Atlanta's leaders boasted about the eighty-two thousand rooms available in the city.

While numerous financial analysts suggested that the city's supply of hotel rooms was overbuilt, an increased number of visitors continued to fill these rooms. According to the Atlanta Convention and Visitors Bureau, in 1998 the city hosted 3,057 meetings attended by more than 3,423,000 people. This growth in the number of conventions led to the fourth enlargement of the Georgia World Congress Center since its opening in 1971. When completed in 2002, the expanded convention facility had 1.4 million square feet of space, making the World Congress Center competitive in size with newly enlarged convention centers in Orlando and New Orleans. The facility helped boost hotel occupancy downtown by enabling Atlanta to host two conventions of fifty thousand visitors at the same time while a third meeting of the same size is setting up. This means less "down time" at the convention facility and more meetings being held. With the increase in visitors to the city, related tourism businesses such as restaurants will continue to thrive. In 1999, Atlanta could boast of having more than eight thousand restaurants to feed the appetites of tourists and local residents.[29]

What has drawn these crowds of visitors to Atlanta? It is the same combination that served the city throughout its history. As the head of the Georgia Hospitality and Travel Association, Lloyd Webre, said, "Organizations prefer Atlanta to host their events for its accessibility, hospitality and the diversions it has to offer to visitors." Atlanta began as the crossroads of the rail lines, and while the railroads no longer bring passengers to the city, Hartsfield International Airport makes it possible for 80 percent of the United States population to reach Atlanta within a two hours' flight. Tourism officials such as Webre also boast of Atlanta's hospitality, "which is well-known from hosting major events like the Olympics and the Super Bowl—and that no matter what time of year you come here, there will be major league sports events, you can see why Atlanta is in the forefront of people's minds."[30]

The convention business became one of Atlanta's basic industries and a major source of dollars pumped into the local economy. The International Association of Conventions and Visitors estimated that each convention visitor to the city spent an average of $1,200 to attend a meeting. Using the ACVB's estimate for the number of visitors to the city in 1998, Atlanta received more than $4 billion that year from the convention business. When other forms of tourism were added, the estimated economic impact on the Atlanta metropolitan area for 1998 was more than $18 billion.[31] Yet, with many tourism businesses such as hotels, restaurants, and amusements owned by national and international corporations, much of this revenue did not remain in the local economy. Atlanta's tourism businesses were also an important source of employment for the central city and metropolitan area with more than 100,000 jobs dependent on the city's visitors.[32] While racial minorities and women held many of these positions in hospitality businesses, most were low-skill and low-wage jobs that provided little chance for upward mobility.

With the constant promotional efforts of organizations such as the ACVB, the Chamber of Commerce, and the local media, the benefits of a tourism economy were often overestimated. At the same time, the costs of tourism to the city were often understated. In a typical article in the *Atlanta Constitution*, the spending by convention visitors was described as "a financial windfall for the city." The same article quoted civic leaders as saying the cost to the city residents of the convention business was "surprisingly little." When a major convention came to town, the paper described the impact as a significant increase in the ridership of Atlanta's rapid transit system, but no additional deployment of police officers was usually needed to handle traffic and crowd control. The issues of congestion and crowding were treated lightly by the newspaper, with the suggestion that large convention groups might make it difficult for local residents to get into their favorite restaurant or to take an additional ten minutes to find a parking space.[33]

The narrative failed to mention the costs of public sector investment in tourism infrastructure by providing convention halls, sports arenas, and entertainment areas such as Underground Atlanta. Few of these generate enough revenue to avoid the need for annual subsidies to pay for their construction and operating costs, while many of the direct benefits of the public sector investments go to corporate owners. Also not mentioned are the costs of additional crowding in low-income neighborhoods as housing was destroyed to create space for facilities such as the Georgia Dome and the Olympic Stadium (now Turner Field).

Nevertheless, estimates of the number of visitors to Atlanta increased each year since 1996. One of the results local leaders anticipated from the Olympics was that publicity generated by the games would promote the image of Atlanta as a place to visit. Since the games, more of the city's visitors have come from overseas. In 1999, Atlanta hosted 538,000 international tourists, which gave the city a ranking of twelfth among U.S. destinations behind the top locations such as New York, Los Angeles, Miami, Orlando, and San Francisco. Atlanta became increasingly popular with travelers from Canada, France, the United Kingdom, and Latin America.[34] Despite the fact that the games failed to fulfill all the "Olympic dreams" of local planners, they provided a major boost to the business of tourism and to the city's growth.[35]

Atlanta's experience hosting the Olympic Games provided some lessons for other cities in the region. First, the business of hospitality produced substantial economic growth for the city. Much of this investment was by national and international corporations as businesses and employment were added to the local economy. The initiative for hosting tourism activities, ranging from conventions to major events such as the Super Bowl or the Olympics, generally came from the private sector. However, the cooperation of the public sector was essential to the process. Convention facilities, sports arenas, and transportation infrastructure resulted from large public sector investments to support hospitality businesses. Atlanta's experience showed that even the largest-scale tourism events did not solve deeply rooted social and economic problems. Issues of race and class were not addressed, so that few of the benefits of tourism-related growth trickled down to the poor black residents who bore much of the cost of this development. As they had throughout the city's history, local leaders combined hard work and constant promotion to shape Atlanta's growth as a tourist city. But with the Olympic Games, their efforts brought increased attention from around the globe.

11
Nobody Knows the Troubles I've Seen, but Does Anybody Want to Hear about Them When They're on Vacation?

Ted Ownby

The essays in this collection investigate the most important questions schol-ars are asking about tourism in the twentieth-century South. Why did people with money to spend travel to, or within, the South? What did local people do to attract tourists? And how did the interaction of tourists and the tour-ism industry change everyday life, social ideals, economics, architecture, and the environment?

This essay asks how, and if, some of the basic categories from southern history have relevance in the development of southern tourism. One might think that promoters of tourism would be relatively unconcerned with his-tory, since their job is to attract visitors however they can. But since history is a big part of the attraction for visitors in many places, including the South, many tourism promoters take on the job of becoming amateur historians. This essay also evaluates the visions of history they are offering and offers a suggestion or two about how professional historians and tourism promoters acting as amateur historians might work together.

"Land is the only thing in the world that amounts to anything."[1]

Margaret Mitchell wrote these words, but it was David O. Selznick, producer, media mogul, and not a southerner, who made them memorable as the theme of the film version of *Gone with the Wind*. Non-southerners have been at-tracted to southern land not just for the profits but also for its physical beauty and for a range of qualities it seems to embody about life. The idea of South as garden is very old, dating at least from colonial pamphlets that told Europeans that the southern colonies had climates and landscapes that would make life easy.[2] Of course, gardens mean different things to different people. Some, like David O. Selznick, see in the southern land opportunities for endurance and strength. Some people want to cultivate their own garden as a safe place where they control the natural world, prune out the strange parts, and arrange the prettiest parts in appealing ways. Others want gardens growing wild, on mountains, near rivers, on beaches. They want a freedom from order.

Many people do not just go to the garden to enjoy the natural world; they attach personal or cultural characteristics to a visit to natural settings. Beaches are not just scenic and hot, they offer ease—and many Americans have long associated ease with the southern upper class.[3] And mountains are not just huge and wild and beautiful; they isolate people from parts of the world that seem impermanent and crass and overly controlled. Since at least the late 1800s, visitors to American mountains have made connections between the majesty of the mountains and the special purity—religious, aesthetic, and cultural purity—they see in mountain people. The Great Smoky Mountains National Park is the largest such attraction—considered so pure, so beautiful, so close to timeless in its beauty that it needs to be preserved—and part of the attraction lies not just in the hills but in the hillbillies.[4] As the essay by Brooks Blevins in this volume attests, many Americans, southern and non-southern, believed mountains offered a closeness to God.[5]

Since the late 1800s, the southern garden has also been a place for non-southerners to take advantage of wilderness for sale. Unlikely places made real profits by letting some of the world's richest people shoot bear or panther or something else that, like southern people, seemed almost too weird to be true. It is widely known, for example, that Theodore Roosevelt went west looking for a rugged life he found lacking in northeastern cities. He also toured the South on hunting excursions. More recently, advertisements for contemporary tourism offer the South to a robust America that can rush to the region with sporting gear handy, ready to raft, boat, spelunk, hike, fish, and hunt. And golf. Above all, southern golf offers year-round play in spectacularly shaped natural settings. Some of the most ambitious efforts at stimulating southern tourism have been at Pinehurst, North Carolina, the Robert Trent Jones Golf Trail in Alabama, the Bear Trace golf courses in Tennessee, the Callaway Gardens in Georgia, and many other golf developments. Advertisements for such courses always stress natural beauty. Fairways are lush, sometimes the hills are rolling and sometimes towering mountains offer breathtaking vistas, rivers rush, brooks bubble, lakes are tranquil, and despite extraordinary feats of engineering, landscapes, according to the advertisements, remain rugged and untouched.

Our Contemporary Ancestors

In 1899 William Goodell Frost wrote an essay arguing that Appalachian people were "Our Contemporary Ancestors." Frost claimed that culture, language, music, handicrafts, and the like all got stuck in the hills, remaining blissfully isolated from economic, technological, or demographic change. Frost's notion had some ugly racial connotations; he suggested that Anglo-Saxon stock in the isolated mountains remained "pure" while the rest of America was suffering from intermingling with new immigrants from eastern and southern Europe.[6] But his larger point, that isolated parts of the South retained qualities that were vanishing in many other parts of the United States, has been attractive among both southerners and non-southerners. In the 1920s, the Vanderbilt Agrarians seized on the idea of the strength of a southern culture rooted in farm, family, and community and blissfully separated from the goods and expectations of industrialization and consumer culture. As the most nostalgic of the Agrarians, Donald Davidson wrote, "The South has been rich in the folk-arts, and is still rich in them—in ballads, country songs and dances, in hymns and spirituals, in folk tales, in the folk crafts of weaving, quilting, furniture-making."[7] In the late nineteenth century and especially the early twentieth century, lovers of such traditions started coming south to celebrate, collect, record, document, and buy, and they're still coming.[8]

Today's tourist guidebooks continue to suggest that going among southerners means going into the past. A 1994 Hippocrene U.S.A. travel guide describes the people of eastern Kentucky as "mountain people," explaining that the term "refers not only to their Appalachian habitat but also to a rather basic and unadorned way of life that developed in isolation removed from the mainstream of American culture." And it is not just Appalachia that represents an appealing, untouched cultural past. The same book introduces travel in Alabama with a happy agrarian theme: "A pronounced small-town and rural flavor dominates Alabama. . . . The small towns, seemingly self-contained and remote from the greater world beyond, live in a sort of sleepy isolation."[9] A handbook for traveling in Virginia claims that the tourist who "ventures beyond the interstates and must-see hordes will quickly discover Virginia's true treasure: her inhabitants, most of whom are, for lack of a better word, just so darned *nice*."[10]

Pleasure shopping—one of the primary sports of recent American life—has become a kind of heritage tourism. People go looking for connections to the past in roadside stands that offer food, local crafts, and frequently some kind of local attraction.[11] And as small-town America suffers serious economic decline, the stores that seem to thrive in what were once active downtown business districts are junk stores, secondhand stores, and antique stores. Shopping for old stuff offers connection to the past both in the goods themselves—preowned, obviously reminiscent of another life—and even in the stores themselves, which are small buildings with creaking wood floors, slow-talking owners, and smells that seem left over from the nineteenth century.[12]

The dramatic growth of accommodations known as bed and breakfasts offers the clearest example of the interest in tourism that relies on the South's folk and family identity. Many guidebooks discuss bed and breakfasts at great length, with the clear suggestion that the travelers who stay in a bed and breakfast are not really strangers in a faceless, prefabricated, predictable room in a motel chain. Instead, people who stay in bed and breakfasts seem to be guests in people's homes, and the whole event becomes a kind of play about hospitality. The architecture, furniture, food, and conversation rely on categories of a tangible past, and the fact that one is staying there helps embody the past. The past is not in a museum, a book, or a battlefield; we can sleep there and have breakfast.

The Burden of Southern History

In 1958, C. Vann Woodward described four features of the burden of southern history: military defeat and its consequences, poverty, racial conflict and guilt, and a sense of limits and historical consciousness that the first three helped create and sustain. For Woodward, looking, thinking, writing about the American South meant contemplating pain and, perhaps, gaining some sort of wisdom and strength through the process.[13]

Does such a vision offer any help in thinking about the appeal of the South for tourists in the twenty-first century? Do people come south looking to experience the emotional depth they fear may be lacking in their lives? Can they come south wanting to connect to struggle and endurance? Or are Woodward's categories just too depressing for tourists, most of whom are trying to escape limits and worries in order to relax and have fun? Does cultural tourism in the South have to choose between depressing honesty and cheerful lies, worst represented by the many pilgrimages to antebellum mansions that avoid serious mention of slavery?[14]

Travel to Civil War battlefields might seem a serious form of vacation-time political engagement, and for many it may be. Battlefield travel means visiting scenes of drama and death, battle strategy, and military technology. However, as David Blight has shown in his study of Civil War memory, most white Americans had by the early twentieth century found ways to depoliticize that death and drama, celebrating valor without dwelling on issues of slavery, emancipation, Reconstruction, or race relations. The problem is that most Americans have not wanted much politics and moral complexity on vacation, so travel to war sites became a way to remember part of the past without connecting it to the most central burdens of southern history.[15] It is worth noting that while there are more Civil War museums than you can shake a musket at, there is no American Museum of Reconstruction.

Surely the most intense, most troubling, most untrivializable, most uncertain topic for tourism is how to deal with the horrors of slavery, the consequences of the Civil War, the inequities of race relations, and the heroism of civil rights activists. The issue arose recently with concerns over plans for a Disney theme park bordering Civil War battle sites in Virginia and even more recently with discussions about museums and exhibits dedicated to the experience of slavery. Both cases evoked much preachy moral certainty, and many historians and others suggested there is real history that is serious and perhaps sacred, and then there are ways people should enjoy themselves separate from the real history. The furor led Disney to cancel its plans for a theme park in 1994. More recent discussions make unclear the future of museums about the slave experience. In the mid-1990s, a program Colonial Williamsburg developed on a slave auction drew protest from the NAACP, but more recent efforts to dramatize slave owners breaking up slave families and disrupting slave gatherings have been more popular. The United States does not have a museum dedicated to slaves, largely because of uncertainty about how to build, fund, and publicize such a thing. While many museum and tourism leaders think a slavery museum would be popular—some cite the importance of the Holocaust Museum—others worry that slavery does not translate well into a happy outing in a commercialized setting. Howard University scholar Russell Adams, for example, warned against any slavery museum that might be "too close to the hamburgers. . . . You don't have somebody eating cotton candy, watch an auction, have a Coke and then watch another auction or whipping."[16]

All southern states today offer African American history elements as part of their appeals to tourists. The sites mentioned in state-supported African American heritage tourism programs tend to emphasize things that are reasonably non-controversial: historic firsts, notable individuals and their homes, churches, schools, colleges, and hospitals. Many go further. A Sea Island, Georgia, site, for example, describes the Sea Island Festival, the Sea Island Singers, a discussion of Gullah dialect, the site of a "mass drowning" of Africans who refused to become slaves, a few slave cabins, a slave trading ship, the story of a man who risked his life to retrieve the body of his owner, a monument that *Chicago Defender* founder Robert Abbott established to remember his family, a plantation museum about rice cultivation, and a park on the site of an African American industrial school.[17] Writers of professional guidebooks have been slower than many state tourism organizations to discuss African American history as part of tourist attractions. They seem to begin with the long-held expectations that tourists want sun, sand, and big houses and have only recently begun to add civil rights sites to lists of tourist attractions.

It is right to worry that an approach to tourism that includes all groups and all experiences is often uncertain and awkward. Such an approach often seems too grim to attract those who don't want grimness on their vacations, and sometimes it seems too safe and reassuring to be both honest and significant. Some attempts to attract tourists by connecting them to the painful sides of southern history border on the bizarre, and some push on past that border. Consider, for example, the Shack Up Inn, located on Hopson Plantation outside Clarksdale, Mississippi. Billing itself as "Mississippi's Oldest B & B (Bed & Beer)," the Shack Up Inn allows tourists the chance to spend the night in "authentic sharecropper shacks" with tin roofs, shotgun designs, and other architectural features that "will conjure visions of a bygone era."[18] Still, the recent emphasis on African American heritage tourism is surely preferable to many previous efforts at attracting tourists to the South. For example, African Americans did not appear in the text and photographs of a state-sponsored Mississippi tourism brochure in 1975, which promoted the state's natural beauty and opportunities for recreation, its historic houses and sites, and its happy biracial society—of whites and Native Americans.[19]

Lift Every Voice and Sing

Surely one of the most appealing ways to turn suffering into pleasure, and then to market some of that pleasure to visitors, is in music. The South has been especially successful in developing and now offering jazz in New Orleans, zydeco and Cajun music in Louisiana, blues, soul, and Elvis in Memphis, country in Nashville, patriotic retro-country in Branson, Missouri, and Pigeon Forge, Tennessee, and a self-conscious roots country in Mountain View, Arkansas. Many people come to the South to pay tribute to a music they know only through recordings. The music belongs to them, and signifies something important in their lives, but music on radio, record, or compact disk can be ephemeral, existing only for one of the physical senses. Going and hearing, touring, is making music three-dimensional; it puts the person's body into something that he or she might otherwise only hear. It puts tourists face to face with performers, and while they do not need to stay at the Shack Up Inn, they are in the same place where people turned personal experiences into music. In some ways, sharing musical experiences makes commodities—recorded music—less commodified.

Music also offers one particularly successful form of tourism that unites southern tourists with tourists from outside the region. Southerners go to the Grand Ole Opry or to Graceland or to Jazzfest in New Orleans to be near experiences they consider their own, and they are often surprised that people from New Jersey or Kansas or Paris or Tokyo love the same music.

The troubling thing about musical tourism is that it tends to resemble Mardi Gras without Lent, or Saturday night without the whole week that came before it. It offers a celebration and a release without the experiences that helped give the music its depth and meaning. To quote James Weldon Johnson's "Lift Every Voice and Sing," it offers "a song full of the hope that the present has brought us" without dwelling as well on the "song full of the faith that the dark past has brought us." Going to festivals or blues clubs or musical theme parks allows people to enjoy relief from trouble without doing much to take note of that trouble. It is hard to know how to address this problem. Perhaps Mardi Gras without Lent characterizes much of contemporary American culture, and perhaps, as the home of America's best known

Mardi Gras, the South seems a fitting place to celebrate. Or perhaps many music tourists identify with the pain and emotional depth of their favorite music by relating them to their own troubled lives—their own dark pasts— rather than to the society that helped produce the music.[20] Still, there should be more and better ways to acknowledge and address the lives behind the music.

A South Too Busy

Today the dominant trope of southern tourism is variety. As Richard Starnes discusses in his essay on North Carolina, states love to say they have it all. Guidebooks and travel brochures always say that tourists can find what they expect to find: land, mountains or beaches, old houses, Civil War sites, rural stuff to see and buy, local music. On the other hand, they also stress that tourists can find things they didn't expect: things not so old and not so stereotypically southern. The first page of a glossy publication the state of Alabama sponsored in 2001 is breathlessly state-of-the-art: "Alabama. The eye-popping, golf-ball-chasing, deep-sea-fishing, suntanning, shop-a-holic, outdoorsy, historic, panoramic, bird-watching, Ferris-wheeling, mountain biking, cricket chirping, restaurant-hopping, family-friendly, bed-and-breakfast, can't-wait-to-come-back State."[21]

The appeal is obvious: tourists should come because southern places offer them things they do not have at home. But if they have already done some of those things, or if they have family members who are not interested, come on anyway, and enjoy the range of possibilities. This is the postmodern South—a South that can trade on parts of its own past but also trumpet changes. Try our traditional barbecue; if you don't like it, look, we have all sorts of foods—fast, continental, nouveau, ethnic, or nondescript: please try them all. As the Arkansas Department of Parks and Tourism urges on its 2002 website, "Feast on finger-licking barbecue and fried catfish, steak and seafood, sushi, French, Thai, Mexican, and Italian entrees, topped off by freshly baked treats and specialty coffee."[22] Guidebooks and state agencies likewise urge tourists to look at old houses, but if you don't like old houses or just get tired of them, look, we have attractions just as good as anybody's. We'll play the part of keepers of the past, they say, but if you don't like that, we'll play other parts as well. Look, we have a charming downtown square where you can buy folk art, crafts that look old, and useless stuff that really is old. If you don't like that, heck, just down the road in Alabama, or Florida, or Texas, we have rockets. Look, we have the majesty, serenity, and bears of the Great Smoky Mountains National Park. If you don't like that, we'll sell you homemade fudge and stuffed bears and try to amuse you with water parks, laser tag, and country comics, most of them named Bubba.

State tourism bureaus and professional guidebooks often cannot go a sentence or a paragraph without the variety trope. History, the latest forms of mindless fun, urban life, we've got them all. The 1995 Virginia Is for Lovers Travel Guide announced the state as "a mixture of exciting cities, thrilling theme parks, historic homes and villages and as much recreational activity as you'd care to squeeze into your stay."[23] The more circumspect Mobil Travel Guide describes Tennessee as "a state of mountain ballads and big-city ballet, of waterpowered mills and atomic energy plants."[24] The AAA traveler's guide to Louisiana stresses that the state is "different things to different people, yet its irresistible allure beckons all of us in some way. This is a state of contrasts, with enticements that can be flamboyant or sedate, raucous or discreet. . . . Louisiana is jambalaya and zydeco, breakfast at Brennan's and jazz at Preservation Hall. Come enjoy the spice, the gentility, the worldly sophistication and the Southern hospitality."[25] Mississippi's Official Tour Guide emphasizes a diversity that apparently negates the need for subjects and verbs. "From the antebellum mansions of Natchez to the bustling excitement of metropolitan Jackson. From the sultry sea breezes and sundrenched beaches of the Coast to the bright lights and fast-paced action of Tunica. It all adds up to one great experience. With its unique blend of cities and countrysides, history and contemporary appeal, porch swings and riverboat gaming, Mississippi has something for everyone."[26]

The result of such variety overkill is a kind of cheerful boosterism that reminds one of the southern chambers of commerce James Cobb has described as being willing to give potential investors land, cheap labor, low environmental standards, tax breaks, and whatever else it takes to bring new money into the post-agricultural South.[27] According to the tourism industry, the South of the twenty-first century has no particular identity: it has numerous identities, gained from the land and climate, from some parts of history, from modern economic change, from cultural creativity, and from other sources as well. It is easy to say the variety trope plays it safe, suggesting that all of southern culture is ready to come together to play golf and shop for antiques. But it is not easy to criticize the variety trope, in part because variety is almost always true and in part because it is so much better than emphasizing a South only for its Civil War battlefields and big old houses.

The variety trope is one of the rare points where tourism professionals and historians tend to agree. Tourism professionals and historians are generally at odds, with the former looking for a past that sells, and the latter seeking a past that is true. But for the past generation or so, both have been trying for their own reasons to push beyond traditional boundaries, to include more groups and more experiences. Perhaps the variety trope offers a way historians can actually contribute to improving tourism in the South. Along with pointing out the ways tourism promoters are safe or wrong or narrow-minded, historians can also offer stories and experiences to broaden the range of things tourists might find interesting. We can broaden the civil rights story, combining the well-known stories of a few martyrs with stories that emphasize movement, excitement, and everyday heroism. We can broaden the story of cultural life, calling attention to the many forms of creativity that do not conform to conventional expectations of folksiness. We can tell stories about music and the lives behind music.

We live in an interesting world, and we should encourage people to come see it. But let's show it all, including the troubles we've seen.

Notes

Introduction

1. Richard E. Foglesong, *Married to the Mouse: Walt Disney World and Orlando* (New Haven: Yale University Press, 2001); and Richard Handler and Eric Gable, *The New History in an Old Museum: Creating the Past at Colonial Williamsburg* (Durham, N.C.: Duke University Press, 1997). For a more detailed typology of tourism, see Valene L. Smith, ed., *Hosts and Guests: The Anthropology of Tourism*, 2d ed. (Philadelphia: University of Pennsylvania Press, 1989), 4–6.

2. For more on literature of tourism outside the United States, see Gilbert Sigaux, *History of Tourism* (London: Leisure Arts, 1966); Malcolm Crick, "Representations of International Tourism in the Social Sciences: Sun, Sex, Sights, Savings, and Servility," *Annual Review of Anthropology* 18 (1989): 307–44; Jafar Jafari, "Tourism and the Social Sciences," *Annals of Tourism Research* 6:2 (1979): 149–78; and Maxine Feiffer, *Tourism in History: From Imperial Rome to the Present* (London: Macmillan, 1984). For a call for an integrated history of world tourism and its effects, see David Engerman, "Research Agenda for the History of Tourism: Towards an International Social History," *American Studies International* 32 (October 1994): 3–31.

3. For an introduction to the study of tourism, see Dean MacCannell, *The Tourist: A New Theory of the Leisure Class* (New York: Schocken Books, 1976); and John Jakle, *The Tourist: Travel in Twentieth-Century North America* (Lincoln: University of Nebraska Press, 1985).

4. Cindy S. Aron, *Working at Play: A History of Vacations in the United States* (New York: Oxford University Press, 1999); Dona Brown, *Inventing New England: Regional Tourism in the Nineteenth Century* (Washington, D.C.: Smithsonian Institution Press, 1995); Michael C. Kammen, *Mystic Chords of Memory: The Transformation of Tradition in American Culture* (New York: Alfred A. Knopf, 1991); Hal K. Rothman, *Devil's Bargains: Tourism in the Twentieth Century American West* (Lawrence: University Press of Kansas, 1998); John F. Sears, *Sacred Places: American*

Tourist Attractions in the Nineteenth Century (New York: Oxford University Press, 1989); Marguerite S. Shaffer, *See America First: Tourism and National Identity, 1880–1940* (Washington, D.C.: Smithsonian Institution Press, 2001); and David M. Wrobel and Patrick T. Long, eds., *Seeing and Being Seen: Tourism in the American West* (Lawrence: University Press of Kansas, 2001).

5. Rembert W. Patrick, "The Mobile Frontier," *Journal of Southern History* 29 (February 1963): 3–18. For an early, but often-impressionistic account of tourism's influence in the modern South, see Thomas D. Clark, *The Emerging South* (New York: Oxford University Press, 1961), especially chap. 10. Much of the research on southern tourism remains unpublished. A partial bibliography of works on or closely related to southern tourism includes Jane S. Becker, *Selling Tradition: Appalachia and the Construction of an American Folk, 1930–1940* (Chapel Hill: University of North Carolina Press, 1998); Rodger Lyle Brown, *Ghost Dancing on the Cracker Circuit: The Culture of Festivals in the American South* (Jackson: University Press of Mississippi, 1997); W. Fitzhugh Brundage, ed., *Where These Memories Grow: History, Memory, and Southern Identity* (Chapel Hill: University of North Carolina Press, 2000); Tim Hollis, *Dixie Before Disney: 100 Years of Roadside Fun* (Jackson: University Press of Mississippi, 1999); Lynn Morrow and Linda Myers-Phinney, *Shepherd of the Hills Country: Tourism Transforms the Ozarks, 1880s–1930s* (Fayetteville: University of Arkansas Press, 1999); C. Brenden Martin, "Selling the Southern Highlands: Tourism and Community Development in the Mountain South" (Ph.D. diss., University of Tennessee, 1997); Anne V. Mitchell, "Parkway Politics: Class, Culture, and Tourism in the Blue Ridge" (Ph.D. diss., University of North Carolina, 1997); Harvey K. Newman, *Southern Hospitality: Tourism and the Growth of Atlanta* (Tuscaloosa: University of Alabama Press, 1999); Daniel S. Pierce, *The Great Smokies: From Natural Habitat to National Park* (Knoxville: University of Tennessee Press, 2000); Howard L. Preston, *Dirt Roads to Dixie: Accessibility and Modernization in the South, 1885–1935* (Knoxville: University of Tennessee Press, 1991); Richard D. Starnes, "Creating the Land of the Sky: Tourism and Society in Western North Carolina" (Ph.D. diss., Auburn University, 1999); Patsy West, *The Enduring Seminoles: From Alligator Wrestling to Ecotourism* (Gainesville: University Press of Florida, 1998); and Stephanie E. Yuhl, "High Culture in the Low Country: Arts, Identity, and Tourism in Charleston, South Carolina, 1920–1940" (Ph.D. diss., Duke University, 1998). For primary material from the visitor's perspective, scholars should consult Thomas D. Clark, ed., *Travels in the Old South: A Bibliography*, 3 vols. (Norman: University of Oklahoma Press, 1956–59); and Thomas D. Clark, ed., *Travels in the New South: A Bibliography*, 2 vols. (Norman: University of Oklahoma Press, 1962). See also Gary D. Ford, "Tourism," in *The Encyclopedia of Southern Culture*, ed. Charles Reagan Wilson and William Ferris (Chapel Hill: University of North Carolina Press, 1989), 1244–45.

6. Lawrence F. Brewster, *Summer Migrations and Resorts of South Carolina Low-Country Planters* (Durham, N.C.: Duke University Press, 1947), 1–6, 53–62; Charlene Marie Lewis, "Ladies and Gentlemen on Display: Planter Society at the Virginia Springs, 1790–1860" (Ph.D. diss., University of Virginia, 1997), passim; and

Thomas E. Chambers, "Fashionable Dis-Ease: Promoting Health and Leisure at Sara-toga Springs, New York and the Virginia Springs, 1790–1860" (Ph.D. diss., The College of William and Mary, 1999), chaps. 3 and 4. Some planters even traveled north in search of the company of their peers. See Daniel Kilbride, "The Cosmo-politan South: Privileged Southerners, and the Fashionable Tour in the Antebellum Era," *Journal of Urban History* 26 (July 2000): 563–90. For the role of resorts in influencing public opinion on issues such as secession, see John C. Inscoe, *Mountain Masters, Slavery, and the Sectional Crisis in Western North Carolina* (Knoxville: Uni-versity of Tennessee Press, 1989), 31–36. Interestingly, travel accounts have been some of the most frequently cited sources on antebellum southern history, but the nature and significance of travel itself eluded scholars of the region.

7. Edward L. Ayers, *The Promise of the New South: Life after Reconstruction* (New York: Oxford University Press, 1992), 61; Nina L. Silber, *The Romance of Re-union: Northerners and the South, 1865–1900* (Chapel Hill: University of North Carolina Press, 1993), chap. 3, quote on 67.

8. William Bean Kennedy, "Montreat: An Educational Center of the Presbyte-rian Church," *American Presbyterians: Journal of Presbyterian History* 74 (summer 1996): 93–106; Mary-Ruth Marshall, "Handling Dynamite: Young People, Race, and Montreat," *American Presbyterians: Journal of Presbyterian History* 74 (summer 1996): 141–53; and Ted Ownby, *Subduing Satan: Religion, Recreation, and Manhood in the Rural South* (Chapel Hill: University of North Carolina Press, 1990), 169, 174.

9. George B. Tindall, *Emergence of the New South, 1913–1945* (Baton Rouge: Louisiana State University Press, 1967), chap. 7; Clark, *Emerging South*, 140; Pres-ton, *Dirt Roads to Dixie*, chap. 2.

10. W. E. B. Du Bois, *Darkwater: Voices from Within the Veil* (New York: AMS Press, 1920), 228–30. Marsha Dean Phelts, *An American Beach for African Ameri-cans* (Gainesville: University Press of Florida, 1997); Russ Rymer, *American Beach: How 'Progress' Robbed a Black Town—and a Nation—of History, Wealth, and Power* (New York: HarperPerennial, 2000). For a full discussion of traveling conditions for black southerners, see Grace Elizabeth Hale, *Making Whiteness: The Culture of Seg-regation in the South, 1890–1940* (New York: Pantheon Books, 1998), 130–34.

11. Steven William Foster, *The Past is Another Country: Representation, Historical Consciousness, and Resistance in the Blue Ridge* (Berkeley: University of California Press, 1988), 194. The literature on tourism workers is particularly small. For an in-troduction, see Michal Smith, *Behind the Glitter: The Impact of Tourism on Rural Women of the Southeast* (Lexington: Southeast Women's Employment Commission, 1989).

12. Jack E. Davis, *Race Against Time: Culture and Separation in Natchez Since 1930* (Baton Rouge: Louisiana State University Press, 2001), chap. 2; Grace Eliza-beth Hale, "Granite Stopped Time: The Stone Mountain Memorial and Represen-tations of White Southern Identity," *Georgia Historical Quarterly* 81 (spring 1998): 22–44; and Clark, *Emerging South*, 142.

13. For an introduction to such issues, see John Shelton Reed, *My Tears Spoiled*

My Aim and Other Reflections on Southern Culture (Columbia: University of Missouri Press, 1993), 5–28, 65–74; James C. Cobb, *The Selling of the South: The Southern Crusade for Industrial Development, 1936–1990*, 2d ed. (Urbana: University of Illinois Press, 1993), 1–4, 279–81.

Chapter 1

1. Charles Dudley Warner, "New Orleans," *Harper's New Monthly Magazine*, January 1887, 186–205.

2. Ibid.

3. *The Mascot*, January 22, 1887.

4. Ibid.; *The New Orleans Item*, February 10, 1910.

5. The ordinances that created and defined the boundaries of the vice district are Ord. 13,032 C.S. and Ord. 13,485 C.S., both passed in 1897. On Behrman's support of the Storyville status quo, see Martin Behrman, *Martin Behrman of New Orleans: Memoirs of a City Boss*, ed. John R. Kemp (Baton Rouge: Louisiana State University Press, 1977), 302–16; George M. Reynolds, *Machine Politics in New Orleans, 1897–1926* (1936; reprint, New York: AMS Press, 1968), 156–61.

6. See Al Rose, *Storyville, New Orleans: Being an Authentic, Illustrated Account of the Notorious Red-Light District* (Tuscaloosa: University of Alabama Press, 1974) for the most commonly referred to rendering of Storyville as unique. Many scholars of the South have chosen not to consider New Orleans in regional histories because they believe its size or racial complexities make it atypical. See for example Howard N. Rabinowitz, *Race Relations in the Urban South, 1865–1890* (New York: Oxford University Press, 1978). While they do not focus on New Orleans, several recent works make explicit connections between race and sexuality in other parts of the South. See for example Glenda Elizabeth Gilmore, *Gender and Jim Crow: Women and the Politics of White Supremacy in North Carolina, 1896–1920* (Chapel Hill: University of North Carolina Press, 1996); Martha Hodes, *White Women, Black Men: Illicit Sex in the 19th-Century South* (New Haven: Yale University Press, 1997).

7. For further exploration of these themes, see Alecia P. Long, "The Great Southern Babylon: Sexuality, Race, and Reform in New Orleans, 1865–1920" (Ph.D. diss., University of Delaware, 2001).

8. *Daily-Picayune*, January 1, 1898; Herbert Asbury, *The French Quarter: An Informal History of the New Orleans Underworld* (New York: Alfred A. Knopf, 1936), 323–25.

9. Behrman, *Martin Behrman of New Orleans*, 302–16; Reynolds, *Machine Politics in New Orleans*, 156–61.

10. Ord. 1615 N.C.S., February 10, 1903.

11. *Architectural Art and Its Allies*, August 1905. See also Keith L. Bryant, "Cathedrals, Castles, and Roman Baths: Railway Station Architecture in the Urban South," *Journal of Urban History* (February 1976): 195–230.

12. *Times-Democrat*, June 1, 1908.

13. For elaboration on the idea of Storyville as an amusement park, see Emily Landau, "'Spectacular Wickedness': New Orleans, Prostitution, and the Politics of Sex" (Ph.D. diss., Yale University, in progress). See also *George L'Hote v. City of New Orleans et al.* (1897), Civil District Court, Division B, Docket No. 54533, hereafter cited as *"L'Hote v. City of New Orleans*, 1897," New Orleans City Archives, New Orleans Public Library (NOCA NOPL); Isadore Dyer, *The Municipal Control of Prostitution in the United States* (Brussels: H. Lamertin, 1900), 2–3.

14. Dyer, *Municipal Control of Prostitution*, 26.

15. Julian Ralph, "New Orleans, Our Southern Capitol," *Harper's New Monthly Magazine*, February 1899, 364–65.

16. *Daily-Picayune*, June 28, 1900.

17. Between June and December of 1900, Mayor Paul Capdeville received at least ten letters from citizens who complained about brothels and assignation houses that remained in their neighborhoods. Even some prostitutes wrote letters to the mayor asking that they be given additional time before moving into the district. See Correspondence of Mayor Paul Capdeville, NOCA NOPL.

18. *Daily-Picayune*, January 18, 1908.

19. New Orleans Travelers' Aid Society Papers, 365, Manuscripts Department, Howard-Tilton Library, Tulane University, hereafter cited as "Travelers' Aid Society MSS." For information on the historical context that led the New Orleans Travelers' Aid Society and similar groups of reformers to engage in antiprostitution efforts nationwide, see John D'Emilio and Estelle B. Freedman, *Intimate Matters: A History of Sexuality in America* (New York: Harper & Row, 1988), 208–15.

20. For a consideration of the relationship between sexuality and Mardi Gras, see Karen Leathem, "'A Carnival According to Their Own Desires': Gender and Mardi Gras in New Orleans, 1870–1941" (Ph.D. diss., University of North Carolina, Chapel Hill, 1994), 7, 214.

21. Ted Ownby, *Subduing Satan: Religion, Recreation, and Manhood in the Rural South, 1865–1920* (Chapel Hill: University of North Carolina Press, 1990), 39, 167. I thank Dr. Ownby for his suggestion that I consider New Orleans as a regional safety valve. See also William Ivy Hair, *Carnival of Fury: Robert Charles and the New Orleans Race Riot of 1900* (Baton Rouge: Louisiana State University Press, 1976), 69–70.

22. On the sexual double standard and the belief that prostitutes provided a necessary safety valve for naturally virulent male sexuality, see D'Emilio and Freedman, *Intimate Matters*, 178–88. For accounts of southern pastors in Storyville, see Reid Mitchell, *All on a Mardi Gras Day: Episodes in the History of New Orleans Carnival* (Cambridge: Harvard University Press, 1995), 2; Ownby, *Subduing Satan*, 39, 167; Hazelhurst *Weekly Copiahan*, March 15, 1884, cited in Hair, *Carnival of Fury*, 76, 80.

23. Leathem, "A Carnival According to Their Own Desires," 185–91.

24. The Williams Research Center at The Historic New Orleans Collection (WRC THNOC) has the most complete collection of extant "Blue Books." See also

Pamela Arceneaux, "Guidebooks to Sin: The Blue Books of Storyville," *Louisiana History* (fall 1987): 397–405; Rose, *Storyville*, 135–46.

25. Arceneaux, "Guidebooks to Sin," 399; Joseph Roach, "Slave Spectacles and Tragic Octoroons: A Cultural Genealogy of Antebellum Performance," *Theatre Survey* (November 1992): 183.

26. See the collection of "Blue Books," WRC THNOC; Rose, *Storyville*, 134–46. See also Landau, "'Spectacular Wickedness': New Orleans, Prostitution, and the Politics of Sex, 1898–1917."

27. *L'Hote v. City of New Orleans*, 1897; Sanborn Fire Insurance Map, 1896.

28. W. C. Handy, *Father of the Blues: An Autobiography* (1941; reprint, New York: Collier, 1971), 77–78, cited in Edward L. Ayers, *The Promise of the New South: Life after Reconstruction* (New York: Oxford University Press, 1992), 388.

29. The *Sunday Sun* article is reproduced in Rose, *Storyville*, 208.

30. "The Red Book—A Complete Directory of the Tenderloin," WRC THNOC; *Wentworth's Souvenir Sporting Guide* (New York: n.p., 1885), cited in Kathie D. Williams, "The 'Painted Inmate' and the 'Aggressive Savage': Sexual and Racial Segregation in Louisville, Kentucky" (paper presented at the Fifth Southern Conference on Women's History, Richmond, Virginia, June 15, 2000); Ayers, *Promise of the New South*, 388.

31. Leathem, "A Carnival According to Their Own Desires," 33.

32. New Orleans Chamber of Commerce Records, RG 66, Special Collections, Earl K. Long Library, University of New Orleans, hereafter cited as "Chamber of Commerce Records."

33. Chamber of Commerce Records.

34. Ibid.; *New Orleans: What to See and How to See It: A Standard Guide to the City of New Orleans* (New Orleans: The New Orleans Progressive Union Press, 1910).

35. Chamber of Commerce Records; Leathem, "A Carnival According to Their Own Desires," 213.

36. Chamber of Commerce Records; Will Irwin, "The American Saloon," excerpted in Rose, *Storyville*, 46.

37. Irwin, "The American Saloon."

38. Thomas Mackey, "Red Lights Out: A Legal History of Prostitution, Disorderly Houses and Vice Districts, 1870–1917" (Ph.D. diss., Rice University, 1984), 2, 15. See also D'Emilio and Freedman, *Intimate Matters*, 210.

39. Act. No. 176, *Acts Passed by the General Assembly of the State of Louisiana at the Regular Session* (Baton Rouge: n.p., 1908), 238–39. See also Leathem, "A Carnival According to Their Own Desires," 226; Reynolds, *Machine Politics in New Orleans*, 161.

40. *Daily-Picayune*, January 7, 1909, cited in Leathem, "A Carnival According to Their Own Desires," 226.

41. Ibid.

42. Chamber of Commerce Records.

43. See Long, "The Great Southern Babylon" for an extended discussion of the connections between the city's sinful reputation and the success of its tourist industry.

44. *The Item*, February 10, 1910.

45. Ibid., February 2, 15, 1910.

46. Ibid.

47. Ibid., and March 22, 1910.

48. Ibid.

49. Ibid.; Chamber of Commerce Records; Ord. 6701 N.C.S., August 2, 1910.

50. *The Item*, October 30, 31, 1910.

51. Ibid., November 1, 1910.

52. Behrman, *Martin Behrman of New Orleans*, 304-5.

53. Ibid., 306-7; Committee of Fifteen for the Suppression of Commercial Vice in Louisiana, *Prostitution: An Appeal to the People of Louisiana* (New Orleans: Hauser Printing Co., 1913). See also Committee on Social Hygiene, *Segregation versus Morality* (New Orleans: New Orleans City Federation of Clubs, ca. 1909); "Resume of Legislation upon Matters Relating to Social Hygiene Considered by the Various States during 1914," *Social Hygiene* (December 1914), 105-6.

54. "Cribs" Broadside, copy in possession of the author.

55. Chamber of Commerce Records.

56. Travelers' Aid Society MSS.

57. Records of the War Department General and Special Staffs, War College Division and War Plans Division, Subordinate Offices—Education and Recreation Branch, Commission on Training Camp Activities, Entry 395, REPORTS RELATING TO TRAINING CAMP ACTIVITIES, 1917 (National Archives), Record Group 165, Box 8, "Kentucky to Louisiana."

58. Ibid. Being "unfit for service" was a euphemism for contracting a venereal infection. See Allan Brandt, *No Magic Bullet: A Social History of Venereal Disease in the United States since 1880* (1985; reprint, New York: Oxford University Press, 1987), 52-95.

59. Brandt, *No Magic Bullet*, 52-95; Joseph Mayer, "The Passing of the Red Light District—Vice Investigations and Results," *Social Hygiene* (1918): 207.

60. Mark Thomas Connelly, *The Response to Prostitution in the Progressive Era* (Chapel Hill: University of North Carolina Press, 1980), 139.

61. Behrman, *Martin Behrman of New Orleans*, 312.

62. *Times-Picayune*, February 22, 1917.

63. Warner, "New Orleans," 201.

64. *Times-Picayune*, January 27, 1921; Reynolds, *Machine Politics in New Orleans*, 231.

65. See Sanford Jarrell, *New Orleans—The Civilized and Lively City* (n.p., ca. 1929); "Tourism, Miscellany," Rare Vertical File, Louisiana Division, NOPL; Edward Anderson, "Uncovering the Vice Cesspool of New Orleans," *Real Detective*, March 1935, 40-43, 66, 68; Marquis W. Childs, "New Orleans is a Wicked City," *Vanity Fair*, November 1934, 62, 72.

66. Roach, "Slave Spectacles and Tragic Octoroons," 186.

67. See for example the pictorial "Mardi Gras 2000," *Playboy*, March 2000, 78–85. Local reaction to the *Playboy* story can be found in the *Times-Picayune*, February 24, 27, 29, and March 3, 2000.

Chapter 2

1. "Biographical Sketches of Harold Sherman," File 3, Box 1 of Subseries 1—Subseries 1, Harold M. Sherman Papers, University of Central Arkansas Archives, Conway; Harold Sherman, "They All Come Back," *Heritage of Stone* 2 (fall 1978): 9–14.

2. *Stone County Leader*, February 8, 1962, 1.

3. Harold Sherman to Wilbur D. Mills, March 15, 1957, File 1, Box 1 of Subseries 3—Series 1, Sherman Papers.

4. "Land of the Cross-Bow," undated press release from the Arkansas Publicity and Information Department, Little Rock, File 3, Box 1 of Subseries 1—Series 1, Sherman Papers.

5. "Preliminary Overall Economic Development Program for North Central Arkansas," August 1961; Leo Rainey, "Summary of Work in the Five-County Area, July 1, 1961–June 30, 1962," Folder 1, Box 4, Leo Rainey Papers, University of Arkansas Special Collections, Fayetteville.

6. See Jane S. Becker, *Selling Tradition: Appalachia and the Construction of an American Folk, 1930–1940* (Chapel Hill: University of North Carolina Press, 1998.)

7. Untitled and undated bulletin, Folder 6, Box 3, Rainey Papers; Leo Rainey, "The Arkansas Traveller Folk Theatre," theater handbill (Hardy, Ark., 1978), Lyon College Library, 5; Rainey to Glen Hinkle, September 21, 1973, Folder 1, Box 11; Rainey, "Summary of Work in the Five-County Area," Folder 1, Box 4; Rainey, Untitled bulletin, February 5, 1962, Folder 6, Box 3, Rainey Papers; "Narrative Report of County Extension Workers—Baxter County, 1962"; "Narrative Report of County Extension Workers—Sharp County, 1962," Box 464, Federal Extension Service Records—Arkansas (FESRA), National Archives Southwest, Fort Worth, Tex.

8. John Fleming, *The Blanchard Springs Caverns Story* (Little Rock: Gallinule Society, 1973), 3, 35, 42; Sherman to Mills, August 18, 1963; November 7, 1963, File 2, Box 1, Subseries 2—Series 1, Sherman Papers.

9. "Narrative Report of County Extension Workers—Stone County, 1962," Box 464, FESRA; Rainey, Untitled bulletin, February 5, 1962, Folder 6, Box 3, Rainey Papers; *Stone County Leader*, April 12, 1962, 1; January 18, 1962, 1; March 1, 1962, 1; March 29, 1962, 1; *Melbourne Times*, April 12, 1962, 1.

10. Rainey to Hinkle, September 21, 1973, Folder 1, Box 11, Rainey Papers; W. K. McNeil, *Ozark Country*, Folklife in the South Series (Jackson: University Press of Mississippi, 1995), 168–69.

11. Ann Davenport Lucas, "The Music of Jimmy Driftwood," *Mid-America Folk-*

lore 15 (spring 1987): 27; Robert M. Anderson, "Jimmy Driftwood: Poet Laureate with a Banjo," *Arkansas Times*, October 1979, 62; Ernie Deane, "Folk Songs Preserve Our Heritage," *Arkansas Gazette*, April 28, 1963, 5E.

12. Samm Woolley Combs, *A Pickin' and a Grinnin' on the Courthouse Square: An Ozark Family Album* (Mountain View: Decisive Moments Press, 1990), 20–21; *Stone County Leader*, February 28, 1963, 1; April 25, 1963, 1; *Batesville Guard*, March 29, 1963, 1 (quote).

13. McNeil, *Ozark Country*, 169; Craig Ogilvie, "Ozark Traditions: Folk Culture, Blanchard Springs, Created Stone County Tourism Industry," *Batesville Guard*, January 25, 1994, 10; *Stone County Leader*, April 24, 1975, 2; Leo Rainey, interview with author, Batesville, Ark., October 9, 1998, Ozark Oral History Program, Ozark Cultural Resource Center, Ozark Folk Center, Mountain View, Ark.

14. I refer to the original Arkansas Folk Festival as "pure" and "earnest," though I am aware that the event represented the commoditization of folk culture, which according to sociologist Dean MacCannell inherently rendered the folk arts presented less authentic. But, as sociologist Erik Cohen asserts, "commoditization does not necessarily destroy the meaning of cultural products. . . . " MacCannell, "Staged Authenticity: Arrangements of Social Space in Tourist Settings," *American Journal of Sociology* 79 (November 1973): 589–603; Cohen, "Authenticity and Commoditization in Tourism," *Annals of Tourism Research* 15 (1988): 383.

15. Jack Temple Kirby, *Rural Worlds Lost: The American South 1920–1960* (Baton Rouge: Louisiana State University Press, 1987), 80.

16. George Fersh and Mildred Fersh, *Bessie Moore: A Biography* (Little Rock: August House, 1986), 181; McNeil, *Ozark Country*, 169; Rainey to Hinkle, September 21, 1973, Folder 1, Box 11, Rainey Papers; *Batesville Guard*, March 31, 1995, 3; David E. Whisnant, *Modernizing the Mountaineer: People, Power, and Planning in Appalachia* (Boone, N.C.: Appalachian Consortium Press, 1980), 72.

17. Combs, *A Pickin' and a Grinnin'*, 19.

18. Fersh and Fersh, *Bessie Moore*, 181, 178; McNeil, *Ozark Country*, 170.

19. McNeil, *Ozark Country*, 169, 170; Fersh and Fersh, *Bessie Moore*, 179, 178.

20. McNeil, *Ozark Country*, 171; Diane O. Tebbetts, *Resident and Tourist Perceptions of the Ozark Folk Center*, Arkansas Agricultural Experiment Station Special Report No. 24 (Fayetteville: A.A.E.S., 1976), 2–3; *Stone County Leader*, May 29, 1975, 2.

21. Tebbetts, *Perceptions*, 3–4; *Stone County Leader*, September 25, 1975, 2; October 2, 1975, 1.

22. H. Page Stephens, "The Case of the Missing Folk Music: A Study of Aspects of Musical Life in Stone County, Arkansas from 1890–1980," *Mid-America Folklore* 10 (fall–winter 1982): 63, 64.

23. *Stone County Leader*, September 18, 1975, 1; April 24, 1975, 2; May 22, 1975, 1, 2; July 10, 1975, 1; July 17, 1975, 1; September 25, 1975, 1.

24. Ibid., May 29, 1975, 2.

25. Tebbetts, *Perceptions*, 3; Leo Rainey, et al., *Songs of the Ozark Folk* (Branson, Mo.: Ozarks Mountaineer, 1972), 35; Rex Harral, interview with author, Wilburn, Ark., July 21, 1993, Ozark Oral History Program, Mountain View, Ark.

26. McNeil, *Ozark Country*, 171; *Stone County Leader*, July 31, 1975, 1 (quote).

27. *Arkansas Gazette*, June 20, 1969, 1B; *Horseshoe Progress*, May 30, 1969, 1; July 4, 1969, 1; August 30, 1969, 1; June 29, 1970, 14; March 31, 1971, 1. Although beyond the bounds of this essay, the growth of tourism and the development of Ozark retirement communities shared common themes. Both took advantage of the region's appealing physical characteristics and low cost of living. Community developers and tourism entrepreneurs also looked to the Midwest for common clients.

28. Rainey interview. The Arkansas Traveller legend, which spawned a song, play, sketching, and variations of each, involved an educated, antebellum traveler's venture into the Arkansas hills and a humorous exchange with a resident Ozarker.

29. *Arkansas Gazette*, January 6, 1967, 1B. Bob Burns was a nationally known, depression-era vaudeville and radio comedian whose hillbilly stage persona capitalized on his Arkansas origins.

30. Donald Harington, *Let Us Build Us a City: Eleven Lost Towns* (1975; reprint, New York: Harcourt Brace Jovanovich, Harvest, 1987), 98.

31. *Arkansas Gazette*, January 4, 1967, 1B; January 6, 1967, 1B.

32. Harington, *Let Us Build Us a City*, 110.

33. *The Informer and Newton County Times*, October 6, 1967, 1; May 17, 1968, 1; May 24, 1968, 1; *Arkansas Gazette*, May 19, 1968, 3A (quote).

34. *Arkansas Gazette*, October 28, 1968, 1A, 2A, 6A; January 9, 1969, 1A; May 4, 1969, 10A; Roy Reed, *Faubus: The Life and Times of an American Prodigal* (Fayetteville: University of Arkansas Press, 1997), 329.

35. Silver Dollar City is an Ozark, pioneer-themed amusement park near Branson, Missouri. Established in 1960 by Mary Herschend, it was designed to be a Midwestern Colonial Williamsburg. Milton D. Rafferty, *The Ozarks: Land and Life* (Norman: University of Oklahoma Press, 1980), 216.

36. Otto Ernest Rayburn, *The Eureka Springs Story* (1954; reprint, Eureka Springs: Wheeler Printing, 1982), 74; Paul Faris, *Ozark Log Cabin Folks: The Way They Were* (Little Rock: Rose Publishing, 1983), 66.

37. Evan Booth to Rayburn, February 17, 1957, Folder 12, Box 1, Otto Ernest Rayburn Collection, University of Arkansas Special Collections, Fayetteville; Otto Ernest Rayburn, *Forty Years in the Ozarks: An Autobiography* (1957; reprint, Eureka Springs: Wheeler Printing, 1983), 89.

38. Glen Jeansonne, *Gerald L. K. Smith: Minister of Hate* (New Haven: Yale University Press, 1988), 2, 11, 188, 189.

39. Ibid., 190–92.

40. Ibid., 193, 196, 199.

41. Ibid., 200, 201.

42. Charles F. Keyes and Pierre L. van den Berghe, "Tourism and Re-created Ethnicity," *Annals of Tourism Research* 11 (1984): 346.

43. Jim Creighton, "'Tis a Gift to Be Free," *St. Louis Post-Dispatch*, April 28, 1974, 16F.

44. In his study of the Missouri Ozarks, Edgar D. McKinney found a similar development. The success of Harold Bell Wright's *Shepherd of the Hills* brought a degree of tourism-inspired modernization and commercialism to Branson's Taney County that was scarcely experienced in the more agriculturally and economically "progressive" plateau sections of south central Missouri. Edgar D. McKinney, "Images, Realities, and Cultural Transformation in the Missouri Ozarks, 1920–1960" (Ph.D. diss., University of Missouri, Columbia, 1990), 52–53.

Chapter 3

1. Although the role tourism has played in the history of Florida has been dealt with in a number of general studies, there remains much work to do on the topic itself. Some books that will give the reader an understanding of the context in which the tourist industry developed are Michael Gannon, *Florida: A Short History* (Gainesville: University Press of Florida, 1993); Gloria Jahoda, *Florida: A Bicentennial History* (New York: W. W. Norton, 1976); and Charlton W. Tebeau, *A History of Florida* (Coral Gables, Fla.: University of Miami Press, 1971).

2. A general account of pre–World War II land development schemes in Florida can be found in the WPA Federal Writers' Project guide to the state that was published in 1939. See *Florida: A Guide to the Southernmost State* (Tallahassee, Fla., 1939). A good analysis of some of the more important development efforts is David Nolan, *Fifty Feet in Paradise: The Booming of Florida* (San Diego: Harcourt Brace Jovanovich, 1984). For a social and environmental history of Florida, see Mark Derr, *Some Kind of Paradise: A Chronicle of Man and the Land in Florida* (New York: William Morrow, 1989).

3. *Florida: A Guide to the Southernmost State*, 61–63; Gannon, *Florida: A Short History*, 77–82; Jahoda, *Florida: A Bicentennial History*, 113–31; and Tebeau, *A History of Florida*, 377–93.

4. While there is no good account of tourism and land development along the Panhandle coast, residents of the area have collected and published personal accounts that supply important information on the evolution of the region. See Carol McCrite, "C. H. McGee: Mr. Seagrove," in *The Way We Were: Recollections of South Walton Pioneers* (Santa Rosa Beach, Fla.: South Walton Three Arts Alliance, 1996), 130–33. See also Harvey H. Jackson III, "Birmingham and the Beach," *Birmingham News*, April 9, 2000.

5. McCrite, "C. H. McGee," 130–33.

6. Ibid. My grandmother, Minnie Edwards Jackson, and my aunt, Sarah Ellen Jackson, both from Deatsville, Alabama, bought property at Seagrove Beach in 1953. In 1955, C. H. McGee, Jr., built a house for them there. Until their deaths in the 1970s they spent a great deal of time at Seagrove, and I visited them often. Other members of our family, including my father, purchased land in the development, and

today another aunt and uncle live there year round. Therefore, much of the information about early Seagrove comes from personal experiences and from letters and documents now in my possession. Today I own the house McGee built and it was my base of operation when I researched and wrote this article.

7. "Time Stands Still in Seagrove Beach," *The Seaside Times*, winter 1992; "Covenant" attached to the "Abstract of Title" to Lot 10, Block D, Seagrove First Addition, April 21, 1953, Jackson File, in possession of the author.

8. Wanda Ruffin, "Sand in Their Shoes: Paul and Margaret Benedict," in *The Way We Were*, 135–38; "Time Stands Still in Seagrove Beach."

9. Carl P. Heartburg to Minnie E. Jackson, December 30, 1956; and Minnie E. Jackson to Richard Simpson, January 2, 1957. Heartburg, vice president of the First National Bank of Birmingham and a homeowner in Seagrove, was organizing the letter writing campaign to oppose the beach route. Richard Simpson was the chairman of the Florida State Road Department. Both letters are in the author's possession.

10. Local newspapers are filled with accounts of the storm. See also Norma Joan Howard, "Hurricane," in *Of Days Gone By: Reflections of South Walton County, Florida* (Santa Rosa Beach, Fla.: South Walton Three Arts Alliance, 1999). A booklet entitled "Hurricane Eloise" was published to document Nature's fury. A copy of this is in the author's possession.

11. "Covenant" attached to the "Abstract of Title." One of the condos also failed and its units were disposed of in a bankruptcy sale.

12. Steven Brooke, *Seaside* (Gretna, La.: Pelican Publishing, 1995), 13–14; Kurt Andersen, "Oldfangled New Towns," *Time*, May 20, 1991, 52–55.

13. Brooke, *Seaside*, 12–14.

14. Ibid., 15–18; Henry Leifermann, "Oz by the Sea or Is It Kansas?" *Sunshine*, December 22, 1985, 12–18; "Seaside: An Attempt to Make Development a Community," unidentified clipping in the 1980 scrapbook, Seaside Archives; Philip Langdon, "A Good Place to Live," *Atlantic Monthly*, March 1988, 39–60; interview with Marietta Lovell, Seagrove Beach, Fla., July 13, 1996.

15. Brooke, *Seaside*, 14–17; Linda Marx, "One Man's Dreamland," *Palm Beach Life*, July 1988, 45, 48, 69–70; *Pensacola News-Journal*, September 1, 1985; *Fort Walton Playground Daily News*, March 15, 1981; "Seaside Development Receives County Approval," unidentified clipping in the 1983 scrapbook, Seaside Archives.

16. Interview with Bill Wright, Seagrove Beach, Fla., July 16, 1996; Lovell interview; Marx, "One Man's Dreamland," 44–45; Langdon, "Good Place to Live," 42; "Seaside: An Attempt to Make Development a Community," 1983; Brooke, *Seaside*, 17.

17. *Panama City News-Herald*, August 16, 1981; *Destin Log*, November 6, 1982; Phil Patton, "In Seaside, Florida, the Forward Thing is Looking Back," *Smithsonian*, January 1991, 90; Concerned Citizens of Walton County to Mr. Robert Davis, October 1981, scrapbook in Seaside Archives; Brooke, *Seaside*, 17–19. The term "Redneck Riviera" was supposedly coined by *New York Times* writer Howell Raines, in an article on the Alabama Gulf Coast. The term stuck and was soon applied, indis-

criminately, to the Florida Panhandle as well—much to the distress of many of its residents. See Howell Raines, *Fly Fishing through the Midlife Crisis* (New York: Anchor Books, 1993), 43–44.

18. *Panama City News-Herald*, August 16, 1981; *Destin Log*, June 8, June 22, July 2, August 10, August 13, 1983; *DeFuniak Springs Herald-Breeze*, August 23, 1983; *Seaside Times*, autumn 1994; Lovell interview. The picture of Robert Davis at the womanless beauty pageant is in Carol McCrite, "Burgers, Beer, and Seaside Saturday Sunset," in *Of Days Gone By*, 22. Before the picture was published its existence was revealed to me by Ken and Cobb Sheriff, Seagrove Beach, Florida.

19. L. Joyner, "Lazy Living on the Gulf," *Southern Living*, June 1984, 102-5; *Destin Log*, November 6, 1982; Davis Mohney and Keller Easterling, eds., *Seaside: Making a Town in America* (Princeton: Princeton Architectural Press, 1991), 46, 72.

20. Brooke, *Seaside*, 21; interview with Robert Davis, Seaside, Fla., August 13, 1996; Lovell interview; Wright interview. During the first year, a lot in Seaside could be purchased from Davis for between $15,000 and $20,000. See George Parsons and Judith Van Cleve, *Destinations: Opportunities for Economic Development in the American Small Town* (Mississipi State: Mississippi State University Community/Economic Development Center, 1993), 26.

21. Although there was some early mention of apartments over stores and a bed-and-breakfast inn, the first advertisement for rentals seems to have been in *Southern Living* in July of 1984. Later that year a Seaside brochure mentioned "vacation rentals," but almost as an afterthought. It was not until the summer of 1985 that the big push began. See *Alabama*, July 1985, 16–17; *Panama City News Journal*, August 5, 1984; interview with Robert Davis, Seaside, Fla., May 7, 1996; Wright interview. Most of the rentals are still handled through Seaside's own rental agency, though in recent years some of the homeowners have decided to list their property with another company.

22. Lovell interview; Wright interview. Apart from sales, the largest source of income for Davis came from his ownership of the buildings in the Town Center and later in Ruskin Place. Once all the town lots are sold, this and his rental arrangements will be his only revenue source, but it will be a lucrative one. Although Davis has been criticized for his control over the stores and their merchandise and for his "home-town socialism" approach to competition, his financial success is difficult to argue against.

23. Lovell interview; Wright interview; interview with Joan Fitzpatrick, Seagrove Beach, Fla., March 25, 1996; Davis interview, May 7, 1996; Boles, "Robert Davis"; Marx, "One Man's Dreamland," 68–69; Leifermann, "Oz by the Sea," 16; Langdon, "A Good Place to Live," 45; Brooke, *Seaside*, 7; John Craddock, "Seaside: A Panorama of the Past," *Florida Trend*, January 1986, n.p.; *Seaside Times*, summer 1995; "Rental Program is Critical to Seaside's Viability," *Seaside Community Report*, June 1992, copy in Seaside Archives.

24. Lovell interview; Davis interview, May 7, 1986; *Jacksonville Times-Union*, March 1, 1986; Marx, "One Man's Dreamland," 68–69; John Dorschner, "Back to

the Future," *Tropic*, February 21, 1988, 13; "Town of the Future," unidentified clipping in the 1988 scrapbook, Seaside Archives. Today the impact of Seaside has been such that rental prices in neighboring towns have escalated to the point that workers cannot afford to live there either, and there is talk of setting up a shuttle service to get employees to the coast from their homes inland.

25. *Time*, November 4, 1985, 81; Leifermann, "Oz by the Sea," 12, 15–16.

26. Leifermann, "Oz by the Sea," 18; Langdon, "A Good Place to Live," 42; Wright interview.

27. Clippings in the Seaside Scrapbooks, 1983 to 1996, some unidentified, but most coming from local newspapers. Also various editions of the *Seaside Times* and promotional brochures (in particular see the one for 1984). See also *New York Times*, August 1, 1993.

28. *St. Petersburg Times*, June 15, 1986; *Destin Log*, February 8, 1984; *Building*, 22. Micah's birth was announced in the first "Seaside Special," a newsletter for employees, November 1987. For a review of the increasing number of activities for children, see later issues of the *Seaside Times*. See also Langdon, "A Good Place to Live," 42.

29. *Seaside Times*, fall 1991, announces Davis's return and includes a lengthy letter in which the developer told of his new plans for Seaside. These ideas (including the train and ponies) were expanded later in a letter from Robert Davis to Seasiders, May 12, 1992, a copy of which is in the Seaside Archives. The next month Seaside's newly formed Town Council objected to the rides, but Davis went ahead with his plans. The concessions were discontinued after a year because of lack of profits. See *Seaside Times*, winter 1992; *Seaside Community Report*, June 1992. For other examples of tensions between the developer and the homeowners, as well as support for Davis, see *Seaside Times*, spring 1989; "Dog Days, 1990," spring 1991; *Seaside Community Report*, January, April, July, and October 1993; interview with town manager Connie McFarland, Seaside, Fla., August 12, 1996; interview with Norwood Hodges, Anniston, Ala., June 3, 1996; Davis interview, May 7, 1996; Wright interview. See also *Destin Log*, February 8, 1992, and June 30, 1993; and Charles Oberdorf, "Seaside: The Little Resort on the Florida Panhandle That's Changing the Streetscapes of New Towns Everywhere," *City and Country Home*, April 1990, 64. According to figures provided by the Seaside Community Development Corporation, by 1996 the amount spent on accommodations had more than doubled.

30. Davis interview, May 7, 1996; Patton, "In Seaside," 88–89, 92–93; Marx, "One Man's Dreamland," 70–71; *Panama City News-Journal* clipping in the 1988 scrapbook, Seaside Archives.

31. The spring 1989 issue of the *Seaside Times* announced the creation of the Seaside Institute, and from that point forward it chronicles the organization's activities. The *Seaside Community Report* is also a good source for Institute activities from the homeowners' perspective. See also McFarland interview; and Lovell interview.

32. *The Wall Street Journal*, June 7, 1995, contained the critical article. Responses to it can be found in *The Wall Street Journal*, *Florida Journal*, August 16,

1995, and in the *Seaside Times*, summer 1995. See also Millie Ball, "Florida's Seaside: An Architectural Disney World," *New Orleans Times-Picayune*, October 9, 1994; and Robert Davis to Millie Ball, *New Orleans Times-Picayune*, November 20, 1994. For evidence that Davis still wanted to create a resident community with a diverse population, see Robert Davis, "Seaside, South Walton & 21st Century Urbanism," *Foresight: 1000 Friends of Florida* (spring 1994): 2, 13–15; and "Affordable Housing at Seaside," *Seaside Times*, autumn 1994. That fall the "Seeing Red Wine, Music & Art Festival" selected Habitat for Humanity as its official charity.

33. Started in 1992, the activities of "Escape to Create" are highlighted in the *Seaside Times*. See also Wright interview.

34. *Destin Log*, February 19, 1992; *Seaside Times*, early summer 1992. "From the Founder," *Seaside Times*, winter 1995, and Kenneth M. Ford and Robert S. Davis, "The Lukeion—A Collaboration Between a Small Town & University," *Seaside Times*, spring 1996, outlines the *Lukeion* idea and the arrangements with West Florida.

35. "From the Founder," *Seaside Times*, winter 1995, and Ford and Davis, "The Lukeion," *Seaside Times*, spring 1996. Davis speech to Seaside homeowners at Homeowners Weekend, October 26, 1996.

36. Davis speech to Seaside homeowners. Although Davis spoke of schools often in the early days of the development, activity really picked up when Micah was born. The story of the creation of the Seaside Neighborhood School can be followed in the pages of the *Seaside Times*, the *Seaside Community Report*, the *Beach Breeze*, and the *Destin Log*. See also Wright interview and Davis interview, May 7, 1996. Conversation with Christy Gibson, July 2, 1998. For the latest development in the story of the Neighborhood Schools, see "Second Seaside Charter School Approved," *Seaside Times*, winter 2000.

37. *Tallahassee Democrat*, September 21, 1986; Patton, "In Seaside," 92–93; Davis speech to Seaside homeowners.

38. Peter Applebome, *Dixie Rising: How the South is Shaping American Values, Politics, and Culture* (New York: Harvest Books, 1996), 21.

39. In the summer of 1998 the *Seaside Times* devoted an entire issue to *The Truman Show*, and included in it Davis's defense of the town, entitled "Illusion and Reality." The movie and its Seaside location were also subjects of numerous newspaper and magazine articles.

40. *Seaside Times*, summer 1998.

41. *Seaside Times*, early summer 1998, describes the work of the Congress for the New Urbanism and announces that Davis has been selected to chair the organization for the coming year.

42. "Beach Home Alabama," *Birmingham News*, March 12, 2000; "Birmingham and the Beach," *Birmingham News*, April 9, 2000.

43. Pricing and other information on Watercolor was provided at the development sales office in March 2000. Prices are subject to change and will probably be higher when this book is published. All other information on Watercolor is from the

promotional material available at that office. For some prices of Seaside houses, see the *Seaside Times,* winter 2000. In that paper a 2 bedroom, 1 bath, 1,008 square foot cottage was offered at $510,000. The most expensive house listed was a 4 bedroom, 2 1/2 bath, 2,145 square foot offered at $985,000.

44. "Birmingham and the Beach," *Birmingham News,* April 9, 2000.

45. Promotional material provided by Watercolor. See also Watercolor's advertisements in *Southern Living,* May 2000, and *Coastal Living,* May–June 2000.

46. Although comparative results can often be misleading, it might be noted that one of few remaining Gulf-front lots, located just east of Seagrove Beach, is currently advertised in *Coastal Living* (May–June 2000) for $650,000. A similar lot, twenty years ago, could have been bought for a tenth of that. There are only a few Gulf-front lots in Watercolor, and they sell for $1 million each.

47. *Seaside Times,* summer 1998. Information on homeownership and rentals was provided by Seaside Town Manager Connie McFarland and Seaside Public Relations Manager Christy Gibson.

48. Watercolor promotional material.

Chapter 4

Space constraints have dictated that the notes that follow be in the briefest possible form. Therefore, most specific references to particular letters have been dropped in favor of general references to manuscript collections, and titles of newspaper articles have been eliminated in favor of a simple reference to the date of the relevant issue of the paper. The maximum possible use of abbreviations has also been made.

Abbreviations

AC	*Asheville Citizen*
ACT	*Asheville Citizen-Times*
AT	*Asheville Times*
BRPA	Blue Ridge Parkway Archives, Asheville, N.C.
CO	*Charlotte Observer*
FOC	Francis O. Clarkson
FOCP	Francis O. Clarkson Papers, Southern Historical Collection, University of North Carolina at Chapel Hill
HC	Heriot Clarkson
HCP	Heriot Clarkson Papers, Southern Historical Collection, University of North Carolina at Chapel Hill
LC	Library of Congress, Washington, D.C.
N&O	Raleigh *News and Observer*
NCC, UNC	North Carolina Collection, Wilson Library, University of North Carolina at Chapel Hill
NCSA	North Carolina State Archives, Raleigh, N.C.
NPS	National Park Service

SC   Switzerland Company
SHCRWD   State Highway Commission, Right of Way Department, Blue Ridge
            Parkway Collection; North Carolina State Archives, Raleigh, N.C.
UNC   University of North Carolina

1. Richard D. Starnes, "Creating the Land of the Sky: Tourism and Society in Western North Carolina" (Ph.D. diss., Auburn University, 1999), 198; C. Brenden Martin, "Selling the Southern Highlands: Tourism and Community Development in the Mountain South" (Ph.D. diss., University of Tennessee, Knoxville, 1997).

2. Anne V. Mitchell, "Parkway Politics: Class, Culture, and Tourism in the Blue Ridge" (Ph.D. diss., University of North Carolina at Chapel Hill, 1997).

3. John A. Jakle, The Tourist: Travel in Twentieth-Century North America (Lincoln and London: University of Nebraska Press, 1985), 135–37; Phil Patton, Open Road: A Celebration of the American Highway (New York: Simon and Schuster, 1986), 66; NPS, "Regulations and Procedure to Govern the Acquisition of Rights-of-Way for National Parkways," February 8, 1935, SHCRWD, Box 1, NCSA.

4. Edward H. Abbuehl, "History of the Blue Ridge Parkway," February 8, 1948, RG 5, Series 38, Box 48, Folder 6, BRPA; NPS, "Regulations and Procedure," February 8, 1935.

5. NPS, "National Park Service Statistical Abstract 1999" (Denver, Colo.: NPS Public Use Statistics Office, 1999), 4–11, 36, 45–46.

6. Katherine Ledford, "Two Views from Grassy Mountain: Founding and Development of Little Switzerland, North Carolina," unpublished paper in possession of author.

7. William S. Powell, ed., Dictionary of North Carolina Biography, vol. 1 (Chapel Hill: University of North Carolina Press, 1979); Johnnie Virginia Anderson, "Heriot Clarkson: A Social Engineer of North Carolina" (master's thesis, Wake Forest University, 1972); various materials in HCP, Boxes 1 and 4; Capus Waynick, North Carolina Roads and Their Builders (Raleigh: Superior Stone Co., 1952), 39; Harry Wilson McKown, Jr., "Roads and Reform: The Good Roads Movement in North Carolina, 1885–1921" (master's thesis, University of North Carolina at Chapel Hill, 1972), 96–100; Paul Escott, Many Excellent People: Power and Privilege in North Carolina, 1850–1900 (Chapel Hill: University of North Carolina Press, 1985), 259–60; George B. Tindall, "Business Progressivism: Southern Politics in the Twenties," South Atlantic Quarterly 62 (1963): 92–106.

8. Louisa DeSaussure Duls, The Story of Little Switzerland (Richmond, Va.: Whittet and Shepperson, 1982); advertising copy for Little Switzerland, The Eastern National Park-to-Park Highway Magazine, Good Will Tour Edition (Asheville, N.C., 1935), 14 ff; Little Switzerland, North Carolina, Nature's Playground, The Beauty Spot of the Blue Ridge on the Scenic Highway State Route No. 19, Advertising pamphlet, July 1, 1931, NCC, UNC.

9. Duls, Story of Little Switzerland, 3, 5–10.

10. Ibid., 11–23.

11. Ibid., 23–29, 178.

12. Ibid., 30; SC, Taliaferro and Clarkson, Attorneys, "Memorandum Brief and Authorities to Mr. Taylor M. Landford, Internal Revenue Agent, Treasury Department, Internal Revenue Service, Raleigh, NC," January 17, 1944, FOCP.

13. Duls, *Story of Little Switzerland,* 33–39; see also correspondence in FOCP on Route 19 controversy in the 1920s; Cecil Kenneth Brown, *The State Highway System of North Carolina: Its Evolution and Present Status* (Chapel Hill: University of North Carolina Press, 1931), 167–68; Frank L. Dunlap to FOC, August 27, 1937, FOCP.

14. Ledford, "Two Views," 7–8; HC to Athan Hollifield, May 11, 1937, FOCP; *Switzerland Company v. North Carolina State Highway and Public Works Commission,* 216 NC 450 (1939), *North Carolina Appeal Record,* 35.

15. *The Eastern National Park-to-Park Highway Magazine,* Good Will Tour Edition (Asheville, N.C., 1935), 14 ff.

16. Committee of Mass Meeting of Little Switzerland Community, *What Citizens Think about Attorney Chas. Ross' Attack on the Switzerland Co. and Its Stockholders,* Pamphlet, August 1938, NCC, UNC; Duls, *Story of Little Switzerland,* 2–38.

17. ACT, July 5, 1936; Duls, *Story of Little Switzerland,* 244–46.

18. Duls, *Story of Little Switzerland,* 14–19, 23–25; SC financial records, 1936 and 1941, FOCP; ACT, July 5, 1936.

19. Duls, *Story of Little Switzerland,* 90–94.

20. Ibid., 81–90, 104.

21. ACT, July 25, 1937.

22. Ibid.

23. AC, June 19, 1938.

24. CO, September 26, 1937.

25. CO, June 15, 1941.

26. CO, August 15, 1937.

27. Heriot Clarkson's involvement with the Parkway movement is detailed in correspondence and other documents in: FOCP; Ehringhaus Papers, NCSA; Josephus Daniels Papers, LC; ACT, June 24, 1934; HCP; RG 79, NARA. Quotation from FOC to R. Getty Browning, August 18, 1937, FOCP.

28. HC to R. Getty Browning, June 29, 1935, SHCRWD Papers; HC to J. P. Dodge, May 11, 1937, and May 22, 1937, FOCP; ACT, July 25, 1937; CO, August 15, 1937; ACT, July 5, 1936.

29. HC to R. Getty Browning, March 21, 1936, FOCP; ACT, July 5, 1936; CO, August 15, 1937; SC financial records, 1937 and 1944, FOCP; *What Citizens Think.*

30. Articles advertising Little Switzerland appeared frequently throughout the 1930s in both the Asheville and Charlotte newspapers, and in 1935 Clarkson had had an observation platform, Kilmichael Tower, built on one of the peaks at Little Switzerland to attract more visitors; AC, June 19, 1938.

31. HC to R. Getty Browning, June 29, 1935, SHCRWD Papers, Box 1; and Parkway correspondence, 1936–37, in the FOCP.

32. James R. Hollowell to R. Getty Browning, May 10, 1936, and R. Getty Browning to J. R. Hollowell, May 13, 1936, both from the SHCRWD Papers, Box 11; R. Getty Browning to William M. Austin, June 2, 1936, SHCRWD Papers, Box 2; Capus M. Waynick to Arno B. Cammerer, November 3, 1936, RG 79, Box 2714, NARA.

33. Stanley W. Abbott to Lynn Harriss (cc to R. Getty Browning), November 18, 1936, and J. P. Dodge to Lynn M. Harriss, December 3, 1936, both from SHCRWD Papers, Box 11; J. P. Dodge to F. O. Clarkson, September 2, 1937, FOCP.

34. From the FOCP: HC to J. P. Dodge, May 22, 1937; SC and James H. Walker, Brief for the North Carolina Highway Commission, April 30, 1962; HC to J. P. Dodge, June 4, 1937; J. P. Dodge to F. O. Clarkson, September 2, 1937; and FOC to J. P. Dodge, August 7, 1937, HCP, Box 4.

35. The per-acre average paid by North Carolina crept upward through the late 1930s but always remained between $30 and $40; R. Getty Browning to FOC, August 20, 1937, and Frank L. Dunlap to FOC, August 27, 1937, both from FOCP.

36. N&O, July 6, 1938; N&O, July 8, 1938; SC and James H. Walker, Brief for the North Carolina Highway Commission, April 30, 1962, FOCP.

37. Correspondence, 1938–39, in FOCP and SHCRWD Papers, Box 3; N&O, December 17, 1938; Tri-County News (Spruce Pine, N.C.), April 6, 1939. All discussion of arguments and legal maneuvers in the case is informed by the official transcripts and records of the case itself: Switzerland Company v. North Carolina State Highway and Public Works Commission, 216 NC 450 (1939), contained in the North Carolina Appeal Record and the decision, from North Carolina Reports v. 216.

38. Clarkson employed this image frequently. See for example N&O, July 8, 1938.

39. FOC to Jonathan Daniels, November 18, 1939, FOCP.

40. HC to Ida C. Jones, November 1, 1937, FOCP; SC and James H. Walker, Brief for the North Carolina Highway Commission, April 30, 1962, FOCP; the specific losses that the Clarksons cited are discussed in various correspondence in HCP, Box 4, FOCP, N&O, July 8, 1938, and N&O, September 18, 1938; FOC to Jonathan Daniels, November 18, 1939, FOCP. This letter was later printed as a letter to the editor: N&O, November 28, 1939.

41. N&O, July 6, 1938.

42. N&O, July 8, 1938; Frank L. Dunlap to FOC, August 27, 1937, FOCP.

43. Correspondence from 1937 in FOCP; N&O, July 14, 1938.

44. Discussion of the accesses at Little Switzerland is contained in 1937–39 and 1962 correspondence in the FOCP and the SHCRWD Papers, Box 11. See also N&O, July 6, 1938; N&O, July 14, 1938; Charles Ross to A. E. Demaray, February 10, 1939, SHCRWD Papers, Box 11; 1939 and 1941 correspondence, RG 79, Boxes 2733, 2768, and 2737, NARA; and especially the legal documents, transcripts and other records from Switzerland Company v. North Carolina State Highway and Public Works Commission, 216 NC 450 (1939). Especially important here is the "Cooperative Agreement" between the North Carolina State Highway and Public

Works Commission and the Interior Department "Relating to the Relocation, Abandonment, and Maintenance of Public Roads on Parkway Lands, Section 2-L," August 30, 1938, included on page 271 of the trial record.

45. The opinion in the Supreme Court case is: *Switzerland Company v. North Carolina State Highway and Public Works Commission*, 216 NC 450 (1939). AT, November 8, 1939; *N&O*, November 9, 1939; SC and James H. Walker, Brief for the North Carolina Highway Commission, April 30, 1962, FOCP; SC financial records, 1939, FOCP.

46. 1939 correspondence and SC financial records in FOCP; 1940 correspondence, HCP, Box 4.

47. HC to FOC, April 18, 1939, FOCP; 1940 correspondence in FOCP and HCP, Box 4; Duls, *Story of Little Switzerland*, 195; see for example *Tri-County News* (Spruce Pine and Burnsville, N.C.), June 12, 1941.

48. Duls, *Story of Little Switzerland*, 193–215, 216–21; ACT, July 27, 1958.

49. 1938–39 correspondence and 1939 SC financial records in HCP, Box 4, and FOCP.

50. See *N&O*, September 18, 1938; and FOC to E. B. Jeffress, December 26, 1938, FOCP; *N&O*, July 6, 1938; *N&O*, September 10, 1938.

51. *N&O*, July 8, 1938; *N&O*, July 14, 1938.

52. HC to FOC, July 20, 1938, FOCP; FOC to J. C. B. Ehringhaus, July 28, 1938, FOCP; *N&O*, August 3, 1938.

53. HC to FOC, July 20, 1938, FOCP; Clarkson had already employed a version of this strategy a year before: see FOC to J. P. Dodge, August 7, 1937, HCP, Box 4.

54. Report of Meeting, August 1, 1938, HCP, Box 4; *What Citizens Think*; Duls, *Story of Little Switzerland*, 108–10; "List of Plaintiff's Witnesses in the Superior Court, March–April Term 1939," and "Mitchell County; List of Plaintiff's Witnesses before the Commissioners," 1939, both in FOCP.

55. HC to FOC, August 3, 1938, FOCP; *What Citizens Think*; 1938 correspondence, FOCP; *N&O*, September 6, 1938.

56. *N&O*, September 6, 1938; *What Citizens Think* and discussion of pamphlet in *N&O*, September 10, 1938.

57. *N&O*, September 10, 1938; FOC to Editor, *N&O*, September 14, 1938, FOCP.

58. FOC to Editor, *N&O*, September 14, 1938, FOCP; *N&O*, September 18, 1938; 1938 correspondence in FOCP; *N&O*, October 2, 1938.

59. 1938–39 correspondence, FOCP; and *N&O*, November 28, 1939.

60. HC to FOC, May 3, 1938, FOCP; HC to FOC, September 28, 1938, and HC to Clyde R. Hoey, May 23, 1939, both from FOCP.

61. *N&O*, July 8, 1938, September 6, 1938, and September 10, 1938; *What Citizens Think*.

62. FOC to J. C. B. Ehringhaus, October 29, 1938, FOCP; HC to Clyde R. Hoey, May 23, 1939, FOCP; HC to Thos. S. Clarkson, May 14, 1940, HCP, Box 4; HC to FOC, February 15, 1940, HCP, Box 4.

63. *N&O*, July 8, 1938.

64. R. Floyd Crouse to FOC, August 17, 1938, and FOC to R. F. Crouse, August 15, 1938, both in FOCP.

65. FOC to E. B. Jeffress, December 26, 1938, FOCP; HC to FOC, May 14, 1938, FOCP; FOC to Jonathan Daniels, January 3, 1939, and FOC to John A. Park, January 17, 1939, both in FOCP; HC to R. Getty Browning, January 12, 1939, FOCP.

66. HC to Judge Wilson Warlick, April 11, 1939, and HC to FOC, April 10, 1939, both in FOCP; *Tri-County News* (Spruce Pine, N.C.), April 13, 1939.

67. The sign affair is described in 1940–41 correspondence and documents in the following locations: RG 79, Boxes 2768, 2733, 2737, NARA.

68. FOC to Newton B. Drury, December 16, 1940, RG 79, Box 2737, NARA; FOC to A. E. Demaray, February 13, 1941, RG 79, Box 2768, NARA; and FOC to A. E. Demaray, February 13, 1941, RG 79, Box 2737, NARA.

69. Stanley W. Abbott to A. E. Demaray, August 21, 1940, RG 79, Box 2737, NARA; see 1940–41 correspondence in: RG 79, Boxes 2768 and 2737, NARA.

70. Capus M. Waynick to Arno B. Cammerer, November 3, 1936, RG 79, Box 2714, NARA.

71. Daniel S. Pierce, "Boosters, Bureaucrats, Politicians and Philanthropists: Coalition Building in the Establishment of the Great Smoky Mountains National Park" (Ph.D. diss., University of Tennessee, Knoxville, 1995), 223–34. Although the Park Service had long been at one level a "tourist development" agency, its mission went beyond catering to the narrow interests of private, local entrepreneurs to focus on opening, enhancing, and preserving national spaces for a broad spectrum of American travelers. See Hal K. Rothman, *Devil's Bargains: Tourism in the Twentieth Century American West* (Lawrence: University Press of Kansas, 1998). Richard West Sellars, *Preserving Nature in the National Parks: A History* (New Haven: Yale University Press, 1997), 280–90, discusses the Park Service as an agency that pursued "development and management of parks for public use, enjoyment, and education," rather than scientific preservation of natural resources.

Chapter 5

1. David R. Goldfield, "The City as Southern History: The Past and the Promise of Tomorrow," in *The Future South: A Historical Perspective for the Twenty-First Century*, ed. Joe P. Dunn and Howard L. Preston (Urbana: University of Illinois Press, 1991), 32; conversation with Kent B. Germany, January 25, 2001. An excellent point of departure for the study of the social and cultural impact of tourism is Hal K. Rothman, *Devil's Bargains: Tourism in the Twentieth Century American West* (Lawrence: University Press of Kansas, 1998).

2. *Polk's 1940 New Orleans City Directory* (New York: R. L. Polk & Co., 1940); Thomas Griffin, "The French Quarter," *Holiday* (March 1954): 52.

3. Walter G. Cowan and John Wilds, manuscript biography of Lester E. Kaba-

coff, ca. 1990, Lester E. Kabacoff Papers, New Orleans [privately held]; Jerry E. Strahan, *Andrew Jackson Higgins and the Boats That Won World War II* (Baton Rouge: Louisiana State University Press, 1994), 51, 64; Morroe Berger to Paula Wainer, January 20, 1943, in Morroe Berger, "Letters from New Orleans," *Annual Review of Jazz Studies* 7 (1994–95): 52; W. H. Russell, "I Ain't Gonna Study War No More," *Jazz* [New York], 1:3 (August 1942): 22; Ken Hulsizer, "New Orleans in Wartime," in *Jazz Review*, ed. Max Jones and Albert McCarthy (London: Jazz Music Books, 1945), 3, 4.

4. *Times-Picayune/New Orleans States Magazine*, February 27, 1949, 46–47; quoted in Calvin Trillin, "A Reporter at Large: The Zulus," *New Yorker*, June 20, 1964, 53, 103.

5. Quoted in Trillin, "A Reporter at Large," 105.

6. Allan P. Merriam and Raymond W. Mack, "The Jazz Community," *Social Forces*, 38:3 (March 1960): 213; Bruce Boyd Raeburn, "New Orleans Style: The Awakening of American Jazz Scholarship and Its Cultural Implications" (Ph.D. diss., Tulane University, 1991), 268–70; Charles Edward Smith, "Land of Dreams," in *Jazzmen*, ed. Frederic Ramsey, Jr., and Charles Edward Smith (London: Sidgwick and Jackson, 1957), 268; Morroe Berger to Paula Wainer, January 23, 1943, in Berger, "Letters from New Orleans," 64; Hulsizer, "New Orleans in Wartime," 6; George Hartman, "New Orleans Today," *The Jazz Record* (January 1945): 4.

7. Eugene Williams, "New Orleans Today: A Wealth of Talent is Concealed," 65, unidentified article found in Vertical File: World War II and Jazz, William Ransom Hogan Jazz Archive, Tulane University (hereafter cited as HJA); Smith, "Land of Dreams," 268; Orin Blackstone, "Down in New Orleans," *H.R.S. Society Rag* (December 1940): 8; Blackstone, "From the Birthplace of Jazz," *Pickup* [Birmingham, England], 1:1 (January 1946): 4.

8. Raeburn, "New Orleans Style," 295–301; Michael Edmonds, "Around New Orleans," *Jazz Music* [London], 4:1 (1949): 6.

9. *Where to Go in and around New Orleans*, May 1, 1968, in Vertical File: French Quarter, HJA.

10. See *This Week in New Orleans*, the official periodical New Orleans tourist guide published in the years after World War II, in HJA.

11. *Vieux Carré Courier*, November 24, 1967; "Quarter's Joker," *Vieux Carré Courier*, April 12, 1968. I trace the intersection of tourism and the struggle against crime and disorder in greater detail in "City in Amber: Race, Culture, and the Tourist Transformation of New Orleans, 1945–1995" (Ph.D. diss., Tulane University, 2002).

12. Alex S. Waller, Jr., "Joy Still Reigns on Bourbon Street," *Chicago Tribune*, April 24, 1960; Charles Suhor, "The Unique, Syncopated Non-Jet Set Rhythm of New Orleans," *Gentlemen's Quarterly*, April 1970, 118; Mac Rebennack [Dr. John], *Under a Hoodoo Moon: The Life of the Night Tripper* (New York: St. Martin's, 1994), 112–13.

13. "Bourbon Street Losing Its Lures," *New York Times*, September 5, 1965;

Jason Berry, Jonathan Foose, and Tad Jones, *Up from the Cradle of Jazz: New Orleans Music since World War II* (Athens: University of Georgia Press, 1986); John F. Henahan, "Bourbon St.: Nobody Here but Us Lemmings," *The Village Voice* [New York], May 7, 1964; *States-Item*, April 20, 1966.

14. Wood Simpson, "Council Passes Anti-Corncob Law," *Vieux Carré Courier*, October 10, 1969; Howard Jacobs, "Remoulade: Bourbon Street Held 'Eden of Epidermis,'" *Times-Picayune*, August 21, 1973.

15. Joe Mares, Jr., interview by William Russell, April 8, 1960, taped interview digest, p. 2, HJA; Bruce Raeburn, conversation with author, January 3, 2001; Joe Mares, Jr., interview by Walt Richter, September 1966, taped interview digest, 9–10, HJA; *The Second Line* (November–December 1954): 29–30; "Johnny St. Cyr Back at Top," *The Second Line* (September–October 1961): 18; "Mares Sends All-Stars to Disneyland," *The Second Line* (January–February 1963): 7; "Who Said Dixieland Was Dying?" *The Second Line* (September–October 1967): 101, 103, 132.

16. William Carter, *Preservation Hall: Music from the Heart* (New York and London: W. W. Norton, 1991), 110–12, 114–16, 132, 204; John Norris, "Way Down Yonder in New Orleans," *Coda* [Toronto], 4:8 (December 1961): 28; Jack V. Buerkle and Danny Barker, *Bourbon Street Black: The New Orleans Black Jazzman* (New York: Oxford University Press, 1973), 91, 108, 116.

17. Carter, *Preservation Hall*, 188, 199–202.

18. Ibid., 184–87, 233–34, 245, 263; Louisiana Tourist Development Commission press release (1969) in Vertical File: Tourism, HJA; New Orleans *States-Item*, July 14, 1970. For a discussion of the growing postwar American nostalgia for yesteryear and its influence on various forms of heritage preservation, see Michael Kammen, *Mystic Chords of Memory: The Transformation of Tradition in American Culture* (New York: Alfred A. Knopf, 1991), especially chap. 16.

19. Harvey K. Newman, *Southern Hospitality: Tourism and the Growth of Atlanta* (Tuscaloosa: University of Alabama Press, 1999), 137–38, 142; Ronald H. Bayor, *Race and the Shaping of Twentieth-Century Atlanta* (Chapel Hill: University of North Carolina Press, 1996).

20. Thaddiola Savoie [St. Charles Hotel employee, ca. 1950], telephone interviews by author, New Orleans, November 15–16, 2000; Harold Toomer [Banquet waiter, Fairmont Hotel], telephone interview by author, New Orleans, November 27, 2000.

21. Tad Jones, "'Separate But Equal': The Laws of Segregation and Their Effect on New Orleans Black Musicians, 1950–1964," *Living Blues Magazine* 77 (December 1987): 27; "Why Louis Armstrong Can't Go Home Again: 'Unconstitutional' La. Law Nixes Satchmo's Mixed Band," *Jet* (November 26, 1959): 57–58.

22. Edward F. Haas, *DeLesseps S. Morrison and the Image of Reform: New Orleans Politics, 1946–1961* (Baton Rouge: Louisiana State University Press, 1974), 250–51; Glen Douthit, Mayor's Office Public Relations Director, to Morrison, May 27, 1954, Folder "Mayoralty-Reading File, May 27, 1954," Box 52, deLesseps S. Morrison Papers, Department of Special Collections, Tulane University; Douthit to Morrison,

September 8, 1954, Folder "Mayoralty-Reading File, September 8, 1954," Box 53, Morrison Papers-Tulane (quote).

23. Morrison to Claude Sitton, December 2, 1960, Folder "Integration School Crisis (6)," Box SPR60-3, deLesseps S. Morrison Papers, New Orleans Public Library (hereafter cited as NOPL); Dr. Leonard L. Burns, taped interviews by Kim Lacy Rogers, May 14, 1979, July 13, 1988, Amistad Research Center, New Orleans; "U.S. Officers Told to Shun Meeting: Pentagon Acts as Hotel in New Orleans Bars Negro," *New York Times,* April 28, 1964; Paul Atkinson, "Trade Group to Move Last Two Sessions," *Times-Picayune,* May 13, 1964.

24. "Protest by Negro Gridders Cancels N.O. All-Star Game," *Times-Picayune,* January 11, 1965; "21 Negroes' Act Causes Regret," *Times-Picayune,* January 12, 1965; Anthony Gagliano, President, New Orleans Coalition, to James A. Nassikas, President, Greater New Orleans Hotel and Motel Association, November 4, 1969, Folder "Public Accommodations (Correspondence)"; Herman J. Penn, Manager, The Rivergate, letter to the editor, *Progress,* December 1969, Folder "Progress— 1969–1970," HRC pamphlet, Folder "Public Accommodations Ordinance," Box 3, Human Relations Committee Records, NOPL.

25. Bill Rushton, "Cityscape: Disneyland's 'New Orleans Square,'" *Vieux Carré Courier,* September 15–21, 1972; *Chicago Daily News* quoted in *Vieux Carré Courier,* March 17, 1967.

26. *Atlanta Weekly,* November 6, 1983.

27. Moon Landrieu, interview by author, New Orleans, November 12, 1999.

28. *Vieux Carré Courier,* September 25, 1970; Anthony C. Marino [President, Vieux Carré Property Owners, Residents and Associates, Inc.], interview by author, New Orleans, October 18, 2000.

29. Charlotte Hays, "The Changing Pace of Decatur Street," *Vieux Carré Courier,* May 20–27, 1971; French Market Corporation press releases, Vertical File: French Quarter, HJA; Folders 382, 392, 399, 401, French Market Corporation Subject Files, NOPL.

30. Calvin Trillin, "U.S. Journal: New Orleans: On the Possibility of Houstonization," *New Yorker,* February 17, 1975, 94–96; David F. Dixon to Darwin S. Fenner, January 9, 1967, Folder "Domed Stadium—1967," and "A New Orleans Theme Park," Folder "Domed Stadium (2)—1967," Box S67-5, Victor H. Schiro Collection, NOPL.

31. "Tourist Commission to Operate Sound & Light Show in French Quarter," *Times-Picayune,* April 26, 1973; "Gagnard Views N.O. Mayor's Sound & Light Show in Jackson Square," *Times-Picayune,* April 29, 1973 (1st quote); "How Do You Like 'Sound and Light'?" *Vieux Carré Courier,* January 22, 1965; Philip D. Carter, "Does Gen. Jackson Need Show Biz?" *Vieux Carré Courier,* June 1–7, 1973; Mary Morrison, "What's Happening at the Vieux Carre Commission?" *Vieux Carré Courier,* May 25–31, 1973 (2nd quote).

32. "Suit Attacks Son et Lumière," *Times-Picayune,* August 18, 1973; "Judge Stops Sound-Light until Plan Satisfies Laws," *Times-Picayune,* October 25, 1973;

"VCC Okays Sound-Light Idea," *Times-Picayune*, January 23, 1974; *Times-Picayune*, June 19, 1975; "1,000 Citizens Boo 'Sound & Light' Show," *Times-Picayune*, July 20, 1975; James G. Derbes [French Quarter attorney and activist], telephone conversation with author, May 31, 2000; "Squaring Off," *Vieux Carré Courier*, July 31–August 6, 1975; "New Orleans!" ca. 1979 brochure in Vertical File: Tourism, HJA; "Jubilee," ca. 1978 brochure in Vertical File: Tourism, HJA (quote).

33. *This Week in New Orleans*, HJA; Greater New Orleans Tourist and Convention Commission, *Annual Report*, 1970–1984, NOPL.

34. For examples of other southern cities' racially motivated urban renewal schemes, see especially Ronald H. Bayor, *Race and the Shaping of Twentieth-Century Atlanta* (Chapel Hill: University of North Carolina Press, 1996); Raymond A. Mohl, "Making the Second Ghetto in Metropolitan Miami, 1940–1960," *Journal of Urban History* 21 (1995): 395–427; Gary R. Mormino and George E. Pozzetta, *The Immigrant World of Ybor City: Italians and Their Latin Neighbors in Tampa, 1885–1985* (Urbana: University of Illinois Press, 1990).

35. Dwight Ott, "Tremé Group Demands Half Culture Center Jobs," *Times-Picayune*, March 5, 1972; Maren Rudolph, "Jazz-Creole Culture Hurt," *Times-Picayune*, May 23, 1973; Allan Katz, "Satchmo Tribute Asked," *States-Item*, June 30, 1972; "Who Cares about Louis Armstrong?" *Louisiana Weekly*, June 27, 1964.

36. "Satchmo Park Given Boost by Uncle Sam," *States-Item*, April 20, 1973; Paul Atkinson, "Park to Honor Satchmo OK'd," *Times-Picayune*, July 26, 1973; Emile Lafourcade, "Storm of Protests Brewing over Armstrong Park Plans," *Times-Picayune*, August 12, 1973; Bruce Eggler, "Park Factions Collide?" *States-Item*, September 13, 1973 (quote).

37. Paul Atkinson, "Jazz Event to Dedicate Park," *Times-Picayune*, March 8, 1980; John Pope, "Armstrong Park: Opener Swings from Politics to Jazz, and No Turning Back," *States-Item*, April 16, 1980; "'Spectaculars' Producer Eyes Armstrong Job," *Times-Picayune*, November 28, 1981; "Top Bid to Develop Armstrong Park is Jazzy $96 Million," *Times-Picayune*, February 1, 1983; "Morial Favors Bid of $96 Million for Armstrong Park," *Times-Picayune*, February 25, 1983; Gayle Ashton, "Private Group Offers to Run Armstrong," *Times-Picayune*, March 8, 1984.

Chapter 6

1. Harvey K. Newman, *Southern Hospitality: Tourism and the Growth of Atlanta* (Tuscaloosa: University of Alabama Press, 1999), 5–10, 289–305.

2. *North Carolina: The Pacemaker in Industry, Agriculture, and Substantial Progress* (Raleigh: Department of Conservation and Development, 1926), 11; Howard L. Preston, *Dirt Roads to Dixie: Accessibility and Modernization in the South, 1885–1935* (Knoxville: University of Tennessee Press, 1991), 23–29; George B. Tindall, "Business Progressivism: Southern Politics in the Twenties," *South Atlantic Quarterly* 62 (winter 1963), 96–106; James C. Cobb, *Industrialization and Southern Society, 1877–1984* (Lexington: University Press of Kentucky, 1984), 27–33; Cobb, *The Selling of*

the South: The Southern Crusade for Industrial Development, 1936–1990, 2d ed. (Urbana: University of Illinois Press, 1993), 1–4; and "Potentialities of Western North Carolina," Public Papers and Letters of Angus Wilton McLean, 1925–1929 (Raleigh: Edward and Broughton Company, 1931), 229–32 (quote).

3. Telegram from O. Max Gardner to George L. Lemmer, ca. May 1931; telegram from New York Evening Post to Gardner, May 18, 1931; and Radio Broadcast Transcript by Gardner, WMAQ-Chicago, May 18, 1929, Administrative Reports and Correspondence Files, 1926–1935, North Carolina Department of Conservation and Development Records, North Carolina Division of Archives and History, hereafter cited as NCDCD Records, NCDAH.

4. Report of the Organizational Meeting of The Carolinas, Inc., Charlotte, N.C., June 20, 1934; "The Carolinas Offer $100,000,000 Travel Market," unpublished paper by Coleman Roberts, and "The World is Waiting to Know More About the Carolinas," advertisement, ca. 1934, The Carolinas, Inc. File, Miscellaneous Subject Files, 1920–1936, NCDCD Records, NCDAH.

5. Coleman W. Roberts to Members of The Carolinas, Inc., February 9, 1935, The Carolinas, Inc. File, Miscellaneous Subject Files, 1920–1936; and Semi-annual Report of R. Bruce Etheridge, Director, July 1, 1937–January 1, 1938, Administrative Reports and Correspondence File, 1936–1941, NCDCD Records, NCDAH.

6. Report of the Director of State Advertising, July 1, 1938; Report of the Director of Conservation and Development, July 11–12, 1938; Semi-annual Report of R. Bruce Etheridge, Director, January 1, 1940–July 1, 1940, Director's Files, NCDCD, NCDAH.

7. "Promoting North Carolina," Radio Transcript, ca. 1938, Advertising Talks File; and Robert L. Thompson to Edmund McLaurin, May 29, 1940, Advertising 1938 File, Activities of the Department File, 1937–41, NCDCD, NCDAH. Cherokee County leaders specifically cited state advertising as a factor in tourism-related growth in the 1930s. See Cherokee Scout, July 14, 1938, July 21, 1938.

8. "Western North Carolina on the March: Address Delivered before a Meeting of the Board of Conservation and Development," Asheville, October 13, 1947, Addresses and Papers of Governor Robert Gregg Cherry, 1945–1947 (Raleigh: Council of State, 1951), 726–31; Cobb, Selling the South, 73, 171–73; "Notes for Talk to Organizational Committee of the North Carolina Tourist Council Meeting," August 24, 1955, General Correspondence Files, 1954–1955, Governor Luther H. Hodges Papers, NCDAH. For more on the changing nature of tourism after World War II, see John A. Jakle, Keith A. Sculle, and Jefferson S. Rogers, The Motel in America (Baltimore: Johns Hopkins University Press, 1996); Howard E. Morgan, The Motel Industry in the United States: Small Business in Transition (Tucson: University of Arizona Bureau of Business and Public Research, 1964); and John A. Jakle, The Tourist: Travel in Twentieth-Century North America (Lincoln and London: University of Nebraska Press, 1985), 75–103. See also John A. Jakle and Keith A. Sculle, The Gas Station in America (Baltimore: Johns Hopkins University Press, 1994), 40–81.

9. Capus Waynick to Luther H. Hodges, August 2, 1955; Susan Frances Hunter

to Ben E. Douglas (transcript), September 4, 1955; Ben E. Douglas to Susan Frances Hunter, September 6, 1955; "State Travel Bulletin, Volume 8, Number 9," December 27, 1955, General Correspondence Files, 1954–1955, Governor Luther H. Hodges Papers, NCDAH; and Greensboro *Daily News*, December 22, 1955.

10. Capus Maynick, "Promotion of Tourism in North Carolina," August 1, 1955, General Correspondence Files, 1954–1955, Governor Luther H. Hodges Papers, NCDAH.

11. Nina L. Anderson, "A History of the Western North Carolina Associated Communities," unpublished manuscript in possession of author, 4–5; George L. Simpson, Harriet L. Herring, and Maurice B. Morrill, *Western North Carolina Associated Communities* (Cherokee: Cherokee Historical Association, 1956), 3–4; and Sylva *Herald*, July 4, 1946. Jackson, Macon, Swain, Graham, Haywood, Buncombe, Madison, Transylvania, Cherokee, and Clay counties were represented at the first meeting, as were Western Carolina College and the Cherokee Indian Reservation. The group issued a special invitation to Henderson County and voted to include the resort community of Lake Lure in Polk County, a testament to the organization's tourism orientation.

12. Sylva *Herald*, July 28, 1949, August 22, 1957, September 12, 1957; Simpson, Herring, and Morrill, *Western North Carolina Associated Communities*, 3–15; Anderson, "A History of the Western North Carolina Associated Communities," 20–51.

13. Simpson, Herring, and Morrill, *Western North Carolina Associated Communities*, 35–36; "Special Bulletin from WNCAC for Hotel Owners and Operators, Tourist Court Operators, Restaurant Operators," June 9, 1949 (quote); "Western North Carolina Tourist Association Board of Directors," June 23, 1949; Minutes of the Board of Directors, June 23, 1949, Western North Carolina Tourist Association Minutes, Western North Carolina Associated Communities Records, WCU; and Sylva *Herald*, June 23, 1949. Later, the organization offered associate memberships to department stores, supermarkets, and other retail concerns. For more on the interdependent nature of tourism businesses, see Uel Blank, *The Community Tourism Industry Imperative* (State College, Pa.: Venture Publishing, 1989), 65–98; Donald E. Lundberg, M. Krishnamoorthy, and Mink H. Stavenga, *Tourism Economics* (New York: John Wiley and Sons, 1995), 135–48; and Peter E. Murphy, *Tourism: A Community Approach* (New York: Methuen, 1985), 77–116.

14. Minutes of the Meeting of the Board of Directors, July 7, 1949, July 25, 1949 (quote); Notice of Meeting, December 3, 1949; WNCTA Minutes, WNCAC Records, WCU. WNCAC leaders urged members to "list facilities of such a poor type that you would not want to refer visitors to them."

15. H. Leslie Furr and Wayne E. Williams, "Grandfather Mountain: An Outdoor Tourism Experiment," *Leisure Today* (October 1988): 44–47; Hugh Morton, "Grandfather Mountain and the USS *North Carolina*," in *The Travel Industry in North Carolina*, ed. James H. Bearden (Greenville, N.C.: East Carolina College, 1964), 103–5.

16. Robert Rierson, "Tweetsie Railroad," and R. B. Cogburn, "Ghost Town and

Frontier Land," in *Travel Industry in North Carolina*, 97–101, 109–13; Barry Buxton, *A Village Tapestry: A History of Blowing Rock* (Boone, N.C.: Appalachian Consortium Press, 1989), 183–88; Charles Alan Watkins, "Somewhere over Beech Mountain: Contemporary Appalachian Artifacts in the Land of Oz," in *Contemporary Appalachia: In Search of a Usable Past*, ed. Carl Ross (Boone, N.C.: Appalachian Consortium Press, 1987), 106–15. For more on southern mountain theme parks, see C. Brenden Martin, "Selling the Southern Highlands: Tourism and Community Development in the Mountain South" (Ph.D. diss., University of Tennessee, 1997), 146–47. Novelist Lee Smith explored mountain theme parks and tourism in *Oral History* (New York: Putnam, 1983). See also Nancy C. Parris, "'Ghostland': Tourism in Lee Smith's *Oral History*," *Southern Quarterly* 32 (winter 1994): 37–47. Most other southern states shared this phenomenon. See Tim Hollis, *Dixie Before Disney: 100 Years of Roadside Fun* (Jackson: University Press of Mississippi, 1999), 89–106.

17. Michael L. Kammen, *Mystic Chords of Memory: The Transformation of Tradition in American Culture* (New York: Alfred A. Knopf, 1991), 464–74, 534–40.

18. Wallace Randolph Umberger, Jr., "A History of *Unto These Hills*, 1941 to 1968" (Ph.D. diss., Tulane University, 1970), 1–2.

19. *Asheville Citizen-Times*, July 10, 1950; Rocky Mount *Evening Telegram*, July 15, 1950; *Unto These Hills Souvenir Program*, 1950 (Cherokee: Cherokee Historical Association, 1950), 1–7; Umberger, "A History of *Unto These Hills*," 72–80.

20. *Asheville Citizen-Times*, February 27, 1952; Anderson, "A History of the Western North Carolina Associated Communities," 67–69; Sylva *Herald*, June 13, 1945, May 16, 1957, June 13, 1957; "Cherokee Tourism Development Plan," Unpublished report, Department of the Interior, Bureau of Indian Affairs, 1945; *Overall Economic Development Plan* (Cherokee, N.C.: Eastern Band of the Cherokee Indians, 1976), 5–19; Mark E. Welch, *Environmental Health Profile and Priority Projection for the Cherokee Indian Reservation* (Cherokee, N.C.: Cherokee Service Unit, 1993), 43–49; John R. Finger, *Cherokee Americans: The Eastern Band of Cherokees in the Twentieth Century* (Lincoln: University of Nebraska Press, 1991), 78–98, 137–38, 160–65.

21. *Asheville Citizen-Times*, May 19, 1979; Finger, *Cherokee Americans*, 161–63, 181. A few "princesses" and "princes" have occasionally appeared along Cherokee's main thoroughfares, but almost always as a companion to a "chief."

22. R. F. Stamper, "Letter to the Editor," ca. June 1979, quoted in Pat Arnow, "Tourons in Wallyworld," *Now and Then* 8 (spring 1991): 2. See also Larry R. Stucki, "Will the 'Real Indian' Survive?: Tourism and Affluence at Cherokee, North Carolina," in *Affluence and Cultural Survival*, ed. Richard F. Salisbury and Elizabeth Tooker (Washington, D.C.: American Ethnological Society, 1984).

23. Fred Bauer, *The Land of the North Carolina Cherokee* (Brevard, N.C.: Buchanan Press, 1970), 55; Laurence French, "Tourism and Indian Exploitation," *The Indian Historian* 10 (fall 1977), 19–24.

24. The history of black tourism is largely unwritten. See Russ Rymer, *American Beach: A Saga of Race, Wealth, and Memory* (New York: HarperCollins, 1998).

25. Robert Liverman to Luther Hodges, August 27, 1957; Affidavit of Howard R. Matzkin, March 6, 1956; John R. Pottle to Robert Liverman, January 21, 1957; E. L. Rankin to Robert Liverman, September 24, 1957; and W. P. Saunders to Robert Liverman, October 8, 1957 in General Correspondence, 1957 Files, Hodges Papers, NCDAH.

26. R. Graham Dozier to Ed Rankin, September 26, 1957, General Correspondence, 1956 Files, and Joseph L. Bailey to Luther H. Hodges, October 8, 1955, General Correspondence, 1954–1955 Files, Hodges Papers, NCDAH.

27. Dorothy Spruill Redford, with Micheal D'Orso, *Somerset Homecoming: Recovering a Lost Heritage* (New York: Doubleday, 1988), 205–37, 241; and Raleigh *News and Observer*, August 9, 1999.

28. Lewis C. Copeland, *North Carolina's Statewide Travel Business, 1960* (Raleigh: Travel Council of North Carolina, 1961), 22, 35; Terry Sanford, "A Look to North Carolina's Travel Future," in *Travel Industry in North Carolina*, 121; Raleigh *News and Observer*, March 18, 1993, March 28, 2000; *1993 Governor's Conference on Travel and Tourism* (Raleigh: Division of Travel and Tourism, 1993), 2–12, 33–35; and Rodger Lyle Brown, *Ghost Dancing on the Cracker Circuit: The Culture of Festivals in the American South* (Jackson: University Press of Mississippi, 1997), 29–44, 179–92. By 2000, Harrah's Cherokee Casino on the Cherokee Indian Reservation surpassed Carowinds as the state's most popular man-made attraction.

29. Minutes of the Meeting of the Board of Directors, Western North Carolina Tourist Association, February 6, 1951, WNCTA Minutes, WNCAC Records, WCU; "September Average Hourly and Weekly Earnings in Leading Industrial Groups," October 20, 1958; "Study of Workers in Eastern and Western North Carolina, 1948," both in North Carolina Department of Labor, Statistics and Inspection Division, Miscellaneous Files, 1934–1959, Box 1, NCDAH.

30. Mrs. Doyle D. Alley to Dr. Paul Reid, April 6, 1951; Maurice Morrill to Mrs. Doyle D. Alley, October 1, 1951; O. A. Fetch to Maurice Morrill, October 11, 1951, Correspondence Files, WNCAC Records, WCU; *Comprehensive Plan—Volume I: Population and Economic Study, Eastern Band of the Cherokee Indians* (Cherokee, N.C.: Eastern Band of the Cherokee Indians, 1974), 91–124; Michal Smith, *Behind the Glitter: The Impact of Tourism on Rural Women of the Southeast* (Lexington: Southeast Women's Employment Coalition, 1989); and Raleigh *News and Observer*, November 15, 1993. More recently Hispanic immigrants of both genders have replaced blacks in the ranks of tourism workers, a fact that changed the demographic composition of resort areas such as Asheville, Wilmington, and Southern Pines.

31. Appalachian Land Ownership Task Force, *Who Owns Appalachia?: Landownership and Its Impact* (Lexington: University Press of Kentucky, 1983), 74–99; L. Alex Tooman, "The Evolving Impact of Tourism on the Greater Smoky Mountain Region of East Tennessee and Western North Carolina" (Ph.D. diss., University of Tennessee, 1995), 210–94; James Branscome and Peggy Matthews, "Selling the Mountains," *Southern Exposure* 2 (fall 1974): 122–29; *The Impact of Recreational Development in the North Carolina Mountains* (Durham: North Carolina Public Interest

Research Group, 1975), 26–36; Joanna Mack, *Growth Management and the Future of Western North Carolina* (Cullowhee, N.C.: Center for the Improvement of Mountain Living, 1981), 8–38; George L. Hicks, *Appalachian Valley* (New York: Holt, Rinehart, and Winston, 1976), 60–61; and John Gregory Peck and Alice Shear Lepie, "Tourism and Development in Three North Carolina Coastal Towns," in *Hosts and Guests: An Anthropology of Tourism*, ed. Valene Smith, 2d ed. (Philadelphia: University of Pennsylvania Press, 1989), 212–22. See also Jeffery Wayne Neff, "A Geographical Analysis of the Characteristics and Development Trends of the Non-Metropolitan Tourist-Recreation Industry of Appalachia" (Ph.D. diss., University of Tennessee, 1975); *A Quest for Mountain Resource Management Policies: North Carolina's Component of the Tri-State Southern Highland Plan* (Raleigh: North Carolina Department of Administration Office of State Planning, 1974), 44–83; Joy Lamm, "So, You Want a Land Use Bill? The Case of the North Carolina Mountain Area Land Management Act," *Southern Exposure* 2 (fall 1974): 52–62; and Mack, *Growth Management and the Future of Western North Carolina*, 90–104.

32. *Impacts and Influences on the Great Smoky Mountains National Park: An Annotated Bibliography with a Discussion and Review of Selected Findings, Recommendations, and Conclusions* (Atlanta: National Park Service Southeast Regional Office, 1982), 39.

33. *Charlotte Observer*, January 23, 1983; *Asheville Citizen*, May 10, 1984; *Winston-Salem Journal*, March 20, 1983; Milton S. Heath, Jr., "The North Carolina Mountain Ridge Protection Act," *North Carolina Law Review* 63 (November 1984): 183–96; and Robert M. Kessler, "North Carolina's Ridge Law: No View from the Top," *North Carolina Law Review* 63 (November 1984): 197–221.

34. Waynesville *Mountaineer*, August 20, 1953; *Land Development Plan, Maggie Valley, North Carolina* (Maggie Valley: Planning and Zoning Board, 1977), 3–52; Tooman, "The Evolving Economic Impact of Tourism," 238–39. For more on coastal communities, see Peck and Lepie, "Tourism and Development in Three North Carolina Coastal Towns," in *Hosts and Guests*, 203–22.

35. Peck and Lepie, "Tourism and Development in Three North Carolina Coastal Towns," in *Hosts and Guests*, 215; and Steven William Foster, *The Past is Another Country: Representation, Historical Consciousness, and Resistance in the Blue Ridge* (Berkeley: University of California Press, 1988), 194.

36. Bud Altmayer, *As I Recall Blowing Rock, North Carolina* (Johnson City, Tenn.: The Overmountain Press, 1991), 202–3.

Chapter 7

1. "They Nabbed This New York Tourist and Sent Him off to Jekyll Island," *Atlanta Constitution*, June 2, 1962. The authors would like to thank Tallu Fish Scott for lending us the scrapbooks in which her mother, Tallu Fish, curator of Jekyll Island's museum, conscientiously collected articles about all phases of Jekyll's development between 1954 and 1971.

2. For information on the early years of Jekyll Island and the founding of the club, see June Hall McCash, *The Jekyll Island Cottage Colony* (Athens: University of Georgia Press, 1998), 9–38. See also William Barton McCash and June Hall McCash, *The Jekyll Island Club: Southern Haven for America's Millionaires* (Athens: University of Georgia Press, 1989), 1–13.

3. Lucy Ferguson to Richard A. Everett, May 1, 1965, Everett Collections, Coastal Georgia Historical Society.

4. *Brunswick—The City by the Sea. A Pamphlet Descriptive of Brunswick and Glynn County, Georgia* (Brunswick, Ga.: BAA, 1885), 9, 21. Copy in Brunswick Library.

5. On du Bignon's business interests, see McCash, *Jekyll Island Cottage Colony*, 26–29.

6. Henry B. Hyde to Oliver Kane King, December 16, 1885, Letterpress book A-22, Henry B. Hyde Papers, Baker Library, Harvard University Graduate School of Business Administration, Boston, Massachusetts.

7. *New York Times*, April 4, 1886.

8. Samuel M. Williams, "A Millionaire's Paradise," *Munsey's Magazine* 30:5 (February 1904): 641–46.

9. Records of the hunts were scrupulously kept in the Jekyll Island Club game book, which has been preserved in the Jekyll Island Museum.

10. David H. King built a private swimming pool in the atrium of his cottage, which he had constructed in 1897 and sold three years later to Edwin Gould, son of Jay Gould. However, the club pool, open to all members and guests, was not built until 1926, under the administration of club president Walter James. The pool opened for the 1927 season.

11. *New York Times*, April 4, 1886.

12. See McCash and McCash, *Jekyll Island Club*, 190–93.

13. John Claflin, the last of the original members, died on June 12, 1938, but his last season on Jekyll was the winter of 1934.

14. Bernon Prentice to Alfred W. Jones, June 9, 1942, September 23, 1942, Sea Island Company Files, Sea Island, Georgia.

15. Bernon S. Prentice to Bill Jones, August 5, 1943, Sea Island Company Files.

16. Memorandum from M. N. F. [Marion Fisher] "RE Jekyll Island Club," January 17, 1945, Sea Island Company Files.

17. Bill Jones to Bernon Prentice, November 26, 1943, Sea Island Company Files. Although the unusually candid letter is marked "Never sent," it clearly reflects Jones's thinking at the time on various issues under discussion.

18. Prentice to Jones, August 5, 1946, cited in McCash and McCash, *Jekyll Island Club*, 11.

19. J. D. Compton to Bill Jones, recounting a telephone conversation with Charles Gowen, August 19, 1946, Sea Island Company Files.

20. *Brunswick News*, September 26, 1946. The two who resisted were Margaret Maurice, the owner with her three surviving sisters of the cottage Hollybourne, and

Lawrence Condon, a New York lawyer who had only recently acquired the Villa Marianna as a consequence of his handling the estate of Frank Miller Gould.

21. Harold Paulk Henderson, "The Accidental Governor," *Georgia Journal* (winter 1992): 10–13, 75.

22. Unidentified newspaper clipping, June 19, 1947, Everett Collection, Coastal Georgia Historical Society.

23. *Atlanta Constitution*, June 4, 1947.

24. *New York, N.Y. News*, September 7, 1947.

25. *Brunswick News*, October 15, 1947; Arthur Watson, "Exclusive Jekyll Island Site May be a New Coney Island," *Atlanta Journal*, June 15, 1947.

26. Jones to Prentice, May 6, 1948, Sea Island Company Files.

27. *Brunswick News*, October 7, 1947, 8.

28. "Hotel on Jekyll to Open March 1 for 300 Guests," *Atlanta Journal*, February 1, 1948; Morgan Blake, "Jekyll Island Proves an Ideal Spot for a Fascinating and Inexpensive Vacation," *Atlanta Journal*, September 22, 1948; *Savannah Morning News*, July 14, 1949, 7; Jekyll Island Authority Minutes (hereafter cited as JIA Minutes), October 5, 1950.

29. *Savannah Morning News*, March 18, 1949, 1.

30. Jekyll Island State Park Authority Act, Georgia Laws, 1950, 152, approved February 13, 1950.

31. Oral interview by Brenden Martin and June McCash on June 2, 2000; Alfred W. Jones, Sr., reminiscence, "From Public to Private Beach at Sea Island and from Private Club to State Beach Park at Jekyll," 1982, Sea Island Company Archives; Charles L. Gowen to Alfred W. Jones, February 8, 1982, Sea Island Company Archives.

32. JIA Minutes, April 26, 1952; telephone interview by Brenden Martin with Andrew E. Steiner, May 27, 2000. Subsequent master plans, the most recent done in 1995, have supplemented the Robert and Company plan. None has significantly modified the configurations of the original.

33. JIA Minutes, October 5, 1950.

34. Andrew Sparks, "Georgia's Padlocked Island," *Atlanta Journal and Constitution*, May 25, 1952.

35. The legislative resolution is mentioned in JIA Minutes, March 7, 1953. Hoke Smith's hiring is recorded in JIA Minutes, April 21, 1951.

36. *Brunswick News*, October 25, 1947. See "Negro Beach House at Jekyll to Open," *Atlanta Journal*, September 13, 1956.

37. JIA Minutes, August 23, 1952. The aforementioned telephone interview with Steiner (see n. 32) revealed that the motives for relegating the south end of the island to Africa Americans were precisely because it was the most separated from previously developed areas.

38. JIA Minutes, July 30, 1955, September 24, 1955. The first applicant for the St. Andrews subdivision was Joe Malone of Albany, Georgia.

39. "Sen. Dykes Moves to Spread His Jekyll Island Empire," *Atlanta Constitution,* July 22, 1956.

40. Jack Nelson, "Jekyll Authority Employee Bought Supplies from His Own Company," *Atlanta Constitution,* July 27, 1956.

41. Charles Pou, "Dykes Record Bared on Jekyll Hotel Tie," *Atlanta Journal,* n.d., 1, 11. The hotel lease was approved in the name of L. L. Phillips of Cochran, Georgia, for Jekyll Island Hotels, Inc., at the JIA meeting of May 14, 1955.

42. "Sen. Dykes Moves to Spread His Jekyll Island Empire," *Atlanta Constitution,* July 22, 1956; "Jekyll to Need Another $500,000, Barrett Tells Investigating Committee," *Brunswick News,* September 17, 1955.

43. Nelson, "Jekyll Authority Employee Bought Supplies From His Own Company"; "Sen. Dykes Moves to Spread His Jekyll Island Empire"; JIA Minutes, July 30, 1955. At the meeting following Compton's resignation, the Authority passed a resolution thanking him for his efforts and expressing deep appreciation for the "very large part" he played "in the creation of the authority's general Development Plan for Jekyll Island." JIA Minutes, August 27, 1955.

44. "Solons Demand Jekyll Authority Be Abolished," *Brunswick News,* December 10, 1955.

45. Charles Pou, "Low Jekyll Price Scale Urged by Rep. Bentley," *Atlanta Journal,* n.d.

46. "An Expert Gives His Opinion On Jekyll Island Lot Titles," *Brunswick News,* July 5, 1955; "Governor to Ask Sale of Jekyll Island Lots," *Brunswick News,* November 14, 1955.

47. "Griffin Asks Jekyll Sale Reserve Beach for State," *Atlanta Constitution,* July 23, 1956.

48. Jack Nelson, "Beer Sold at Jekyll after License is Denied," *Atlanta Constitution,* July 22, 1956; Jack Nelson, "Jekyll Island Sale Favored, Opposed by State Leaders," *Atlanta Journal and Constitution,* July 27, 1956.

49. "Jekyll Boom Attributed to Curiosity," *Brunswick News,* July 31, 1956; Roy LeCraw, letter to the editor, *Atlanta Constitution,* n.d.; Bruce Galphin, "Aldred Says 'Hecklers' Hurt Jekyll," *Atlanta Constitution,* October 19, 1956.

50. Jack Nelson, "Jekyll—A Golden Elephant," *Atlanta Journal and Constitution,* August 31, 1958; Jekyll Island State Park Authority Act, Act No. 464, H.B. No. 171, 1957 Session of the General Assembly.

51. Willard Neal, "Fabulous Jekyll Island," *Atlanta Journal and Constitution,* May 19, 1957; Nelson, "A Golden Elephant."

52. "Jekyll Authority to Follow Plan of Development," *Brunswick News,* April 25, 1957.

53. "Thrasher Assails Selling Lots on Jekyll Island," *Brunswick News,* February 2, 1957; "Three on Jeykll Authority Disagree over Lot Sales," *Atlanta Journal,* May 7, 1957.

54. "Probe of Dykes' Leases Ordered," *Brunswick News,* April 15, 1957; "Owes

Jekyll No Rent, Dykes Insists in Court," *Atlanta Constitution,* May 21, 1957. See also JIA Minutes, April 15, 1957. At the Authority meeting of June 17, 1957, minutes note that Dykes has now paid all rents in full. A telephone interview on June 3, 2000, by June McCash with Madelyn Neill, JIA secretary for twenty-five years, clarified the issue of the quit claim deed. Dykes, living once again in Cochran, Georgia, and allegedly in a state of depression, committed suicide in December 1966. "Cochran's James Dykes Found Dead, Gun Near," *Atlanta Constitution,* December 29, 1966.

55. *Atlanta Constitution,* June 29, 1964; "Jekyll Oceanfront Road Closed to Make Room for Apartments," *Atlanta Journal and Constitution,* June 18, 1972. Figures concerning the number of homes owned by state political officials or former officials is from "Liquor and Segregation Fading as Resort Problems," *Atlanta Constitution,* June 29, 1964. Several other political figures had at one time owned leases at Jekyll, but had allowed them to expire.

56. "Georgia Sets Plan to Compete For Florida's Tourist Dollars," *Florida Times-Union,* August 29, 1961; *Atlanta Constitution,* November 15, 1962; "$600,000 Earnings Expected on Jekyll," *Brunswick News,* April 13, 1965. "Georgia Tourism at $385 Million Now," *Free Press,* Thomaston, Georgia, July 19, 1965.

57. See JIA Minutes, April 8, 1963, March 23, 1964. Telephone interview by Brenden Martin with Henry Armstrong, May 17, 2000; "Folks Can't Wait for Jekyll Edifice," *Atlanta Journal,* May 5, 1961, 18.

58. Gene Britton, "Jekyll Unit Is Cautious on Closing," *Atlanta Constitution,* May 21, 1960.

59. "Desegregation at Jekyll Asked by Biracial Unit," *Atlanta Journal,* March 13, 1963; "Group Plans Court Action over Jekyll," *Brunswick News,* March 25, 1963.

60. *Brunswick News,* June 13, 1964; "Judge Signs Jekyll Isle Racial Edict," *Florida Times-Union,* July 28, 1964.

61. "Half-Million Earmarked To Remodel Jekyll Motel," *Brunswick News,* December 31, 1966.

62. Ernest Rogers, "Percentage Sam Reports Jekyll is No Sahara," *Atlanta Journal and Constitution,* May 21, 1961; William O. Smith, "Jekyll Motel Suit Likely in Liquor Permit Controversy," *Atlanta Constitution,* September 19, 1965; *Atlanta Constitution,* May 20, 1971; *Atlanta Constitution,* June 19, 1971; see JIA Minutes, April 15, 1971, and June 4, 1971.

63. Among them was the splendid home of Joseph Pulitzer, which suffered a small fire and was demolished in 1951. Bricks from the Pulitzer house were later used to construct a golf house.

64. JIA Minutes, June 13, 1951. Tallu Fish was a recently widowed native of Waycross, Georgia, and the politically well-connected editor of the *Democratic Women's Journal of Kentucky.* From 1954 until shortly before her death in 1971, she served, in addition to her capacity as curator of the museum, as the island's public relations director and publicist, promoting an interest in Jekyll's historical importance with press releases and tourist brochures. Interview with Tallu Fish Scott, May 23, 2000.

The JIA also later executed leases with Dewey Scarboro for Villa Ospo and Crane Cottage, which he restored, furnished, and opened to the public for a charge.

65. *Brunswick News*, March 1, 1960; JIA Minutes, July 8, 1963; *Atlanta Constitution*, October 19, 1956; *Atlanta Journal*, August 16, 1963; *Brunswick News*, December 12, 1965. Interview with Tallu Fish Scott, May 23, 2000.

66. JIA Minutes, June 13, 1966; "Virginia Architect Named to Restore Jekyll Village," *Brunswick News*, July 19, 1966; "Restoration of the Rockefeller House, Jekyll Island Museum," Roger Beedle's address to the National Society of Interior Decorators, April 1970, Beedle File, Jekyll Island Museum; *Atlanta Journal and Constitution*, June 18, 1972. Clarmont Lee joined the project in 1970.

67. JIA minutes, March 7, 1983.

68. Interviews by June McCash and Brenden Martin with Warren Murphey, June 1, 2000, and with Larry Evans, May 25, 2000; JIA Minutes, February 22, 1985. Murphey attributes the success of the project in large measure to the leadership of JIA Chair, John McTier.

69. Although club officials had earlier brought in experts to review the erosion problem, Bill Jones cites it as one of his major concerns when Sea Island was considering purchasing Jekyll after World War II. See McCash and McCash, *Jekyll Island Club*, 204.

70. John Pennington, "Jekyll Ocean Front Lots Go in Hurry," *Atlanta Journal*, January 28, 1955; Marjorie Smith, "Fabled Jekyll of Millionaires, Pirates Thrown Open to Public," *Atlanta Journal and Constitution*, December 12, 1954; *Brunswick News*, June 28, 1962; *Brunswick News*, September 22, 1964; JIA Minutes, January 7, 1964.

71. *Atlanta Constitution*, September 19, 1971; *Atlanta Journal and Constitution*, June 18, 1972.

72. "Golf Course Construction Halted," *Brunswick News*, January 12, 1995; "Jekyll Authority Chief Quits," *Florida Times-Union*, February 1, 1995; David Layman, "Miller Signs Jekyll Bill," *Brunswick News*, March 15, 1995.

73. Oral interview by June McCash and Brenden Martin with JIA Executive Director, Bill Donohue, May 31, 2000; "Final Master Plan for the Management, Preservation, Protection, and Development of Jekyll Island," Robert Charles Lesser & Co. and Tunnell-Spangler & Associates, June 30, 1996; oral interview by Brenden Martin with Jean and Leonard Poleszak, May 24, 2000.

Chapter 8

1. This work draws heavily from Margaret A. Shannon's master's thesis, on which Stephen W. Taylor served as research assistant. The process of assembling and rewriting the material for presentation in this essay was a joint endeavor. See Margaret A. Shannon, "From Tomato Fields to Tourists: Hilton Head Island and Beaufort County, South Carolina, 1950–1983" (master's thesis, University of Tennessee, 1996).

2. This is especially true of one otherwise excellent study, Michael N. Danielson with Patricia R. F. Danielson, *Profits and Politics in Paradise: The Development of Hilton Head Island* (Columbia: University of South Carolina Press, 1995), which examines the development of the tourist economy at Hilton Head Island. That work portrays blacks, when they appear at all, as passive background figures in the remarkable transformation wrought by Fred Hack, Charles Fraser, and other developers upon the island.

3. James C. Cobb, *The Selling of the South: The Southern Crusade for Industrial Development, 1936–1990,* 2d ed. (Urbana: University of Illinois Press, 1993.)

4. Arthur Simon, "Conservation Collides with the Jobless: Battle of Beaufort," *New Republic,* May 23, 1970.

5. "An Editorial," Beaufort (S.C.) *Gazette,* December 11, 1969.

6. "Shrimp Co-Op Makes Blacks Their Own Bosses: South Carolinians Now Control Fishing Fleet," *Ebony,* November 1969, 106–8; Vernie Singleton, "A Venture into Shrimp," *Southern Exposure,* November–December 1983, 48–49; "Shrimp Boats Are A-Comin'," *American Forests,* May 1970, 26; "Officials Waiting for Requirements," Beaufort (S.C.) *Gazette,* April 9, 1970; "BASF Reconfirms Plans to Build Here: Officials Deny Rumor," Beaufort (S.C.) *Gazette,* April 16, 1970; "BASF Officials Answer Pollution Charges," Beaufort (S.C.) *Gazette,* March 12, 1970.

7. "Island Group Files Suit against BASF," Beaufort (S.C.) *Gazette,* March 19, 1970.

8. "If BASF Pulls Out: Area Developers Announce Plans for Tourist Center," Beaufort (S.C.) *Gazette,* April 2, 1970.

9. The Department of Agricultural Economics and Rural Sociology and the Water Resources Research Institute, Clemson University, *Economic Evaluation of the Development of Industrial Facilities in the Port Victoria-Hilton Head Area of Beaufort County, South Carolina* (preliminary draft) (Clemson, S.C., January 1971) (hereafter cited as BASF report), 94.

10. "BASF Will Not Locate in County; Returns the Site," Beaufort (S.C.) *Gazette,* January 21, 1971.

11. BASF report, 94–95.

12. Ibid., 95.

13. "Alternative to BASF: Natural Development," *Hilton Head Island Packet,* September 10, 1970, 7; Skidmore, Owings & Merrill, Inc., *Master Plan for Hilton Head Island* (Washington, D.C.: Hilton Head Company, June 1972), 1–2, 21. Compare to BASF report results, 93–95.

14. "Hilton Head: A Contest of Cultures," Palm Beach (Fla.) *Post-Times,* December 30, 1973.

15. These factors are cited in Lawrence J. Hanks, *The Struggle for Black Political Empowerment in Three Georgia Counties* (Knoxville: University of Tennessee Press, 1987), 152–53, as essential ingredients for successful empowerment of black voters in the South.

16. Danielson, *Profits and Politics in Paradise*, 100–105, 115–19, and passim.

17. Leo McGee and Robert Boone, "Introduction," in *The Black Rural Land-owner—Endangered Species: Social, Political, and Economic Implications*, ed. Leo McGee and Robert Boone (Westport, Conn.: Greenwood Press, 1979), xvii–xviii; The Black Economic Research Center, *Only Six Million Acres: The Decline of Black Owned Land in the Rural South* (New York: The Black Economic Research Center, 1973), 25; William F. Nelson, Jr., "Black Rural Land Decline and Political Power," in *Black Rural Landowner*, 83–84.

18. Rupert S. Holland, ed., *Letters and Diary of Laura M. Towne, written from the Sea Islands of South Carolina, 1862–1884* (New York: Negro Universities Press, 1969), passim; Elizabeth Hyde Botume, *First Days Amongst the Contrabands* (New York: Arno Press, 1969), passim; Willie Lee Rose, *Rehearsal for Reconstruction: The Port Royal Experiment* (Indianapolis: Bobbs-Merrill, 1964), passim; "No Place in the Sun for the Hired Help," *Southern Exposure*, May–June 1982, 35–36.

19. Leo McGee and Robert Boone, "A Study of Rural Landownership, Control Problems, and Attitudes of Blacks Toward Rural Land," in *Black Rural Landowner*, 64; Black Economic Research Center, *Only Six Million Acres*, 51–57.

20. McGee and Boone, "A Study of Rural Landownership, Control Problems, and Attitudes of Blacks toward Rural Land," 64; *Only Six Million Acres*, 51–53.

21. "Quieting" a title to land is a legal maneuver by which one owner of a share of jointly—or severally—owned land will sue to force a sale of the tract, the proceeds being divided between the owners according to the size of their share. Here, the Penn Center was complaining about developers who sued to quiet land titles in order to force sale of the entire tract at auction at which they would be the highest bidder. "Report on the Black Land Services Project" (Appendix K) in *Only Six Million Acres*, K1-K3. Another organization, the Emergency Land Fund (ELF) helps out by keeping a revolving fund to bid up prices at tax auctions, so that even if ELF is unable to save the land, it is able to ensure that the owners get fair market value for it; see Charles H. Marbury, "The Decline in Black-Owned Rural Land: Challenge to the Historically Black Institutions of Higher Education," in McGee and Boone, *Black Rural Landowner*, 102. For a discussion of the history of the Penn Center, see Rose, *Rehearsal for Reconstruction*; see also Holland, *Letters and Diary of Laura M. Towne*.

22. Harold R. Washington with P. Andrew Patterson and Charles W. Brown, *Black Land Manual: "Got Land Problems?"* (Frogmore, S.C.: Penn Community Services, 1973), 5.

23. "We are an Endangered Species," *Southern Exposure*, May–June 1982, 37–39; "Sea Island Plantations Revisited," *Southern Exposure*, May–June 1982, 33–34; "No Place in the Sun for the Hired Help," 35–36; Peter Applebome, "Tourism Enriches an Island Resort, but Hilton Head Blacks Feel Left Out," *New York Times*, September 2, 1994, National Edition.

24. Jack Bowle, "Blacks Take Zoning Complaints to Council," *Hilton Head Island Packet*, May 11, 1972.

25. "NAACP Meeting," *Hilton Head Island Packet*, October 19, 1972.

26. Terry Plumb, "JPC Hearing Draws Variety of Comments," *Hilton Head Island Packet*, July 23, 1978.

27. Ibid.

28. Chris Porter, "Land Use Plan Met with Skepticism by Blacks," *Hilton Head Island Packet*, September 29, 1981.

29. Porter, "Land Use Plan Met with Skepticism by Blacks"; "The Issue of Hilton Head's Incorporation," *Penn News* (Frogmore, S.C.), November 30, 1983.

30. Chris Porter, "Moratorium Move Dies," *Hilton Head Island Packet*, February 25, 1982.

31. "JPC Chairman Backs Moratorium," *Hilton Head Island Packet*, March 23, 1982; Chris Porter, "Moratorium Bid Fails Second Time," *Hilton Head Island Packet*, March 25, 1982; Chris Porter, "JPC Holds off High Density Construction," *Hilton Head Island Packet*, April 1, 1982.

32. Julia Cass, "Newcomers and Natives Square off on Hilton Head," *Philadelphia Inquirer*, July 3, 1983.

33. Ibid.

34. F. Fred Grimm, "Culture vs. Condos," *Miami Herald*, June 27, 1988.

35. Cass, "Newcomers and Natives Square off on Hilton Head."

36. For a discussion of the problems wrought by increasing development, see R. Michael Easterwood, *Incorporation as an Option for Hilton Head Island, South Carolina: A Preliminary Analysis* (Columbia, S.C.: Bureau of Governmental Research and Service, 1982), 4, 8–9.

37. Easterwood, *Incorporation as an Option*, 7.

38. Ibid., 1; Michael L. M. Jordan and Horace W. Fleming, Jr., "Chapter One," in Horace W. Fleming, Jr., et al., *Hilton Head Island Government: Analysis and Alternatives* (Hilton Head Island, S.C.: Hilton Head Community Association, Inc., and Harold W. Fleming, Jr., 1974), 16.

39. Fleming, et al., *Hilton Head Island Government*, i–iii.

40. Jack Bowie, "Community Undecided as March 20 Meeting Nears," *Hilton Head Island Packet*, March 15, 1973; "Harvey Postpones Bill Vote to Hear NAACP Comment," *Hilton Head Island Packet*, April 12, 1973; Jack Bowie, "'Fruitful' Meeting Does Not Relieve NAACP Opposition to Council Plan," *Hilton Head Island Packet*, April 19, 1973; Jordan and Fleming, "Chapter Two," 1–3; "Joe Brown Declares Council Concept is Unsound, Undemocratic, Selfish," *Hilton Head Island Packet*, March 1, 1973; "NAACP Opts for Municipal Government," *Hilton Head Island Packet*, March 22, 1973.

41. Fran Smith, "Unique Proposal Going to Referendum," *Hilton Head Island Packet*, October 17, 1974.

42. "Island NAACP Issues Statement vs. Planning Referendum," *Hilton Head Island Packet*, October 31, 1974.

43. Fleming, et al., *Hilton Head Island Government*, 210–314; Smith, "Unique Proposal Going to Referendum," *Hilton Head Island Packet*, October 17, 1974;

"Racusin Hopes for Approval of Island Commission Proposal," *Hilton Head Island Packet*, November 12, 1974; Fran Smith, "Council Senses 'Opposition' to Commission," *Hilton Head Island Packet*, November 18, 1974; Fran Smith, "Grant Calls for 'Happy Medium' on Island Commission Proposal," *Hilton Head Island Packet*, December 30, 1974.

44. Fran Smith, "NAACP to Fight Commission Proposal," *Hilton Head Island Packet*, November 13, 1975; Fran Smith, "Grant Calls for 'Happy Medium' on Island Commission Proposal," *Hilton Head Island Packet*, December 30, 1974.

45. Smith, "Unique Proposal Going to Referendum"; "Island NAACP Issues Statement vs. Planning Referendum," *Hilton Head Island Packet*, October 31, 1974; "Racusin Hopes for Approval of Island Commission Proposal," *Hilton Head Island Packet*, November 12, 1974; "Perry White Appointed to JPC," *Hilton Head Island Packet*, January 14, 1975; "Ecology Dispute over S.C. Plant Nears End," *Hilton Head Island Packet*, March 4, 1975.

46. In 1970, there were a total of 2,456 people living on the island, and by 1980 that figure had increased by 74.2 percent to 11,344 residents. In 1975, there were 5,212 whites and 1,299 blacks. By 1980, the population of whites had increased 85.3 percent to 9,659, while the black population had increased only by 29.7 percent to 1,685. See Jordan and Fleming, "Chapter One," 5.

47. George Cathcart, "Abe Grant, Buck Smith Win Races," *Hilton Head Island Packet*, June 10, 1976; Joint Center for Political Studies, *National Roster of Black Elected Officials, 1973–1982* (Washington, D.C.: Joint Center for Political Studies, 1973–1982.)

48. Fran Smith, "Islanders Approve Commission," *Hilton Head Island Packet*, February 25, 1982; Chris Porter, "Commission Makeup Change Proposed," *Hilton Head Island Packet*, May 11, 1982.

49. Easterwood, *Incorporation as an Option*, 4, 5, 7, 8.

50. Jordan and Fleming, "Chapter One," 5–6.

51. Ibid., 8; Jordan and Fleming, appendix entitled "Committee on Self-Government Options," Section No. 36, n.p.

52. Jordan and Fleming, "Chapter One," 9, Household Characteristics, 1980. For example, native South Carolinians composed only 23.7 percent of Hilton Head's population, and while 93.4 percent of the island's population was over the poverty line, the split was 95 percent for whites and 83.7 for blacks, with median incomes of $38,488 for whites and $18,129 for blacks, a difference of more than $20,000. Whites had greater school enrollments, also, with 74.9 percent of white children three or older attending school and only 25.1 percent of black.

53. Jordan and Fleming, "Chapter Four: Home Rule," 10–11; Joe Gray, "A General Air of Optimism," *Islander* 13 (January 1979): 5–13.

54. Jordan and Fleming, "Chapter One," 6–7. This concern about their dwindling proportion was manifested in other ways as well. For example, during the years that Hilton Head was just a sleepy rural island, education was kept alive by its black residents. But as more whites moved to the area, black prominence in education de-

clined. After 1970, when legal school segregation ended in Beaufort County, blacks dominated the school systems as teachers and administrators. Since then, however, coinciding with the growth of the white population at Hilton Head, a trend of replacing retiring or departing black teachers with whites began to be apparent, sparking controversies. Should hiring decisions be made to favor blacks, thus committing reverse discrimination? An example is the hiring of Steve Gottfried, a white man, as assistant principal of Hilton Head Elementary School. "Vast development on Hilton Head has overrun everything public there. The black native population is lagging. Public schools are the hope of the blacks," NAACP president Perry White observed, echoing the feeling of many black Hilton Headers that they were being overwhelmed and their concern for black role models for the children ignored by whites with stronger numbers; see "Gottfried's Hiring Shows Trend," *Hilton Head Island Packet*, July 30, 1981.

55. "Voters say 'yes' to Town," *Hilton Head Island Packet*, May 12, 1983.

56. Jordan and Fleming, appendix entitled "NAACP Lawsuit," sections 1–7, 10, 23.

57. Ibid.; David Stacks, "Candidate Calls for Cooperation," *Hilton Head Island Packet*, June 14, 1983; "NAACP Renews Efforts in Federal Court," *Hilton Head Island Packet*, August 2, 1983; David Stacks, "New Town Government Won by Majority Votes," *Hilton Head Island Packet*, August 9, 1983.

Chapter 9

1. The two best accounts on the "Road to Nowhere" and the surrounding issues can be found in Margaret Brown, *The Wild East: A Biography of the Great Smoky Mountains* (Gainesville: University Press of Florida, 2000), 267–74, 309–11; and Stephen W. Taylor, "Building the Back of Beyond: Government Authority, Community Life, and Economic Development in the Upper Little Tennessee Valley" (Ph.D. diss., University of Tennessee, 1996), 166–90.

2. *Asheville Citizen-Times*, November 2, 2000.

3. Alfred Runte, *National Parks: The American Experience* (Lincoln: University of Nebraska Press, 1987), 104.

4. Richard D. Starnes, "Creating the Land of the Sky: Tourism and Society in Western North Carolina" (Ph.D. diss., Auburn University, 1999), 14–30.

5. Ibid., 27.

6. Ibid.

7. Francis Butler Simkins, *The South, Old and New: A History, 1820–1947* (New York: Alfred A. Knopf, 1947), 374.

8. Howard L. Preston, *Dirt Roads to Dixie: Accessibility and Modernization in the South, 1885–1935* (Knoxville: University of Tennessee Press, 1991), 109–27.

9. *Knoxville Sentinel*, October 10, 1923.

10. Carlos Campbell, *Birth of a National Park in the Great Smoky Mountains*, rev. ed. (Knoxville: University of Tennessee Press, 1969), 17.

11. Runte, *National Parks*, 167–71.

12. *Knoxville Journal*, December 8, 1925; and *Asheville Citizen*, December 7, 1925.

13. Horace Albright to Harvey Broome, October 1931, in Box 310, File 630, Record Group (hereafter cited as RG) 79, National Archives and Records Administration II, College Park, Maryland (hereafter cited as NA).

14. J. R. Eakin to Horace Albright, February 16, 1932, in Box 310, File 630, RG 79, NA.

15. John Finger, *Cherokee Americans: The Eastern Band of Cherokees in the Twentieth Century* (Lincoln: University of Nebraska Press, 1991), 78–79.

16. J. R. Eakin to Horace Albright, February 16, 1932, in Box 310, File 630, RG 79, NA.

17. Harris Reynolds to Arno Cammerer, September 6, 1932, in Box 311, File 631-1, RG 79, NA; Horace Albright, "Memorandum for the Staff," November 14, 1932, in Box 310, File 630, RG 79, NA; Harlan Kelsey to Horace Albright, November 19, 1932, in Box 311, File 630, RG 79, NA.

18. Harvey Broome to Horace Albright, October 14, 1932, in Harvey Papers, McClung Historical Collection, Lawson McGhee Library, Knoxville, Tennessee (hereafter cited as MHC).

19. Arno Cammerer to Phillip Ayres, December 6, 1932, in Box 311, File 630, RG 79, NA.

20. Harlan Kelsey to Horace Albright, November 30, 1932, in Box 311, File 630, RG 79, NA.

21. Paul Sutter, "Driven Wild: The Intellectual and Cultural Origins of Wilderness Advocacy during the Interwar Years" (Ph.D. diss., University of Kansas, 1997), 1–4; and *Knoxville News-Sentinel*, October 20, 1934.

22. Sutter, "Driven Wild," 1–2; and Copy of Wilderness Society Charter with Broome's handwritten corrections, in Harvey Broome Papers, MHC.

23. Stephen Fox, *John Muir and His Legacy: The American Conservation Movement* (Boston: Little, Brown, 1981), 209.

24. Robert Marshall, "Memorandum for the Secretary," July 9, 1935, in Box 1081, File 201, RG 79, NA.

25. Arno Cammerer, "Memorandum for the Secretary," July 15, 1935, in Box 2012, File 12-22, RG 48, NA.

26. T. H. Watkins, *Righteous Pilgrim: The Life and Times of Harold Ickes, 1874–1952* (New York: Henry Holt and Co., 1990), 471–72.

27. C. Brenden Martin, "Selling the Southern Highlands: Tourism and Economic Development in the Mountain South" (Ph.D. diss., University of Tennessee, 1997).

28. Finger, *Cherokee Americans*, 113 and 116.

29. Brown, *Wild East*, 174–175; Finger, *Cherokee Americans*, 138.

30. Daniel S. Pierce, *The Great Smokies: From Natural Habitat to National Park* (Knoxville: University of Tennessee Press, 2000), 199.

31. Ibid.; Taylor, "Building the Back of Beyond," 175.

32. Department of the Interior, "Transportation Concepts: Great Smoky Mountains National Park," 1971, Great Smoky Mountains National Park Library and Archives, Gatlinburg, Tennessee (hereafter cited as GSMNP); Taylor, "Building the Back of Beyond," 166–90; and Asheville Citizen, February 24, 1952.

33. An extensive file of letters and clippings on the Highway 228 controversy can be found at Management Records, Box VI, Folder 1, GSMNP; Newton Drury to Monroe Redden, November 8, 1950, Management Records, Box VI, Folder 1, GSMNP; Taylor, "Building the Back of Beyond," 168; and Asheville Citizen, February 24, 1952.

34. Assistant Regional Director (William) Zimmer, memo "Conference with R. Getty Browning, North Carolina Senior Engineer on Great Smoky Mountains National Park Road Problems," Management Records, Box VI, Folder 1, GSMNP; E. T. Scogen, Acting Director NPS to (N.C.) Governor Luther Hodges, November 12, 1957, Management Records, Box VI, Folder 2, GSMNP; Henry Wilson to Stewart Udall, May 9, 1962, Management Records, Box VI, Folder 5, GSMNP; Taylor, "Building the Back of Beyond," 170–71.

35. Wilson to Udall, May 9, 1962; and Taylor, "Building the Back of Beyond," 174.

36. Asheville Citizen, September 3, 1960.

37. Several folders of letters and clippings related to the construction difficulties encountered by the Park Service can be found in Management Records, Box VI, Folders 5, 6, and 7; Nashville Tennessean, October 23, 1966; Department of the Interior, "Transportation Concepts"; Asheville Citizen, October 2 and 4, 1965; and Taylor, "Building the Back of Beyond," 177.

38. Runte, National Parks, 173; Department of the Interior, "Transportation Concepts"; George Fry, George Fry: The Legend (self-published, 1994), 229; Brown, Wild East, 216–17, 222.

39. Brown, Wild East, 222; Asheville Citizen, June 13 and 16, 1966; Knoxville News-Sentinel, June 13, 14, and 15, 1966.

40. Knoxville News-Sentinel, June 14, 1966; Asheville Citizen, October 24, 1966; and Brown, Wild East, 221.

41. Knoxville News-Sentinel, June 16, 1966; Asheville Citizen, June 16, 1966; Brown, Wild East, 225; New York Times, December 5, 1965, copy of editorial found in GSMNP Vertical File, Folder marked "Northshore Road" along with numerous letters and articles opposing the transmountain road.

42. Nashville Tennessean, October 23, 1966; Asheville Citizen, June 16 and 17, 1966, and May 5, 1966.

43. Fox, John Muir, 319; Asheville Citizen, October 24, 1966; Knoxville New-Sentinel, October 23 and 24, 1966; and Harvey Broome, Out under the Sky of the Great Smokies (Knoxville: Greenbriar Press, 1975), 282–85.

44. Department of the Interior, "Briefing Statement: North Shore Road Issue Settlement," January 11, 1995, in Vertical File GSMNP.

45. *Asheville Citizen,* March 28, 1984.

46. Department of the Interior, "Briefing Statement"; and *Asheville Citizen-Times,* October 25, 2000.

47. *Asheville Citizen-Times,* November 2, 2000.

48. Ibid.

49. Aldo Leopold, *A Sand County Almanac* (New York: Oxford University Press, 1966), 101.

Chapter 10

1. *Southern Hotel Journal,* June 1916, 26.

2. Bradley R. Rice, "If Dixie Were Atlanta," in *Sunbelt Cities: Politics and Growth since World War II,* ed. Richard M. Bernard and Bradley R. Rice (Austin: University of Texas Press, 1983), 31–32.

3. J. O. Wyatt, Jr., interview by author, January 14, 1998.

4. Atlanta Convention and Visitors Bureau, Annual Reports, 1960 and 1970.

5. Dana F. White and Timothy J. Crimmins, "How Atlanta Grew: Cool Heads, Hot Air, and Hard Work," *Atlanta Economic Review* 28 (January–February 1978): 7–15; and Clarence N. Stone, *Regime Politics: Governing Atlanta, 1946–1988* (Lawrence: University Press of Kansas, 1989).

6. *Atlanta Constitution,* May 16, 1983, B-1; and May 17, 1983, A-1.

7. Ibid., August 6, 2000, B-1.

8. Ibid., January 17, 1999, B-1 to 3.

9. Ibid.

10. Ibid., September 19, 1999, H-6.

11. Harvey K. Newman, *Southern Hospitality: Tourism and the Growth of Atlanta* (Tuscaloosa: University of Alabama Press, 1999), 257.

12. Larry Keating, *Atlanta: Race, Class, and Urban Expansion* (Philadelphia: Temple University Press, 2001), 148–52.

13. Matthew J. Burbank, Charles H. Heying, and Greg Andranovich, "Anti-Growth Politics or Piecemeal Resistance? Citizen Opposition to Olympic-Related Economic Growth," *Urban Affairs Review* 35 (January 2000): 344–48.

14. Larry Keating and Carol A. Flores, "Sixty and Out: Techwood Homes Transformed by Enemies and Friends," *Journal of Urban History* 26 (March 2000): 300–301.

15. Larry Keating, Max Creighton, and Jon Abercrombie, "Essay Two: Community Development: Building on a New Foundation," in Research Atlanta, Inc., *The Olympic Legacy: Building on What Was Achieved* (Atlanta: Policy Research Center, Georgia State University, 1996), 1 and 4.

16. Atlanta Committee for the Olympic Games, *The Official Report of the Centennial Olympic Games, vol. 1: Planning and Organizing* (Atlanta: Peachtree Publishers, 1997), 47.

17. Rebecca Poynor Burns, "Welcome to Sex City (Hope You Brought Cash)," *Atlanta Magazine,* March 2000, 75–78.

18. John R. Logan and Harvey L. Molotch, *Urban Fortunes: The Political Economy of Place* (Berkeley: University of California Press, 1987).

19. C. Richard Yarbrough, *And They Call Them Games: An Inside View of the 1996 Olympics* (Macon, Ga.: Mercer University Press, 2000), 108.

20. *Atlanta Constitution*, August 13, 2000, G-8 and 9.

21. Ibid., October 12, 1995, C-1.

22. Newman, *Southern Hospitality*, 277.

23. *New York Times*, August 4, 1996, 1 and 23.

24. *Atlanta Constitution*, August 11, 1996, A-1, C-5, and February 9, 1997, C-5.

25. Ibid., November 17, G-10, November 18, 1996, B-1.

26. See Edward G. Goetz, "The Politics of Poverty Deconcentration," *Journal of Urban Affairs* 22 (2000): 157–73.

27. *Atlanta Constitution*, August 14, 1996, E-2, September 28, 1996, E-3, and December 17, 1996, D-1.

28. Ibid., July 20, 1998, E-2.

29. Ibid., July 20, 2000, JE-1 and 4.

30. Ibid.

31. Ibid., July 5, 1999, F-5.

32. Estimating the number of jobs in the tourism industry is a difficult task since these jobs do not fall within a single employment classification. For a discussion of the problem, see Newman, *Southern Hospitality*, 203–5.

33. *Atlanta Constitution*, July 29, 2000, JE-1 and 4.

34. Ibid., September 13, 2000, F-1 and 4.

35. Matthew J. Burbank, Greg Andranovich, and Charles H. Heying, *Olympic Dreams: The Impact of Mega-Events on Local Politics* (Boulder, Colo.: Lynne Rienner Publishers, 2001).

Chapter 11

1. Margaret Mitchell, *Gone with the Wind* (New York: Avon Books, 1973), 38.

2. See Thomas Nairne and John Norris, *Selling a New World: Two Colonial South Carolina Promotional Pamphlets*, ed. Jack P. Greene (Columbia: University of South Carolina Press, 1989).

3. William R. Taylor, *Cavalier and Yankee: The Old South and American National Character* (Garden City, N.Y.: Anchor Books, 1961); David Bertelson, *The Lazy South* (New York: Oxford University Press, 1967).

4. Michael Frome, *Strangers in High Places: The Story of the Great Smoky Mountains*, rev. ed. (Knoxville: University of Tennessee Press, 1980).

5. See also Catherine L. Albanese, *Nature Religion in America: From the Algonkian Indians to the New Age* (Chicago: University of Chicago Press, 1990); Lynn Morrow and Linda Myers-Phinney, *Shepherd of the Hills Country: Tourism Transforms the Ozarks, 1880s–1930s* (Fayetteville: University of Arkansas Press, 1999); Lori

Robbins, "A'Lyin' to Them Tourists: Tourism in Branson, Missouri" (master's thesis, University of Mississippi, 1999).

6. William Goodell Frost, "Our Contemporary Ancestors in the Southern Mountains," in W. K. McNeil, ed., *Appalachian Images in Folk and Popular Culture* (Ann Arbor, Mich.: UMI Research Press, 1989), 91–107.

7. Donald Davidson, "A Mirror for Artists," in Twelve Southerners, *I'll Take My Stand: The South and the Agrarian Tradition* (Baton Rouge: Louisiana State University Press, 1977), 55.

8. See Benjamin Filene, *Romancing the Folk: Public Memory & American Roots Music* (Chapel Hill: University of North Carolina Press, 2000); Henry D. Shapiro, *Appalachia on Our Minds: The Southern Mountains and Mountaineers in the American Consciousness, 1870–1920* (Chapel Hill: University of North Carolina Press, 1978); David E. Whisnant, *All That Is Native and Fine: The Politics of Culture in an American Region* (Chapel Hill: University of North Carolina Press, 1983).

9. Tom Weil, *Hippocrene U.S.A. Guide to America's South: The Gulf and the Mississippi States* (New York: Hippocrene Books, 1994), 150, 3.

10. Julian Smith, *Virginia Handbook* (Chico, Calif.: Moon Travel Handbooks, 1999), 1.

11. Tim Hollis, *Dixie Before Disney: 100 Years of Roadside Fun* (Jackson: University Press of Mississippi, 1999).

12. Ted Ownby, *American Dreams in Mississippi: Consumers, Poverty, and Culture, 1830–1998* (Chapel Hill: University of North Carolina Press, 1999), 165–68.

13. C. Vann Woodward, *The Burden of Southern History*, enl. ed. (Baton Rouge: Louisiana State University Press, 1968), 3–26.

14. Jack E. Davis, *Race Against Time: Culture and Separation in Natchez Since 1930* (Baton Rouge: Louisiana State University Press, 2001).

15. David D. Blight, *Race and Reunion: The Civil War in American Memory* (Cambridge: Belknap Press of Harvard University Press, 2001).

16. Quoted in Allen G. Breed, "Slave Museum Plans Pit History, Commerce," *Memphis Commercial Appeal*, February 17, 2002, E7.

17. Brunswick and the Golden Isles of Georgia website, African-American Heritage, 2002, www.bgivb.com.

18. Shack Up Inn website at www.shackupinn.com. My thanks to Warren Ables for this reference.

19. Mississippi Agricultural and Industrial Board Travel and Tourism Department, *Mississippi: Your Guide to Travel* (Jackson: Mississippi Agricultural and Industrial Board, 1975).

20. See Bill C. Malone, *Singing Cowboys and Musical Mountaineers: Southern Culture and the Roots of Country Music* (Athens: University of Georgia Press, 1993).

21. Alabama Tourism, *Now this You've Gotta See*, 2001, first page.

22. Arkansas, The Natural State, website designed by the Arkansas Department of Parks and Tourism, 2002, www.arkansas.com, first page.

23. 1995 Virginia is for Lovers Travel Guide, page 2.

24. *Mobil 1998 Travel Guide: Southeast* (New York: Fodor's Travel Publications, 1998), 327.

25. *AAA Alabama Louisiana Mississippi* (Heathrow, Fla.: AAA Publishing, 1999), 80.

26. Mississippi Tourism Association, *The Official Tour Guide for Mississippi* (Jackson: Mississippi Tourism Association, 2001), 15.

27. James C. Cobb, *The Selling of the South: The Southern Crusade for Industrial Development, 1936–1990*, 2d ed. (Urbana: University of Illinois Press, 1993).

Selected Bibliography

Appalachian Land Ownership Task Force. *Who Owns Appalachia? Landownership and Its Impact*. Lexington: University Press of Kentucky, 1983.

Arceneaux, Pamela. "Guidebooks to Sin: The Blue Books of Storyville." *Louisiana History* (fall 1987): 397–405.

Aron, Cindy S. *Working at Play: A History of Vacations in the United States*. New York: Oxford University Press, 1999.

Ayers, Edward L. *The Promise of the New South: Life after Reconstruction*. New York: Oxford University Press, 1992.

Becker, Jane S. *Selling Tradition: Appalachia and the Construction of an American Folk, 1930–1940*. Chapel Hill: University of North Carolina Press, 1998.

Blevins, Brooks. *Hill Folks: A History of Arkansas Ozarkers and Their Image*. Chapel Hill: University of North Carolina Press, 2002.

Brewster, Lawrence F. *Summer Migrations and Resorts of South Carolina Low-Country Planters*. Durham, N.C.: Duke University Press, 1947.

Brown, Dona. *Inventing New England: Regional Tourism in the Nineteenth Century*. Washington, D.C.: Smithsonian Institution Press, 1995.

Brown, Margaret. *The Wild East: A Biography of the Great Smoky Mountains*. Gainesville: University Press of Florida, 2000.

Brown, Rodger Lyle. *Ghost Dancing on the Cracker Circuit: The Culture of Festivals in the American South*. Jackson: University Press of Mississippi, 1997.

Brundage, W. Fitzhugh, ed. *Where These Memories Grow: History, Memory, and Southern Identity*. Chapel Hill: University of North Carolina Press, 2000.

Chambers, Thomas E. "Fashionable Dis-Ease: Promoting Health and Leisure at Saratoga Springs, New York and the Virginia Springs, 1790–1860." Ph.D. diss., The College of William and Mary, 1999.

Clark, Thomas D. *The Emerging South*. New York: Oxford University Press, 1961.

———, ed. *Travels in the New South: A Bibliography*. 2 vols. Norman: University of Oklahoma Press, 1962.

———. *Travels in the Old South: A Bibliography.* 3 vols. Norman: University of Oklahoma Press, 1956–59.

Cobb, James C. *The Selling of the South: The Southern Crusade for Industrial Development, 1936–1990.* 2d ed. Urbana: University of Illinois Press, 1993.

Cohen, Erik. "Authenticity and Commoditization in Tourism." *Annals of Tourism Research* 15 (1988): 383.

Crick, Malcolm. "Representations of International Tourism in the Social Sciences: Sun, Sex, Sights, Savings, and Servility." *Annual Review of Anthropology* 18 (1989): 307–44.

Danielson, Michael N. with Patricia R. F. Danielson, *Profits and Politics in Paradise: The Development of Hilton Head Island.* Columbia: University of South Carolina Press, 1995.

Davis, Jack E. *Race Against Time: Culture and Separation in Natchez Since 1930.* Baton Rouge: Louisiana State University Press, 2001.

Derr, Mark. *Some Kind of Paradise: A Chronicle of Man and the Land in Florida.* New York: William Morrow, 1989.

Engerman, David. "Research Agenda for the History of Tourism: Towards an International Social History." *American Studies International* 32 (October 1994): 3–31.

Feiffer, Maxine. *Tourism in History: From Imperial Rome to the Present.* London: Macmillan, 1984.

Filene, Benjamin. *Romancing the Folk: Public Memory & American Roots Music.* Chapel Hill: University of North Carolina Press, 2000.

Finger, John. *Cherokee Americans: The Eastern Band of Cherokees in the Twentieth Century.* Lincoln: University of Nebraska Press, 1991.

Foglesong, Richard E. *Married to the Mouse: Walt Disney World and Orlando.* New Haven: Yale University Press, 2001.

Ford, Gary D. "Tourism." In *The Encyclopedia of Southern Culture,* edited by Charles Reagan Wilson and William Ferris. Chapel Hill: University of North Carolina Press, 1989, 1244–45.

Foster, Steven William. *The Past is Another Country: Representation, Historical Consciousness, and Resistance in the Blue Ridge.* Berkeley: University of California Press, 1988.

Gannon, Michael. *Florida: A Short History.* Gainesville: University Press of Florida, 1993.

Hale, Grace Elizabeth. "Granite Stopped Time: The Stone Mountain Memorial and Representations of White Southern Identity." *Georgia Historical Quarterly* 81 (spring 1998): 22–44.

———. *Making Whiteness: The Culture of Segregation in the South, 1890–1940.* New York: Pantheon Books, 1998.

Handler, Richard, and Eric Gable. *The New History in an Old Museum: Creating the Past at Colonial Williamsburg.* Durham, N.C.: Duke University Press, 1997.

Hollis, Tim. *Dixie Before Disney: 100 Years of Roadside Fun.* Jackson: University Press of Mississippi, 1999.

Inscoe, John C. *Mountain Masters, Slavery, and the Sectional Crisis in Western North Carolina*. Knoxville: University of Tennessee Press, 1989.

Jafari, Jafar. "Tourism and the Social Sciences." *Annals of Tourism Research* 6, vol. 2 (1979): 149–78.

Jakle, John. *The Tourist: Travel in Twentieth-Century North America*. Lincoln and London: University of Nebraska Press, 1985.

Jakle, John A., and Keith A. Sculle. *The Gas Station in America*. Baltimore: Johns Hopkins University Press, 1994.

Jakle, John A., Keith A. Sculle, and Jefferson S. Rogers. *The Motel in America*. Baltimore: Johns Hopkins University Press, 1996.

Kammen, Michael C. *Mystic Chords of Memory: The Transformation of Tradition in American Culture*. New York: Alfred A. Knopf, 1991.

Kilbride, Daniel. "The Cosmopolitan South: Privileged Southerners, and the Fashionable Tour in the Antebellum Era." *Journal of Urban History* 26 (July 2000): 563–90.

Lewis, Charlene Marie. "Ladies and Gentlemen on Display: Planter Society at the Virginia Springs, 1790–1860." Ph.D. diss., University of Virginia, 1997.

Long, Alecia P. "The Great Southern Babylon: Sexuality, Race, and Reform in New Orleans, 1865–1920." Ph.D. diss., University of Delaware, 2001.

MacCannell, Dean. "Staged Authenticity: Arrangements of Social Space in Tourist Settings." *American Journal of Sociology* 79 (November 1973): 589–603.

———. *The Tourist: A New Theory of the Leisure Class*. New York: Schocken Books, 1976.

Martin, C. Brenden. "Selling the Southern Highlands: Tourism and Community Development in the Mountain South." Ph.D. diss., University of Tennessee, 1997.

McCash, June Hall. *The Jekyll Island Cottage Colony*. Athens: University of Georgia Press, 1998.

McCash, William Barton, and June Hall McCash. *The Jekyll Island Club: Southern Haven for America's Millionaires*. Athens: University of Georgia Press, 1989.

Mitchell, Anne V. "Parkway Politics: Class, Culture, and Tourism in the Blue Ridge." Ph.D. diss., University of North Carolina, 1997.

Mitchell, Reid. *All on a Mardi Gras Day: Episodes in the History of New Orleans Carnival*. Cambridge: Harvard University Press, 1995.

Morrow, Lynn, and Linda Myers-Phinney. *Shepherd of the Hills Country: Tourism Transforms the Ozarks, 1880s–1930s*. Fayetteville: University of Arkansas Press, 1999.

Newman, Harvey K. *Southern Hospitality: Tourism and the Growth of Atlanta*. Tuscaloosa: University of Alabama Press, 1999.

Nolan, David. *Fifty Feet in Paradise: The Booming of Florida*. San Diego: Harcourt Brace Jovanovich, 1984.

Ownby, Ted. *American Dreams in Mississippi: Consumers, Poverty, and Culture, 1830–1998*. Chapel Hill: University of North Carolina Press, 1999.

———. *Subduing Satan: Religion, Recreation, and Manhood in the Rural South, 1865–1920.* Chapel Hill: University of North Carolina Press, 1990.

Patrick, Rembert W. "The Mobile Frontier." *Journal of Southern History* 29 (February 1963): 3–18.

Patton, Phil. *Open Road: A Celebration of the American Highway.* New York: Simon and Schuster, 1986.

Phelts, Marsha Dean. *An American Beach for African Americans.* Gainesville: University Press of Florida, 1997.

Pierce, Daniel S. *The Great Smokies: From Natural Habitat to National Park.* Knoxville: University of Tennessee Press, 2000.

Preston, Howard L. *Dirt Roads to Dixie: Accessibility and Modernization in the South, 1885–1935.* Knoxville: University of Tennessee Press, 1991.

Rose, Al. *Storyville, New Orleans: Being an Authentic, Illustrated Account of the Notorious Red-Light District.* Tuscaloosa: University of Alabama Press, 1974.

Rothman, Hal K. *Devil's Bargains: Tourism in the Twentieth Century American West.* Lawrence: University Press of Kansas, 1998.

Rymer, Russ. *American Beach: How 'Progress' Robbed a Black Town—and a Nation—of History, Wealth, and Power.* New York: HarperPerennial, 2000.

Sears, John F. *Sacred Places: American Tourist Attractions in the Nineteenth Century.* New York: Oxford University Press, 1989.

Sellars, Richard West. *Preserving Nature in the National Parks: A History.* New Haven: Yale University Press, 1997.

Shaffer, Marguerite S. *See America First: Tourism and National Identity, 1880–1940.* Washington, D.C.: Smithsonian Institution Press, 2001.

Sigaux, Gilbert. *History of Tourism.* London: Leisure Arts, 1966.

Silber, Nina L. *The Romance of Reunion: Northerners and the South, 1865–1900.* Chapel Hill: University of North Carolina Press, 1993.

Smith, Michal. *Behind the Glitter: The Impact of Tourism on Rural Women of the Southeast.* Lexington: Southeast Women's Employment Commission, 1989.

Smith, Stephen A. "The Old South Myth as a Contemporary Southern Commodity." *Journal of Popular Culture* 16 (winter 1982): 22–29.

Smith, Valene L., ed. *Hosts and Guests: The Anthropology of Tourism.* 2d ed. Philadelphia: University of Pennsylvania Press, 1989.

Starnes, Richard D. "Creating the Land of the Sky: Tourism and Society in Western North Carolina." Ph.D. diss., Auburn University, 1999.

Taylor, Stephen W. *The New South's New Frontier: A Social History of Economic Development in Southwestern North Carolina.* Gainesville: University Press of Florida, 2001.

Thomas, June Manning. "The Impact of Corporate Tourism on Gullah Blacks: Notes on the Issue of Employment." *Phylon* 41 (spring 1980): 1–11.

Tindall, George B. *Emergence of the New South, 1913–1945.* Baton Rouge: Louisiana State University Press, 1967.

Tooman, L. Alex. "The Evolving Impact of Tourism on the Greater Smoky Mountain Region of East Tennessee and Western North Carolina." Ph.D. diss., University of Tennessee, 1995.

West, Patsy. *The Enduring Seminoles: From Alligator Wrestling to Ecotourism*. Gainesville: University Press of Florida, 1998.

Whisnant, David E. *All That Is Native and Fine: The Politics of Culture in an American Region*. Chapel Hill: University of North Carolina Press, 1983.

———. *Modernizing the Mountaineer: People, Power, and Planning in Appalachia*. Boone, N.C.: Appalachian Consortium Press, 1980.

Wrobel, David M., and Patrick T. Long, eds. *Seeing and Being Seen: Tourism in the American West*. Lawrence: University Press of Kansas, 2001.

Yarbrough, C. Richard. *And They Call Them Games: An Inside View of the 1996 Olympics*. Macon, Ga.: Mercer University Press, 2000.

Yuhl, Stephanie E. "High Culture in the Low Country: Arts, Identity, and Tourism in Charleston, South Carolina, 1920–1940." Ph.D. diss., Duke University, 1998.

Contributors

Brooks Blevins is director of regional studies at Lyon College. A native of Arkansas, he is author of *Cattle in the Cotton Fields: A History of Cattle-Raising in Alabama* (University of Alabama Press, 1999) and *Hill Folks: A History of Arkansas Ozarkers and Their Image* (University of North Carolina Press, 2002).

Harvey H. Jackson III is professor of history at Jacksonville State University. His books include *Rivers of History: Life on the Coosa, Tallapoosa, and Alabama* (University of Alabama Press, 1995) and *Putting "Loafing Streams" to Work: The Building of Lay, Mitchell, Martin, and Jordan Dams, 1917–1929* (University of Alabama Press, 1997). He is working on a larger study of the Florida panhandle titled "The Rise and Decline of the Redneck Riviera."

Alecia P. Long is a historian at the Louisiana State Museum and holds a Ph.D. in history from the University of Delaware. Her dissertation is titled "The Great Southern Babylon: Sexuality, Race, and Reform in New Orleans, 1865–1920," and will be published as a book by the Louisiana State University Press.

C. Brenden Martin is assistant professor of history at Middle Tennessee State University. He holds a Ph.D. in history from the University of Tennessee and has published several articles on the history of southern tourism.

June Hall McCash holds a Ph.D. in comparative literature from Emory University and is professor of foreign languages at Middle Tennessee State

University. Among her published works is *The Jekyll Island Cottage Colony* (University of Georgia Press, 1998).

HARVEY K. NEWMAN is associate professor of urban studies at Georgia State University and author of *Southern Hospitality: Tourism and the Growth of Atlanta* (University of Alabama Press, 1999).

TED OWNBY is professor of history and southern studies at the University of Mississippi. His works include *Subduing Satan: Religion, Recreation, and Manhood in the Rural South, 1865–1920* (University of North Carolina Press, 1990) and *American Dreams in Mississippi: Consumers, Poverty, and Culture, 1830–1998* (University of North Carolina Press, 1999).

DANIEL S. PIERCE is assistant professor of history at the University of North Carolina at Asheville and author of *The Great Smokies: From Natural Habitat to National Park* (University of Tennessee Press, 2000).

MARGARET A. SHANNON is an independent scholar. She holds master's degrees in history and economic philosophy from the University of Tennessee.

J. Mark Souther received his Ph.D. in history from Tulane University. His dissertation is titled "City in Amber: Race, Culture, and the Tourist Transformation of New Orleans, 1945–1995." He teaches at Cleveland State University.

RICHARD D. STARNES is assistant professor of history at Western Carolina University. He is the author of a forthcoming study of tourism in the North Carolina mountains.

STEPHEN W. TAYLOR holds a Ph.D. in history from the University of Tennessee and teaches history at Macon State College. His publications include *The New South's New Frontier: A Social History of Economic Development in Southwestern North Carolina* (University Press of Florida, 2001).

ANNE MITCHELL WHISNANT is the Mellon Project Officer at the John Hope Franklin Humanities Institute at Duke University. She received her Ph.D. from the University of North Carolina at Chapel Hill and is currently revising her dissertation for publication.

Index